Register for Free Membership to

solutions@syngress.com

Over the last few years, Syngress has published many best-selling and critically acclaimed books, including Tom Shinder's *Configuring ISA Server 2000*, Brian Caswell and Jay Beale's *Snort 2.0 Intrusion Detection*, and Angela Orebaugh and Gilbert Ramirez's *Ethereal Packet Sniffing*. One of the reasons for the success of these books has been our unique **solutions@syngress.com** program. Through this site, we've been able to provide readers a real time extension to the printed book.

As a registered owner of this book, you will qualify for free access to our members-only solutions@syngress.com program. Once you have registered, you will enjoy several benefits, including:

- Four downloadable e-booklets on topics related to the book. Each booklet is approximately 20-30 pages in Adobe PDF format. They have been selected by our editors from other best-selling Syngress books as providing topic coverage that is directly related to the coverage in this book.

- A comprehensive FAQ page that consolidates all of the key points of this book into an easy to search web page, providing you with the concise, easy to access data you need to perform your job.

- A "From the Author" Forum that allows the authors of this book to post timely updates links to related sites, or additional topic coverage that may have been requested by readers.

Just visit us at **www.syngress.com/solutions** and follow the simple registration process. You will need to have this book with you when you register.

Thank you for giving us the opportunity to serve your needs. And be sure to let us know if there is anything else we can do to make your job easier.

SYNGRESS®

SYNGRESS®

SECURITY SAGE'S Guide to

Hardening the Network Infrastructure

Steven Andrés

Brian Kenyon

Foreword by
Erik Pace Birkholz
Series Editor

Jody Marc Cohn
Nate Johnson
Justin Dolly

KEY	SERIAL NUMBER
001	KLBR4D87NF
002	829KM8NJH2
003	JOY723E3E3
004	67MCHHH798
005	CVPL3GH398
006	V5T5T53455
007	HJJE5768NK
008	2987KGHUIN
009	6P5SDJT77Y
010	I295T6TGHN

PUBLISHED BY
Syngress Publishing, Inc.
800 Hingham Street
Rockland, MA 02370

Security Sage's Guide to Hardening the Network Infrastructure

Printed in the United States of America
1 2 3 4 5 6 7 8 9 0
ISBN: 1-931836-01-9

Series Editor: Erik Pace Birkholz   Cover Designer: Michael Kavish
Technical Editor: Justin Dolly   Copy Editor: Beth Roberts
Page Layout and Art: Patricia Lupien   Indexer: Nara Wood

Distributed by O'Reilly & Associates in the United States and Jaguar Book Group in Canada.

Acknowledgments

We would like to acknowledge the following people for their kindness and support in making this book possible.

Ping Look and Jeff Moss of Black Hat for their invaluable insight into the world of computer security and their support of the Syngress publishing program.

Syngress books are now distributed in the United States by O'Reilly & Associates, Inc. The enthusiasm and work ethic at ORA is incredible and we would like to thank everyone there for their time and efforts to bring Syngress books to market: Tim O'Reilly, Laura Baldwin, Mark Brokering, Mike Leonard, Donna Selenko, Bonnie Sheehan, Cindy Davis, Grant Kikkert, Opol Matsutaro, Lynn Schwartz, Steve Hazelwood, Mark Wilson, Rick Brown, Leslie Becker, Jill Lothrop, Tim Hinton, Kyle Hart, Sara Winge, C. J. Rayhill, Peter Pardo, Leslie Crandell, Valerie Dow, Regina Aggio, Pascal Honscher, Preston Paull, Susan Thompson, Bruce Stewart, Laura Schmier, Sue Willing, Mark Jacobsen, Betsy Waliszewski, Dawn Mann, Cindy Wetterlund, Kathryn Barrett, and to all the others who work with us. A thumbs up to Rob Bullington for all his help of late.

The incredibly hard working team at Elsevier Science, including Jonathan Bunkell, Ian Seager, Duncan Enright, David Burton, Rosanna Ramacciotti, Robert Fairbrother, Miguel Sanchez, Klaus Beran, Emma Wyatt, Rosie Moss, Chris Hossack, and Krista Leppiko, for making certain that our vision remains worldwide in scope.

David Buckland, Daniel Loh, Marie Chieng, Lucy Chong, Leslie Lim, Audrey Gan, Pang Ai Hua, and Joseph Chan of STP Distributors for the enthusiasm with which they receive our books.

Kwon Sung June at Acorn Publishing for his support.

Jackie Gross, Gayle Voycey, Alexia Penny, Anik Robitaille, Craig Siddall, Iolanda Miller, Jane Mackay, and Marie Skelly at Jackie Gross & Associates for all their help and enthusiasm representing our product in Canada.

Lois Fraser, Connie McMenemy, Shannon Russell, and the rest of the great folks at Jaguar Book Group for their help with distribution of Syngress books in Canada.

David Scott, Tricia Wilden, Marilla Burgess, Annette Scott, Geoff Ebbs, Hedley Partis, Bec Lowe, Andrew Swaffer, Stephen O'Donoghue and Mark Langley of Woodslane for distributing our books throughout Australia, New Zealand, Papua New Guinea, Fiji Tonga, Solomon Islands, and the Cook Islands.

Winston Lim of Global Publishing for his help and support with distribution of Syngress books in the Philippines.

Authors

Steven Andrés (CISSP, CCNP, CNE, MCSE, CCSP, CCSE, INFOSEC), is the Director of Technical Operations at Foundstone, Inc., a leading information security software and services firm based in Southern California. He principally manages the infrastructure and ensures the confidentiality of sensitive client data within the Foundstone Managed Service. Steven is the co-inventor of the award-winning FS1000 Appliance, and in his role as Chief Architect, he continues to lead the development and innovation of the entire Foundstone Appliance product line. Additionally, as Manager of Product Fulfillment, Steven oversees all aspects of product licensing and electronic distribution of software and periodic threat intelligence updates to customers and worldwide partners.

Prior to Foundstone, Steven designed secure networks for the managed hosting division of the largest, private Tier-1 Internet Service Provider in the nation. In previous employment, he managed the largest fully-switched Ethernet network in the nation, encompassing over a dozen buildings in a campus-wide connectivity solution. Steven has nine years of experience managing high-availability networks in the Entertainment, Health Care, Financial, and Higher Education industries, and is frequently invited to speak on security issues and provide insight for webcasts on newly announced vulnerabilities.

His other works include the best-selling *Hacking Exposed: Network Security Secrets & Solutions, Fourth Edition* (ISBN 0-072227-42-7) as well as a contributing author for *Special Ops: Network and Host Security for Microsoft, Oracle and UNIX* (Syngress Publishing, ISBN 1-931836-69-8). Steven has earned the Certified Information Systems Security Professional (CISSP) designation, as well as vendor certifications such as the Cisco Certified Network Professional (CCNP), Novell Certified Netware Engineer (CNE), Microsoft Certified Systems Engineer (MCSE-2000), Cisco Certified Security Professional (CCSP), Checkpoint Certified Security Engineer (CCSE), Nokia

Security Administrator, and was awarded the INFOSEC Professional designation, jointly-issued by the U.S. National Security Agency (NSA) and the Committee on National Security Systems (CNSS). Steven earned a Bachelor of the Arts degree from the University of California, Los Angeles (UCLA).

Brian Kenyon (CCNA, MCSE) is the Director of Product Services for Foundstone, Inc., a leading information security software and services firm based in Southern California. Foundstone offers a unique combination of software, hardware, professional services, and education to continuously and measurably protect an organization's most important assets from the most critical threats.

Since joining Foundstone in 2001, the company has leveraged Brian's deep domain expertise across a variety of functional areas including professional services, hardware innovation and software development. Brian is the Chief Architect of Foundstone's Security Operations Center, which monitors vulnerabilities at client sites, and has been integral in designing and developing Foundstone's cutting-edge hardware solutions, including the award-winning and highly acclaimed FS1000. Brian is also responsible for the development and expansion of the company's entire Product Service line—a key strategic growth area for the company. Brian is considered to be an industry expert on vulnerability management best practices and is frequently invited to speak and train.

Prior to Foundstone, Brian specialized in designing and securing large e-commerce infrastructures for two technology start-ups. Over the course of his ten-year IT career, Brian has consulted for a number of firms providing architecture insight and project planning services. Brian is a contributing author on network architecture for *Special Ops: Network and Host Security for Microsoft, Oracle and UNIX* (Syngress Publishing, ISBN: 1-931836-69-8) and frequently hosts popular webcasts across a wide range of network security topics. Brian holds a Bachelor of the Arts degree from Loyola Marymount University.

Contributors

Jody Marc Cohn (CNE, CCNA) currently works as a network engineer for a private consulting company. During his 18 years in information technology, he has installed and maintained cutting-edge networks based on Ethernet, Token Ring, ATM, FDDI, and CDDI technologies. Prior to consulting, he worked for the University of California, Los Angeles (UCLA), helping to maintain what was currently the largest switched Ethernet network in the world. From there, he moved to network administration for a premier network switch manufacturer, and then worked as the IT Manager for the leading Health & Fitness publisher. Jody has a Bachelor of Arts degree from UCLA.

Nathan Johnson (MCSE) is a founder and CTO of RIS Technology Inc. (www.ristech.net), an Internet application hosting company focused on custom hosting and managed services. RIS Technology offers its customers an inclusive package of ultra-high quality data center space, top-tier Internet connectivity, redundant network infrastructure, and managed security and systems administrative services. RIS Technology hosts high traffic websites for clients like the National Academy of Recording Arts and Sciences who put on the Grammy Awards as well as complicated Internet applications like business networking site ZeroDegrees.com.

Nate has deep technical experience with designing high availability network infrastructures. In his 10-year career in IT, Nate has designed and implemented the internal network infrastructure for corporations and financial institutions, as well as the Internet network architectures for many large e-commerce sites and ISPs. Nate holds a degree in Computer Science from the University of California, Riverside

Matt Wagenknecht (CISSP, MCSE, MCP+I) is a Senior Security Administrator with Quantum Corporation. He is key contributor to a team responsible for incident response, intrusion detection, vulnerability assessment, penetration audits, and firewall management for Quantum's global infrastructure. His specialties include Microsoft Windows security, intrusion detection, forensics, network troubleshooting, Virtual Private Network architecture and design, and firewall architecture and design.

Matt lives in Colorado with his wife, Janelle, and his children, Kiersten, Amber, Hunter, and Dylan. Matt is passionate about security, but passion alone did not write his contribution to this book. Without support and encouragement from his wife, his kids would have overtaken him and driven him to hours of therapy. Janelle, thanks for supporting him in everything he does and for keeping the kids at bay. Kids, thanks for the chaos and for reminding him what's important.

Technical Editor

Justin Dolly is the Information Security Officer at Macromedia. In this role, Justin has global responsibility for ensuring the security and integrity of information, infrastructure, and intellectual property at Macromedia.

He is also heavily involved with product security, risk management, audit compliance, and business continuity planning initiatives. He is a founding member of SecMet, the Security Metrics Consortium (http://www.secmet.org), a non-vendor and industry-neutral group of security executives. SecMet's goal is to seek to empower security professionals with the ability to continually measure their organization's security posture by defining real-world, standardized metrics. Previously, Justin held a variety of technical and engineering positions at Wells Fargo Bank. He has nine years experience in network engineering and design; infrastructure, information and Web security. Justin holds a Bachelor of Arts degree from the National University of Ireland and Le Mirail-Toulouse, France.

Series Editor

Erik Pace Birkholz (CISSP, MCSE) is a Principal Consultant for
Foundstone, and the founder of Special Ops Security
(www.SpecialOpsSecurity.com), an elite force of tactical and strategic
security luminaries around the globe. He is the author of the best-selling
book, *Special Ops: Host and Network Security for Microsoft, UNIX and Oracle*
(Syngress, ISBN: 1-931836-69-8). He is also a contributing author of *SQL
Server Security* and on four of the six books in the international best-selling
Hacking Exposed series. He can be contacted directly at
erik@Foundstone.com

Erik is a subject matter expert in information assurance with the
Information Assurance Technology Analysis Center (IATAC). IATAC is a
Department of Defense entity that belongs to the Defense Technical
Information Center (DTIC). Throughout his career, he has presented
hacking methodologies and techniques to members of major United
States government agencies, including the Federal Bureau of Investigation,
National Security Agency, and various branches of the Department of
Defense. He has presented at three Black Hat Windows Security Briefings,
SANS Institute, Microsoft, WCSF, RSA, and TISC. Before accepting the
role of Principal Consultant at Foundstone, he served as the West Coast
Assessment Lead for Internet Security Systems (ISS), a Senior Consultant
for Ernst & Young's National Attack and Penetration team and a
Consultant for KPMG's Information Risk Management group.

In 2002, Erik was invited by Microsoft to present Hacking
Exposed: Live to over 500 Windows developers at their corporate
headquarters in Redmond. Later that year, he was invited to present
Hacking NT Exposed to over 3000 Microsoft employees from
around the globe at the 2002 Microsoft Global Briefings. Evaluated
against over 500 presentations by over 9,500 attendees, his presentation was rated first place. Based on that success, he was a VIP
Speaker at the Microsoft MEC 2002 conference. In 2003, Erik was
awarded "Best Speaker" for his presentation of Special Ops: The Art
of Attack and Penetration at the 6th Annual West Coast Security

Forum (WCSF) in Vancouver, Canada. In 2004, Erik is scheduled to speak at RSA, the Black Hat Briefings, ISACA, and for the North Atlantic Treaty Organization (NATO).

Erik holds a Bachelor's of Science degree in Computer Science from Dickinson College in Carlisle, PA. In 1999, he was named a Metzger Conway Fellow, an annual award presented to a distinguished Dickinson alumnus who has achieved excellence in his or her field of study.

Contents

Foreword

When I created the book *Special Ops: Host and Network Security for Microsoft, UNIX and Oracle*, I attempted to include a chapter to cover each common yet critical component of a corporate network. More specifically, I coined the phrase *internal network security*; which was really just an asset-centric approach to securing your hosts and networks from the inside-out. After the release of *Special Ops* it became clear (to Syngress and me) that some of the topics covered in Special Ops warranted an entire book. To satisfy this need, we have created the exciting new series entitled: *Security Sage's Guides.*

Security Sage's Guide to Hardening the Network Infrastructure is the first book in this series; concentrating on the bottom OSI layers that provide a solid foundation to any sound security posture. The next book in the series is *Security Sage's Guide to Attacking and Defending Windows Server 2003.* This book will give readers the practical knowledge they need to defend their resources from both a management and operational level using Microsoft's new Windows Server 2003. In *Hacking Exposed* I stated, "The majority of my (security) concerns, in most cases, are not a result of poor products but products being implemented poorly." The *Security Sage's Guides* aim to deliver you the information you need to fight host and network negligence.

Drawing from their extensive real world experiences and showcasing their successes as well as their failures, Steven Andrés and Brian Kenyon provide the reader with a comprehensive tactical and strategic guide to securing the core of the network infrastructure. This book details how to attack, defend and securely deploy routers, firewalls, switches, Intrusion Detection Systems (IDS), and the network protocols that utilize them. The goal was to create a readable and usable book that would empower its readers to mitigate risk by reducing attack vectors, remediation of known vulnerabilities, and segmenting critical assets from known threats. *Security Sage's Guide to Hardening the Network Infrastructure* is an indispensable reference for anyone responsible for the confidentiality, integrity, and availability of critical business data.

UNIX or Windows? Apache or IIS? Oracle or MySQL? . . .Regardless of where you draw your political line, you need a solid foundation to communicate securely and reliably with your corporation's networks, servers, and users. Network infrastructure is the foundation and underlying base of all organizations. Unless you were blessed by the Network Fairy, it is likely you are faced with supporting, securing, and monitoring an infrastructure designed for usability rather than security. Shifting this network paradigm is not a simple task; expect heavy resistance from users and administrators while reducing their usability to increase their security.

> A great network doesn't just happen—but a bad one does. Some of the worst network designs have reared their ugly heads because of a lack of forethought as to how the network should ultimately look. Instead, someone said, 'Get these machines on the network as cheaply and quickly as possible.'
> —Chapter 11 "Internal Network Design"

On January 28th 1986, a similar mentality cost America the lives of seven pioneers when the space shuttle Challenger exploded just 73 seconds into its mission. The real tragedy was that the whole thing was avoidable; the potential for cold temperature O-ring failure was a known vulnerability. The engineers at Thiokol issued a written recommendation advising against a shuttle launch in temperatures below 53 degrees Fahrenheit. Some would argue it was a break down in the communication process that held these facts from the final decision makers, but others point to the fact that the previous three launch cancellations had severely damaged the image and publicity of the whole event; in turn affecting potential future funding of NASA. Whatever the case, the temperature on January 28th was a shivery 36 degrees and usability won out at the cost of security.

Over the past two years, network based worms opened the eyes of executives in boardrooms around the globe. From management's perspective; the security of a corporate network can exist in two states; *working* and *not working*. When business operations halt due to a security issue, management is forced to re-assess the funds and resources they allocated to ensure they are adequately protecting their critical host and network based operations. In this case, wealthy corporations won't hesitate to throw money at the problem of security;

expecting to find a panacea in the industry's newest security solution. Alternatively, corporations concerned with ROI and TCO for IT investments would be better served to empower their InfoSec staff; Asking them to assess their current network architecture and rearchitect low cost yet secure solutions that keep the corporate packets moving securely, day after day.

The good news is that everyone is finally thinking about security; now is our time to execute. *Security Sage's Guide to Hardening the Network Infrastructure* is dedicated to delivering the most up-to-date network layer attacks and mitigation techniques across a wide assortment of vendors, and not just the typical attention paid to market leaders such as Cisco and Checkpoint (although these are obviously covered in great detail). This expanded breadth will help reach a wider range of network engineers who may not have the budget to purchase and install best-of-breed hardware, but want to know how to make the most out of what they do have.

In the early parts of my career I worked as a young auditor for two of the Big 5 accounting firms. I assisted the audit teams by reviewing the effectiveness of information security controls as part of the larger General Control Reviews (GCR). Large client after large client, I found the state of InfoSec controls was worse than I could have imagined.

I would find critical choke routers protecting the financial servers, and was able to gain complete control of the router with default SNMP community strings of *private*. This little oversight allowed me to download or modify router configurations and access control lists. Frequently, financial servers were running on Windows and were therefore part of an NT Domain. After a cursory assessment of the PDC or BDC, I would find *Domain Admin* accounts with weak or blank passwords. I developed quite a talent for divining privileged windows accounts with poor passwords. As an all-powerful *Domain Admin*, I connected directly to the financial servers with the ability to view, modify or delete critical corporate data. Finally, I can't count how many poor Solaris boxes running an Oracle database were easily compromised because the administrator didn't bother to change the password for the Oracle user account. Our running joke was something about how all you needed to know to hack UNIX was *oracle:oracle*.

After each engagement I would carefully document my findings and deliver them as draft to my manager or the regional partner for inclusion in the audit report. What a joke. Did my ineffective security control findings cause the auditors to take a closer look at the integrity of this data the controls were failing to protect? Not even close, the information was "adjusted" up the line before it ever saw a genuine audit report. How bad was it? Let's just say that no matter how many high risk or critical vulnerabilities I uncovered, the end result communicated to the audit team and eventually the customer was always effective internal controls.

New SEC legislation such as Sarbanes-Oxley will force infrastructure accountability by requiring management to report on the effectiveness of their corporate internal controls over financial data and systems. Hopefully, the days of ineffective control "adjustments" will dwindle once executives are accountable for the disclosure and integrity of these controls. Just maybe this new found accountability will force companies to create, review, implement and enforce effective corporate security policies and procedures supported by securely architected network infrastructures. If it does and you have read this book; executing on your infrastructure initiatives should be a snap.

—*Erik Pace Birkholz*, CISSP
Series Editor
Foundstone Inc. & Special Ops Security
Author of *Special Ops: Host and Network Security for Microsoft, UNIX and Oracle*
Co-author of *SQL Server Security* and *Hacking Exposed*

Chapter 1

Defining Perimeter and Internal Segments

Solutions in this Chapter:

- Internal versus External Segments
- Footprinting: Finding the IP Addresses Assigned to Your Company

Related Chapters:

- Chapter 2 Assessing Your Current Network
- Chapter 10 Perimeter Network Design
- Chapter 11 Internal Network Design

☑ Summary

☑ Solutions Fast Track

☑ Frequently Asked Questions

Introduction

With the proliferation of wireless access points (WAPs), virtual private networks (VPNs), and extranets, it's becoming increasingly difficult to determine where your network begins and ends. Add this complexity to common economic factors, such as company mergers and acquisitions, and now you have a tangled web of interconnected segments and networks that you will need to understand. While this book aims at providing you the necessary tools to protect your network infrastructure assets, it is imperative that before we dive into the details you have a good understanding of how your network is designed.

Having a commanding knowledge of your network topology today is no simple feat. We are often reminded of a financial services company at which we performed some consulting work. This company has grown over the past few years by acquiring related financial companies. At the end of the day, this team of network engineers had to manage over 300 Frame Relay lines, over 100 Microsoft Windows NT 4.0 domains, and numerous Internet access points (IAPs). To add insult to injury, these networks are not static environments; in fact, there are numerous routing changes and firewall modifications made on a daily basis. The only saving grace this team of dedicated foot soldiers has are solid topology diagrams detailing each Frame Relay network and IAP, and a comprehensive list of all of their outwardly facing IP addresses.

While these tools sound like networking basics, we are constantly surprised at the number of IT departments that are without this information. Without knowing how your network is laid out, or understanding which segments touch the Internet directly, it will be nearly impossible for you to begin locking down your network devices. If you are not armed with these tools already, this chapter will help you find your external IP address presence and help you get a handle on understanding the differences between your core network segments and those that lie on your perimeter. Chapter 2, "Assessing Your Current Network," will help provide you with those all-important topology maps if you aren't fortunate enough to have them in your toolbox already. Furthermore, the end goal of this chapter is to arrive at common language that can be easily understood, and used throughout the entirety of the book.

Internal versus External Segments

Most of the time it might be quite simple to define your network segments as internal or external, core or perimeter; in larger, more heterogeneous organizations, this is not an easy task. Corporate acquisitions, multiple Internet service providers (ISPs), and remote offices offer areas of complexity that might result in some uncertainty as to which network is connected and where it leads. The following section will help you define and piece together those segments that will lead to a better understanding of your network topology.

Explaining the External Segment or Perimeter Segment

Simply defined, an external, or perimeter segment, is any network that exists in a low security zone of your environment. In other words, any network that connects your physical environment to another untrusted network, such as the Internet. A good example could be a network that is attached to the external interface of your firewall and connects to the external interface of you ISP's router. In this scenario, the network is untrusted from the standpoint of your organization because it is ultimately controlled by the ISP.

This definition could extend to other network segments as well, such as a demilitarized zone (DMZ) that houses and provides Web or application services to other untrusted networks. In many cases, this type of network would be considered external, or on the perimeter, since many of those services map directly to external or public IP addresses. This class of service would still fit in our description because the firewall is passing certain types of untrusted traffic to that DMZ network; thus, you cannot always guarantee the safety of those devices from Internet traffic.

If you begin to think about your network from the perspective of a potential attacker on the Internet, the definition of the external segment will become clearer. An untrusted Internet attacker will only have access to devices or services that are directly connected to the Internet. With this in mind, you now have a clear picture of what we would consider a perimeter network or device. Does it serve content to the Internet? Can anyone PING or connect to the device?

Wireless Access Points: Extending the Perimeter

As wireless technology has matured over the years, so has its acceptance in corporate America. More and more, companies are turning to wireless technology to extend usability to employees and management. While this increase in usability can drive efficiency in the workplace, it also adds risk to the IT department that is working to protect the corporate assets.

Without diving into too much detail on how WAPs work, each device emits a radio frequency (RF) that is used to pass network communication and protocols. Many of these devices have a substantial range, meaning that people who are physically located far from the access point will still be able to communicate with it. Additionally, in many companies these WAPs are located on internal segments, providing connectivity to corporate mail servers, payrolls servers, intranet sites, and potentially users' desktops.

The inherent risk from these devices comes from that fact that they might not be properly secured. Unsecured WAPs provide a gateway into the internal network for untrusted users. Potential attackers could take advantage of misconfigurations or lax security policies on these devices and begin to communicate on your internal network. Because of the increased range capabilities of these devices, the untrusted user might be walking by your building, sitting in your parking lot, or on a different floor in your office building. Regardless of the user's location, this unsecured device just opened the door to your internal network.

So, how do WAPs extend the perimeter? If you recall our basic definition of an external segment (providing services or connectivity to an untrusted network or user), this technology falls into that scenario. This device could potentially allow an untrusted user with no privilege access to your company's internal assets and resources, thereby extending the perimeter onto your internal segments. What's worse is that any type of elaborate firewall setup (that might be air-tight) has been completely circumvented and done so from the comfort of the untrusted user's '83 Toyota across the street.

The Internal Segment Explained

Using the information already presented in this chapter, it is quite simple to deduce what the definition of an internal segment is. For the purposes of this book, we define an internal segment as any network that resides in the secured portion of your environment and provides resources or services that are only for internal use (that is, should not be accessible by untrusted Internet users).

Similar to how we thought about our external properties, if you think about the internal segments as providing resources only to internal assets, you will get a clearer picture of how the network should be defined. Most of the networks within your corporate environment will be internal, as many companies have only a few IAPs.

Assigning Criticality to Internal Segments

Since most of your networks are going to be internal segments, they cannot all have the same importance for your organization. Prioritizing these segments is an important step in aligning your network for security and business continuity plans. For example, many of your network segments will only house employee desktops or laptops, while some might contain mission-critical servers, such as mail, payroll, software development source code, customer databases, or HR applications. While you will want to provide the most comprehensive security policy and defense for your entire environment, it is not practical when the latest security tsunami hits.

Assigning network and device criticality is an essential step in planning for how you are going to handle security patches, network recovery, and continuity. For example, a few months ago a serious design flaw was discovered in the Cisco Internet Operating System (IOS) that runs on all Cisco routers and some other Cisco network devices. Many organizations have hundreds, if not thousands, of Cisco routers in use on their network. Instantly, those companies had a massive project on their hands. The use of network and device criticality helped those administrators put together a plan of action on which Cisco devices needed to be updated first and which were less important.

For the perfect example, we refer back to our favorite financial services company that we previously mentioned. When the Cisco IPv4 vulnerability hit the wire in July 2003, this company was not prepared for the chaos and damage that could potentially ensue from such a threat. With nearly 700 Cisco devices deployed across their worldwide enterprise, this bank only had a few spreadsheets with asset information, mainly comprised of IP addresses and physical asset location. What's worse, the security team had zero information as to which department or person was in charge of the maintenance of each device. Any inkling of network device criticality at this point was nothing but a distant dream.

Within a few hours, reports started to surface as to the dire circumstances surrounding this vulnerability. The security team was feverishly trying to make heads or tails of the asset inventory information they did possess. Questions similar to, "Is that our router or does the Telco maintain it?" were shouted from offices. Spreadsheets were being circulated through e-mail like a bad Outlook virus! Alas, IT personnel had very few answers and a tremendous amount of questions. Almost four hours into the crisis, they had made zero progress on their remediation efforts.

All told, it took nearly six business days for the bank to fully remediate their Cisco devices. The main reason for this delay was not policy or change control, but rather, the network engineers did not have accurate inventories of the network device assets and their respective owners/maintainers. Essentially, it took them six days just to find all of their routers and the corresponding individual who administered the device. It was not an impressive showing, but thankfully the vulnerability turned out to be nothing more of a scare, so little damage was actually realized.

Nevertheless, had they moved on from this incident without learning anything this anecdote would not have made the pages of this book. The security staff spent many weeks after the Cisco scare working on assembling all of the asset information into a consolidated spreadsheet. They documented their network architectures and spent time going through all of their telecommunications contracts to understand where their responsibilities ended and the ISP demarcation began. Their data collection did not stop with networking devices, but stretched to the desktop where they inventoried systems down to the OS revision. With this information in hand, they began to decide which devices and networks were most important to the business. While this information didn't prove useful immediately, it wasn't long until the next Microsoft worm exploded onto the scene.

When the Microsoft Messenger Service Buffer Overflow began to make headlines in October 2003, this security team was well poised to respond. Even with thousands more Windows devices to patch (compared to only 700 Cisco devices), the total time for complete remediation was only three days–a significant improvement in their processes. Part of the reason why they were able to act so swiftly this time was the asset inventory spreadsheets and the asset criticality information. Rather than spinning their wheels on less critical Microsoft systems, they focused on the business-critical servers and workstations first, and then broadened their approach outward as resources became available. This allowed them to ensure the continuity of the business through the security threat, and lessen the potential impact across the enterprise.

As you begin to map out your network, it would be wise to begin thinking about how important that segment is to your business. Documenting this information will help when crisis strikes and you and your team need to act swiftly.

Footprinting: Finding the IP Addresses Assigned to Your Company

Now that you have a clear understanding of where your perimeter networks are, and more importantly what they are connected to, the next important step is to ensure that you haven't missed any of them. Since your perimeter networks should be the only gateway for untrusted Internet attackers to enter your network, you will want to make certain that there aren't any other IAPs out there that were acquired through a business merger or a new remote office. The following sections will help you begin to collect information about the public IP addresses assigned to your organization.

Using *whois* to Understand Who You Are

The International Corporation for Assigned Names and Numbers, better known as ICANN, defines the Address Supporting Organization (ASO), which maintains databases of assigned public IP addresses. These databases are broken down into Regional Internet Registries (RIR). Each geographic region has an organization that is responsible for tying the publicly assigned IP addresses with the corresponding company. In other words, when you or your ISP purchases a new network block, the company and contact information is stored in these databases. These providers correlate the IP address block information with your public company information. The following is some sample output of a RIR IP block record:

```
OrgName:    BrianCorp Inc.
OrgID:      BrianCI
Address:    One Brian Way
City:       Newport Beach
StateProv:  CA
PostalCode: 92660
Country:    US

NetRange:   192.0.2.0 - 192.0.2.255
CIDR:       192.0.2.0/24
NetName:    BCorp
NetHandle:  NET-192-0-2-0-1
Parent:     NET-192-0-0-0-0
```

```
NetType:     Direct Assignment
NameServer:  NS1.US.bkhome.COM
NameServer:  NS2.US.bkhome.COM
Comment:
RegDate:     2002-09-26
Updated:     2004-03-01


TechHandle:  BK763
TechName:    Kenyon, Brian
TechPhone:
TechEmail:   dns@bkhome.com


# ARIN WHOIS database, last updated 2004-03-03 19:15
# Enter ? for additional hints on searching ARIN's WHOIS database.
```

There are currently four active RIRs and one pending approval. The RIRs are as follows:

- **ARIN** North and South America Registry also serving parts of Sub-Sahara Africa
- **APNIC** Registry serving the Asia Pacific region
- **LACNIC** Latin America and parts of the Caribbean
- **RIPE** Registry for Europe, Middle East, Central Asia, and parts of Africa
- **AfriNIC** Pending approval, will serve African regions

Unless your organization is located in several different countries, you will most likely be using ARIN for the majority of *whois* queries.

RIRs can be queried by using IP address or domain name to provide specific company information. Only UNIX-based operating systems come with an embedded *whois* client; however, there are several freeware utilities available for the Windows platform. For the most part, you could use various Web sites to handle the *whois* query for you, such as www.network-tools.com or www.dnsstuff.com. The Network-Tools site will allow you to search through the ARIN, RIPE, and APNIC databases only, while the DnsStuff site will attempt to ascertain the appropriate RIR to query before giving you an error. For further searching capabilities you can go directly to the particular RIR's Web site, such as www.arin.net or www.apnic.net.

Using DNS Interrogation for More Information

What happens if you do not know all of the domains or IP addresses that might be assigned by your company? If your organization, or parent company, is a publicly traded company, you can use the U.S. Securities and Exchange Commission's (SEC) Web site to gather information about potential subsidiaries. The SEC has a search utility named EDGAR used for searching through public SEC filings. Using this utility, you can query your company name for a detailed list of all the SEC filings. For simplicity, we typically look at the 10-Q filings for any given organization. These filings take place each quarter and will have the most up-to-date information. Once you open the filing, search for the term *subsidiary*, or any variation of it, to find other related entities to your organization.

For example, a search on a fictional company, BrianCorp Inc, might yield the subsidiary, Brian-Ventures. With this information, we are going to do a little more digging.

Using the utility NSLOOKUP, which is on all versions of Windows and UNIX operating systems, do a quick lookup for Brian-Ventures.com, Brian-Ventures.org, and so forth.

```
C:\>nslookup brian-ventures.com
Server:   dns.bkhome.com
Address:  192.0.2.111


Non-authoritative answer:
Name:     brian-ventures.com
Address:  192.0.2.21
```

Our results show that the domain brian-ventures.com does exist and it resides at the IP address 192.0.2.21 (not a public IP address and used for example only). Using this information we go to the ARIN Web site and do a quick lookup on the IP address to see what the entire network block is and to determine if it actually belongs to the company. The following is some sample output:

```
Search results for: 192.0.2.21


OrgName:    BrianCorp Inc.
OrgID:      BrianCI
Address:    One Brian Way
City:       Newport Beach
```

```
StateProv:    CA
PostalCode:   92660
Country:      US


NetRange:     192.0.2.0 - 192.0.2.255
CIDR:         192.0.2.0/24
NetName:      BCorp
NetHandle:    NET-192-0-2-0-1
Parent:       NET-192-0-0-0-0
NetType:      Direct Assignment
NameServer:   NS1.US.bkhome.COM
NameServer:   NS2.US.bkhome.COM
Comment:
RegDate:      2002-09-26
Updated:      2004-03-01


TechHandle:   BK763
TechName:     Kenyon, Brian
TechPhone:
TechEmail:    dns@bkhome.com


# ARIN WHOIS database, last updated 2004-03-03 19:15
```

From this information provided by the ARIN database, we are able to ascertain that the Web site is owned by BrianCorp, and we own the entire 192.0.2.0 Class B network. Keep in mind, however, that BrianCorp might not own the entire Class B range, as they might just lease a small subset of the Class B from their upstream ISP or Web hosting provider. However, with this information we can cross-reference our network topologies and make sure that we accounted for this public (external facing) network.

Tools & Traps...

The DNS Zone Transfer

DNS has always provided a volume of information regarding which domains belong to a company and on which network it resides. While this information is generally used so that the general public can access your public Web sites by mapping an IP address to the domain name, it can also provide a lot of useful information in tracking down which domains are owned by the company.

If you do not have access to your DNS zone information, you can try to obtain it through a common DNS feature called the *zone transfer*. Zone transfers were previously used to share updated information with other DNS servers, primarily for redundancy in case the primary DNS server were to fail. While open Internet zone transfers aren't common practice anymore, some DNS servers and networks are still misconfigured to allow this. The most common attribute of a DNS server that allows zone transfers is the presence of TCP port 53 being open. Since common DNS queries are performed on UDP port 53, TCP does not need to be open and can be blocked, thereby disabling zone transfers on the network layer.

Using a utility like NSLOOKUP will provide the mechanism for the zone transfer.

```
C:\>nslookup
Default Server:  dns.corp.com
Address:  10.22.164.12


> server dns.bkhome.com
Default Server:  dns.bkhome.com
Address:  192.0.2.111
> set type=any
> ls -d bkhome.com
[dns.bkhome.com]
bkhome.com           SOA       dns.bkhome.com
bkhome.com           MX        30    mail.bkhome.com
bkhome.com           NS        dns.bkhome.com
bkhome.com           A         192.0.2.2
```

Continued

```
mail                    A       192.0.2.3

www                     A       192.0.2.2

brian-ventures          A       10.162.183.21

brian-invest            A       10.162.183.22
```

The preceding output shows all the subdomains and the mail record for the bkhome.com domain. From this information, we can see that there are two different networks that are providing Web services: 192.0.2.0 and 10.162.183.0.

While we used this for internal IP address allocation reasons, attackers can use this information to learn about your networks and your topology. As a general rule, you want to disable zone transfers from both the Internet and internal segments.

DNS zone transfers can be disabled both from a networking and an application perspective. To block zone transfers on the network you can filter TCP port 53 to the DNS server. While this will block the zone transfer from occurring over the network, the DNS application would still allow it if you could connect to the server on that port. Each DNS application, such as the Windows DNS implementation and BIND (Berkley Internet Name Domain) for UNIX, have different remediation steps to disable zone transfers. The zone transfer can be disabled entirely, or it can be enabled to only allow transfers to particular hosts, which is a more common implementation method.

Checklist

- Take the time to make an accurate diagram of your network infrastructure, including IAPs and leased lines from your telecommunications provider.

- Use vulnerability assessment (VA) tools, or port scanners to discover and record devices on your network.

- Using VA tools look for WAPs and examine their security policies.

- Check Regional Internet Registries (RIRs) for detailed information on your company's network blocks and assigned IP addresses.

- Query and examine your DNS servers regularly to determine if there is any unneeded information leakage or the possibility of zone transfers.

Summary

This chapter helped provide some of the basic information that can later be used in diagramming and understanding the network topology. While much of this information is not ground breaking, we have established a common language that will be used throughout the book. The use of *external* or *perimeter segments* will be used to refer to untrusted networks, or those that can be easily accessed from the Internet, while the *internal segment* will be used to describe the protected internal company networks.

We also provided some valuable information on tracking down domains and rogue networks that your IT department might not be aware of. The Regional Internet Registries will provide detailed information on the network blocks owned by your company. This information is extremely valuable, as it will help you understand what is publicly available and to where your perimeter extends. Additionally, we touched on the notion of assigning a criticality value to each of your internal and external network segments. This data will help you decide how to react when a serious security vulnerability emerges and you are forced to react to protect you company's networks.

Ultimately, having these data points will help you apply the techniques and procedures in this book. Having a solid knowledge of where all your devices are and how they interconnect will be essential in providing a solid defense-in-depth strategy to protecting your environment.

Solutions Fast Track

Internal versus External Segments

☑ External or perimeter segments are networks that are directly connected to an untrusted network, such as the Internet.

☑ Internal segments are networks that are highly protected and secured and provide interior resources that should not be available to untrusted networks.

☑ Wireless access points (WAPs) extend the perimeter into the internal segments, as they can allow untrusted and unprivileged users access to internal resources.

☑ Network and asset criticality is an important data point allowing you to prioritize your work in remediating security vulnerabilities across the enterprise.

Footprinting: Finding the IP Addresses Assigned to Your Company

☑ Regional Internet Registries (RIRs) provide detailed information regarding IP blocks assigned to your company.

☑ These RIRs can be queried using a *whois* client or through various Web sites.

☑ DNS information can be a valuable source in finding rogue domains and networks in use by your company.

Links to Sites

■ **www.arin.net** The RIR site for North America.

■ **www.apnic.net** The RIR site for the Asia Pacific region.

■ **www.ripe.net** The RIR site for Europe, the Middle East, and Africa regions.

■ **www.lacnic.net** The RIR site for Latin America.

■ **www.network-tools.com** A basic network management site featuring multiple network lookup features.

■ **www.dnsstuff.com** A site with various CGI network management and DNS-related tools.

■ **www.sec.gov** The U.S. Government Securities and Exchange Commission used for publicly traded companies and their filings.

■ **www.freeedgar.com** A site dedicated to searching the SEC filings.

Mailing Lists

■ **www.apnic.net/community/lists/index.html** Provides general discussions on the APNIC registry.

- **www.arin.net/mailing_lists/index.html** Provides numerous mailing lists regarding the North America Internet registry.
- **www.cisco.com/offer/newsletter/123668_1** This Cisco mailing list provides quick information on Cisco products and vulnerabilities.

Frequently Asked Questions

The following Frequently Asked Questions, answered by the authors of this book, are designed to both measure your understanding of the concepts presented in this chapter and to assist you with real-life implementation of these concepts. To have your questions about this chapter answered by the author, browse to **www.syngress.com/solutions** and click on the **"Ask the Author"** form. You will also gain access to thousands of other FAQs at ITFAQnet.com.

Q: How should I begin to discover and map devices on my network?

A: Port scanners and vulnerability assessment tools offer a great way to discover live devices on your network. Most tools allow you to export the results into a CSV or XML for further manipulation. Refer to Chapter 2 for more details.

Q: I have multiple Frame Relay lines in my network, but very little information on them; what should I do?

A: As boring as this sounds, digging up and reading your telecommunication contracts can be extremely beneficial in uncovering details about your leased lines.

Q: I do not have a DMZ and do not provide any services out to the Internet, so do I have a perimeter?

A: Yes, you do. Even if you have a drop-all policy on your firewall, and no DMZ connected to it, you still have devices that are connected to the Internet and could potentially be compromised. For example, at the very least your firewall has an untrusted interface connected to the Internet. This interface can fall victim to some firewall exploits and provide a door into your internal network. If you have a router connected to your Internet lines, that would be a perimeter device and poses some risk to your infrastructure.

Q: All of my network segments are critical; how can I differentiate them and assign different values?

A: This is actually simpler than you might think. Take some time and set up a meeting with your CFO or Risk Management person and ask him or her what the most critical aspects of the business are, and what could potentially cause your business to come to a crashing halt if it were to stop working or become unavailable. Then, examine your networks with these factors in mind. When you isolate those segments or devices that provide value to those vital business factors, than you have decided on which are most critical networks and devices. Everything else cascades down from there.

Chapter 2

Assessing Your Current Networks

Solutions in this Chapter:

- Monitoring Traffic
- Looking at Logical Layouts
- Performing Security Audits
- Examining the Physical Security

Related Chapters:

- Chapter 7 Network Switching
- Chapter 11 Internal Network Design
- Chapter 12 Secure Network Monitoring

☑ Summary

☑ Solutions Fast Track

☑ Frequently Asked Questions

Introduction

"Nothing in the world is more dangerous than sincere ignorance and conscientious stupidity."
—Martin Luther King, Jr.

Dr. King's words ring true even in the case of your humble network. You can't start to defend your network if you don't know everything about it. Before you skip this chapter and say, "Oh, come on—of course I know everything about my network. I am the admin, the ruler of the CAT5; I am the *One*" (*Matrix*-like stunts aside), you might want to rethink that statement. Although most administrators can immediately tell you what type of network they run (a stable one, right?) and where their important servers are located, the less physical manifestations of their digital domain might escape them. From this, sincere ignorance as to the dangers that might lurk in their network develops quite easily. This chapter will answer "what" you need to secure, and we'll see the "how" to secure portions in other chapters.

To fully assess your network, you need to examine more than just the servers. Every path that a network packet could take should be reviewed and documented. Yes, the evil word: *documentation*. You've spent most of your waking hours avoiding it, but now is the time to set aside an hour or two and get it done We're going to show you some methods in this chapter to make that chore a bit more bearable. After a few dozen pages, you'll have enviable documentation that will impress absolutely no one at a bar on weekends, but will provide the basis of a security roadmap.

Our journey of discovery starts with listening in on the wire to find out what is really happening. We discuss a handful of tools that make this task both simple and educational. We also show the statistical counters that will be the odometer for our network and give us a method to see trends in our network month to month. Examining the logical layout of your network will give us a good framework for understanding what's wrong with the network later. Vulnerability Assessment (VA) tools will be our main provider of security information for our network, and as such, we review most of the major players in the market in both software and managed service varieties. Remediation of the issues discovered is discussed as well as patch management. We finish the chapter with a discussion of creative physical security techniques that should be a part of every network.

Monitoring Traffic

An effective security plan is not going to happen if you're flying blind. You need to have visibility into your network to find out how to secure against any threats that might endanger your data. How do we discover the invisible world of 1s and 0s zipping across wires? Staring into the strands of fiber is only going to blind you, and putting your ear up to the CAT5 punch-down block won't get you very far either. There are only a couple of methods to peer into the wired world, but many tools to accomplish that task. The two common methods we explore in this chapter are:

- Sniffing the wire
- Checking the statistical data of the wire usage

Sniffing

Not only will you get strange looks from the CEO when you tell him you're going to sniff some wires in the back closet, you'll likely be asked for a urine sample for drug testing. Besides the funny name, a network sniffer (or, as they are referred to by corporate types, "network packet analyzers") are an essential part of any network administrator's toolkit.

Notes from the Underground...

Sniffer versus Sniffing

Sniffer is a product; sniffer is a type of product. The capitalization distinction is important. *Sniffer* has emerged as a proprietary eponym for network packet analyzers. Network General originally developed the product, which Network Associates now owns through its acquisition of Network General back in the late 1990s. Network engineers generically use the word to refer to all network packet analyzers, similarly to how people ask for a Kleenex when they really just want a facial tissue.

Network Sniffing Basics

In its simplest form, a sniffer is the computer network equivalent of a doctor's stethoscope. Much like the doctor puts his stethoscope on a patient's chest to investigate the symptoms pestering the patient, a sniffer can give a network engineer valuable insight into performance bottlenecks in your network. We seek to display the characteristics of packets zooming past our computer, and to peer inside these packets to examine their data.

In essence, all we ask the basic sniffer to do is to copy the packets that enter our network interface card (NIC) to the screen, hopefully in a format we can understand (seeing binary information would be of little use—interpreting that binary into ASCII characters is a minimum requirement).

Some sniffers don't stop there, and instead provide packet header information and protocol decodes. The latter is almost always found in your more expensive sniffers and is one of the many features that set them apart from their free counterparts.

Sniffing Challenges

Sounds pretty simple, right? A packet comes into the NIC, gets passed up the operating system layers, and eventually the packet driver (whether built into the sniffer or a third-party tool) receives the information. Once at the packet driver, the sniffer examines the packet and performs some formatting on it for display on your screen. Easy as pie.

Snoop on Your Neighbor

But wait—there's more! More complications, that is. This example works great if the packet were actually destined for your NIC (as determined by the destination MAC address). Remember that Ethernet is a logical bus topology. This means that every host within a particular collision domain (see Chapter 7, "Network Switching," for a complete discussion on topologies and collision domains) will "hear" or receive all packets on the network, including ones that aren't destined for your NIC. By design, the MAC layer will examine the incoming packet and if it is not addressed to itself (and not a multicast or broadcast packet, intended for all hosts), it will discard the packet before any other system components get a chance to see it.

Only seeing the packets destined for your machine would still be interesting, but it would only help you diagnose the traffic going to or coming from one machine and wouldn't give you a complete picture of the traffic traversing your network. Luckily, there is a way to prevent the MAC layer from discarding these extra packets.

Since this would basically enable your machine to be "nosey" and view all packets on the shared data bus, the term *promiscuous mode* is used to describe this special condition. The first task a sniffer has is to instruct the NIC to enter promiscuous mode so that all the packets will be captured and none will be discarded. To do this on a small percentage of troublesome NICs, a special driver is needed. For the most part, your sniffer will be able to easily start promiscuous mode.

Damage & Defense...

Password Sniffing

Even though it's been said thousands of times, now is a good time to remind you that clear-text protocols such as Telnet, POP3, and FTP really will transmit your password in broad daylight on the wire. When you begin sniffing, you'll start to see these passwords zipping by your sniffer at an alarming rate. If your users enjoy instant messaging or "chat" programs, you'll not only be able to see their IM passwords, but also the content of their conversations (and hopefully they're not discussing confidential client data in clear text).

If you've been having trouble convincing management that blocking IM traffic is a good security measure, just leave your sniffer running for a few days. Then, send e-mails to all those who opposed you using your new-found knowledge, like "I sure hope that rash clears up so that we can approve the new IM firewall rules," or "I know you're really busy, what with juggling a wife, two kids, and a mistress in Encino, but I'd really like to get consensus on this instant messaging traffic on our network." It works like a charm!

Snoop on the Whole Neighborhood

Perfect—so now we're listening in on the party line conversation thanks to promiscuous mode. We can hear our neighbor (on the local subnet), but we might not be able to hear the whole neighborhood (the entire network). To properly assess your network, you need to have your ears open to everything on the network, not just the local subnet. If your network is a switched network (meaning it employs network switches to divide the large logical bus into smaller collision domains), your NIC will only see packets specifically addressed to you, from you, or broadcast packets. A more detailed description of switching technologies can be found in Chapter 7, but for our purposes all we need to know is that we want to turn our big expensive network switch into a cheap five-dollar hub.

The reason for this is that on a hub, all ports see the packets for all other ports (horrible for network performance, but fantastic for network sniffing). On most managed switches, there is a configuration command especially designed for sniffing and other network monitoring (such as Intrusion Detection Systems—see Chapter 9 for more information). Cisco calls this feature a "SPAN" (switched port analyzer) port, while the rest of the world refers to it as "port mirroring." This command should be used with caution and only enabled on one or two ports that are directly under your control. It would be a security breach if someone were to get into your network switch's configuration and set himself up with a SPAN port—make sure you guard your passwords! Figure 2.1 shows a number of popular network switches. For the purposes of our configuration example, we will be using port 24 on the Cisco Catalyst switch as our SPAN port.

Figure 2.1 Front View of the Cisco Catalyst 2924XL, Extreme Networks Summit24, and Dell PowerConnect 3024 Network Switches

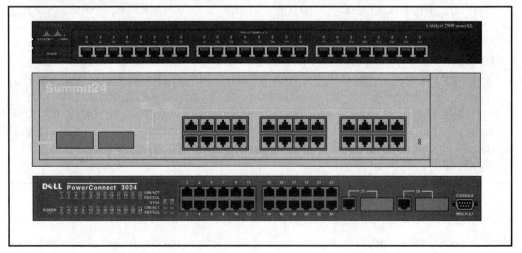

We begin by connecting to the switch (using the console serial port, Telnet, or SSH). The connection to the switch is unimportant and covered in much greater detail in your manufacturer's documentation. We're going to jump ahead and get to the good stuff. Once you have entered the configuration mode (on a Cisco Catalyst, this would be the "enable" mode), you would enter something similar to the following:

```
Switch (enable) set span 1/1-23 1/24
      Destination : Port 1/24
      Admin Source : Port 1/1-23
      Oper Source : Port 1/1-23
      Direction : transmit/receive
      Incoming Packets: disabled
      Learning : enabled
      Multicast : enabled
      Filter : -
      Status : active
%SYS-5-SPAN_CFGSTATECHG:local span session active for destination port 1/24
```

This would enable port 24 (the rightmost port on our Cisco 2924XL) as a SPAN port, for switches that run the CatOS, the Cisco embedded operating system for Catalyst switches. Some Cisco switches do not use CatOS, and instead run the IOS normally found on routers. In that case, we would use a configuration similar to:

```
Switch(config)# interface FastEthernet0/24
Switch(config-if)# port monitor FastEthernet0/1-0/24
Switch(config-if)#
```

Here, again, we designated port 24 as our SPAN port. Cisco's higher-end switches, such as a Cisco 12000 Global Switching Router, or GSR, usually run a variation of IOS, rather than the lower-end switches that run on CatOS.

Remember that when you're done with your sniffing activities, you should always disable the SPAN port, remove the SPAN feature from that port, or just always reserve that port for sniffing activities and never assign it to a user or other networking device. If you did allow a user's workstation to connect to the SPAN port, not only would that user suffer a high percentage of collisions (after all, his network card would be receiving traffic from all over the network), but you would also be opening up a security risk. That user would just have to use any of a number of packet analyzers to read sensitive information directly off the wire.

The Sniffers

Now that we have the challenges out of the way, we can move on to working with the actual sniffer software. As with most useful network utilities, the software ranges from open source to expensive and from command-line to extensive GUI-based applications. While not an exhaustive list by any stretch of the imagination, here we present some popular sniffers and some quick info on each.

- Ethereal
- TcpDump/WinDump
- Snort
- Microsoft Network Monitor
- eEye Iris
- TamoSoft CommView
- WildPackets EtherPeek
- Network Associates Netasyst

Remember most of all that your selection of sniffer depends more on just price—the features that you value should also be taken into consideration. Even if you are just curious, or need an occasional view of your network, your needs will differ from someone who wants a full-featured sniffer package with all the bells and whistles. Don't let anyone tell you which is best; try all of them first (they all allow for free trials) and choose the one that suits you.

Tools & Traps…

From Italy with Love

All sniffing tools (and indeed, other open source products as well) rely on a packet capture driver that takes the information off the NIC input buffer and exposes it to an application. This allows the author of the tool to concentrate on the interpretation of the network data, and not have to worry with the particulars of how to get the data off the wire. One extremely popular packet driver is called WinPCap (known as LibPCap for UNIX) produced by the Netgroup division of the Politecnico di Torino university, in Torino, Italy. This gem is a requirement for some of the tools discussed next, and can be downloaded and installed quite easily from the Netgroup Web site (http://netgroup-serv.polito.it). So, next time you're enjoying the powerful features of one of the open source tools, remember to thank our friends in Italy—or better yet, make a donation on their Web site (http://winpcap.polito.it/misc/wlist.htm) to thank them for their benevolent contributions to the security community.

Ethereal

We really wanted to mention Ethereal first just because it is so versatile and it is the *de facto* open source tool for sniffing. Not only can it sniff off the wire, it can also import sniff dump files from other programs such as TcpDump, Network Associates' Sniffer, Microsoft's Network Monitor, WildPacket's EtherPeek (and AiroPeek), and many more. Add to this flexibility the power to decode 407 protocols and you really get a feel for just how much collaborative effort went into this tool (see Figure 2.2 and Table 2.1).

Figure 2.2 Ethereal Network Analyzer, Showing Captured DNS Traffic

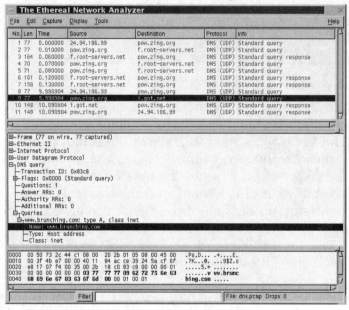

Table 2.1 Ethereal at-a-Glance

Web site	www.ethereal.com
Cost	Free (open source, GNU General Public License)
Notes	Requires WinPCap

NOTE

Interested in learning more about the Ethereal Packet Sniffer? We recommend the book *Ethereal Packet Sniffing* available from Syngress Publishing (ISBN: 1-932266-82-8).

WinDump (derived from TcpDump)

Yes, the same Italians who gave us the WinPCap driver also have provided a great Windows port of the venerable UNIX *tcpdump* command. This is as raw as sniffing gets; packets are read off the wire and spooled to your stdout (your screen). The nice part is that people who are very used to using TcpDump in the UNIX world will feel right at home with WinDump. The same syntax is used so even your old scripts should work with WinDump. If you're troubleshooting at a client site and don't have your laptop full of commercial sniffer software with you, WinDump does the trick. On many occasions, we've saved the client many hours' worth of troubleshooting by downloading WinDump, WinPCap, and taking a look on the wire. WinDump supports the entire rich filtering features of TcpDump, so you can view exactly what you're looking for. In Figure 2.3, we're trying to find any Yahoo! Messenger traffic, to see what the VP of Development has planned.

Figure 2.3 WinDump Capture of ICMP Traffic to 192.168.10.1

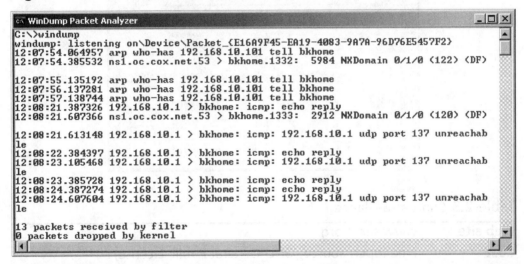

Table 2.2 WinDump at-a-Glance

Web site	http://windump.polito.it
Cost	Free (open source, GNU General Public License)
Notes	Requires WinPCap

Snort

While primarily an Intrusion Detection (IDS) tool, Marty Roesch's wonderfully useful Snort can also be used as a command-line sniffer much like WinDump. Rather than use filters to trigger alarms, you can simply output the packets to the display. Using the –d –e –v switches will give you the most sniffer-like view of data, showing the raw packet as well as the decoded information. Snort is discussed further in Chapter 9, "Intrusion Detection Systems." In Figure 2.4 we show an example of Snort listening for any TCP port 5190 (AOL) port traffic. Yes, we're hunting for AOL Instant Messenger gems (see Table 2.3).

Figure 2.4 Snort Log of ICMP Traffic to 192.168.10.101

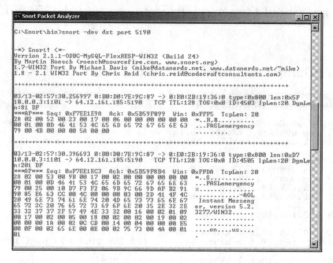

Table 2.3 Snort at-a-Glance

Web site	www.snort.org
Cost	Free (open source, GNU General Public License)
Notes	Requires WinPCap

Tools & Traps…

Foundstone SuperScan 4

Recently improved in version 4, Foundstone SuperScan is a Swiss army knife tool that belongs in every security professional's bag of tricks. Combining a rudimentary port scanner, OS identification, Windows NetBIOS enumeration, and a host of quick WHOIS, DNS, and HTTP lookup tools, SuperScan is useful when you just need a quick scanning solution in a nice GUI. This tool is great for junior administrators and those just getting started; they can get their feet wet without causing a whole lot of damage. Since no attack methods are in the tool, you don't have to worry as much about interns using the tool, versus arming them with an eEye Retina or ISS Internet Scanner (with which they could launch intrusive vulnerability checks against your sensitive servers by mistake). This free tool does not require WinPCap, and you can grab it at www.foundstone.com/resources/freetools.

Microsoft Network Monitor

An easy way (albeit less powerful than the previous two sniffers) to get started with monitoring your network is with the Microsoft Network Monitor, bundled together with Microsoft Systems Management Server (SMS). A limited version of the tool, available in Windows NT Server and Windows 2000 Server, only allows monitoring of traffic to and from the local machine (instead of the entire network segment). As with most sniffers, capture filters can be defined to narrow the focus to just the traffic that is interesting to you. Microsoft Knowledge Base Article 148942 discusses this at length. One particularly interesting feature of Network Monitor is that when you start using it, a notification packet will be broadcast to the local subnet. Other users of Network Monitor will be able to know when you start sniffing the wire. This was intended by Microsoft to be a deterrent to having just anyone sniff your network without knowing, but as a security information gathering tool, it really blows your covert cover! (See Figure 2.5 and Table 2.4.)

Figure 2.5 Microsoft Network Monitor Displaying Network Interface Statistics

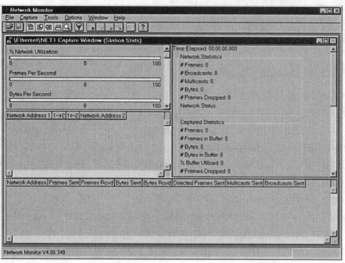

Table 2.4 Network Monitor at-a-Glance

Web site	www.microsoft.com/windowsserversystem
Cost	Free (included with server operating systems)
Notes	Sends out notification to others on the network when you use it

TamoSoft CommView

One of our favorite network sniffers, the TamoSoft CommView product is really well written. An IP Statistics window shows you all the active conversations on the wire from a very high-level view; this is very useful to just leave running and look at during different times of the day. A user who is usurping the company T1 line to download the latest Red Hat Linux distribution CD-ROM is going to stand out quickly on a display such as this. When switching over to the real packet-sniffing portion of the program, you can pick an individual packet and examine the raw data in a built-in viewer. More useful, however, is allowing the program to decode the packet into the various protocol portions and do the data translation for you. If you right-click on a packet, you can select the entire "conversation" (where it selects all the packets that were involved in the back-and-forth of the selected host with the remote server). This is much easier than trying to set up a filter. Once highlighted, you can save just those packets for later analysis (over 100 protocols can be decoded) or replay the packets on the wire (very useful for forensic analysis but potentially destructive if you are replaying the packets involved in an attack). If you're trying to perform monitoring on a very large network, you'll appreciate the remote agent monitoring capabilities; install a small agent on a machine in the target network and sit back at your desk and perform all the packet analysis—without balancing the laptop on your knee in the fourth floor wiring closet! (See Figure 2.6 and Table 2.5.)

Figure 2.6 TamoSoft CommView Sniffer Captures and Reconstructs Entire TCP Communication

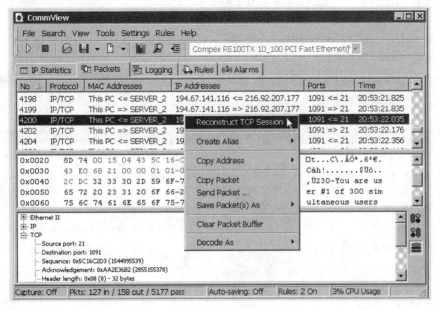

Table 2.5 CommView at-a-Glance

Web site	www.tamos.com/products/commview
Cost	Home user (noncommercial) license is $129, enterprise license is $249; demo version available
Notes	Remote agent available for monitoring many points in your network

eEye Iris Network Traffic Analyzer

Originally purchased in summer 2000 from SpyNet, the CaptureNet product was reworked and renamed to Iris, fitting the rest of eEye's product line. The user interface is deceptively simple; there is a lot packed into this program. Your standard set of capture filters is enhanced by a number of extras: the ability to create your own packet and transmit on the wire is especially useful for any security pro tinkering on a test network. One of the most entertaining features is the ability to mark a set of packets (a "conversation") and right-click on them to "send to decode." This will attempt to reconstruct the order of the packets and the end result. Do this on some HTTP traffic and Iris will render the actual HTML in a window for you. Therefore, not only can you find out who is visiting the job listing sites, you can actually see the results of their searches from the comfort of your own office. (See Figure 2.7 and Table 2.6.)

Figure 2.7 eEye Iris Network Analyzer Demonstrating the Flexibility of Decoding Raw Packets

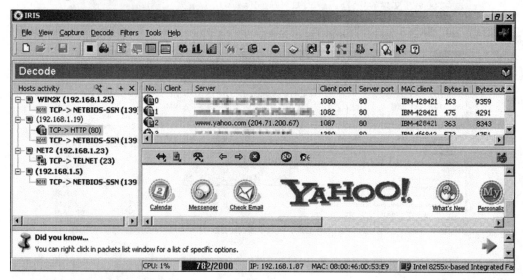

Table 2.6 Iris at-a-Glance

Web site	www.eEye.com/html/Products/Iris
Cost	With one-year maintenance, $995; free trial available
Notes	Uses its own packet driver (WinPCap not needed), easy-to-use graphical interface

WildPackets EtherPeek

One very popular protocol analyzer that has been featured in more technical books than we can imagine is EtherPeek. Its excellent GUI (with distinctive speedometer-like analog gauges in the corner) and a very easy-to-understand decode panel walk you through every part of a selected packet—truly an excellent way to learn about the inner workings of network communications. EtherPeek manages to offer all of the decoding, filtering, and diagnostics of a high-end analyzer in a well thought-out interface that beginners can digest easily. A decade after the company was founded, the AG Group renamed themselves "WildPackets" in September 2000, and has since introduced new products such as AiroPeek (the version of EtherPeek for wireless networks) and EtherPeek NX, the expert edition of their sniffer. (See Figure 2.8 and Table 2.7.)

Figure 2.8 WildPackets EtherPeek Dashboard Displaying Network Traffic Analysis

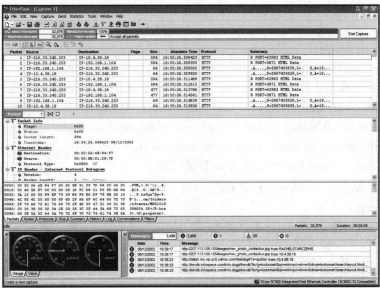

Table 2.7 EtherPeek at-a-Glance

Web site	www.wildpackets.com/products/etherpeek
Cost	With one-year maintenance, $995; demo version available
Notes	Uses its own packet drivers, good dashboard showing network health

Network Associates Netasyst

No review of network packet analyzers would be complete without giving credit to the sniffer that has been on the market (in one form or another) for the past 15 years. Those readers with experience measured in decades will remember the old Sniffer luggable appliances that looked more like carry-on luggage than a sensitive network-troubleshooting device. The product has evolved from a 50-pound shared resource to an advanced suite of applications that can be loaded on a network engineer's laptop. In addition to the familiar Sniffer Mobile, Sniffer Portable, Sniffer Voice, and Sniffer Distributed, Network Associates released a new younger brother to the family: Netasyst. Targeted at the small and medium-sized business (SMB) customers who need powerful analysis at an entry-level price, the product line replaces Sniffer Pro. In addition to the standard fare of filters and packet decode capabilities you would expect from the product that started the industry, the latest offering includes some advanced quasi-human intelligence dubbed "Expert Analysis" that attempts to analyze and interpret streams of packet capture information as a skilled network engineer would (an engineer with 15 years of experience, at that!). Netasyst can be purchased in wired-only, wireless-only, and wired/wireless combinations, as well as with or without the optional Expert Analysis. Additional add-on modules such as Netasyst Voice can detect and decode Voice-over-IP (VoIP) packets, and the wireless editions of Netasyst can decode wired equivalency protected (WEP) traffic, either during capture or post-capture, so that you can analyze encrypted communications. (See Figure 2.9 and Table 2.8.)

Figure 2.9 Network Associates Netasyst Graphs and Charts Depicting Your Network Traffic

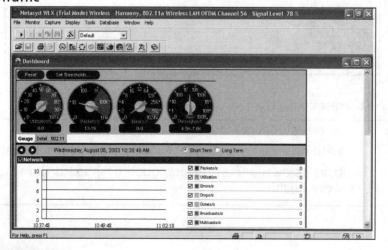

Table 2.8 Netasyst at-a-Glance

Web site	www.networkassociates.com
Cost	Pricing starts at $1,395 (without "Expert Analysis") or $3,295
Notes	The most expensive commercial packet analyzer out there

Sniffing the Air

A relatively recent variation on the sniffing theme has come about due to the proliferation with wireless networks. Although we won't specifically discuss assessing your network for wireless devices (that could be an entire book in itself), we should point out the unique challenges involved in wireless sniffing. Indeed, a great primer into wireless sniffing is found in Chapter 15 of the book *Special Ops: Host and Network Security for Microsoft, UNIX, and Oracle* (ISBN 1-931836-69-8).

To get started, you'll need specialized software and hardware. The sniffing tools that we described previously are for wired sniffing. Some vendors, like WildPackets, have wireless versions of their software. Still other vendors specialize in only wireless sniffing. Next, you might need a special wireless NIC. Some software will only work on wireless network cards that are based on the PRISM3 chipset. Still other software is more restrictive and will only work on certain models and brands of NICs. Consult the vendor Web sites for more information and make sure to read Chapter 15 of *Special Ops: Host and Network Security for Microsoft, UNIX, and Oracle*, Syngress Publishing ISBN 1-931836-69-8. It goes into depth about the differences between PRISM3 network cards and different antennae styles.

Counting the Counters

A fair amount of statistical knowledge can be gleaned quite easily by using the counters that are present in most network devices and even Windows 2000. While they won't provide as clear a picture as a sniffer will, a performance counter will be able to give you a snapshot of the state of your network.

Network Device Counters

Most managed network devices such as routers, switches, and firewalls will have some type of counter mechanism where they track important statistics about the packets that are flowing through them. This information is particularly important if the device is a gateway to the Internet or placed in your network where it is near a heavily used server. In both cases, this device will see a large percentage of your network's packets and can therefore be a good source of statistical information.

Some of the information that might be of interest is the number of "runts" (fragments) and oversized packets that have traversed your network. Moreover, it can show you how many collisions the network device has tracked. All these are very important indicators of network performance. You should get into the habit of zeroing-out the counters on a monthly or quarterly basis, and then measuring each month/quarter against the previous one. With this raw information, trends can be found easily and network growth forecasting is much simpler.

Figure 2.10 is an example of the counters built in to the Cisco Internetworking Operating System (IOS), which can be found on Cisco routers. While only high-end Cisco switches run versions of IOS, the CatOS also has the same network counters built in.

Figure 2.10 Code Listing Showing Cisco IOS and Its Counters

```
Router# show interface counters

Port            InOctets    InUcastPkts    InMcastPkts    InBcastPkts
Fe0/1           23324617          10376         185709         126020
Fe0/2                  0              0              0              0


Port            OutOctets   OutUcastPkts   OutMcastPkts   OutBcastPkts
Fe0/1            4990607          28079          21122             10
Fe0/2            1621568          25337              0              0


Router# show interface counters errors

Port          Align-Err    FCS-Err    Xmit-Err    Rcv-Err    UnderSize
Fe0/1                 0          0           0          0          0
FE0/2                 0          0           0          0          0


Port       Single-Col Multi-Col  Late-Col Excess-Col Carri-Sen  Runts
Giants
Fe0/1              0         0         0         0         0         0         0
Fe0/2              0         0         0         0         0         0         0
```

Make note of these counters, as they can be an early warning indicator to poor physical infrastructure (perhaps bad wiring or rodents in the walls eating away at your CAT5). If you see a sharp rise in error packets and retransmissions, you should check the cabling with a decent CAT5 tester—sometimes called a *reflectionometer* because it sends a signal out on the wire and measures the round-trip time it takes the electrical impulse to bounce back to the source.

SNMP Counters

Most network devices will also provide their counter information by exposing them through SNMP. This can be useful by retrieving the same error and collision packet information as mentioned in the previous section. The added benefit is if an automated task is collecting this SNMP information, it can dynamically graph these counters for you and present it on a Web page for you to review (see Chapter 6, "Secure Network Management," for examples of this).

Windows 2000 Performance Monitor

Your server's operating system might also have counter functionality. Microsoft Windows 2000 and Windows Server 2003 have performance counters built in to most of their services and hardware interactions. These counters can be accessed by using the Performance Monitor application located in the Administrative Tools section of your Start menu.

Once you start Performance Monitor, immediately you will see that it has very little to report to you. That's because we haven't asked it to track anything yet. Click on the "+" icon on the toolbar and select from a wide assortment of performance counters. Some particular ones that you will find interesting include:

- "Network Interface" object
  - Output Queue Length
  - Packets Outbound Discarded
  - Packets Outbound Errors
  - Packets Received Discarded
  - Packets Received Errors
  - Packets/sec
- "TCP" object
  - Connection Failures

- Segments Retransmitted/sec
- "UDP" object
    - Datagrams No Port/sec
    - Datagrams Received Errors
- "IP" object
    - Fragment Reassembly Failures
    - Fragmentation Failures
    - Datagrams Outbound No Route
    - Datagrams Outbound Discarded

After adding a few counters, you'll have a large number of line graphs all over your screen, as shown in Figure 2.11. You need to adjust the scale of the graph and the multiplier of the values (to scale down really large values or scale up really small values) so that it fits nicely. Once set, however, you can save your settings and call them up at a later time. Performance Monitor is one of those nice, free tools that you can leave on display on some large plasma screen in your NOC (preferably behind smoked glass) to wow your nontechnical folks and investors.

Figure 2.11 Microsoft Performance Monitor with Several Network-Related Counters

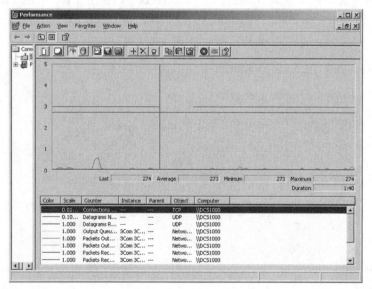

Looking at Logical Layouts

While not overly time-consuming, looking at the logical layout of your network is important in any assessment, as it will come into play later when we redesign the network (see Chapter 11, "Internal Network Design"). This shouldn't take very long to accomplish, as there are a number of quality tools out there that do automated mapping. Other times, you will find a network-mapping component in other tools, such as a wizard buried within Microsoft Visio or as a component of a vulnerability assessment (VA) tool such as Foundstone Professional.

Get on the Bus

To make things easy, start out assuming your network is a logical bus topology, because that's what most Ethernet networks are. Even though they are physically wired as a star topology (with workstations going directly back to a central switch on each floor), logically and electrically the voltage travels in a bus. Notable exceptions to this are FDDI and Token Ring networks that are logically ring configurations, yet wired as star topologies. In terms of what you will see physically in any corporate network this side of the millennium, the most common would be a physical star network. The other types are physical bus topology, ring, and mesh.

Bus Topology

A relic from the networking days of the late 1980s and early 1990s, the bus still lives on in the electrical wiring of modern Ethernet networks (see Figure 2.12). Thankfully, you won't find the bus topology in its physical form in most networks. In a bus topology, all workstations connect to one backbone cable that snakes through the entire network. Because of the electrical properties in which the packets are sent over this backbone, the ends of the bus need to be capped with "terminators," which prevent the packets from bouncing and reflecting back on the wire (causing a storm of packet echoes). These little 50-ohm devices look a bit larger than a thimble and can bring your network to a halt if they were to be removed (see Figure 2.13).

Figure 2.12 Typical Ancient Bus Architecture

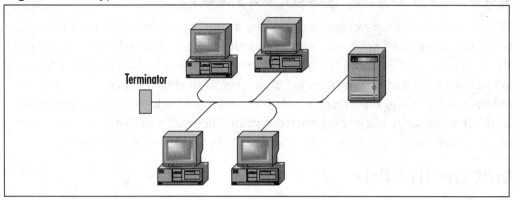

Figure 2.13 T-Connector (left) Used in Bus Topology, along with 50-ohm "Terminator" (right)

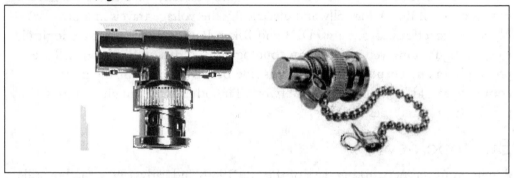

Ring Topology

While FDDI and Token Ring still use a logical ring topology, it is cumbersome to wire a physical ring. In this setup, each host is wired directly to the next downstream host, with the last host linked back to the first host (thus making the ring). Each host is only allowed to send packets on the network during its assigned time slice. This is usually represented by a "token" being received by the workstation. When the token arrives (much like that cool vacuum tube at some old banks), a message can be placed in it (if the token is empty) and forwarded along the ring. When the token returns (from the bank teller, for instance), you remove the contents (money, data, whatever) and send the packet along the ring for someone else to use. Rings were useful at a time when proper segmentation and network switching (VLANs and so forth) were not an option. Their allure came from the fact that they were *deterministic*: you knew exactly how long it would take for the token to come back to you. This was very attractive for scientists developing early video-streaming systems for research and medicine (you don't want to drop packets in the middle of a live brain surgery video stream), but has been deprecated by high-bandwidth solutions such as fiber. In the 21st century, you're not likely to run into a Token Ring network unless you work in government or education. (See Figure 2.14.)

Figure 2.14 The Ring Architecture, the Network Historian's Favorite

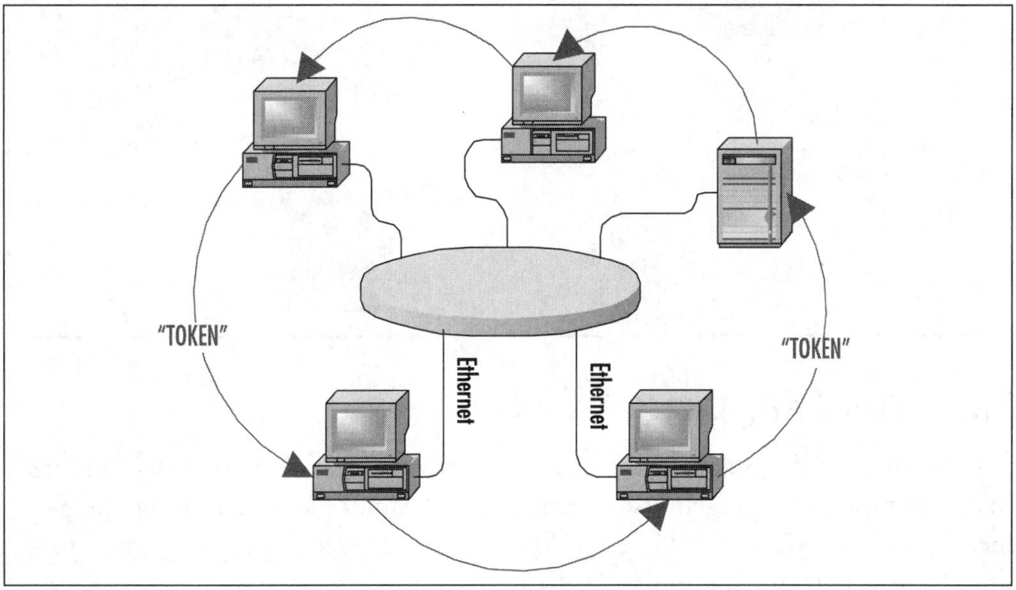

Mesh Topology

Much like the bus topology, mesh architectures are rarely used and are more of an anecdote in networking publications (such as this one). In a mesh topology, every host is connected to every other host in the network. As you can imagine, this can get annoying after 6 or 7 hosts (15 to 21 individual connections), and downright impossible after 18 or 19 hosts (153 to 171 connections). Excluding the lonely hobbyist who had a lot of CAT5 laying around and an urge to prove us wrong, nobody in his right mind has ever deployed a mesh network. If you have the time to crimp 171 CAT5 cables, we doubt you have the money to fund that many NICs in each host. Prove us wrong—check the Syngress Web site and click on "Ask the Author." We'd love to see actual photos of an operating mesh network. Prizes will be handed out in the second edition. (See Figure 2.15.)

Figure 2.15 The Last Mesh Topology You Will Ever See

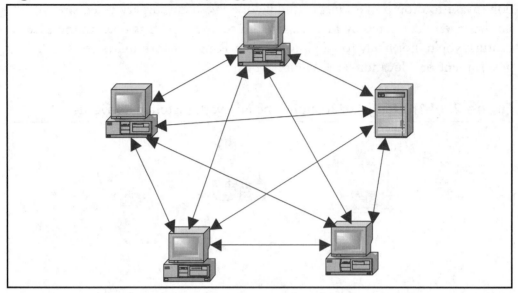

Network Mapping 1-2-3

A staple of good documentation is an eye-catching network map. When disaster strikes and the network grinds to a halt due to a faulty piece of routing equipment, your network map will be the first thing you reach for to triage the situation. Here we present some tools that can make the job easier.

Vulnerability Assessment Tools

Nearly all VA tools will present some form of a graphical map. Since the section "Performing Security Audits" goes into detail about these tools, we won't list them again. Unlike dedicated network mapping tools that scour your network, VA tools will usually only create network maps on the portions of your LAN or WAN that you have asked them to scan for vulnerabilities.

Mapping-Only Tools

These tools were designed from the ground up for network mapping and thus may have more flexibility or mapping features than their VA counterparts.

Cheops

One of the older tools (dating back to at least 1998) is the Cheops Network User Interface. The most recent release of this tool—version 0.61, released September 2001—seems to be the last one that Mark Spencer is planning on updating. This venerable Linux tool has been recently superceded by *cheops-ng* (for "next generation"), written by Brent Priddy and available as version 0.1.12 (released May 2003). (See Figure 2.16 and Table 2.9.)

Figure 2.16 Cheops 0.61 Network Mapping

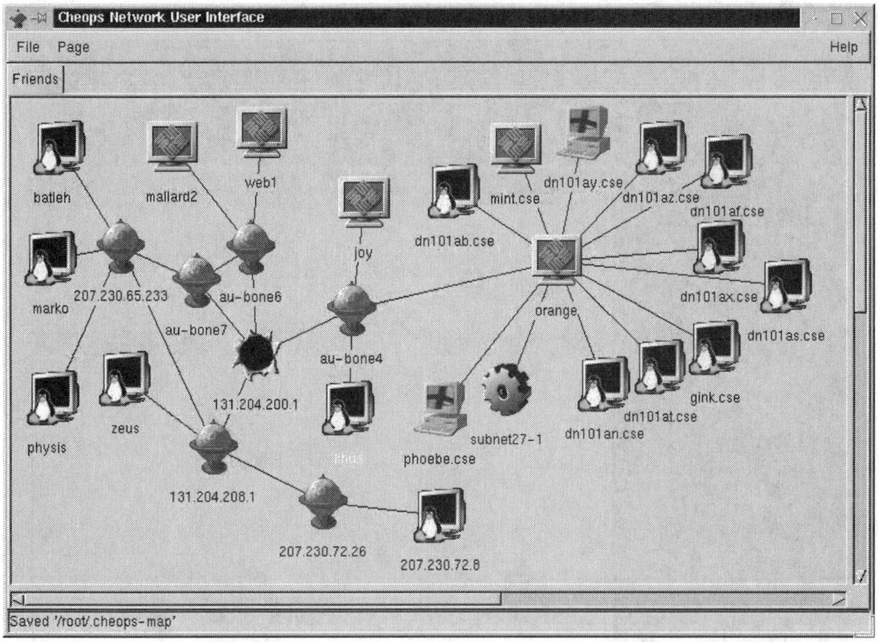

Table 2.9 Cheops at-a-Glance

Web site	http://cheops-ng.sourceforge.net
Cost	Free (open source, GNU General Public License)
Notes	Core engine hasn't been updated since 2001

NTObjectives Fire & Water Toolkit

Ntomap is a simple command-line tool capable of creating robust HTML-based network maps (see Figure 2.17 and Table 2.10). While flexible and powerful enough to map even the largest networks, the real strength of ntomap is its capability to seamlessly integrate with the Fire & Water Toolkit—a set of XML-based network tools that share data between one another. The toolkit's comprehensive HTML reporting allows one to graphically view your network architecture, while linking all data to compressive host information, including vulnerabilities, network/application services, information trending, and more. This information can be viewed in its standard HTML format, which can even be modified through the provided XSLT templates, or used discreetly through its XML files. As a command-line tool, ntomap can easily be uploaded to remote hosts.

Figure 2.17 Ntomap Displaying Basic Network Maps from Traceroutes

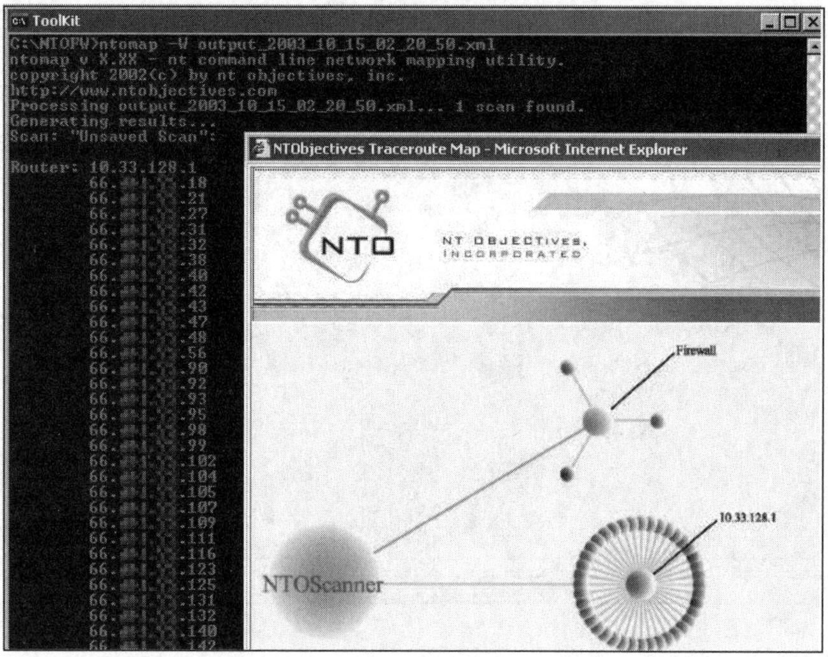

Table 2.10 Ntomap at-a-Glance

Web site	www.networkassociates.com
Cost	Free for noncommercial use
Notes	As part of an XML-based toolkit, you can chain the output of one tool with the input of another.

Qualys FreeMap Service

Qualys, a provider of network security auditing and vulnerability management services (and covered later in this chapter), provides a free mapping service to anyone with a Java-enabled Web browser at http://freemap.qualys.com. Since the promotion started in May 2003, they have received a large amount of visitors looking for a quick peek at their network from an external point of view. To sign up, you simply enter a valid e-mail address, a range of 255 addresses, and agree to a standard license agreement. Minutes later, the probe packets start flowing from their Redwood Shores data center. As the service is scanning your network, the objects that are detected are populated into an animated dynamic network map (shown in Figure 2.18). Clicking on a router will show the hosts detected behind that router hop, causing them to animate across the screen and explode out from the router. After spending time playing with the Java animation of your network (and believe us, you *will* find yourself playing with it and rearranging your network on the screen), you can run a one-time vulnerability scan of the network range to find any security holes. (See Table 2.11.)

Figure 2.18 Qualys FreeMap Service

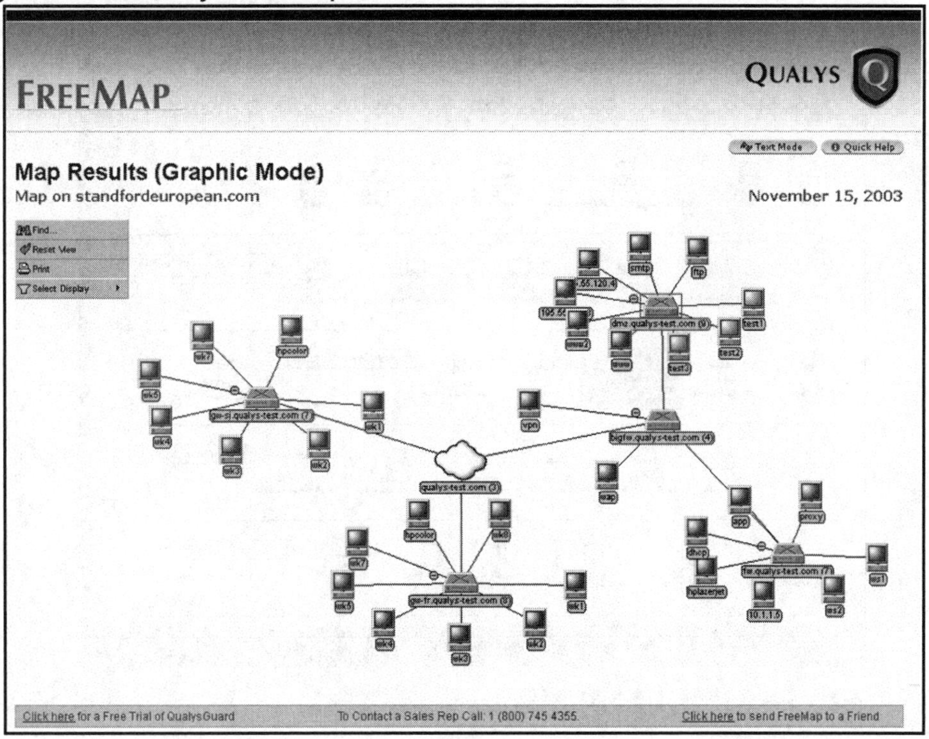

Table 2.11 FreeMap at-a-Glance

Web site	http://freemap.qualys.com
Cost	Free
Notes	Interactive Java-based UI

NetworkView

One of only two tools listed here that is not free, NetworkView is a powerful mapping utility that has an impressive SNMP and MAC database of over 11,000 entities—yet still fits on a single floppy disk. What's truly amazing is that all this power is contained in one very compact executable with no supporting DLLs or database files needed. This makes it very attractive to be another valuable item in your day-to-day toolbox of utilities. Like most mapping tools, NetworkView will use tracerouting to determine the logical layout of your network, and then proceed to probe each responding host to determine which of 19 types (router, workstation, server, printer, etc.) it is. Right-clicking on any object will allow you to perform individual port scanning on that node. (See Figure 2.19 and Table 2.12.)

Figure 2.19 NetworkView Topology Map

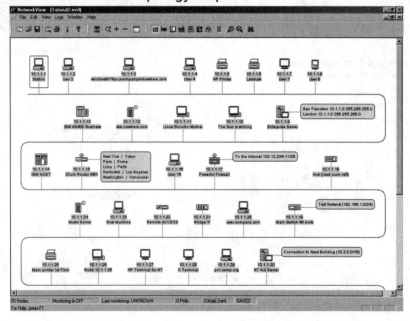

Table 2.12 NetworkView at-a-Glance

Web site	www.networkview.com
Cost	Personal licenses start at $59; demo version available
Notes	If you leave the program running, it can even serve as a rudimentary network monitoring tool.

NOTE

Interested in learning more about network monitoring tools? Chapter 6, "Secure Network Management," has a wealth of information regarding these and other complementary tools.

Microsoft Visio

The humble workhorse of any network administrator, Microsoft Visio has always been on the short list of "must have" programs for day-to-day survival. One particularly convenient feature was the Network AutoDiscovery wizard that would search the local subnet (using SNMP) or import the objects in a Novell NDS Tree or Microsoft Active Directory tree and populate your diagram automatically. Available in Visio 2000 Enterprise Edition and wildly popular, this feature was inexplicably yanked from later versions of Visio. The Visio 2003 FAQs states that due to customer feedback, they invested their resources in other areas on the product and refer you to use other third-party tools for your mapping needs. So, if you happen to have an older version of Visio 2000 Enterprise, hang on to it. The rest of us with Visio 2003 might ask you to bring your laptop over and do some diagramming for us. (See Table 2.13.)

Table 2.13 Visio at-a-Glance

Web site	www.microsoft.com/visio
Cost	$168 for Visio 2003 Standard; $460 for Visio 2003 Professional
Notes	Comes with hundreds of stencils and icons to help make excellent network maps (how do you think we made all of the illustrations in this book?).

Performing Security Audits

If you have read this far into this chapter, security is high on your list of priorities. One of the most important activities in any network assessment is a review of the current (and trust us, you have some) security vulnerabilities that exist in your network. This can be accomplished using a local application or a third-party hosted (managed) security service. The former is the choice of large corporations or consultant groups that have the time and the energy needed to devote to these systems. The latter is best suited for very tight IT budgets (and shrinking IT staff head count) that need a quick way to examine their external, Internet-facing server vulnerabilities.

Vulnerability Assessment

Having a well-designed firewall policy is not enough to fully protect your network; all you have done is fortify your perimeter defenses. However, what can happen with just the few ports that you have allowed through the firewall? Certainly, the NIMDA and Code Red worms of 2001 have shown that even with just the HTTP (port 80) open, your network is still exposed to plenty of external threats. What VA attempts to do is examine your network for weaknesses and find as-yet-unexploited deficiencies in your current software. Much in the way a home inspection will tell you if you'll likely need to replace the roof in a couple years simply by inspecting the termite damage on the cross-beams, a good VA package can examine the running processes and revision levels on your servers and clue you in to areas where you might have issues in the future. Better to proactively patch up your servers today than reactively run around shutting down infected machines tomorrow.

Notes from the Underground…

Reading Tea Leaves

OS identification is an art form, not a science. What you are basically asking software to do is to ascertain the operating system that is running by looking at the peculiarities of the way they construct their packets. They aren't triggering on anything that is screaming out the OS name—

Continued

there is no universal OS identification string included in your transmission. What we're asking is a little like determining someone's future by reading tea leaves or tarot cards. We're looking at the artifacts of network transmissions and making inferences based on that.

All software (that isn't based on pre-installed agents) is taking its "best guess" at the remote OS. In some cases, guessing correctly is impossible; there is no difference between Macintosh OS X, 10.1, and 10.2, for example. Other times, there are two OS types that are very similar and the software guesses incorrectly. Most of the software mentioned here provides for a way of tweaking the OS identification process to better fit your network. In some cases, it's as simple as weighing one OS more heavily than another in ranking tables (thereby influencing the vote one way or another).

All major vendors welcome customer input, and if you are consistently getting erroneous results, or if you have a peculiar device on your network that they might not have had access to in their testing, contact them so that they can include it in their databases during a maintenance release or update package.

Local Application

The products in this group are meant to run on your laptop (if you're a traveling network security consultant) or on a dedicated server in your infrastructure (for larger installations). All of them have a method of updating their internal database of vulnerability checks on a regular basis (much like anti-virus software) so that you are always scanning your network with the most current information. Most software offerings have three major parts:

- **Discovery**, where the VA tool attempts to determine which of the IP addresses you entered as targets are actually alive on the network, and which services those live machines have running.

- **Vulnerability assessment**, where each running service is probed from a repository of known attack sequences.

- **Reporting** the results of the assessment in an easy-to-read format (usually HTML with plenty of pie graphs and charts).

Some of the VA tools try to differentiate their product offering from the rest of the industry (and especially the commercial offerings need to differentiate themselves from Nessus, the open-source alternative) by adding unique features, faster performance, more usability, or providing more vulnerability tests (often referred to as "checks" or "check count"). Here we will briefly review the six most prevalent VA tools on the market, but there are certainly more.

Nessus

In earlier sections we saw how commercial sniffers must convince users to pay for their products, while (seemingly) getting similar results from an open-source tool (Ethereal, WinDump, etc.). They accomplish this by adding advanced features on top of a core set of functionality, but they are always compared to their open-source older brothers. The VA tool market is much the same, with commercial tools constantly trying to outdo the yardstick for the industry: the open-source Nessus vulnerability scanner. In line with the communal thinking of the open-source movement, Nessus has an open database where anyone can contribute vulnerability checks to the product, using a special Nessus Attack Scripting Language (NASL). Much like the worldwide Internet user community support of the Snort IDS (where new checks are available hours after a new attack is detected), the NASL database of checks keeps growing. However, since checks are written by people with different levels of experience, your mileage may vary.

Nessus has smart service recognition and won't be fooled by "security through obscurity" techniques (such as running your Web server on port 8080 instead of 80). Another interesting feature is Nessus' built-in network intrusion detection system (NIDS) evasion techniques, which takes many of the common methods used by attackers to avoid detection (see Chapter 9 for more information about IDS and IPS) and makes them one-click simplicity. Report output from Nessus is available as ASCII, HTML, or LaTeX (that can be converted to PDF).

Nessus 2.0 was the current stable build as of the publication date of this book, and is available for UNIX environments. Windows users can install a native client application to connect to a UNIX server running *Nessusd*, but there is no native version of the Nessus server for Windows environments. (See Figure 2.20 and Table 2.14.)

Figure 2.20 Nessus NG Console Showing NetBIOS Vulnerabilities

Table 2.14 Nessus at-a-Glance

Web site	www.nessus.org/download.html
Cost	Free
Notes	Subject to false-positives with open-source vulnerability scripts

NeWT

If you fell in love with Nessus when you worked at a UNIX-centric data center, but now live in the Windows world, Tenable Network Security has ported Nessus into a product called NeWT. The GUI is easy to use and resembles the simplicity of the Microsoft Baseline Security Advisor. NeWT includes many things that make penetration testing very easy, such as an address book of common targets, customizable security tests, and live updates of new checks. If you don't like one of NeWT's canned reports, you can write a new XML style sheet or import your data directly into Microsoft Office. The basic edition of NeWT is licensed per machine (not target address) and can scan whichever Class C network segment the machine is currently attached to (meaning that you can travel from network to network, but you can only scan 256 IP addresses in one shot). NeWT Pro has no IP address limitation and also has the capability to act as a Nessus daemon (and receive requests from Nessus clients). (See Figure 2.21 and Table 2.15.)

Figure 2.21 Tenable Security NeWT Security Scanner in Action

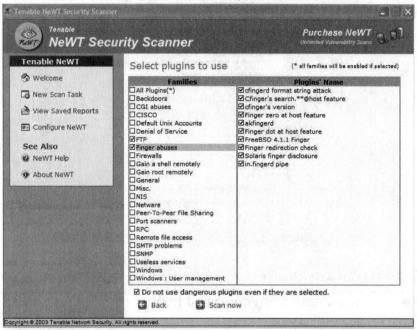

Table 2.15 NeWT at-a-Glance

Web site	www.tenablesecurity.com/newt.html
Cost	$500 for 256 addresses; NeWT Pro also available for $3,000 (unlimited scanning)
Notes	Based on Nessus, has a huge amount of community support for the latest vulnerabilities

**Passive Vulnerability Scanning:
Never Ask for Permission or Forgiveness**

Anyone who has done vulnerability scanning has most likely had to either ask for permission to scan a network, or explain why a certain scan crashed a key network resource. Tenable's NeVO passive scanner changes this. It determines vulnerabilities completely through passive analysis of the network traffic. It's deployed like a sniffer, but gives you data as if it came right from Nessus. Tenable has written NeVO to produce output compatible with the Nessus vulnerability scanner. NeVO can identify hosts, their OS, their services, their applications, and the vulnerabilities found in those applications. More information about NeVO is available at www.tenablesecurity.com/nevo.html.

eEye Retina

Retina from eEye has a slick GUI wrapped around a powerful VA scanner. You might have heard of eEye in your monthly Microsoft security bulletins; their research and development teams pride themselves on the amount of vulnerabilities in Microsoft software they discover. You can find a nod of thanks embedded in Microsoft Security Bulletins MS03-036, MS03-039, and others. Because of their expertise in vulnerability analysis, updates to Retina happen almost daily, while other products update weekly or semi-monthly. Like Nessus, Retina makes no assumptions that a Web server will answer on port 80; instead, it will analyze the traffic and determine the service running regardless of its use (or more likely, nonuse) of standard IANA-assigned port numbers. For OS detection, Retina has licensed the popular NMap database of OS fingerprints, which is very extensive. To further differentiate their product offering, eEye includes wireless access point (AP) detection and a fuzzy logic vulnerability detection system they call CHAM—Common Hacker Attack Methods. Retina, like most VA tools, is licensed based on the amount of target IP addresses you intend to scan. See Figure 2.22 and Table 2.16.)

Figure 2.22 eEye Retina Showing an IIS Vulnerability

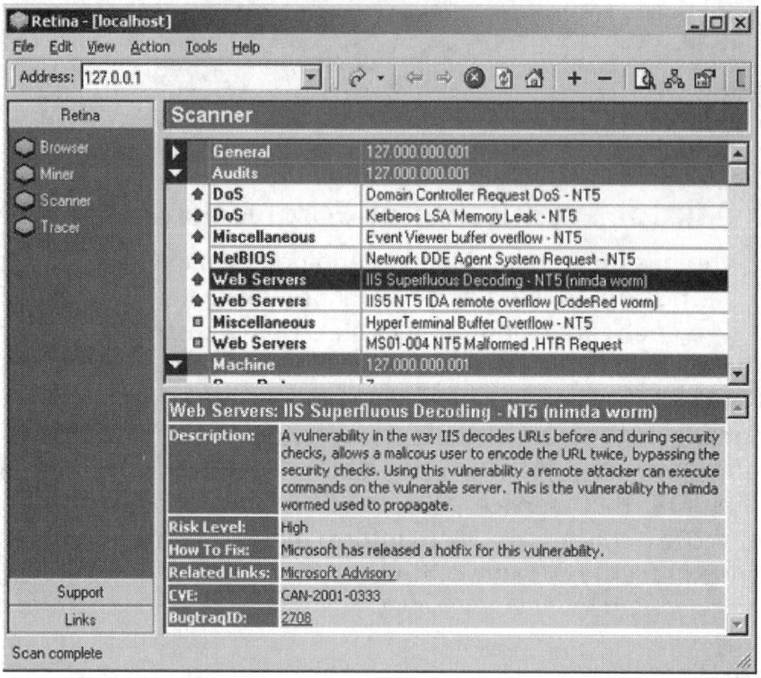

Table 2.16 Retina at-a-Glance

Web site	www.eEye.com/html/Products/Retina
Cost	$995 for 16 IP addresses; $6,520 for 256 IP addresses
Notes	With the talented eEye Research team churning out new Microsoft vulnerabilities at a steady pace, this scanner will have an arsenal of information for each check.

eEye REM

Worth noting are the enterprise-level capabilities of REM, the eEye Remote Enterprise Management module. While not a VA tool itself, it allows many copies of Retina (as well as other eEye products such as SecureIIS and Blink) to plug in to one central console for advanced reporting and management. Using REM allows an organization to use the ticketing system to assign remediation tasks (install patch, etc.) to various users within a large IT department. With different levels of user authority and differing "scopes" of responsibility for each user account, you can quickly concentrate each technician on your staff to his or her vulnerabilities. (See Table 2.17.)

Table 2.17 REM at-a-Glance

Web site	www.eEye.com/html/Products/REM
Cost	Contact vendor for customized price breakdown for your environment
Notes	Combine the power of many copies of Retina into one central console

Foundstone Professional

Designed for the small office or the network security professional on the go, Foundstone Professional is the portable edition of Foundstone's full-strength vulnerability assessment tool, Foundstone Enterprise. The core engine is built for speed and can scan a 65,000+ address Class B network segment in about six hours; a huge 16 million+ address Class A segment takes about 48 hours. After detecting the active machines on your network, the library of Foundstone Scripting Language (FSL) checks are launched at the targets where appropriate (checks intended for UNIX systems will not be wasted on detected Windows systems).

Vulnerability probes begin with less-intrusive checks and escalate in sophistication (much like a real attacker would) across all targets. An FSL developer class is available that can teach you how to author custom FSL scripts targets for any peculiar network applications or custom Web applications you have in your network. The language is based largely on the extensible ECMAscript standard. Foundstone Professional will generate a detailed network map showing which machines and subnets have high-risk vulnerabilities on them, as well as note any (potentially rogue) wireless APs. By assigning a criticality to each scanned asset, the software can take this into account when determining overall digital risk (you might be more concerned about a medium-risk vulnerability on your accounting server than you would be on a high-risk vulnerability on a secretary's workstation).

Reports with detailed vulnerability analysis and executive-level summaries can be presented in HTML or exported via XML. The Foundstone Professional-TL product is licensed with professional service organizations or freelance security consultants in mind; unlimited scanning on all your customer networks with all results reporting back into one database. This enables the smaller consultants to provide a high level of personal attention to all their clients by reviewing all the results across the entire Professional-TL database. (See Figure 2.23 and Table 2.18.)

Figure 2.23 Foundstone Professional HTML Reports

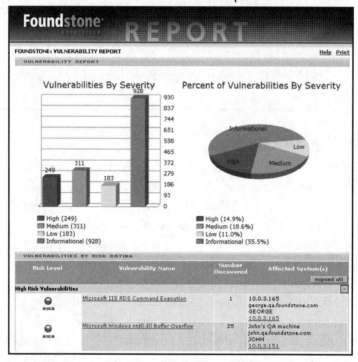

Table 2.18 Foundstone Professional at-a-Glance

Web site	www.foundstone.com/products/pro.htm
Cost	$5,900 for 100 IP addresses; Free trial version available
Notes	Results are stored in a highly relational SQL database, which makes ad hoc reporting or other data mining techniques simple.

Foundstone Enterprise

For larger environments that need an enterprise view of their business risk, Foundstone Enterprise builds on the feature set of Foundstone Professional and adds an interactive Web portal that can manage many scan engines around your WAN. The Foundstone Enterprise Manager portal allows your IT staff to view the results of past scans, track the risk exposure of your network using the trending provided by the Executive Dashboard view, and research the most recent changes (new hosts appearing or new vulnerabilities) in your network. Included with the Enterprise Manager is the Remediation Ticket Center, which opens a new incident or "ticket" for each vulnerability found during the course of a scan. As an administrator, you can assign these tickets as to-do tasks for your technicians, and track their progress, as described in the "Remediation" section later in this chapter.

By purchasing add-on components such as the Threat Correlation Module and Enhanced Reporting Module, you can extend the detailed reporting capabilities of Enterprise. The Threat Correlation Module (shown later, in the "Managed Service" section) is a customized security news feed that will correlate upcoming or potential threats to your digital security with previously obtained vulnerability information on your network.

Foundstone makes good use of their professional services experience in the industry by quantifying your business risk in their Foundstone Security Factors. These include the security ranking called FoundScore, which compares specific aspects of the scanned environment against best practices. This number, ranging much like an exam score from 0 to 100, provides a useful abstraction of security information into a format that can be easily tracked over time. When the board of directors wants to know if your network security is better now than it was last year, you usually would have to find a way to describe the complex mix of vulnerabilities, hosts, and services to a nontechnical audience. With the FoundScore, you can easily track an improvement in network security (noted as an increase in your FoundScore). By comparing your FoundScore with other published industry FoundScores for your industry, you can answer the board's next question: "Are we doing better than our competition?" (See Figure 2.24 and Table 2.19.)

Figure 2.24 Foundstone Enterprise, Showing FoundScore Trending Across Most Recent Scan Jobs

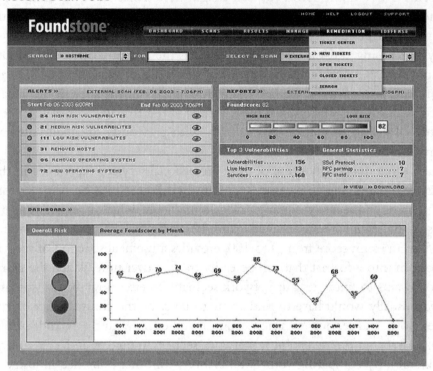

Table 2.19 Foundstone Enterprise at-a-Glance

Web site	www.foundstone.com/products/enterprise.htm
Cost	Contact vendor for customized price breakdown for your environment
Notes	Along with a centralized "dashboard" of your organization's risk, the Web portal allows centralized scheduling of multiple scan engines across the globe.

Tools & Traps…

Apples to Oranges

When considering which VA tool to purchase, you need to take into account more than just raw "check count" (that is, the number of vulnerability checks the software comes with). In order to inflate their numbers, some vendors write two or three checks for the same vulnerability, and give them slightly different names. One excellent way to level the playing field is by using the MITRE Corporation's "Common Vulnerabilities and Exposures" (CVE) universal reference numbers. These index numbers are an excellent way to cross reference what one tool found versus the other, which is very useful when you're evaluating many tools and deciding where to spend your budget dollars. The references also allow you to root out duplicate checks provided by the vendor, for the same CVE entry. Before a particular vulnerability is assigned a CVE number, it undergoes a great deal of scrutiny by the review board. During this period, it is a *candidate* vulnerability and noted as such by the "CAN" prefix. Some of the vulnerabilities listed in the next section have CAN identifiers that will likely be approved and converted to CVE identifiers by publication time. Find out more at http://cve.mitre.org.

Free Tools

Apart from the software listed earlier, many vendors rapidly produce free scanning tools after a major worm or vulnerability is announced. They do this not only because of their own generosity in giving back to the security community, but also in the hopes that you will like their free tool so much that you will at least consider them when you have the budget ready for a real VA package. Quick links to recently released tools (that address problems that are probably still plaguing your network as this book went to press) include:

- Microsoft Messenger Service (CAN-2003-0717)
    - www.eeye.com/html/Research/Tools/MSGSVC.html
    - www.foundstone.com/resources/proddesc/messengerscan.htm
- Microsoft MSBlaster Worm (CAN-2003-0352)

- www.eeye.com/html/Research/Tools/RPCDCOM.html
- www.foundstone.com/resources/proddesc/rpcscan.htm
- http://support.microsoft.com/?kbid=824146
- Cisco Denial of Service (CAN-2003-0567)
  - www.foundstone.com/resources/proddesc/ciscan.htm
- Microsoft SQL Slammer (CAN-2002-0649)
  - www.eeye.com/html/Research/Tools/SapphireSQL.html
  - www.foundstone.com/resources/proddesc/sqlscan.htm
  - http://support.microsoft.com/?kbid=323875

Managed Vulnerability Assessment

When you're short on time and do not want to build out an infrastructure to perform scanning of your network for vulnerabilities, you can benefit from having a managed security service do all the hard work for you. The two solutions listed here perform a pure managed vulnerability assessment, while other solutions (from Guardant, Symantec, and others) mix vulnerability assessment with IDS and firewall management for an all-around outsourced security. If you have enough on your plate with just keeping up with server patches and want to perform security assessments on demand, these solutions are a good fit.

Foundstone Managed Service

The Foundstone Managed Service uses the Foundstone Enterprise software, deployed at one of the company's secure data centers. Customers can purchase a subscription and have a Web portal where they can launch scans as needed or on a schedule. With zero onsite deployment, no administration or maintenance, and very little training, any member of the IT staff can gain control of the exposed vulnerabilities of an organization. The Foundstone Managed Service produces attractive HTML reports that can be downloaded in compressed archives or viewed online. The real power of the system is evident when creating accounts for all the members of your team within the portal. After a scan has completed, each newly found vulnerability is tracked in a Remediation Center (see Figure 2.27) and can be assigned to a member of your team.

A recent addition to the service offering is the Threat Correlation Module, which is continually updated with forward-looking security threat information. Before the next worm becomes an actual vulnerability (with the associated vulnerability check or signature updated in the database), it shows up as a potential vulnerability or *threat* in this correlation module. News stories are updated twice a day from the Foundstone Labs research team, and clicking on any story will link to further detail on the right. The "correlation" part of the name (rather than just being a nifty interface to a security newsletter) is that for each selected threat, the module will scan your *existing* scanned host information and project which machines can or will be victimized by the upcoming threat. If you take the time to rank your critical assets in the portal with a number from 1 to 5, this ranking will be taken into consideration when determining the overall risk for that host (the colored numbers on the bottom left, see Figure 2.25). Long before the Microsoft DCOM vulnerabilities were unleashed on the world in September 2003, there was a threat article warning about impending attacks. Based on correlation information (banner, port, OS, services found) embedded in the news article, your at-risk DCOM installations can be determined and patched before the vulnerability hits the open streets. (See Table 2.20.)

Figure 2.25 Foundstone Managed Service Threat Correlation Module

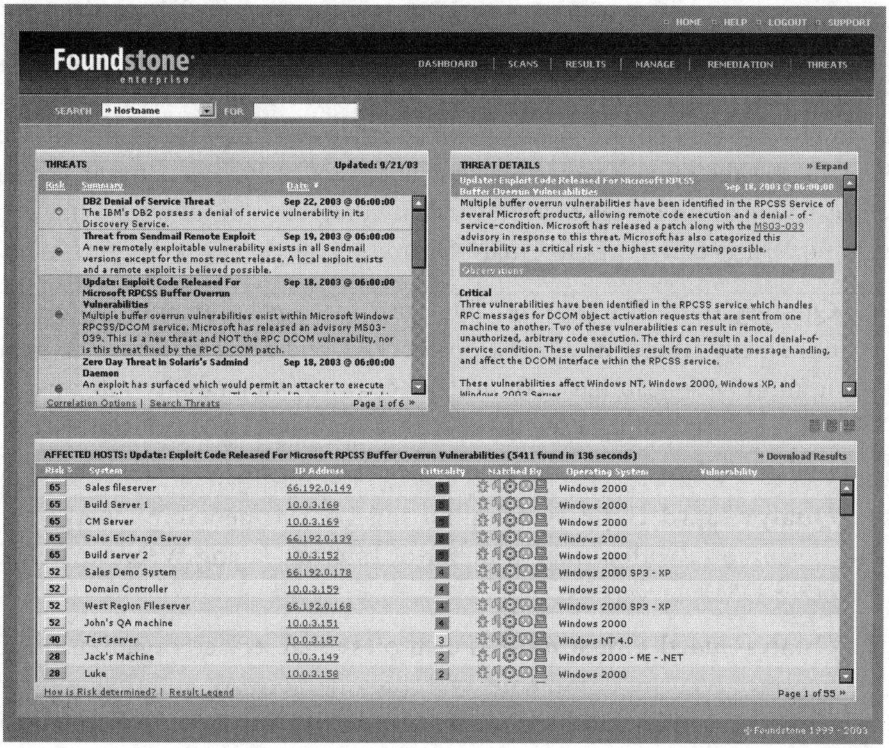

Table 2.20 Foundstone Managed Service at-a-Glance

Web site	www.foundstone.com/products/managedservice.htm
Cost	$2,500/year for five live IP addresses; Free trial subscription available
Notes	Available soon—a Threat Compliance module that will graph an organization's responsiveness to discovered vulnerabilities.

Qualys QualysGuard

Many of Qualys' customers enjoy the immediacy of a Web-delivered vulnerability management service. Customers can simply scan their network perimeter or internal systems without installing software, building out complex systems to protect their sensitive vulnerability data, or investing in more personnel to manage these systems. Qualys' approach to vulnerability management enables customers to perform the complete cycle of network discovery (mapping), vulnerability assessment (scanning), reporting, and remediation all within the QualysGuard system. (See Figure 2.26 and Table 2.12.)

External (perimeter) scans are performed on request or can be scheduled for frequent testing. Qualys maintains an impressive Knowledge Base of unique vulnerabilities—currently totaling over 3000 entries—which allows the QualysGuard service to provide very comprehensive and accurate scanning. Internal scans are performed using the same Knowledge Base and use QualysGuard Intranet scanner appliance(s), which can be easily deployed and configured in minutes. Qualys has three core offerings based on the QualysGuard service:

- **QualysGuard Enterprise** Designed for large, distributed organizations with thousands of desktops, servers, and remote networks, many administrators can have controlled access to vulnerability information, while still providing executives with a high-level view of the enterprise's security status.

- **QualysGuard Express** Ideal for small departmental intranets or an organization with a small number of Internet-facing Web, extranet, and other DMZ servers.

- **QualysGuard Consultant** For professional service organizations or freelance security consultants who provide network auditing and risk-reduction services and require a solution that can be quickly deployed and used remotely.

■ **QualysGuard MSP** Designed for other managed service providers to immediately deploy their own managed service as a stand-alone solution, or as part of an integrated suite of managed security offerings.

Figure 2.26 Qualys QualysGuard Sample HTML Report

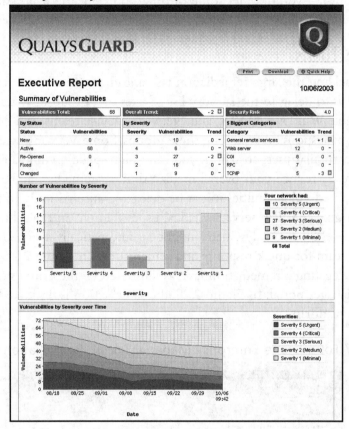

Table 2.21 QualysGuard at-a-Glance

Web site	www.qualys.com/webservices
Cost	$3,495/year for 5 IP addresses (pricing varies on IP address pool size)
Notes	Pay-per scan options are also available.

Remediation

This could be the most obvious step in your overall network assessment. When you find problems in your network, fix them! Rather than carry around a notebook or the ubiquitous spreadsheet of vulnerability data that we all have on our desktops (admit it—you do!), let some of these tools put the *management* in your vulnerability life cycle.

Delegate Tasks

The key to tackling the large remediation task ahead of you after performing a security audit is to delegate the laundry list of fixes to a group of system administrators. Assemble Windows, UNIX, and Network Device teams, and divide up the list according to responsibility among these groups. Some VA tools will allow you to designate particular users to whom you can assign specific vulnerability tasks, which can greatly reduce your overall median time-to-remediation. For example, Web-server related vulnerabilities might be delegated automatically to the IT professional managing the Web servers. Critical issues ("High" in Foundstone Enterprise, "Level 5" in QualysGuard) might be automatically assigned to an internal tiger team for quick response and remediation. In Figure 2.27, we see an example of delegating a remediation task, as illustrated by the Foundstone Enterprise Manager portal. In Figure 2.28, the same action is illustrated within the QualysGuard platform.

Figure 2.27 Foundstone Enterprise Manager Portal, Remediation Center

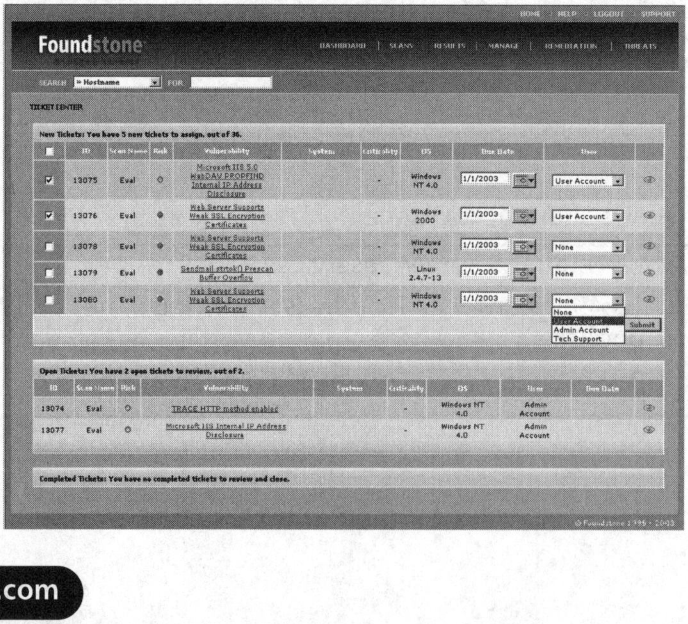

Figure 2.28 Qualys' QualysGuard Vulnerability Management and Ticketing

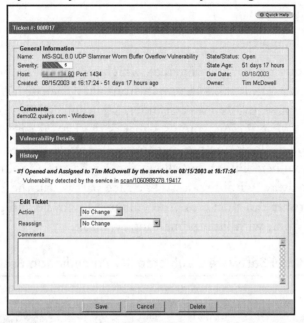

For each vulnerability found, a trouble ticket is created. These tickets can be assigned to users and given a deadline for completion. Much like a full-blown helpdesk application, a history of ticket assignment, notes posted, and activities surrounding that ticket are kept in the database. After a system administrator has fixed a problem, he or she can mark the ticket as closed. These systems can create a "micro-scan" for just that vulnerability and host machine combination to make sure that the issue has truly been resolved. Because micro-scans are highly targeted, they execute very quickly.

Alternatively, the next network scan will also uncover if the vulnerability is still present and re-issue the ticket to the user. The nice part about this is that as the security administrator, you know that any tickets returned to you are truly completed and verified by the system.

Patch Management

Sometimes, the best bet for the ever-present Microsoft hotfix is to purchase software to deal with the problem automatically. While outside the scope of this chapter, we should mention some products that can manage the download, distribution, and reporting of patches across your network, such as:

- Shavlik HFnetchkPro

- Patchlink

- Citadel Hercules

Of special interest is Citadel Hercules, which combines the best of both worlds (see Figure 2.29). It takes the input from your favorite VA tool (including Foundstone Enterprise, ISS Internet Scanner, Microsoft MBSA, Nessus, Qualys QualysGuard, and eEye Retina) and uses that as the basis for patch distribution. This efficient model allows one product to excel at what it does best (the VA tool seeking out vulnerabilities) and allows the remediation tool to make those vulnerabilities go away (within reason). The nice part is that the Hercules patch management software can then close the vulnerability cycle and go from discovery to remediation with little human intervention.

Figure 2.29 Citadel Software's Vulnerability Remediation Best Practices

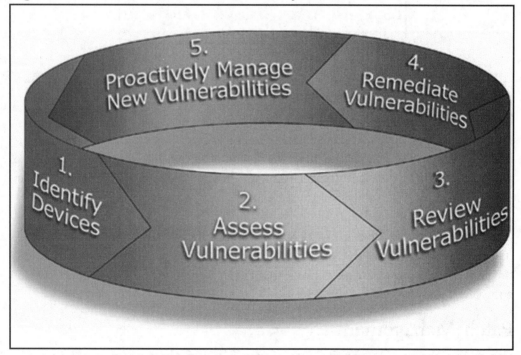

Follow-Up

Essential to any security audit is the scheduling of a follow-up audit. The purpose of this is to see if the state of security in your network has improved or deteriorated. Having a one-time security audit is useful, but not nearly as useful as having a history of quarterly security audits. If you can afford it, monthly audits are even better since they allow you to react on a much faster scale. If you are using enterprise-level VA software that allows for advanced scheduling (eEye REM and Foundstone Enterprise both do), you'll be able to have trending information that shows your recent scans and if the trend is toward a more secure network. Some particularly security-conscious folks might even opt for daily scans of their most valuable externally facing assets just to make sure they are the first to know about a potential flaw instead of the evil-doers of the world.

Examining the Physical Security

After examining everything about your network from a digital point of view, it is necessary to take a good look at the physical attributes of your network. Every safeguard that you take at the network layer won't mean much if your attacker is able to walk in, pick up your firewall, and toss it in the back of his pickup truck.

Who's Knocking on Your NOC?

All of your infrastructure rooms or network operation centers (NOCs) should have proper physical security. First, you must ask yourself if your entire infrastructure is actually enclosed in rooms! How many networks have you seen where a critical hub or switch or router was carelessly placed underneath someone's desk? Your firewall security policy might be first rate, but if the firewall is in danger of being unplugged by someone's foot, you really haven't secured your network.

All sensitive network equipment should be stored in rooms that have most if not all of the following characteristics:

- Locking door
- Dedicated power circuit
- Dedicated, round-the-clock air conditioning, heating (and humidifier/dehumidifier, if necessary)
- Video monitoring (or other log) of entries and exits
- Data-grade fire suppression

Let's face it, how many people can tell the difference between HALON and FM-200 fire suppression? Okay, put your hands down, show-offs. For the rest of us, there's hope. Large data center companies employ highly talented sales engineers to know the intricate differences in heat dissipation, humidity levels, and fire suppression qualities. Even if you're not in the market for collocated rack space, it certainly wouldn't hurt to call up Global Crossing, SBC Data Services, Cable & Wireless, Equinix, or your favorite local hosting provider to pick their brains a bit. Just act interested and smile a lot.

More Is Better

Physical security definitely adheres to the "more is better" approach. In fact, layering methods is usually your best bet to slow down a determined attacker and provide adequate mobility to your staff. Consider starting out with a digital combination lock on the NOC rather than keys. This will allow you to issue unique codes to all of your staff that you can track later. Supplement this with individual rack door locks and only give the appropriate people keys. This way, you still allow your junior-level staff to enter the NOC to monitor the system and do front-line troubleshooting of network outages, while retaining control of the rack to your senior-level staff.

From this basis, you can scale up to having biometrics on the NOC door. This proves that your senior network engineer really is entering the NOC, and not some crafty mailroom worker who has been watching the codes being entered. As a second layer, closed-circuit surveillance cameras recording to tape inside the NOC and aimed at the door will provide a log of who actually entered; although this doesn't prevent the mailroom malcontent from entering, it does document it for later review. A third layer could be to have digital combination locks on the rack doors to cut down on the expense of keys.

Stay Current with Your Electrical Current

With additional hardware known as "intelligent power strips" installed in your rack, you can measure the amount of electrical current that your equipment is drawing from your power circuit. After you blow your first circuit at the data center and have your entire network come to a screeching halt, you'll want to look into measuring your amperage draw from the circuit. Remember that having backup power is good—but if you're drawing more amps than you had originally planned, your UPS will not last as long as expected. In the worst case, you might overload the UPS and then be faced with a hard and very abrupt shutdown of your network (trust us on that one). During the writing of this chapter, one of our racks blew a fuse downstream from the UPS, which resulted in an abrupt shutdown. The UPS batteries were powerless to stop the power failure since the fuse was downstream. Since then, we monitor our amperage *religiously*. Well, maybe not religiously; but definitely monthly.

Extra Ports Equal Extra Headaches

Modern buildings have the benefit of being pre-wired with one or two Ethernet ports in every room. By the same token, modern buildings have the security risk of having an access point to your network in almost every room. How easy would it be for a vendor to be sitting quietly in your conference room, waiting for a meeting to start, and get on your network? If you're using DHCP, all the vendor would need to do is plug in and start browsing your network. Armed with this information, the vendor might use his knowledge of your departmental budget to charge you a high price, or simply sell the information to your competitor should you decline his offer.

Default Disabled

The best strategy for these heavily pre-wired buildings is to "default disable" your ports. This means either do not patch all the available ports, or patch them but have those ports administratively disabled in your switch's configuration. Most people do the former, since it saves them money on ports that will never be used. Some, however, do the latter since they want to be able to remotely enable a port without visiting a wiring closet.

In large data centers, you'll see all ports patched into the switch but administratively disabled. You might even have experienced this school of thought if you've visited a hotel that had Internet service in the rooms. All the ports are patched in, but until you accept the $9.95 charge, your port is not activated.

Conference Room DMZ

One particularly good application of secure network design is to put all conference rooms and other public spaces on their own DMZ within your firewall. This ensures that visiting guests are still provided with Internet access so that they can check their e-mail, but protects your network from unauthorized browsing. Authorized employees who are making a presentation in a conference room can just use the VPN to get to the files that they need. This provides the added benefit of encrypting the information end to end so that the other laptops in the conference room can't sniff the traffic and get their hands on information they really shouldn't have. An in-depth look at proper segmentation of your internal network can be found in Chapter 11, "Internal Network Design."

Checklist

- ☑ Find a sniffer that you are comfortable with and practice examining normal network traffic; you'll need those skills when there are real problems on the network

- ☑ Know how to check and track the built-in performance counters of your networking equipment.

- ☑ Have an updated network map on hand in your "emergency" set of documentation.

- ☑ Perform regular tests for vulnerabilities on your internal networks.

- ☑ Contract with a third-party vendor to test your external networks for vulnerabilities.

- ☑ Purchase automated patch management software to lighten the burden of monthly Microsoft security bulletins.

- ☑ Plan for adequate physical security of your networking devices.

- ☑ Disable anything (ports, services, etc.) that doesn't have a valid business case today; if you need it tomorrow, you can add it later.

Summary

Neither sincere ignorance nor conscientious stupidity has any place in good internal network security. To defend your digital castle, you must have the blueprints. More than likely, when you assumed the keys to the castle on your first day of work, there were no stacks of well-documented network routing maps. Find a good network protocol analyzer that you are comfortable with and begin to understand the makeup of your traffic flows. Use an automated network mapping tool to provide some context for any changes you intend to make to your network later. Without a proper map, the impact of even minor network changes cannot be fully understood. The vulnerability assessment industry has transformed itself into a new practice: vulnerability management. The tools presented in this chapter are excellent ways to proactively manage your organization's digital risk to attack. Using asset-criticality algorithms provided by some vendors, you can triage your problems to ensure you're always protecting the most valuable assets first. Once all high- and medium-level vulnerabilities have been fixed on your high-value servers, consider a remodeling of your organization's physical security. Protecting the castle's inner sanctum only makes sense if you've remembered to bolt the drawbridge door.

Solutions Fast Track

Monitoring Traffic

- ☑ To truly understand network infrastructure, you must study what is actually being transmitted on the wire.

- ☑ Network protocol analyzers or "sniffers" are powerful tools in the network administrator's tool belt.

- ☑ In modern switched networks, sniffing usually involves some preliminary configuration of the switch to copy all packets to one port for monitoring.

- ☑ Sniffers range from the free to the commercial high-power variety; make sure to pick the one that best fits your needs.

- ☑ Built-in network device counters can provide a useful (and free) indicator of pain points in your network and areas where increased bandwidth might be helpful.

Looking at Logical Layouts

☑ Most networks are physically wired as star networks, and the underlying technology is a logical bus (Ethernet), a ring (FDDI), or some derivative of a mesh.

☑ Network mapping tools will help document your network and will save valuable time pinpointing failures when trouble happens on your network.

Performing Security Audits

☑ Regularly test your networks to ensure that no new vulnerabilities or hosts are added.

☑ Use one of the free or commercial tools listed to give your network a thorough checkup.

☑ When a new worm breaks, check the VA vendor Web sites for free detection (and sometimes remediation) tools to quickly scan your entire network to find out just how bad the outbreak is.

☑ If you are short staffed or just enjoy the independent analysis of a third party, consider one of the Managed Vulnerability Assessment Services listed earlier to offload detection of vulnerabilities.

☑ Once you unearth all the vulnerabilities facing your network, formulate a plan to remediate and correct those vulnerabilities. Don't take it all on yourself—delegate tasks to your team.

☑ Use automated patch management software to deploy the never-ending stream of operating system patches out to all your desktops and servers.

Examining the Physical Security

☑ Adequately plan the physical security of your NOC or data center.

☑ Combine multiple technologies (biometric, video recording, door locks) for a layered, defense-in-depth approach.

☑ Invest in environmental monitoring tools—they will save you money in the long run should disaster strike.

☑ Don't overlook your electrical requirements, and heed the guidelines of your electrician.

☑ Disable any unused ports on your switches.

☑ Relegate any general-purpose rooms (conference rooms, kitchen, etc.) to their own DMZ with very little network access.

Links to Sites

- **www.Snort.org** Makers of Snort IDS that can be used as an effective sniffer.

- **http://windump.polito.it** WinDump, a popular raw network sniffer based on UNIX TcpDump.

- **www.tamos.com** Makers of TamoSoft CommView network-sniffing software.

- **www.ethereal.org** Makers of Ethereal network-sniffing software.

- **www.wildpackets.com** Makers of EtherPeek, AiroPeek, and EtherPeek MX sniffer software.

- **www.networkview.com** Makers of NetworkView network-mapping software.

- **www.networkassociates.com** Makers of Netasyst network-sniffing software.

- **http://cheops-ng.sourceforge.net** Cheops-NG, the next-generation freeware network-mapping tool.

- **http://cve.mitre.org** MITRE organization that lists common vulner-abilities and exposures (CVE).

- **www.ntobjectives.com** Makers of the NTO Fire & Water Toolkit, including ntomap network-mapping tool.

- **www.nessus.org** Makers of Nessus freeware VA tool.

- **www.qualys.com** Makers of QualysGuard MSP managed security service and the freemap.qualys.com tool.

- **www.patchlink.com** Makers of PatchLink patch management software.

- **www.shavlik.com** Makers of HFnetchk LT and HFnetchk Pro patch management software.

- **www.eeye.com** Makers of eEye Retina VA tool, and numerous free scanning tools.

- **www.foundstone.com** Makers of Foundstone Enterprise VA tool, and Foundstone Managed Service.

- **www.citadel.com** Makers of Citadel Hercules patch management software.

- **www.cwusa.com/services/facility_services** Cable and Wireless Data Centers.

- **www.sbcdata.com** SBC Communications Data Services.

- **www.globalcrossing.com** Global Crossing Data Centers.

- **www.equinix.com** Equinix Data Centers.

Mailing Lists

- **www.snpx.com** Security News Portal—excellent source for late-breaking security news.

- **sectools@securityfocus.com** The latest security tools from a large community of developers lacking any funds to advertise on their own. (www.securityfocus.com/subscribe?listname=110).

Frequently Asked Questions

The following Frequently Asked Questions, answered by the authors of this book, are designed to both measure your understanding of the concepts presented in this chapter and to assist you with real-life implementation of these concepts. To have your questions about this chapter answered by the author, browse to **www.syngress.com/solutions** and click on the **"Ask the Author"** form. You will also gain access to thousands of other FAQs at ITFAQnet.com.

Q: I've downloaded WinPCap and Ethereal, but I can't see any traffic other than my own. What's wrong?

A: Your network is either not very busy (doubtful) or has network switches upstream from your connection. You will need to configure your port to receive all the packets on your network (sometimes known as a SPAN port) to be able to adequately assess your network traffic.

Q: My network switch is not an expensive managed switch and has no provision for SPAN ports. Am I out of luck?

A: Not entirely. You just have a lot more work to do. Locate the one or two busiest servers on your network, or if you're monitoring outbound usage of the Internet, locate your main border gateway. Unplug that device's NIC (during a scheduled maintenance window) and attach it to one of those micro-hubs that you can find in major electronics stores for $20. Attach your sniffer to the micro-hub and then a third cable back to the server. Presto—you have a $20 wiretap for Ethernet.

Q: I used Foundstone Professional/eEye Retina/ISS Scanner to discover hosts on my network, but it has misidentified a number of my device operating systems. What can I do?

A: OS identification is an art form, not a science. As such, the software takes a "best guess" among several likely OS types. If your networked Sega Dreamcast is often being mislabeled as an Axis Webcam, it might be because both devices use the same low-level device kernel in their electronics. If you only have Dreamcasts on your Ethernet and none of the Axis Webcams, then you can safely rename that entry in the OS type database for major software vendors. In addition, you should e-mail the vendors so they can update their database and benefit all customers worldwide.

Q: I tried using the Visio Network AutoDiscovery wizard, but I can't find it. Where is it?

A: Sadly, support for the AutoDiscovery wizard has been removed from current and future versions of Microsoft Windows software. Visio 2000 Enterprise Edition still has the AutoDiscovery Wizard.

Q: Why would I need a patch management tool like Citadel Hercules when I already get by just fine with the Windows Update notification in the corner of my screen?

A: While the Critical Update Notification Service is useful at an individual host, it loses some of its appeal on a large enterprisewide deployment. The nice thing about Patch Management tools such as Hercules is that you can push out patches to machines and confidently know that they have been applied, rather than just hoping your user community notices the icon in the corner of the screen and double-clicks on it. Furthermore, many Patch Management systems (Hercules included) can push out other files to your machines (anti-virus update files, or similar) in much the same way it transmits patches. Finally, tools like these allow you to push out security configurations (such as disabling exploitable services or adjusting anonymous enumeration settings), which is definitely not something that can be done with WindowsUpdate.

Q: Why should I spend thousands of dollars on commercial VA tools when I have my trusty freeware Nessus? For that matter, why should I spend money on a sniffer when I have my trusty freeware Ethereal?

A: Great question, and one that can only be answered by the person asking it. If all you need is a quick peek at your network now and then, Ethereal will definitely fit your needs and is very easy on the pocketbook. If you want more in-depth packet analysis or remote network monitoring, you'll want to upgrade to a commercial tool such as TamoSoft CommView. Likewise, if you are a one-person security team and just need to quickly scan the network for obvious vulnerabilities, then Nessus will serve you well. However, if you are a larger organization with a dozen or so IT employees who need a way to perform automated and scheduled network security scans, you need a commercial tool such as Foundstone Enterprise.

Chapter 3

Selecting the Correct Firewall

Solutions in this Chapter:

- **Understanding Firewall Basics**
- **Exploring Stateful Packet Firewalls**
- **Explaining Proxy-Based Firewalls**
- **Examining Various Firewall Vendors**

Related Chapters:

- Chapter 4 Attacking Firewalls
- Chapter 7 Network Switching
- Chapter 10 Perimeter Network Design
- Chapter 11 Internal Network Design

☑ Summary

☑ Solutions Fast Track

☑ Frequently Asked Questions

Introduction

Early in human history, people recognized fire as both a tool and a danger. We could easily say the same thing about information—the right information in the wrong hands has probably destroyed almost as many companies as fires have. Therefore, borrowing an architectural term used to denote a structure for containing a potential disaster seems apropos. A *firewall*, when discussed in the realm of computers, prevents unauthorized access to protected networks from users outside the protected network.

Firewalls likely serve as the most important component to network security, second only to the physical security of the network. Prior to the Internet, most firewalls were used in networks that protected high-security installations where employees had distinct security ratings, such as defense contractors. Firewalls were originally employed for the purpose of allowing certain employees to connect to the inner sanctum of the company's data as a form of access control.

The Internet has changed the purpose and function of the firewall. By plugging in a single cable, a network administrator has the potential to make a company's data as accessible to the CEO as it is to the other six billion people on the planet. The new breed of firewall needs to allow a small population of that six billion to have expanded access, and the rest must be stopped at the door. All this must be accomplished with the flexibility to protect against attacks that hackers haven't even invented yet. Of course, a piece of hardware cannot take the place of a well-crafted security policy that incorporates all aspects of the network. However, in many installations the firewall *is* the only manifestation of the security policy.

To that end, we are going to examine the basic building blocks of modern firewalls. Once we understand what makes a firewall tick, we have to find out which of the two major types of firewalls—proxy or stateful inspection—are right for your organization. There's a big difference between the two, and it comes down to a trade-off between functionality and performance. Finally, we'll round out this firewall festival with a discussion on all the major vendors and what makes them so special.

Understanding Firewall Basics

Firewalls need to do more than just protect the good guys from the bad guys. The United States government has taken an active interest in computer security since well before the first integrated circuit rolled off the assembly lines. With this in mind, it makes sense to examine the government's regulations on

firewalls...except there aren't any. Similar to the movie industry, firewall manufacturers police themselves.

Seal of Approval

ICSA Labs, a division of TruSecure Corporation, provides firewall certification
based on the input of the Firewall Product Developer's Consortium (FWPD), a
46-member organization of the who's who in network security
(www.icsalabs.com/html/communities/firewalls/membership). This certification
is an important seal of approval for the industry but does not imply that a particular firewall is fit for your network. The goal of the ICSA Labs certification is to
ensure that what a vendor markets as a firewall actually operates in a firewall
capacity. The network firewall criteria are available for download and center on a
set of feature tests. The specific objectives for personal firewalls spells things out
more clearly:

- Capability to support Microsoft Networking capabilities while providing
  endpoint protection

- Capability to support concurrent dial-up and LAN connectivity

- Capability to block common external network attacks

- Capability to restrict outgoing network communications

- Capability to maintain consistent protection across multiple successive
  dial-up connections

- Capability to log events in a consistent and useful manner

All the firewalls that we discuss later in this chapter have attained ICSA Labs
certification. Being the only barometer for the industry, you should demand that
your next firewall vendor has passed this important baseline certification. Attaining
this certification is not so much an award the vendor receives, but a seal of approval
that their product will perform as anyone would expect a modern firewall to perform. To aid you in selecting a firewall, after reading this chapter you should also
check out the *Firewall Buyers' Guide* produced by ICSA Labs
(www.trusecure.com/cgi-bin/download.cgi?ESCD=W0048&file=doc594.pdf).

A firewall has to do more than just protect a secure network from a less-
secure network. If a firewall only needed to do that, couldn't you just cut the
cable connecting the two networks? That would protect the secure network from
any computer that couldn't lob nuclear missiles. Firewalls need to allow computers from the secure side to access information on the public side: "Packets get

out but they don't get in." All firewalls must allow access to the outside world. Conceivably, this would include full, unfettered access, which some firewalls do provide, but the ICSA 4.0 criteria only test firewalls against the following services: Telnet, Active and Passive FTP, HTTP, HTTPS, SMTP, DNS, POP3, and IMAP. Unless allowed by a security rule, a firewall needs to prevent all access into the network from the outside world.

Security Rules

Every firewall processes traffic based on an ordered set of rules. These rules could be considered the heart of the firewall. A body of security rules specifies not only what can come into a site but also what is allowed to leave a site. Most people would think that a proper security policy concentrates only on what can come into a site. Most network administrators trust their internal networks, so they usually don't consider outgoing traffic a problem. Unfortunately, that assumption is exactly what has made worms such as SQL Slammer, mass-mailing viruses like Melissa, and other malicious traffic possible.

A proper set of security rules should consider what type of traffic needs to leave the organization. A common security policy allows all outbound traffic to be permitted. The reason is simple—at 3 A.M. when configuring the firewall, the last thing you want to do is guess at what services to which your users are going to want access. Sure, it's easy to assume that they will want Web access (outbound HTTP and HTTPS), but what else? Do you want to make a rule for every flavor of instant messaging program that lives on your users' desktops? Certainly not. Therefore, we just allow all forms of traffic outbound and call it a night.

Unfortunately, this means that you've not only allowed legitimate traffic (such as Web browsing and FTP downloads), you also open your network up to Trojan programs. Malicious code writers know that most companies allow everything out, so they create their evil programs and hide them in pretty screen savers. Your users download and execute the screen saver, and in the background, the Trojan program starts up. To communicate back to the author, it starts an outbound session from your network to his machine. Since everything was allowed, the peculiar traffic destined for port 31337 isn't stopped by the firewall because it is traveling *from* the trusted internal network to the *untrusted* external network.

A much better plan would be to follow the "most restrictive" strategy: allow only what your users need and block everything else by default. This *will* result in more phone calls to your helpdesk, but it is the most secure method of operating. Start out with only allowing common outbound services: DNS, FTP, HTTP, and

HTTPS. When a request comes in for additional access (for example, outbound on port 5190 for ICQ chat services), evaluate the request in a business context and determine whether it should be allowed. Document the requestor and his stated purpose for the added access. Then, determine if you would be better served opening up this access to all users (if it's a common request) or just for this user.

This strategy is not limited to user workstations, however. For example, why should your corporate Web server need to access other external Web servers? HTTP traffic on Transmission Control Protocol (TCP) port 80 coming from your Web server and headed toward the Internet could be an indication of an infected host. Some worms (in particular, Code Red and NIMDA) spread by having one Web server contact other Web servers and attempt to infect these foreign targets. A firewall rule that only allows the corporate Web server to respond to Web requests, but not initiate any of its own, would prevent such a problem.

Notes from the Underground...

Outbound 31337 Is Not Very Elite

In August 1998 (yes, ancient by Internet calendars), the smart folks over at the Cult of the Dead Cow group (some would call them hackers) created "Back Orifice," a Trojan program that allows remote attackers to control a victim's machine. Borrowing its name from the Microsoft Windows BackOffice suite of applications, Back Orifice is installed on a machine after it has been compromised, leaving the attacker with back-door access at some point in the future. While the listening port is configurable, many amateur attackers leave the default port of TCP 31337 running. Upon hearing this, one can easily draw the conclusion that any inbound traffic on TCP 31337 showing up in IDS logs is malicious in nature (either someone probing for Back Orifice or someone using Back Orifice). However, this is still reactionary—looking at logs of a problem and taking action (hopefully) after the machine in infected.

The question that sage firewall admins should be asking is, "Does our corporate Web server have *any* reason to be communicating outbound on port 31337? For that matter, does it have any business communicating outbound from any ports other than TCP 80 and 443?" Construct your firewall rules such that Web servers are only allowed specific outbound ports on which to communicate. This will give you an important layer of

Continued

defense should your server fall victim to Back Orifice. And, for those who are curious but haven't figured it out yet, 31337 was picked because if you stare at the numbers long enough (and change 3 to "e," 1 to "l," and 7 to "t"), it spells out the word *elite*, a common term of distinction among the hacker community.

Hardware or Software

Firewalls usually take the form of either a computer running a common operating system (OS) with the firewall software installed on top, or a purpose-built hardware appliance that the manufacturer intended as a firewall from the ground up. Those that fall into the latter category either run on pre-hardened versions of a common, general-purpose OS (such as NetBSD or Solaris), or they run a customized, real-time OS that was only intended to run the firewall. Table 3.1 introduces the major vendors and where their products line up in the marketplace.

Table 3.1 Firewall Vendors and Types

Firewall Vendor	Form	OS
3Com Corporation & SonicWALL	Hardware	Custom
Check Point Software Technologies	Both	Windows, Solaris, IPSO
Cisco Systems, Inc.	Hardware	Custom
CyberGuard	Hardware	Custom
Microsoft	Software	Windows 2000 Server
NetScreen	Hardware	Custom
Novell	Software	NetWare
Secure Computing	Hardware	Custom
Stonesoft, Inc.	Software	Linux
Symantec Corporation	Software	Windows, Solaris
WatchGuard Technologies, Inc.	Hardware	Custom

Microsoft ISA Server and Symantec Enterprise Firewall fall into the software category, while the Cisco PIX firewalls fall into the hardware appliance category. Interestingly enough, Check Point FireWall-1 falls into both categories: it can be installed on a common OS (Solaris or Windows), but through a partnership with Nokia, most Check Point firewalls actually run on Nokia IPSO appliances.

The vendors that do run as pure software installed on a common, general-purpose OS usually employ some form of hardening process so that hackers do not compromise the security of the underlying OS. Rather than try to subvert the firewall, they could just attack the OS that is hosting the firewall and cause that machine to route packets before the firewall sees them, or just obtain a remote terminal session with the desktop and change the security policy altogether.

Axent Raptor, the predecessor to Symantec's Enterprise Firewall, runs a service called "Vulture" to kill any rogue processes (such as viruses, Trojans, or other malicious applications) that attempt to start. Rather than lock the Windows OS down such that outside programs can't infect the server, the Vulture "watchdog" process just makes sure that no new processes start up once the firewall is installed. Similarly, Novell's BorderManager, which runs on NetWare, requires a special version of the NetWare core SERVER.EXE file to prevent access to the console before authenticating to the machine.

Manufacturers that specialize in hardware appliances will often flaunt the security holes in general-purpose OS as a weakness of products that run on those platforms. Furthermore, they'll usually state that hardware appliances have better security since the firmware that runs them has no other function. The argument seems to make sense, but it doesn't cover every situation. Check Point Firewall-1 and Symantec Enterprise Firewall easily exceed the minimum ICSA requirements, while numerous hardware appliances have needed firmware upgrades to fix security holes. Therefore, you cannot make a judgment about a firewall's security based mainly on this one aspect. You do, however, need to know into which category your firewall falls because each type presents a different challenge to hackers.

In the end, the decision of which firewall type to use is more of a personal preference. You should select your firewall according primarily to which features you need. Only as a secondary or tertiary criteria should you consider the delivery format—hardware or software. For many, us included, the ease of a plug-and-play hardware appliance is very attractive. If something goes wrong, just slide in a new appliance and off you go. Others might not want to pay the extra money for a purpose-built custom appliance, and instead would like to repurpose some of their old servers that can be converted to use as a firewall. Depending on your organization and the budget you have for your firewall, you will naturally gravitate to either the hardware (more expensive, usually higher performance) or software (able to repurpose old hardware at substantial savings) types of firewall.

Administrative Interfaces

For the most part, any firewall will not work the way you need it to for your individual organization straight out of the box. Firewalls are not a "one size fits all" solution; each firewall requires individual tinkering and tweaking so that it fits your needs. Therefore, all firewalls require an administrative interface to make these changes to their configuration and security policies. Administrative interfaces can take many forms. Hardware appliances can use a simple serial connection for the initial setup and then allow the user to switch to Telnet or a graphical user interface (GUI) installed on an administrative machine. The GUI could be a proprietary application or an open standard, such as a Web browser. Software firewalls will typically have an interface directly on the machine, but many also allow for remote access configuration. (See Figures 3.1 through 3.4.)

Figure 3.1 Initial Serial Connection

Figure 3.2 SonicWALL Administrative GUI Using a Web Browser

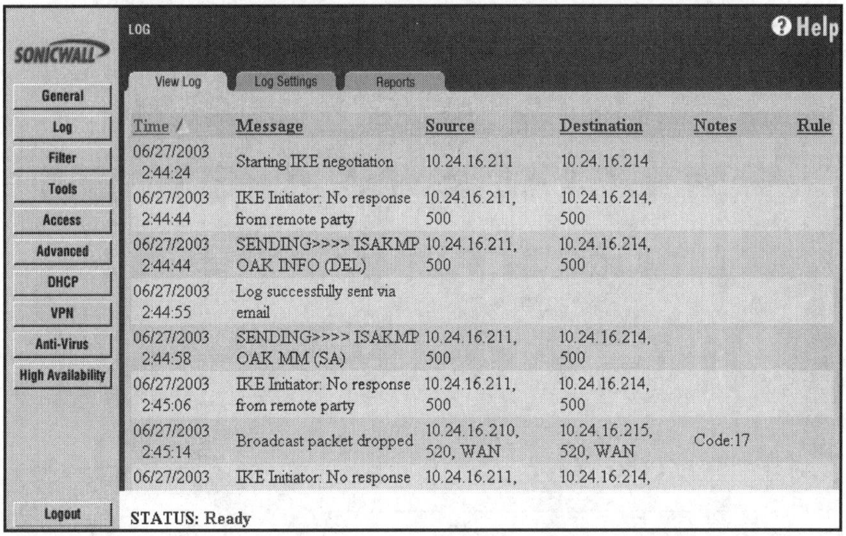

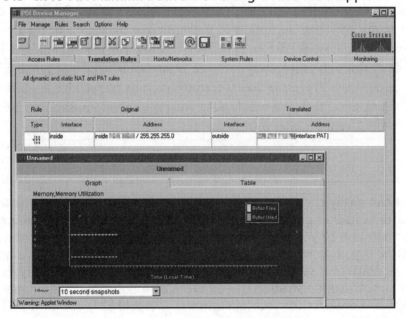

Figure 3.3 Cisco PIX Administrative GUI Using a Java Web Applet

Figure 3.4 Check Point Firewall-1 Administrative GUI Using Proprietary Application

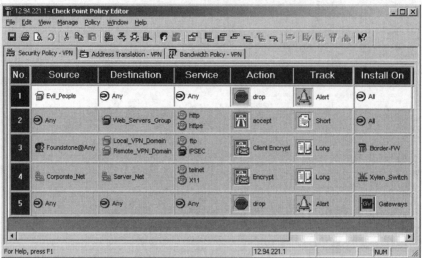

Since the administrative interface allows the user to configure the firewall, this feature needs special security to protect itself from hackers. All decent firewalls need at the very least an option to prevent reconfiguration of the firewall from an untrusted network. Better firewalls will allow for secure remote administration, such as through proprietary software or an open standard such as SSL. You must understand all remote access features of your firewall because hackers will often attack these first. We will look at the types of administrative interfaces for major firewall vendors later in this chapter.

NOTE

If you can easily change your firewall rules from outside your trusted network, a hacker might be able to do the same. Before enabling remote administration of your firewall, carefully weigh the risks versus the rewards. If you work 60 hours a week onsite, you probably have ample time to craft your security policies in the office, so you probably don't need remote administration. If you work as a consultant, administering dozens of networks for your customers, you probably couldn't do your job without it. Moreover, if you're not sure what you have to worry about with remote administration, keep reading...

Traffic Interfaces

Firewalls protect resources by delineating what needs protecting versus from where the attacks could come. Many people refer to this as "us" versus "them." Firewalls usually do this by acting as a highly selective router between the trusted network that needs protecting and the untrusted network full of potential hackers. Standard routers can add a great deal of latency to a network, so a firewall could make this worse. Firewalls work with complex rule sets that require fast processors and fast connections. Network administrators need to make sure that the firewall they choose can process information quickly enough to keep up with their network. Many firewalls now have 100 Mbps interfaces, so network administrators often assume that their firewalls can pass traffic that quickly. In most cases, this simply isn't true. Fortunately, most networks probably don't need a firewall that moves traffic that quickly.

DMZ Interfaces

Network engineers often speak of a network gray area called the "demilitarized zone," or DMZ. The DMZ contains resources that need protecting from the outside world but from which the majority of the inside world needs protecting. For example, a company that hosts its Web server onsite needs to allow traffic from the outside world into the Web server. A typical setup will look something like Figure 3.5.

Figure 3.5 Firewall without a DMZ

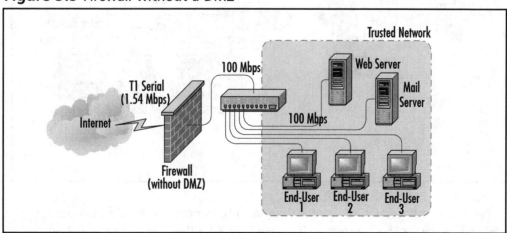

At a minimum, the firewall needs to pass Hypertext Transfer Protocol (HTTP) traffic on TCP port 80. However, what happens when a security hole in the operating system allows a hacker to take control of the Web server through traffic sent as a Web request? Once this happens, the hacker can then use the Web server as a stage to mount an attack against the rest of the network. If we re-examine Figure 3.5, we immediately see that the Web server sits on the trusted network. The firewall cannot protect any of the workstations from the Web server, so once the hacker controls the Web server, all of the attacks come from inside the protected network.

Let's compare this to Figure 3.6. Here, the firewall has a DMZ interface for the Web server so that the Web server is not on the same network as the workstations. Since all traffic from the Web server to the trusted network must travel through the firewall, the network administrator can set up security policies to prevent a rogue machine in the DMZ from compromising the entire network.

Figure 3.6 Firewall with DMZ

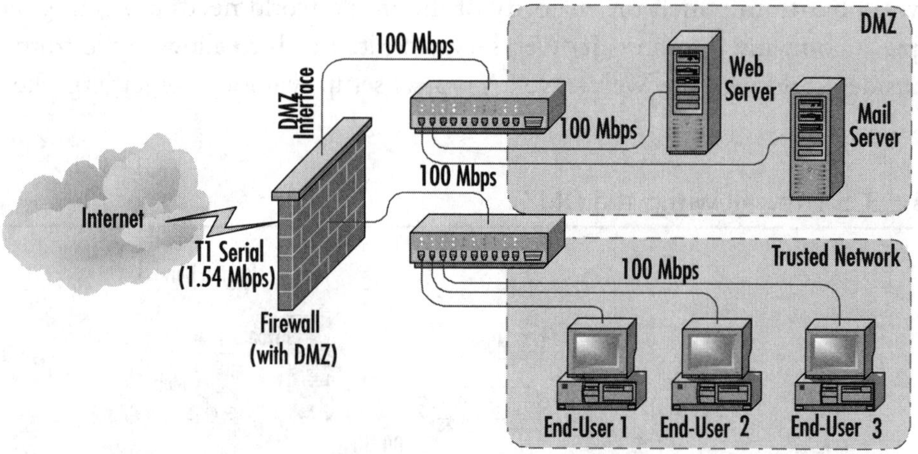

Now, speed becomes an issue. In Figure 3.5, the firewall could only accept traffic to and from the Internet at T1 speeds (1.54 Mbps). Most decent firewalls can handle this amount of traffic without slowing the network. However, in

Figure 3.6, the workstations must go through the firewall to get to the Web server, just as the computers from the Internet. However, unlike the Internet, the path from the trusted network to the Web server use only 100 Mbps links. This presents a network design challenge.

Need for Speed

Almost any firewall will pass the traffic, but only the better firewalls will do it without significantly compromising the speed. Does your network need this much speed? Can your CFO afford this much speed? This is the challenge. Of course, even the best firewall will introduce latency to the network. What if your network needs even more speed than the best firewall can achieve, but you still want a DMZ? Some switch vendors produce equipment that can do multilayer switching (MLS), which you can use to create DMZs that need more speed than security policy flexibility. We'll take a look at these closer in Chapter 7, "Network Switching."

Additional Interfaces

Not all firewalls have the capacity to create a DMZ, while for others the DMZ is not a singular entity. Some firewalls have more than three interfaces allowing for multiple DMZs. Software firewalls usually have an advantage here since most of these are built on computers that can easily accommodate additional network interface cards (NICs), which the firewall turns into the various networks (Figure 3.7). Some firewalls also include an auxiliary port (Cisco even names theirs "AUX") for plain old modem or ISDN backup in case the primary interfaces die.

Figure 3.7 WatchGuard Firebox X1000 Integrated Security Appliance, Showing Multiple DMZ Interfaces

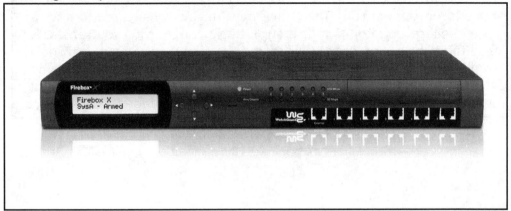

Logging

All firewalls need to keep track of what they see happening on the network. Without a log, an administrator would have little warning of an attack in progress. Low-end firewalls will only log security exceptions and don't have the capacity to keep the logs for an extended period of time. High-end firewalls generally have richer logging features that show both potential problems and usage trends. These enhanced logs can also track the traffic leaving your site. Beyond just security, these logs can give you an idea of how much of your bandwidth is being used, who's using it, and when. These statistics can help you in your next budget meeting with the CFO when you want to ask for a faster connection to the Internet.

Damage & Defense...

You Can't Just Track the Inbound Traffic

Most network administrators take a quick look at the logs to check for hacking attempts, and then ignore them, never realizing that they should also track what leaves the company. Believe it or not, not everyone at work works all of the time—say it ain't so! Santa didn't install the Christmas Light desktop decorations and his little helpers didn't download Elf bowling by themselves. These things might merely annoy you, but some employees take a big step past this and actually commit cyber crimes from within your network. When the police, or the lawyers, or the police with lawyers trace this back, they'll probably only know that it came from your network. Then, they'll eventually come to you to trace it to the real perpetrator. If your firewall tracks this activity, you can easily feed the right person to the wolves and the company can put the whole sordid mess behind it. If your firewall doesn't track this information—and you were overlooked for a promotion last year—you can always just point the authorities at your boss and solve two problems at once!

Optional Features

Just about every firewall has the previous features, but the following optional categories help to differentiate the products:

- Network Address Translation
- Port Address Translation
- Advanced routing
- Point to Point Protocol over Ethernet
- Dynamic Host Configuration Protocol Client and Server
- Virtual private networks
- Clustering and high availability
- URL filtering
- Content filtering
- Antivirus protection

When buying a firewall, nothing substitutes for security, but with all other things being equal, the extras can tip the balance.

Network Address Translation and Port Address Translation

Every machine that communicates across the Internet needs a unique Internet Protocol (IP) address—or so the story goes. Engineers started noticing that even though a 32-bit address space creates up to 4,294,967,294 (2^{32}–2) usable IP addresses, many of these addresses get wasted by organizations taking huge blocks that they barely use. As a result, the rulers of the Internet foresaw a time when we would run out of IP addresses and have to abandon IPv4 (which we all know and love) for IPv6, with a much greater capacity for addresses. In the short term, the Internet Engineering Task Force (IETF) established what eventually evolved into Request For Comment (RFC) 1918.

RFC 1918 (ftp://ftp.rfc-editor.org/in-notes/rfc1918.txt) specifies which IP addresses network administrators can use privately. These addresses allow companies to give each of their machines a unique IP address within the company without having to pay for them and without having to worry about conflicting with another machine at another company. The addresses don't conflict because, as per RFC 1918, Internet routers do not route these IP addresses. Therefore, these IP addresses work fine for companies internally, but they do not allow users to access information on the Internet.

Notes from the Underground…

1918: A Year to Remember?

An important reason to remember RFC 1918 is the near ubiquity with which it is used in internal networks. As you can see from Table 3.2, RFC 1918 provides more than enough address space for even the largest organizations to uniquely identify every network device on their internal network.

Table 3.2 RFC 1918 Private Address Space

IP Address Range	Number of Usable Hosts	Number of Class C Subnets
10.0.0.0–10.255.255.255	16,777,214	65,536
172.16.0.0–172.31.255.255	1,048,574	4,096
192.168.0.0–192.168.255.255	65,534	256

Most people select the 10.0.0.0 network for the simplicity of the numbers involved (it's much easier to remember your corporate IP address space as being "ten-dot-something" instead of "one-nine-two-dot-one-six-eight-dot-something"). However, most organizations never even dream of having more than 16 million network devices. Most home users will recognize the 192.168.0.0 address space because it is most often used with SOHO routers and firewalls.

So, you have RFC 1918 private addresses on your internal hosts, but we just said that these special addresses are not allowed on the Internet. So, how do we convert from private to public address space? Network Address Translation (NAT) solves this by proxying the internal requests for Internet services using a registered public address (or addresses) controlled by the device performing NAT. In short, NAT allows all of the private addresses to act as public addresses for outgoing requests. Since the Internet does not route private addresses, this also adds a layer of security to the workstations since the Internet community never sees the true IP address of the workstations. If a hacker tries to access a NATed workstation using the reported public IP address, the hacker merely attacks the device doing the NATing, which, in the case of firewalls, is designed to withstand these attacks.

Private addresses may add security because no one can route to them, but this would also prevent users from accessing Web servers behind a firewall. NAT takes this into account and can map a public address back to a private address if necessary. In the case of a Web server, an administrator would probably only want to accept HTTP traffic for a Web server not running Secure Sockets Layer (SSL). In this case, only TCP port 80 would get mapped. Many vendors refer to this as *Port Address Translation* (PAT) instead of NAT.

Tools & Traps...

Creative IP Addressing with RFC 1918

You could just take the RFC 1918 private address space at face value and start handing out addresses with the first available one, and continue from there. A much more effective IP addressing schema would be to use the flexibility that all those extra IP addresses provides. For most of our customer networks that we design, we usually set aside distinct class C subnet "chunks" to represent different classes of network devices. For example, 172.16.*x.x* could represent your Los Angeles office, and 172.17.*x.x* could be New York, and so on. Further breaking down the network into "purpose" classes can help administration as well. For example, *x.x*.0.*x* can be networking devices such as routers, *x.x*.8.*x* can be servers, *x.x*.16.*x* can be peripherals like network printers or copiers, and *x.x*.32.*x* can be the average user range. The value comes in later during log analysis. If you get an alert from your SNMP management console (see Chapter 12, "Secure Network Management" for more information), you can instantly tell that a brute-force password attempt coming from 172.17.32.14 is a user workstation in your New York office, and that a high amount of outbound SMTP traffic from any network other than your Los Angeles mail server at 172.16.8.11 should be investigated.

Advanced Routing

Most firewalls also need to act as routers since they usually connect at least two different subnets. A simple network can set up all of the routers to use static routing tables, but a large network needs more flexibility. Since the firewall works as a router, the firewall might also need to run routing protocols such as Routing Information Protocol (RIP) or Open Shortest Path First (OSPF) just as the rest of the networking equipment does. Not all firewalls do this, so if you need this feature, check the specifications carefully.

NOTE

For more information on routing tables and routing protocols, refer to Chapter 5, "Routing Devices and Protocols."

Point to Point Protocol over Ethernet (PPPoE)

Telecommunication providers at the consumer level use PPPoE on Digital Subscriber Line (DSL) broadband connections to force their broadband customers to authenticate their connections as though they're using a dial-up connection. This allows the regional telecommunication providers to only allocate the IP address as a station needs it. This works great for the phone company, but for consumers it's just one more thing to go wrong. Often, firewalls connect directly into the telecommunication provider's DSL modem, which means that the firewall must have PPPoE capabilities for the connection to work.

Fortunately, most business-class DSL services do not use PPPoE, so you probably won't see this in most offices. As for residential broadband, if the DSL provider in your area uses PPPoE, check to see if you can get a cable modem in your area, since those never use PPPoE and the speed is usually as good or better than DSL.

Dynamic Host Configuration Protocol (DHCP) Client and Server

DHCP allows machines to automatically get IP addresses or assign addresses, depending on whether the machine acts as a client or a server. Most firewalls today can do both simultaneously, although from different interfaces. If a site gets a dynamic address from the ISP, the firewall will need to act as a DHCP client on the outside interface. To ease configuration on the inside equipment, many firewalls can dole out private addresses on the inside interface. This can make for easy configurations since the firewall can then dispense information that it gleaned from connecting to the Internet, such as Domain Name Services (DNS) servers, to the machines on the trusted network. Administrators at large networks probably have another machine doing this already (perhaps even one integrated with your Microsoft Active Directory), but smaller networks might need this. Note too, that DHCP does provide a slight information security risk in the ease in which an attacker can receive valuable reconnaissance information about your network. However, each company's individual security policy must balance the ease of use with protection of IP addressing information.

Virtual Private Networks

Virtual private networks (VPNs) allow remote users or remote sites to connect to each other securely over the Internet. In the beginning, companies rolled out VPNs for employees who wanted to work from home, but they still connected remote offices to each other through expensive WAN links, such as point-to-point T1s. Today's VPNs can create secure tunnels to each other using relatively inexpensive links to the Internet instead of paying for a dedicated link between offices.

Some companies produce VPNs as separate products from their firewalls and recommend running these devices in parallel or behind a firewall. These vendors usually recommend removing the VPN functions from the firewall due to the processor-intensive nature of the VPN connections. This makes sense in some situations, but current high-end firewalls have enough processing power to handle both functions. Generally, a firewall with a built-in VPN costs less than a comparable firewall without VPN capabilities and a separate VPN. In addition, it usually takes less effort to configure and maintain one box instead of two.

Clustering and High Availability

Most administrators have heard of clustering servers, but not everyone has heard of clustering firewalls. Any network is only as resilient as its weakest link. Most networks lose access to the Internet when the firewall dies, which might inconvenience many companies, but won't kill the business if it doesn't come up for a few hours. However, if your business involves a Web site taking credit card orders, every minute that customers can't see the site costs your company money. You might have "five nines" uptime on your servers, but—proverbially—if a server falls in the woods with no one around to hear it, will your company have enough cash for your paycheck to clear?

Clustering firewalls allows for a hot-standby firewall to take up the slack if one dies. In some advanced setups, multiple firewalls can load balance, and if any one firewall dies, the remaining firewalls take up the slack. Most times, firewalls are mirrored in an "HA" or *high availability* setup, where one firewall is the "active" member (passing traffic) and the other is the "standby" member waiting in the wings. We cover this topic more later in the section *Stateful Failover*.

URL Filtering, Content Filtering, and Antivirus Protection

Most firewalls can block simple Universal Resource Locators (URLs), but most cannot block specific content or even recognize viruses. Many firewalls, however, have third-party support for companies that compile databases of Web sites and then categorize the sites (WebSense and SurfControl, to name just two). Administrators can then subscribe to this service and download the lists to the firewall. Once the firewall has these lists, the administrator can then determine the type of content permissible for viewing. Usual categories include sexually explicit material, hate sites, gambling, drug use, and things of that nature. High-end firewalls will often allow the administrator to match the content rules to specific workstations based on an IP address, but even better firewalls (or third-party applications) will take this a step further and integrate this information into the company's directory (for example, Microsoft's Active Directory or Novell's eDirectory) and allow the administrator to make exceptions based on users rather than computers.

Notes from the Underground...

Think about the Children

Many network administrators consider inappropriate content a social problem and not a technological one. Everyone's an adult here, so what's the harm? However, if you run a school network, now you have kids accessing the Internet, so everything changes. Some schools will cry poverty and claim that they can't afford filtering software, but the reality is that the poorest schools qualify for Federal subsidies (E-rate) for Internet access. One caveat is, though, that the site must have filtering software installed as per the Children's Internet Protection Act (CIPA), www.sl.universalservice.org/reference/CIPA.asp. For a coherent explanation of E-rate, see www.kelloggllc.com/erate/primer_02.pdf.

Better firewalls will also allow administrators to subscribe to third-party products that scan all traffic for viruses and hostile applets and then kill them before they ever reach the users. Even if you have antivirus protection on the machines, it doesn't hurt to eradicate these bugs before they ever hit your network.

Exploring Stateful Packet Firewalls

Quite possibly, the most underrated feature among modern firewalls is their capability to be "stateful" with their routing and pass/drop decisions. In other words, modern firewalls are able to ascertain if a transmission is in response to a request that originated on the trusted network, or a transmission that originated on the scary "outside" network. This might sound simple since this is what we expect from our firewalls when we write in our security policy "must allow outbound connections but no inbound connections." In reality, what we are asking our firewalls to do is to "allow all outbound connections, allow all inbound responses to those outbound connections, and block all other inbound attempts."

What Is a Stateless Firewall?

Any conversation on stateful firewalls should really begin with a look at how bad it really could be: stateless firewalls. Although you won't find anyone selling a stateless firewall, it does exist as a concept. Basically, it would involve a very literal interpretation to your security policy without much "business logic" to make the device perform adequately. In essence, a stateless firewall would do "what you told it to do and nothing more," when what you really want is a firewall that will "do what I mean, not what I say."

For an example of a stateless firewall, imagine a router that is being forced to perform firewall-like functions. The following example uses notation that appears alarmingly similar to Cisco IOS, but it is purely for illustration. In Cisco's defense, their routers (with the appropriate Firewall Feature Set) include the Adaptive Security Algorithm (ASA), which allows them to operate more securely than the following demonstration. Let's start with a basic security policy for Company XYZ:

```
10. permit outbound from 172.17.0.0/16 on any_port to any_ip on any_port
20. permit inbound from any_ip on any_port to host 172.17.8.11 on smtp
30. permit inbound from any_ip on any_port to host 172.17.8.13 on http
40. deny all
```

Pretty basic—we have two rules to allow Web and e-mail to flow to our servers, we have the obligatory *deny all* statement for completeness at the end, and we have the rule to allow outbound connections from our network to foreign locations on the Internet. We've even gone so far as to practice good security policies by specifying the source network (172.17.*x*.*x*) where our internal hosts are coming from. So, why can't the CEO get to eBay? A quick peek at the firewall log gives us a clue:

```
12:01:14 src=172.17.32.142:1025 dst=4.2.2.2:53 action=PASS rule=10
12:01:15 src=4.2.2.2:53 dst=172.17.32.142:1025 action=DROP rule=40
12:01:16 src=172.17.32.142:1025 dst=4.2.2.2:53 action=PASS rule=10
12:01:17 src=4.2.2.2:53 dst=172.17.32.142:1025 action=DROP rule=40
```

Right away we can see that to get to www.eBay.com, his machine must first do a lookup on his ISP-provided DNS server (4.2.2.2, the Genuity DNS server with the most memorable IP address ever). When the DNS server attempts to respond, the firewall is dropping the packets. Therefore, we add this rule, just above rule 20:

```
19. permit inbound from any_ip on dns to 172.17.0.0/16 on any_port
```

Now, we head over to the CEO, confident in our abilities, and ask him to try it again. Still nothing. Now the CEO is getting steamed because the auction close is coming soon, and he needs a new leather laptop bag. Back to the firewall log:

```
12:08:21 src=172.17.32.142:1027 dst=4.2.2.2:53 action=PASS rule=10
12:08:22 src=4.2.2.2:53 dst=172.17.32.142:1027 action=PASS rule=19
12:08:23 src=172.17.32.142:1027 dst=66.135.208.101:80 action=PASS rule=10
12:08:24 src=66.135.208.101:80 dst=172.17.32.142:1027 action=DROP rule=40
```

We forgot to allow for Web traffic to respond back. With little time to spare, you react without thinking and add another ill-conceived *permit* statement to your access list, and another, and another, until the CEO is able to bid on his item and chat with his daughter on AOL Instant Messenger:

```
16. permit inbound from any_ip on http to 172.17.0.0/16 on any_port
17. permit inbound from any_ip on https to 172.17.0.0/16 on any_port
18. permit inbound from any_ip on 5190 to 172.17.0.0/16 on any_port
```

The CEO is happy, you're happy, and you go home feeling on top of the world. Later that night, the 13-year-old in southern Yemen who just got infected with the latest HTTP-borne worm leaves his computer on while he goes to school. The worm sends packets to your network, infects your Accounting server, infects your CEO's computer, and manages to transmit sensitive documents across e-mail to a hacker in Western Fraudikstan, just outside Moscow. Let's watch that again, in slow motion:

```
23:13:02 src=147.45.35.40:53 dst=172.17.32.142:139 action=PASS rule=19
23:13:03 src=147.45.35.40:80 dst=172.17.8.18:80 action=PASS rule=19
23:13:04 src=172.17.32.142:1034 dst=147.45.35.40:25 action=PASS rule=10
23:13:05 src=172.17.8.18:1026 dst=147.45.35.40:25 action=PASS rule=10
```

The rules you added were *too permissive* and while they did let in the responses to your CEO's Web requests, they also allowed packets that originated outside the firewall to walk right in. Since your outbound policy does not specify that workstations cannot transmit mail directly to the outside world (even though you have a corporate mail server), your trade secrets are now sitting in some evil-doers' Inbox. But what else are you to do? If only there was a way to keep track of the outbound conversations.

Keeping Track of Conversations

We've seen that allowing a broad selection of network traffic (such as HTTP inbound) is a really bad idea due to the security implications. If we instruct the router to keep track of packets (or more specifically, of *conversations*) that exit the network, we will be able to allow the response to those queries to enter the network. This is most commonly implemented in a *sessions table*. Sometimes referred to as a *state table*, this is the essence of "keeping state" of the conversations. This is what separates a simple packet filtering firewall/router from a stateful inspection firewall.

When network requests pass from the internal segment to the external segment, the firewall makes a note of the host that initiated the request, the target, and the corresponding ports (source and destination). Then, it alters the security policy just slightly to allow a "pinhole" entrance for the return traffic. Let's look at our previous example of our CEO attempting to reach eBay, but with a stateful firewall. This time, let's start with the original security policy:

```
10. permit outbound from 172.17.0.0/16 on any_port to any_ip on any_port
20. permit inbound from any_ip on any_port to host 172.17.8.11 on smtp
30. permit inbound from any_ip on any_port to host 172.17.8.13 on http
40. deny all
```

We are allowing everything outbound from our internal network and only allowing external access to our mail and Web server—looks good so far. Now let's watch as our CEO's laptop performs a DNS request to resolve www.eBay.com:

```
14:38:39 src=172.17.32.142:1025 dst=4.2.2.2:53 action=PASS rule=10
```

Upon seeing this traffic exit the router, an entry in the session table will be made, indicating that 172.17.32.142 has sent traffic to 4.2.2.2 on port 53. The result can best be visualized if we assume that the router quickly rewrites the security policy and inserts the following rule at the very top, before rule 10:

```
9. permit inbound from host 4.2.2.2 on dns to host 172.17.32.142 on 1025
```

This "pinhole" window in the security policy is what the DNS server needs to respond to the query. After the traffic passes through the router, from the outside to the internal segment, the rule is immediately deleted to prevent someone from piggybacking on that rule. The response comes back to the CEO's laptop and then a Web request goes out:

```
14:38:40 src=4.2.2.2:53 dst=172.17.32.142:1025 action=PASS rule=9
14:38:41 src=172.17.32.142:1027 dst=66.135.208.101:80 action=PASS rule=10
```

Again, the "pinhole" opens:

```
8. permit inbound from host 66.135.208.101 on http to host 172.17.32.142 on
1027
```

and the return traffic is able to come back in to your network:

```
14:38:43 src=66.135.208.101:80 dst=172.17.32.142:1027 action=PASS rule=8
```

What is most important to realize about this whole transaction is that no administrator intervention was needed to modify the security policy. The best part is that after the return Web traffic reached the laptop, the security policy is back to the original rule set with the pinhole permit statements removed:

```
8.   <deleted>
9.   <deleted>
10.  permit outbound from 172.17.0.0/16 on any_port to any_ip on any_port
20.  permit inbound from any_ip on any_port to host 172.17.8.11 on smtp
30.  permit inbound from any_ip on any_port to host 172.17.8.13 on http
40.  deny all
```

Too Much Chatter

This previous example of processing network traffic works great if you just have one host accessing external resources at any given time. What happens when multiple hosts try to reach external resources simultaneously? Well, the router or firewall must then store the requests in a First in First Out (FIFO) buffer and store more lines in the sessions table. Many modern firewalls can handle incredible amounts of simultaneous conversations measured in the maximum size of their sessions table. The higher-end firewalls have more memory and can store many more sessions than a SOHO firewall that perhaps is better suited for home networks of 10 or less machines.

When the number of sessions exceeds the memory available for the state table, the oldest session is dropped from the table and no longer tracked. This means that when the response to that particular request (perhaps the HTTP traffic back from a Web server) gets to the firewall/router, there will be no pinhole *permit* statement to allow that traffic through the firewall. Thus, the traffic will be dropped and the end user will experience a loss of connectivity.

Stateful Failover

In larger firewall deployments, high availability is mandatory, which means at a minimum, two firewalls in a mirrored configuration. As mentioned previously, you could also cluster firewalls (three or more) to balance the load of traffic across many firewalls. In either case, there needs to be a mechanism to determine when there is a failure in the system. In mirrored firewall configurations, a *heartbeat* function allows the standby firewall(s) to determine if there was a failure in the primary firewall. Most times, this is a simple one-packet "ping" to determine whether the other firewall is online.

If there is a lot of traffic going to the firewalls, there exists a possibility for this ping packet to be lost in the noise of regular traffic. Therefore, most heartbeat implementations will have a dedicated crossover cable between the mirrored pairs so that there is no chance of latency or dropped packets. This dedicated heartbeat network offers a nice secondary benefit: a high-speed data transfer method for state or session table information.

Even if a vendor claims that their firewall has failover capabilities, only the very best will offer *stateful failover*. The difference between the two is simple:

- Normal failover simply boots up the standby firewall when the primary is down.

- Stateful failover means that the session table and other operational information is transferred to the secondary firewall so that it can pick up exactly where the other firewall left off.

When stateful failover happens, the end user should not notice any difference. Many times, the only way to know that a stateful failover happened is by looking at the log file. In contrast, a stateless failover (or just a regular failover) will be noticed by LAN users because they will have a momentary loss of network connection (2 to 10 seconds) and might have to retry their most recent Web request or e-mail transmission. The reason is that in stateless failover, the newly activated firewall (the standby one) springs to life without any prior knowledge of active sessions. Therefore, when HTTP requests leave via the primary firewall, the failover happens, and then HTTP responses come in via the secondary firewall, they will appear to be unauthorized access attempts and will be blocked. If there were any VPN connections to the firewall from remote clients or from distant partner networks, these will have to be manually reestablished and a new key exchange will have to take place. This can introduce a level of latency or LAN-to-LAN VPN failure that is unacceptable to very integrated business partners.

In stateful failover, the newly activated firewall will have an up-to-the-second session table so it will be able to process that return HTTP traffic immediately. VPN sessions and key exchange information will also be preserved so no connections will be dropped. As stated previously, the easiest and most common way that firewall vendors implement this is via a dedicated cross-over cable, as illustrated in Figure 3.8. Part of the heartbeat process includes sending updates of the session table to the secondary firewall so it has a mostly updated table. When the primary reaches a fatal error and needs to shut down, it sends a copy of its routing table, session table, and other pertinent information over the dedicated link and then dies. In the case of a catastrophic failure (such as power failure) where the primary doesn't have a chance to send this last batch of information, at least the secondary firewall has a recent copy of the session table (perhaps 5 to 10 seconds old).

Figure 3.8 Wiring Diagram Showing Stateful Failover Heartbeat Cable between Two Cisco devices

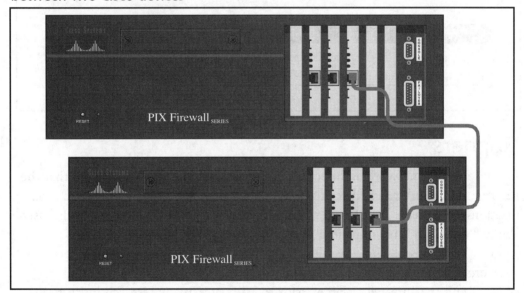

Explaining Proxy-Based Firewalls

Until now, we've discussed the firewalls that examine packets at the lower end of the OSI layers and make their forwarding decisions based on port, protocol, and session information. There exists an entirely separate class of firewall that makes decisions based on very high-level information provided by Layer 7, the application layer. This allows for a richer feature set but at the expense of performance.

A packet filtering firewall will be the best performance possible, but has limited use in today's networks (see the earlier stateless firewalls example). A stateful inspection firewall will always outperform a proxy firewall just based on the amount of work involved for each technology. However, which is better for your organization? Figure 3.9 gives an indication of the performance tradeoff when a firewall performs deep inspection into the upper OSI layers.

Figure 3.9 Tradeoff between Performance and Packet Inspection

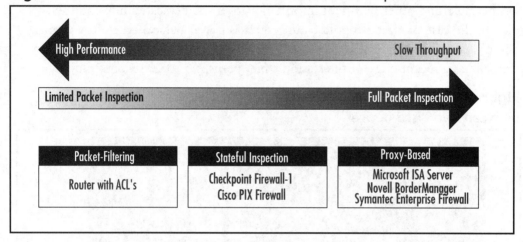

Gophers

If you looked at network architecture in the early 1990s, you would find that the Internet still hadn't reached "critical mass" as a vital part of business. Some organizations didn't have an ISP and managed to turn a profit. The ones that did usually had a dial-up line connected to one machine appropriately called the gateway host. This machine would usually provide the e-mail exchange between your organization's private e-mail (something like the antiquated MS Mail or cc:Mail) and the Internet at large. Prior to Web sites, many research institutions, libraries, and universities ran *gopher* servers to provide information (aptly named both due to the action of "going for" the data, and because most gopher server admins rarely saw the light of day). A gopher server was an efficient method of posting information about your organization in an organized manner. For universities and research institutions, the first inhabitants of the Internet, this was a great place to publish research documents or student theses. As time passed, people inside the LAN wanted access to these gopher servers, but obtaining Internet access for each computer became cost-prohibitive. There, the concept of an Internet proxy was born.

Software, such as Microsoft Proxy Server, would be installed on a dual-homed gateway machine and provide the link from the external network to the internal one. Requests from the inside network would be routed to the proxy. Then, the proxy would establish its own connection to the target gopher server. The response from the gopher server would be sent to the proxy and then the proxy would respond to the original LAN machine. What is very important to note here is that at no point in time are any internal machines (save the gateway machine) connected to the outside world.

Modernization: The Evolution of Gophers

Gopher servers have come and gone, but the Internet has only increased in importance to an organization. The original need for proxy servers has disappeared, but today's proxy-based firewalls are much like their predecessors. When a request comes in from the outside to deliver e-mail to a company's mail server, the proxy-based firewall will actually open another connection, sourced from itself, to the destination mail server. Once the TCP handshake is complete, it will proxy the connection by copying packets from one connection to the other. When the transmission is complete, the firewall will tear down both connections. Again, it is very important to note that at no time is the remote host ever connected to the company's mail server.

Some vendors will tell you that by definition this is more secure. Well, there is always something to be said for security by obscurity, but a malicious attack on a Web server using a Code Red type attack will still be successful if the firewall is copying all packets from one connection to the other. The only way a Code Red attack would be stopped prior to reaching the Web server would be for advanced packet inspection rules to peek into the upper layers of the Web request and note the offending URL string.

Since each packet must be processed at Layer 7, the top of the OSI reference model, the firewall has access to all the packet information. The downside is that processing each layer takes time, with more time taken in the higher layers because data must be interpreted rather than just read; looking at an IP address to match a *permit* list is relatively trivial, but dissecting the parts of an HTTP request searching for a malformed *content-type* string is more CPU intensive. After the packet has been flagged as allowed traffic, it needs to be packaged in all seven layers into another connection. This explains the large performance difference between proxy and packet-filtering firewalls.

Explaining Packet Layers: An Analogy

Any discussion on the benefit of proxy-based firewalls and their ability to peer into the upper layers of a packet must include a definition of these layers. In the early 1980s, the International Standards Organization (www.iso.ch), headquartered in Geneva, Switzerland, designed their Basic Reference Model as part of their suite of networking standards known as Open Systems Interconnection (OSI). The reason why the 147 countries that the ISO represents wanted to define a standard was simple: many very different networking systems were starting to be developed and they needed to connect with one another. What the OSI Basic Reference Model (now known as the seven layers of OSI) provided was a common vocabulary of network transmission components across vendors and technologies. From its humble beginnings designed to enable large, clunky mainframes to talk with one another, the OSI layers still serve a valuable purpose today in explaining complex network communications with a logical abstraction. Every book on networking has a section on OSI—it's almost a law. However, rather than throw figures and tables out, a gastronomical analogy would work much better.

Chips n' Salsa

A Super Bowl party staple is the cacophony of calories that is known as the 7-Layer Dip. This melding of cheese, guacamole, sour cream, and other waist-expanding foods goes great on a chip and has—okay, bear with us here—a rich "feature set" of flavors. In one bite, you're able to examine all the ingredients (from the tortilla chip as the physical layer to the all-important presentation layer with the solitary sliced black olive) and how they interact with one another. This might seem entirely silly, but it does illustrate how proxy-based firewalls are given a lot more ingredients on which to base their forwarding decisions. Just as you can say that you will only enjoy a cheese layer if it is of the cheddar variety and only if the bite occurs on Super Bowl Sunday, you can also be very specific with proxy firewall rules: allow Web traffic but only if it is HTTPS and only on weekends. A packet-filtering firewall is just like salsa—gets the job done but just isn't as rich. Let's look at both methodologies.

Cheddar, American, Swiss, or Jack?

When it comes down to it, cheese is cheese, so who cares what variety is used in our favorite party snack? Well, the answer depends on your security policy. Perhaps your company has stated that it doesn't mind audio files being down-loaded from the Internet, as long as they are WAV and not MP3. In this case, a packet-filtering firewall won't be able to help you because that information is stored in higher levels that are ignored. Figure 3.10 shows the layers involved in an e-mail transmission.

Figure 3.10 Comparing Packet Inspection between Firewall Types

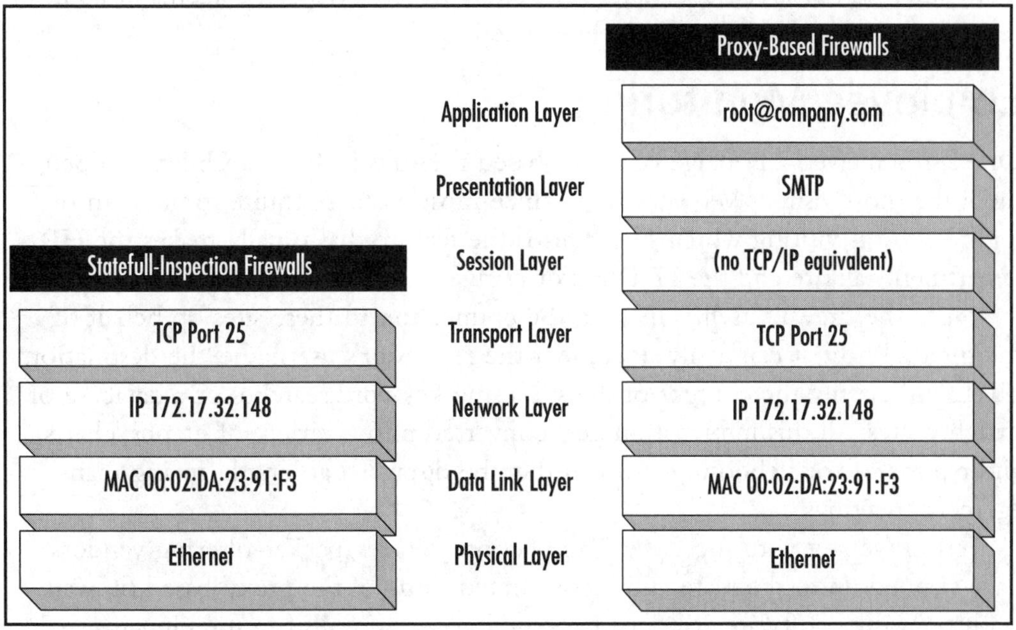

In Figure 3.10, we see the same packet but from the point of view of both firewalls. In most cases, you can get away with just port and protocol information. However, what if we wanted to filter out all e-mail bound for root@company .com? We would have to examine Layer 7 to find out the recipient of the informa-tion. Perhaps you don't want anyone on the outside sending mail to the root account and want to avoid any possibility of a virus infecting that mail account; using a Layer 7 packet inspection rule would work quite nicely.

Mild or Extra Spicy?

Even the humble salsa has undergone a recent makeover. A decade ago, salsa came in "chunky" and "extra chunky" varieties. That seemed a little plain sitting on the coffee table next to the seven-layer dip. Now you have a salsa bar that ranges from mild, extra hot, low sodium, and chipotle blends. The same modernization can be seen in packet filtering firewalls.

The advanced high-level packet inspection that was a strong selling point for proxy-based firewalls has been incorporated into some packet-filtering software. While still fundamentally different from proxy firewalls, the added features do erode some of the advantage that proxy firewall vendors would like you to believe they have. This goes by many names (Stonesoft calls it Multi-Level Inspection, Symantec calls it Full Inspection), but in the end it means a hybrid that combines the speed of stateful inspection with very specific agents or application proxies that can be selectively enabled.

Employee Monitoring

One last perceived advantage of proxy-based firewalls is their capability to document the most visited Web sites and—since most proxies require some form of login—who is visiting which sites. This is the feature that usually makes the HR department salivate and the IT Director cringe.

Since the firewall itself is making the connection to these sites on behalf of the internal host, it can easily document the requestor's username, the destination URL, and classify the content of the site using keyword searches or a database of naughty sites. All this information gets converted into a variety of graphs, charts, and reports of your choosing that can then be discussed at length during management meetings.

Just as we saw with the Layer 7 inspection features, packet-filtering vendors have stepped up to the plate and incorporated some of the proxy-based firewall features in their software. Modern packet-filtering firewalls can use plug-ins such as WebSense and SurfControl to determine inappropriate Web site access. Rather than worrying about the URLs, the firewall will ask the URL filter for permission before completing any outbound HTTP request. These third-party filters are updated on a weekly or daily basis and can offer detailed reporting just as well as their proxy-based counterparts can. Using integration plug-ins between DHCP servers and Microsoft Active Directory or Novell NDS Directory Service, these filters can also correlate a username with a source IP address to document who is visiting the inappropriate sites. Moreover, the user isn't forced to authenticate using yet another username/password. The final decision on proxy versus packet-filtering firewalls rests within your security policy and an informed balance between features and performance.

Examining Various Firewall Vendors

Armed with a thorough overview of what goes into a firewall and the different types of firewalls, the only thing left to do is to select the right one for your needs. Before examining the field from which to choose, you should write down what the "must have" features are for your organization and not get distracted by extra bells and whistles that might be helpful but not necessary. By no means is this an exhaustive list of firewall vendors, but it does represent the majority of products out there.

3Com Corporation and SonicWALL, Inc.

3Com and SonicWALL have similar product offerings; many of the 3Com small office firewalls are really SonicWALL devices that have been re-branded as 3Com products through a partnership agreement. Solid performers, they all have support for VPN tunnels in the same hardware (with the use of an unlocking license code). The Web-based user interface really takes the guesswork out of a complex task like setting up IP Security (IPSec) tunnels, Internet Key Exchange (IKE), and Internet Security Association and Key Management Protocol (ISAKMP) settings. Web filtering is also provided in the same box, which makes this a very compelling choice for small offices that cannot afford a more robust external URL filter. A yearly subscription is required, but updates are downloaded to the firewall weekly and violations to the content filter can be sent via e-mail to an administrator.

One unique offering from 3Com that really brings the concept of "defense in depth" to the market is their Firewall Desktop PCI Card (model 3CRFW200, also available in PCMCIA versions). This allows you to deploy a strong hardware firewall on all of your critical servers without taking any valuable rack space or altering your network infrastructure. Since the OS recognizes the card as just another network card, compatibility is not an issue. All the cards are managed centrally by a Firewall Policy Server to ease administration. The best part is that no "wandering hands" in the data center can accidentally subvert this firewall because it is not inline. It lives within the server case and thus would be very difficult to bypass without obvious detection (server shut down, case opened up, and so forth). (See Table 3.3.)

Table 3.3 3Com / SonicWALL at-a-Glance

Web site	www.3com.com/products/en_US/prodlist.jsp?tab =cat&pathtype=purchase&cat=134482 www.sonicwall.com/products/vpnapp.html
Models	3Com OfficeConnect Internet Firewall 25 3Com SuperStack 3 Firewall 3Com Firewall Server PCI Card SonicWALL SOHO3 Firewall SonicWALL PRO330 Firewall
Pros	Innovative embedded firewall is industry first
Cons	Best suited for smaller networks

Check Point Software Technologies

Depending on which survey you read, the Cisco PIX and Check Point Firewall-1 share market dominance. In our experience, most networks that we run across (that are larger than the SOHO class) have Check Point running on Nokia IPSO appliances. Claiming to have invented stateful inspection, FireWall-1 is a hybrid stateful inspection firewall that has configurable application-layer proxies to perform inspection. The software can be installed on Solaris or Windows NT, but is most often deployed on hardened NetBSD appliances provided by Nokia (formerly manufactured by Ipsilion). (See Table 3.4.)

Table 3.4 Check Point Software Technologies at-a-Glance

Web site	www.checkpoint.com/products/protect/firewall-1.html
Models	Check Point Firewall-1 NG Check Point Provider-1 NG Nokia IPSO 350 appliance Nokia IPSO 650 appliance
Pros	Market leader, high performance with good balance of rich features
Cons	Product licensing is second only to differential calculus in difficulty

The Check Point Policy Editor, their administrative GUI, is very well thought out, with logical groupings of commands and a simple tabular display of security rules in columns with headings in plain English. This management console is so nicely designed and well received by the industry that competitors are starting to duplicate the "look and feel" of the Check Point console. The security policy screen of the Cisco PIX Device Manager (see next section) was modeled heavily after this GUI.

FireWall-1 has an innovative attack-forecasting feature called SmartDefense. Using this technology, your firewall can connect to one of several Internet Storm Centers, such as the one operated by the SANS Institute, Dshield.org. You can contribute anonymous logs to the community effort, but more importantly, you can download a list of top attackers and use that to block future attacks on your network. This mimics the idea of a collaborative blacklist for firewalls, much like the SPAM blacklist services that exist. Using a mixture of hardware accelerators and software enhancements, the SecureXL feature set can enable FireWall-1 to process up to 3.2 Gbps of throughput. Most discomfort in Check Point installations comes from a very restrictive and difficult-to-understand licensing policy.

NOTE

For more dedicated information on the suite of products available from Check Point and Nokia, refer to the following other books also available from Syngress Publishing.

Check Point Next Generation Security Administration, ISBN 1-928994-74-1.

Nokia Network Security Solutions Handbook, 1-931836-70-1.

Check Point NG VPN-1/Firewall-1 Advanced Configuration and Troubleshooting, 1-931836-97-3.

Check Point Next Generation with Application Intelligence Security Administration, 1-932266-89-5.

Cisco Systems, Inc.

Cisco has been known as the most unfriendly but powerful firewall in the industry for quite some time. While certainly not glamorous, the PIX Firewall configuration commands are fairly easy to understand if you have knowledge of the Cisco IOS command set. With the exception of NetScreen, the PIX is the only firewall that runs on a custom real-time operating system (referred to as PIX OS, but in reality it is the brainchild of one of Cisco's acquisitions and they called it Finesse) rather than a hardened off-the-shelf OS. Many people believe in the power and features of PIX, but up until recently, the only way to fully configure the firewall was to use a command-line interface (CLI) on their text-based administrative interface (serial or Telnet connection). This might have been a bit daunting for some users, so Cisco recently introduced a Web-based Java applet called the PIX Device Manager (PDM) that hopes to win back some of the market share that was lost to Check Point based on user interface. (See Table 3.5.)

Table 3.5 Cisco at-a-Glance

Web site	www.cisco.com/en/US/products/hw/vpndevc/ps2030
Models	Cisco PIX 501 Cisco PIX 506 Cisco PIX 515 Cisco PIX 525 Cisco PIX 535
Pros	Market leader, fantastic performance, interacts with Cisco routers; can shun active attacks
Cons	Command line can be difficult for beginners

PIX appliances are all solid-state and have no hard drives in them (unlike the Nokia IPSO). To their advantage, this means fewer parts to wear out or worry about during an abrupt power outage. A slight disadvantage is that firewall logging cannot be performed locally. Instead, the PIX will stream log entries to any SYSLOG dæmon of your choosing.

The PIX product line ranges from the SOHO to large enterprise levels. The PIX 501 is about the size of a VHS cassette tape, yet runs the complete PixOS just like the larger counterparts. The PIX 515, previously the entry point to the PIX product line, is a popular inhabitant of data centers across the country due to its compact, 1U design. For companies that have high demands of their firewalls, the PIX 525 is a good compromise between the sometimes overwhelming power of the 535 and the always overwhelming price tag. The high-end Cisco PIX 535 will provide 1.7 Gbps of throughput and 500,000 simultaneous connections in the session table. Along with Symantec, it also supports the new *Advanced Encryption Standard* (AES, or Rijndael) encryption method for VPN components. Most firewalls only support the older NIST standard, Triple DES. The PIX 520, now obsolete and unsupported, is the last of the PIX models to still "look" like a normal PC, complete with floppy drive in the front. All the newer models are based on purpose-built chassis design.

CyberGuard

This line of proxy-based firewalls is likely one of the best for this category, earning the prestigious *SC Magazine* Best Firewall award (www.westcoast.com/events/awards) for the second year in a row t (2002 and 2003). They stress the importance of protocol and application awareness during the firewall packet-forwarding decision. One of the largest (physically) firewalls out there, this 4U behemoth boasts up to four SCSI drives in a RAID 5 hot-swappable configuration and can support up to 12—yes a dozen—Ethernet 10/100 interfaces running on a derivative of UnixWare. The high end of the CyberGuard spectrum includes some very helpful smart proxies that are preconfigured (for Telnet, HTTPS, and FTP) to click-and-install. The WebSense URL filtering software can be purchased in a bundle to allow for greater control over what your users are doing with their time. Additionally, the F-Secure Anti-Virus system enables scanning for evil e-mail attachments at the gateway. This allows you to regain control over these malicious attachments before they get distributed to the internal e-mail server. (See Table 3.6.)

Table 3.6 CyberGuard at-a-Glance

Web site	www.cyberguard.com/solutions/product_overview.cfm
Models	CyberGuard FS250 CyberGuard SL3200 CyberGuard KS1500
Pros	Common Criteria EAL4+ Fantastic performance Interacts with Cisco routers; can shun active attacks
Cons	Command line can be difficult for beginners

Microsoft ISA Server

Regardless of what the marketing documents say, ISA Server is really nothing more than the old Microsoft Proxy Server with better wizards. However, ISA Server's integration with the Active Directory provides centralized management and control over ISA settings, Windows network username logging for firewall traffic, and built-in availability features based on the resiliency of Active Directory. The "publishing" wizards are helpful in creating a rule set, but are specified using the opposite terminology than the rest of the industry. (See Table 3.7.)

Table 3.7 Microsoft at-a-Glance

Web site	www.microsoft.com/ISAServer
Models	Microsoft Internet Security & Acceleration Server
Pros	Integrated with Active Directory to provide resiliency of firewall information
Cons	Rule sets might be hard for veteran firewall admins to understand; appear to be written from the wrong point of view

NetScreen

NetScreen has always been known for performance. Their high-end packet-filtering firewalls can process an insane 12 Gbps and have earned them the 2003 *Network Magazine* Product of the Year award (www.infoxpress.com/reviewtracker/reprints.asp?page_id=1538). Most of their performance boost can be attributed to their highly optimized ScreenOS operating system and custom ASICs that perform the forwarding decisions for the firewall. NetScreen's high availability solutions include the typical active-standby configurations but also a nice active-active one where the two firewalls share the network load cooperatively. Their SOHO offerings even include an innovative anti-virus scanning functionality usually found on higher-end firewalls. The Trend Micro AV engine is featured on the NetScreen 5GT and can scan SMTP, POP3, and Web traffic. (See Table 3.8.)

Table 3.8 NetScreen at-a-Glance

Web site	www.netscreen.com/products/firewall
Models	NetScreen-25 NetScreen-208 NetScreen-500 NetScreen-5400
Pros	Extremely optimized for speed FIPS as well as Common Criteria certification
Cons	Configuration language hard to use if you have deep understanding of the Cisco IOS command set. Users with no prior IOS experience should not have a problem

Novell

Novell, famous for the very successful NetWare network operating system and later the highly scalable NDS Directory service, also offers a firewall solution called BorderManager. One of the nice features of BorderManager is the tight integration with NDS. We don't mean just integrating firewall logs with user-names from NDS. All the firewall features can be controlled from within your favorite NDS browser, which really cuts down on administrative headache. Starting with version 3.7, BorderManager has the SurfControl content database integrated into the firewall, which makes URL filtering as easy as the 3Com with the power of a third-party solution. BorderManager is still a proxy-based firewall, so performance does suffer. However, if you're an all-Novell shop it is a great solution that will reduce the strain on your IT department. Since BorderManager is offered as part of the Novell Small Business Solution, small offices that don't have an IT department can get a firewall for free with their network operating software package. (See Table 3.9.)

Table 3.9 Novell at-a-Glance

Web site	www.novell.com/products/bordermanager
Models	Novell BorderManager
Pros	Heavily Integrated with Novell NDS and that provides an easy administration task SurfControl for content screening
Cons	Specialized knowledge of NetWare 5.1 or later is required

Secure Computing

Another firewall in the hybrid category, Secure Computing has a stateful packet inspection firewall that has intelligent adaptive proxies that can perform Layer 7 inspection without slowing the network connectivity to the speed of a pure proxy solution. A mature solution, the Sidewinder has been around since 1994 and keeps getting better each year. Their Sidewinder G2 firewall has won the *Network Computing* magazine's Well-Connected Award for 2003 (www.nwcwell-connected.com). Primarily delivered as a ready-to-go hardware appliance, the Sidewinder G2 is different from the other hardware appliances listed here in that it is really just a Dell PowerEdge 2650 server that has been preinstalled with their special SecureOS UNIX variant. The software can also be purchased separately, to run on your own hardware. We would stick to using what they're calling an appliance just to reduce the headache of any strange SCSI card in your flavor of server that might not be supported in SecureOS. (See Table 3.10.)

Table 3.10 Secure Computing at-a-Glance

Web site	www.securecomputing.com/index.cfm?skey=232
Models	Secure Computing Sidewinder G2
Pros	Automated response engine can react in real time to attacks
	EAL4 common criteria certified
Cons	Because of a very detailed method of inspecting packets, Sidewinder is slower than other firewalls
	Lack of a solid state "true" hardware appliance means you might have to manage different hardware platforms for all your different Sidewinder firewalls

Stonesoft, Inc.

Stonesoft products are obsessed with high availability. Everything they do has an eye toward failover, and this doomsday view of life makes for some very robust offerings. StoneGate, their high availability clustered firewall, has a mix of application-layer agents that provide information to their stateful inspection engine (they call this multilayer inspection) that we mentioned earlier. Running on a hardened version of Debian Linux, StoneGate performs heartbeat functions (discussed earlier) with all members (up to 16) of the firewall cluster and has won *SC Magazine*'s Best Buy award (www.stonesoft.com/products/StoneGate/ Certifications_and_Awards/SC_Magazine_-_Best_Buy). StoneGate is also the only firewall offering to be available for the IBM zSeries mainframe. This is a huge plus for financial organizations that might be forced to keep their large mainframes around to support legacy applications, and don't want to manage yet another device in front of the mainframe to protect it from network attacks. In Q2 of 2004 (right around the time you'll be reading this sentence), Stonesoft will have a product offering on Linux, designed to run on the IBM eServer iSeries. (See Table 3.11.)

Table 3.11 Stonesoft at-a-Glance

Web site	www.stonesoft.com/products
Models	Stonesoft StoneGate
Pros	Very strong clustering and high-availability features, based on the work they have done with clustering other vendors' devices as well
	Available for IBM z990 mainframe
Cons	Does not come in its own appliance; users must supply their own server

If the emphasis on high availability seems intense, it's because Stonesoft began by providing third-party clustering solutions (called StoneBeat) for Check Point Firewall-1, Microsoft ISA Server, Raptor (now Symantec Enterprise Firewall), and Secure Computing's Gauntlet. Even if you decide not to use the Stonesoft firewall, you should definitely look into their clustering technology to complement an installation of any of those four products.

Symantec Corporation

Symantec purchased the Raptor firewall product and renamed it Enterprise Firewall. With version 7.0, Enterprise Firewall is EAL-4 certified for Common Criteria compliance (important for government facilities). Symantec describes their firewall as "full inspection" as opposed to stateful inspection firewalls. This just means that they are much like StoneGate and FireWall-1 by being a stateful inspection firewall that has elements of Layer 7 inspection to allow it to make intelligent forwarding decisions. Enterprise Firewall, much like BorderManager, teamed up with a content filtering provider and includes the WebNOT technology with its firewall and is one of only a few vendors that use AES for VPN connections. The software can be installed on Solaris or Windows NT platforms, but is also offered in a VelociRaptor appliance that is more attractive (much like the Nokia IPSO platform). (See Table 3.12.)

Table 3.12 Symantec at-a-Glance

Web Site	http://enterprisesecurity.symantec.com/content/ProductJump.cfm?Product=47&EID=0
Models	Symantec Gateway Security 5200
	Symantec VelociRaptor 1200
	Symantec Enterprise Firewall 100
Pros	As part of the Symantec Gateway Security offering, the firewall component has some good company, including Symantec AntiVirus and other intrusion prevention methods
Cons	User interface can be hard to navigate at times

WatchGuard Technologies, Inc.

With its distinctive bright red appliance chassis, the WatchGuard firewall can be identified from clear across the data center floor. Their lower-end Firebox SOHO 6 Wireless is a great idea for small remote offices that need to connect to headquarters using LAN-to-LAN VPN tunnels. Not only does it allow for IPSec encryption of the wireless and wired sides, but through a partnership with McAfee the Firebox has a VirusScan ASaP subscription to help with virus issues at the remote office with little or no IT support. On the high end of the spectrum, WatchGuard has really stepped up to the ISP and large organization level and introduced their Firebox V200 that can provide up to 2 Gbps of throughput and support up to 40,000 branch office VPN connections. The Firebox 4500, while supporting less capacity, still has an impressive 200 Mbps throughput and uses application layer proxies to complement its stateful inspection engine. They include Web content filtering as well, provided by CyberPatrol. (See Table 3.13.)

Table 3.13 WatchGuard at-a-Glance

Web site	www.watchguard.com/products/wgls.asp
Models	Firebox SOHO 6
	Firebox III
	Firebox X
	Firebox vClass
Pros	With the Firebox X, you can easily grow your firewall in pace with the growth of your networks
	High availability active/active configurations
	Four embedded RISC processors on the vClass line, for extra number crunching power
Cons	Management software is Windows based only

The most exciting product offering from WatchGuard is their new line of Firebox X devices. Distancing themselves from the almost cartoonish front panel design of the Firebox III, the X has a crisp appearance, an LCD screen, and expandable capacity for two to six NICs. As your network grows, entering in a software license activation key will enable the additional NICs and additional capabilities. Spam filtering, antivirus, VPN, intrusion prevention, and Web filtering can also be activated easily, as your company grows, using just an activation key.

Checklist

☑ Decide what is more important to your organization (performance, or packet inspection) and select accordingly.

☑ Plan ahead and don't paint yourself into a corner when doing an eval; know what targets you're trying to hit and clearly articulate these to your vendors.

☑ Understand the pros and cons of each firewall technology.

☑ Visit the vendor Web sites listed in this chapter to find out the features provided on each model.

☑ Visit the mailing lists and message boards listed at the end of this chapter to hear the real skinny from the trenches on using and maintaining different firewall types.

Summary

The firewall is your front lines of defense against attackers on the Internet. Everyone knows that you need a firewall, but who has stopped to examine the reasons behind that need? More than just "keeping the bad guys out," a sound firewall policy will make your network more efficient by only dealing with the traffic that is truly essential to your business operations. In essence, a firewall can concentrate your networking efforts and turn a noisy network into a laser-beam focused data delivery service.

Through the course of this chapter, we explained the different types of firewalls and their inner workings. Certifications, in the firewall industry, are an important way to show third-party acceptance of your product. Restricting your Web servers to only performing Web-related services, and your mail servers restricted to performing mail-delivery services, you will have less cause for alarm at night. This makes both good business and technological sense; you would only give particular employees the key to the NOC, so too should you be particularly discriminating about the ports to which you allow servers to make outbound connections.

While some vendors have a hardware appliance offering, others concentrate on the software only and leave the hardware to the end customer (still a couple of others will offer the software in both variations). All firewalls will have some form of administrative interface or GUI to configure the firewall for your company's particular needs. Most firewalls will provide a third NIC to define a service network, or DMZ, for your mail servers and other trusted-but-feared machines.

The differences between proxy-based and stateful packet inspection firewalls make for good debate. However, other, less controversial issues tend to get equal press in the security publications: logging, VPN, clustering, high availability, content filtering, and antivirus features are all powerful add-ons to look for when choosing your next firewall. Just remember not to sacrifice stable performance and a track record for quality software for the latest and greatest command-line utility that masquerades as a firewall.

Good ol' RFC 1918 makes it easy to segment your network according to functional business units, rather than arcane network address range assignments. Stateful failover, a feature often reserved for very high-end firewalls, is critical in a 24/7 operations center. Finally, go through the Web sites for all the vendors listed here and discover the solution that works best in your environment. Don't be afraid to kick the tires and make sure you're getting what your network needs today and this year. A pushy salesperson convincing your company of 10 employees that they need the PIX 535 is just criminal. Make sure you don't fall victim to the same tactics.

Solutions Fast Track

Understanding Firewall Basics

☑ A firewall must make packet routing decisions based on its preconfigured security profile.

☑ Better firewalls include features like detailed reporting and URL content filtering.

Exploring Stateful Packet Firewalls

☑ Although attributed to Check Point, the advent of stateful packet filtering firewalls allows us to be very restrictive in our security policy and yet know that return traffic will be handled.

Explaining Proxy-Based Firewalls

☑ Proxy firewalls will always be slower than the competition.

☑ Detailed reporting is possible due to the full-packet inspection process involved.

Examining Various Firewall Vendors

☑ Each vendor has its strengths and a weaknesses—what works for your organization will vary.

☑ Look for content filtering software pre-bundled with firewalls today.

☑ Use embedded PCI NIC firewalls for maximum security.

Links to Sites

■ **www.sl.universalservice.org/reference/CIPA.asp**
e-Rate Federal subsidized Internet access for schools.

- **www.websense.com** WebSense provides Web content filtering software that can plug in to firewalls like Cisco PIX.

- **www.surfcontrol.com** SurfControl also provides content filtering software to prevent users from navigating to inappropriate Web sites.

- **www.cyberpatrol.com** CyberPatrol produces content filtering software dubbed "Parental Control Software" due to its home-computer target, rather than Enterprise deployment.

- **www.cisco.com/en/US/products/hw/vpndevc/ps2030** Information on the entire Cisco PIX product line.

- **www.checkpoint.com/products/protect/firewall-1.html** Check Point Firewall-1 is one of the best selling firewalls around.

- **http://secure.dshield.org** By correlating a massive amount of data from user-submitted firewall logs, DShield can show the current "weather" condition of the Internet.

- **www.watchguard.com/products/wgls.asp** More information on the WatchGuard family of firewalls.

- **http://enterprisesecurity.symantec.com/content/ ProductJump.cfm?Product=47&EID=0** Symantec Enterprise Firewall information and detailed product specifications.

- **www.novell.com/products/bordermanager** Novell BorderManager is the only product (oddly enough) to integrate seamlessly with Novell NDS.

- **www.stonesoft.com/products** Stonesoft provides highly redundant firewall architectures.

- **www.netscreen.com/products/firewall** NetScreen firewalls range from small office to data-center grade performance.

- **www.microsoft.com/ISAServer/** Microsoft Internet Security and Acceleration Server information.

- **www.sonicwall.com/products/vpnapp.html** SonicWALL makes a range of firewall appliances to fit any budget, from home office to large company.

- **www.3com.com/products/en_US/productsindex.jsp?tab= cat&pathtype=purchase** Information on the 3Com Firewall Desktop PCI card, allowing all of your servers to have a robust hardware firewall-on-a-NIC.

- **www.icsalabs.com/html/communities/firewalls/** ICSA Certification criteria for network firewalls.

- **www.icsalabs.com/html/communities/pcfirewalls/** ICSA Certification criteria for PC firewalls.

Mailing Lists

- **firewalls@securityfocus.com** A great, vendor-neutral discussion that has contributions from people all over the globe.

- **firewalls@lists.gnac.net** Smaller membership than SecurityFocus, this list also has some useful information.

- **www.snpx.com/newsticker.html** This continuously updating news ticker is specifically geared toward the security industry. You can embed this little applet on your company's intranet and always stay up to the minute on the latest exploits and vulnerabilities.

- **http://honor.icsalabs.com/mailman/listinfo/firewall-wizards** ICSA Labs is the major certification for firewall products, and as such, this mailing list provides many useful tips and tricks from the firewall veterans.

- **www.isc.org/services/public/lists/firewalls.html** ISC, the organization behind the prestigious CISSP certification, maintains a firewall mailing list that tends to be more academic and theory than vendor-specific issues, but it still quite useful.

■ **www.securitynewsportal.com/pagetwo.shtml** The lighter side of the security industry news, this is the place to keep up with the latest gossip or Web site defacements.

Frequently Asked Questions

The following Frequently Asked Questions, answered by the authors of this book, are designed to both measure your understanding of the concepts presented in this chapter and to assist you with real-life implementation of these concepts. To have your questions about this chapter answered by the author, browse to **www.syngress.com/solutions** and click on the **"Ask the Author"** form. You will also gain access to thousands of other FAQs at ITFAQnet.com.

Q: What makes a proxy-based firewall so slow?

A: Remember the diagram explaining OSI layers earlier in the chapter? Of course you do—it was so concise and well written, it's resonating in your brain as we speak. Each time a software process must travel up or down the OSI layers, there is going to be a performance hit. Traveling between layers means either opening the lower layer's data packet "envelope" or wrapping a higher layer's data in its own envelope. To send a packet between two hosts, the proxy-based firewall must unwrap these envelopes all the way up at Layer 7, copy the data to another buffer, and reseal all seven envelopes. Anyone who has worked in accounts payable can tell you—licking that many envelopes will definitely slow you down (and might cause a nasty paper cut on your tongue).

Q: I've heard rumors that Check Point firewalls have back doors built into them; is this true?

A: You should keep out of the Cisco booth at trade shows! There have been rumors floating around for years (mostly from San Jose residents) that the Mossad, the Israeli equivalent of the United States' Central Intelligence Agency, wrote the Check Point software and has a back-door password to get into any Firewall-1 protected network in the world. If such a back door existed, the amount of scrutiny that modern firewalls endure would almost certainly flush out this fact in a number of online forums known for pointing out flaws in security design. While we cannot say anything about Check Point source code with certainty, we know that if you throw enough smart people at an issue (say, for instance, the worldwide population of hackers), you're bound to find out if there's a back door. Check out Chapter 4, "Attacking Firewalls," for a description of a Check Point vulnerability that is more of a "front door" hole than a back door one.

Q: Wow—security software written by Israeli intelligence agencies! This sounds like a Tom Clancy novel. How can I find out more?

A: We're not going to perpetuate any rumors about ties to the Mossad, but we will tell you this: in April 2001, the Mossad published advertisements in major publications, encouraging electronic engineers and computer scientists to apply to their special "Technology Department." The ad stated "The Mossad is open / Only to 13 engineers … The Mossad is open. Not to everyone. Not to many. Maybe to you." You draw your own ending to this novella; just make sure nobody discovers your true identity, 007.

Q: Who invented stateful inspection firewall technology?

A: Again, our friends at the Mossad, er… we mean Check Point take credit for this one. Although nobody really should be allowed to take credit for a type of technology, many Check Point publications reference the assertion that they "invented" this technology. In fact, they do hold the patent on stateful inspection firewall technology—but that does not necessarily mean they invented it. It just means they were the first to patent the technology. It would be the same thing as if we said "We're going to patent the process of logging in to a Web site so that it can show us personalized content." You would say, "You're crazy—that's just a concept. You can't patent the concept of logging in. Any dynamic site on the Internet today has some mechanism of logging in and having pre-stored preferences recalled. I mean, even something as simple as MyYahoo would be infringing upon that patent! You're crazy!" You can stop yelling at us—we won't try to patent that idea. But only because Gateway Computer beat us to it (U.S. Patent 6,530,083). And as soon as you stop yelling about how ridiculous that sounds, remember that the BT Group went to court against the Prodigy online service in February 2002 because they claimed to own the patent on hyperlinks.

Q: Where is future firewall technology headed?

A: If you ask us (and well, we guess you just did), firewalls are going to become smaller and more pervasive. Right now, you'll only find personal firewalls on very smart home users or very security savvy business users. In a year's time, nobody would think of powering on his or her machine without a personal firewall set on "red alert." The emphasis of choke points on your network where all traffic must filter through one device (the firewall) will disappear as that technology gets pushed out to the end points. A real big winner in this field is 3Com; they've already designed the product (the firewall-on-a-NIC described earlier) and are just waiting for the industry to take off. Soon, your data center won't have a single firewall in it! Instead, it will have 85 firewalls, one on each NIC port. They will all report back to a centralized management console and it will provide for the ultimate in granular manageability.

Chapter 4

Firewall Manipulation: Attacks and Defenses

Solutions in this Chapter:

- **Firewall Attack Methods**
- **Check Point Software Attacks and Solutions**
- **Cisco PIX Attacks and Solutions**
- **Microsoft ISA Server Attacks and Solutions**
- **NetScreen Firewall Attacks and Solutions**
- **Novell BorderManager Attacks and Solutions**

Related Chapters:

Introduction

As you read in Chapter 3, "Selecting the Correct Firewall," the concept and underlying technologies of firewalls have changed dramatically over the years. In like manner, the way in which attackers prey on networks and the techniques used have also matured. In previous years, the concept of sharing information or allowing Web services into your network was as foreign a concept as the Anaheim Angels winning the baseball World Series. The firewall policies of old were without complexity and the intricacies of modern business. Generally, these policies consisted of only a "Drop-All" rule that prevented any incoming traffic from the Internet, or your perimeter. This left the firewall itself as the only attack vector available. From an attacker's perspective, this meant that we had to manipulate or subvert the firewall before we could make a move on any of the internal systems or resources.

As time marched on, companies began to offer services to the Internet at large. While not as sexy or complicated as some of the policies in recent times, the services were opened by typically allowing functions like Web, mail, and DNS. Attackers now had multiple attack vectors at their disposal (Web, mail, or DNS servers) and didn't have to primarily focus on compromising the firewall as the main point of entry. Even when we could successfully compromise the internal servers, we still needed other points of entry into the network, prompting us to attack the firewall from the inside out.

Fast forward a few more years to present day and we are faced with the fact that the Anaheim Angels did finally win the World Series, and firewalls are now configured to allow a myriad of protocols and services from the Internet. This allows us, the external attackers, numerous attack vectors and points of entry to the DMZ and internal segments. With this in mind, the need and demand to attack and compromise the firewall device itself is nearly extinct. Instead, current firewall vulnerabilities and exploits provide the missing pieces that allow us to more efficiently attack our target networks and resources. While the vendor vulnerabilities of recent years are much less extensive, the information provided through such attacks is instrumental in helping us chart our course into the internal network.

The following pages will help you understand the different and more prominent firewall attack methodologies and techniques and provide you with multiple vendor vulnerabilities and exploits. With this information, you will be prepared to tune and patch your devices to limit your exposure to the external evildoers.

Firewall Attack Methods

In today's networking climate, there are really only three valid firewall attack methods: *information gathering*, *denial of service*, and *remote system compromise*. Each offer extremely different outcomes, and have differing requirements; however, combined they provide a bulk of the known vulnerabilities and attacks on recent firewall platforms and applications. The following two sections describe these attack methodologies.

Notes from the Underground...

Firewall Hacks: From the Inside Out

It used to be common practice to attack firewalls to provide the main entry point to internal networks. Penetration Testing professionals, and hackers alike, used to work to compromise systems in the DMZ, usually Web servers, mail servers, or DNS. Once compromised, the attacker would move all of his tools and resources to the "owned" box, providing a new launching point for his "Army." To provide further inroads into the internal segments, the attacker would then begin to launch attacks on the firewall from the internal or DMZ segment.

In this context, the intruder is not actually attacking the firewall application, but rather is attacking the underlying operating system (OS). For example, many administrators run the Check Point Firewall-1 application on a Windows 2000, Linux, or Solaris platform. In this scenario, the attacker would be exploiting vulnerabilities present in the Windows OS, or perhaps Solaris, rather than the firewall module.

While this is somewhat outside the scope of this book, it is important to realize that unless you are running your firewall on a completely hardened appliance, there are potentially some underlying vulnerabilities that could compromise your firewall installation.

Attacking for Information

Information disclosure is one of the most pervasive types of attacks used today. Once the exploit is initiated, the attacker is trying to cull as much information about the victim's networks or resources as possible. Typical disclosure includes internal IP addressing schemes, network topologies, and sometimes, through more extensive exploits, firewall rules and policies. With this information at hand, intruders can more efficiently plot their moves and confine their attacks. While this attack provides the necessary footprinting information on our target networks, it does not provide any further footholds for us to compromise deeper into the Lion's Den.

All firewall vendors are susceptible to these types of attacks. In the upcoming sections, we will look at different information disclosure vulnerabilities on several different vendors, including Check Point, Cisco, and NetScreen. While some of these vulnerabilities exist through flaws discovered in the firewall application, many of them are present from common misconfigurations.

Denial-of-Service Attacks

The absolute converse to information gathering would be a DoS style of attack. These attacks are written to disrupt network activity and business productivity by causing resources to be unavailable or unreachable. Attacks of this type generally provide little value in terms of network reconnaissance. Moreover, these attacks are not discrete, as any type of logging or intrusion detection will surely provide enough information to lead administrators to the offending IP address.

Attacks of this type come in many different forms, including buffer overflows, TCP SYN attacks, or through software flaws in the firewall application itself.

Notes from the Underground…

Denial of Service: The Corporate Fire Alarm

DoS attacks can pose an interesting problem when they are being initiated from your own internal segments. We think of these attacks as the equivalent of a high-school student pulling the fire alarm on his way to Algebra class, just so he doesn't have to sit through another boring lecture. If you think of the potential damage these attacks can reap on your internal resources, the analogy is not that far off.

Even in our own "real job" there are meetings that we would rather not attend, and e-mails we surely would not like to answer. How perfect would it be if we downloaded the latest Check Point DoS exploit and unleashed it on our own internal firewalls? That would easily solve all of

Continued

our problems! In like manner, we have found that many of the attacks successfully performed on the internal networks are more often than not DoS. The following are reasons as to why this is true:

- **Increased bandwidth on internal segments** Many DoS attacks require that an immense amount of data be pushed to the target device. While this is technically feasible across the Internet, with the increased speed and resiliency of internal segments, the bandwidth limitation is nonexistent.

- **No need for network reconnaissance** Typically, the internal attacker is an unskilled user who came across an exploit or tool that could invoke such an assault. Using that as our primer, most of these would-be attackers have no use for information disclosure attacks or other mild exploits that only provide limited information or access. In short, they are not in this for the long haul; they just want to knock something over quickly.

- **Relaxed firewall rules or access control lists (ACLs)** More so than the Internet, our users generally have more relaxed per-missions and access controls on the inside. This means that attacks that might be blocked by edge routers will pass unno-ticed on our internal segments.

While all of these characteristics might be true, and present, on your network, it does not necessarily mean that you cannot mitigate against a DoS type of attack. For example, keep your network devices as up to date as possible with the latest OS or software revisions. Additionally, try to use Quality-of-Service (QoS) or bandwidth throttling techniques on all of your critical segments so that users cannot successfully send large amounts of traffic during an exploit.

Remote Firewall Compromise

Perhaps the rarest of all the firewall attacks, the remote system compromise, pro-vides attackers the ability to gain access via the firewall's graphical user interface (GUI), or command-line interface. Either method will yield significant influence over the firewall application or underlying OS, and allow the attacker to make a myriad of modifications.

Typically, these types of attacks exist within flaws in the firewall application itself, and not usually the underlying OS. Nevertheless, it is quite common for the intruder to be able to make modifications to the firewall rule base, thereby altering the security context of the victim's network. With this capability, the attacker will commonly allow all traffic inbound and outbound to his source IP address, and in so doing, open the gates to the fortress. Moreover, a crafty intruder will disable all of the logging for that rule, leaving little trace of the traffic the passes through the device. The only saving grace left is your host-level defenses via an Intrusion Prevention System, or other router and switch ACLs in the environment.

While these attacks are rare, we have seen more research and exploits in this arena in recent months, most notably with Check Point. In the following sections, we detail some of these attack types.

Check Point Software Attacks and Solutions

Depending on which survey you read, the Cisco PIX and Check Point Firewall-1 share market dominance. Claiming to have invented stateful inspection, FireWall-1 is a hybrid stateful inspection firewall that has configurable application-layer proxies to perform inspection. The software can be installed on Solaris or Windows NT, but is most often deployed on hardened NetBSD appliances provided by Nokia (formerly manufactured by Ipsilion). Being one of the major market leaders in the firewall space prompts many vulnerability researchers to focus on your software, and the potential flaws therein. With this in mind, Check Point currently has many vulnerabilities associated with its software offerings. In the next section, we will dissect some of the most critical exploits and exposures.

VPN-1/SecureClient ISAKMP Buffer Overflow

As of print, this is the most recent and potentially damaging attack that affects any of the firewall technologies. Originally discovered by the X-Force team at Internet Security Systems, the vulnerability exists in the virtual private network (VPN) server and clients for Check Point's Firewall-1 product. This functionality allows remote users the ability to VPN to internal networks and resources. While many methods exist to handle the client and server negotiation of the tunnel, this particular vulnerability resides in the code that handles the firewall's certificate exchange. This vulnerability affects Firewall-1 version 4.1 up to Service Pack 5a, and Check Point NG, Feature Packs 0 and 1.

Attacking Check Point VPN with Certificates

For VPN tunnels to be established and secured, the client and server must exchange encryption keys prior to establishing the tunnel. The method to exchange these keys is known as *Internet Key Exchange*, or IKE. The network protocol used to enable this key exchange is known as the Internet Security Association and Key Management Protocol, or ISAKMP. Check Point's implementation of the ISAKMP protocol is where the major vulnerability resides.

The way in which a Check Point VPN server handles how certificates are requested is where the vulnerability lies. Certificates are used to negotiate the security of the VPN tunnel. When an unauthenticated client connects to the VPN server and requests a certificate, if the payload buffer is larger than the server can handle, a routine stack overflow is accomplished and the system is successfully exploited. Since an unauthenticated user is able to perform this attack without knowing a username or password, this exploit is open to all untrusted Internet or internal users who connect to a vulnerable system.

According to the ISS X-Force team, the exploit is extremely easy to execute and has far-reaching impact. Furthermore, X-Force, although not released as of yet, has produced proof-of-concept code that can repeatedly exploit this vulnerability. The inevitable result of this vulnerability allows a remote attacker to have an interactive command-line shell to the firewall device. In this context, the remote attacker can make alterations to the firewall rules policy, thereby potentially compromising the principal security of the remote network. Once the modifications are made, the remote attacker can then use these openings to launch more attacks deeper into the victim's internal networks.

Tools for Attacking Check Point's VPN

At the time of print, the only known working exploit to this vulnerability is within the confines of ISS' X-Force team; however, we would be naïve to think that a public exploit won't be available soon. Since there is no tool to carry out this attack as of yet, the threat to your network infrastructure is relatively mild, giving you ample time to remediate your systems from this vulnerability. By the time this book prints there is likely to be an exploit available. Continue to monitor the following URL for the presence of exploit code: http://www.security-focus.com/bid/9582/exploit/.

Mitigation for Check Point VPN

It is has been stated that the only true way to remediate this vulnerability on your Check Point devices is to upgrade to the latest service or feature pack for your current software versions. If you are running Firewall-1, version 4.1, you can upgrade to Service Pack 6 to remove the vulnerability. If you are already running the Check Point Next Generation (NG) release, you must upgrade to Feature Pack 2. Keep in mind that version 4.1 of Firewall-1 has been relegated to end-of-life by Check Point, meaning there will be no further updates or product releases for that version. If future vulnerabilities arise in the 4.1 version, users will need to upgrade to NG to mitigate the vulnerability.

Another potential remediation tactic exists with limiting the source IP addresses of your VPN users. This mitigates the vulnerability by removing much of the untrusted Internet from being able to exploit the vulnerability. In other words, by locking down your VPN access to only specific IP addresses, the attackers who are not part of the confined group would not be allowed to connect to your VPN server and initiate the exploit. This also means that if any of your corporate users are evildoers, they could still launch the attack, as their IP would be allowed to connect.

This is by no means an effective or efficient workaround if you have more than a few remote VPN users, as you would need to know the source IP address of each of the remote workers. Additionally, this technique does not fully mitigate the vulnerability, as your VPN users could initiate the exploit. However, if you are resource and time constrained, then this might be a quick remediation effort, rather than testing and implementing the latest service pack.

Check Point SecuRemote
Internal Address Disclosure

The Internal Address disclosure is yet another vulnerability that revolved around Check Point's implementation of the VPN. While this vulnerability does not provide the remote system compromise, like the previous Check Point attack, it still provides invaluable information about the internal segments connected to the firewall. With this information, a skilled attacker can plan the next phase of the attack.

Originally discovered by Andy Davis at Information Risk Management in London, the vulnerability provides the IP addresses, and therefore the directly connected networks, of the internal interfaces on the firewall. The vulnerability affects Check Point Firewall-1 versions 4.0 through 4.1 Service Pack 4. Check Point NG is not vulnerable to this attack.

Check Point's IP Disclosure

SecuRemote, the predecessor to Check Point's SecureClient, is an agent that installs on the computers of remote VPN users. SecuRemote handles all of the VPN negotiation with the firewall transparently to the user, until the user needs to enter the VPN credentials. The Firewall-1 application listens on TCP ports 256 and 264 for VPN connections. During the unencrypted communication with the firewall, the VPN server will send the internal IP addresses to the SecuRemote client. While this information is never displayed on the screen, it can be captured via a packet sniffer off of the wire. Since the information is sent in clear-text, it is also possible for remote attackers to be able to see this information being passed when normal SecuRemote activity is taking place.

Since the transfer of the IP address information takes place during the unencrypted portion of the VPN negotiation, it was simple for IRM to determine exactly what nudge the VPN server needed to be able to send the IP information. From this analysis, IRM was able to create a proof-of-concept exploit and publicize their findings.

Tools for Exploiting Check Point's VPN

Two separate exploits are currently available that perform this attack. Again, since this attack is only providing information to the attacker, the exploits are nonintrusive and will generally not set off any Intrusion Detection System (IDS) alarms. Furthermore, typical firewall behavior and traffic will continue without interruption or disturbance.

IRM's proof-of-concept code is named "*fwenum*" and is available for download at their Web site: http://www.irmplc.com/advisories.htm. Their script is quite simple to use, having only one parameter to provide—the IP address of the firewall. Once compiled, the exploit can be run with the following parameter:

```
#fwenum 192.0.2.24
```

In this example, the target firewall has the IP address 192.0.2.24. Once the command is issued, the exploit code queries the target device on TCP port 256 and provides the number of active firewall interfaces and the list of the respective IP addresses.

The second active exploit in the wild was written by Jim Becher and is available at http://www.securityfocus.com/bid/8524/exploit/. Similar in usage and technique, the only differentiator in this exploit is the ability to provide a range of IPs to test this exploit against. In other words, if you are not sure where or how many Check Point firewalls are present on your network, you can simply provide the entire network range and let the exploit test them all. Therefore, in many respects, this exploit is like a mini-port scanner for Check Point firewalls. Once compiled, the exploit can be run with the following parameters:

```
#fw1_getints  192.0.2.1  192.0.2.254
```

Using the same IP range from our previous tool, this exploit will look for the presence of TCP port 256 on Firewall-1 version 4.0 or earlier, and TCP port 264 on version 4.1 or later.

Defending against Internal IP Address Disclosure

There are a few mitigating circumstances for this vulnerability. First, if SecuRemote or VPN access is not necessary on the firewall, TCP ports 256 and 264 can be filtered or disabled. If VPN access is a necessary component, then software updates to Firewall-1 must be performed.

To update version 4.1, you must install Service Pack 6. Currently, version 4.0 of Check Point Firewall-1 is only the end-of-life list from the vendor. If you are running this old version, then you will have to upgrade to version 4.1 Service Pack 6 to be fully patched. To get the latest updates, you must have a current support and maintenance contract with Check Point. As mentioned previously, the Next Generation version is not vulnerable to this information disclosure.

Cisco PIX Attacks and Solutions

We all know of Cisco's reputation as market leader in terms of both market share and quality networking products. However, in the firewall market, the Cisco PIX has taken a backseat to vendors like Check Point and NetScreen, mainly because of the poor user interfaces on previous versions of the firewall. With those follies behind them, Cisco is getting a second wind with their new device manager interface and is beginning to gain market prominence once more.

While their dominance in the industry has earned them many accolades, it has also earned them the interest of vulnerability researchers worldwide—and from this research comes the many vulnerabilities and exploits that we have to understand and defend against. In the next few sections we will look at some of the more recent Cisco PIX vulnerabilities and flaws. The following vulnerabilities were selected for inclusion because of their simplicity and potential damage.

Cisco PIX SNMPv3 Denial of Service

As will be extensively discussed in Chapter 8, "Defending Routers and Switches," Simple Network Management Protocol (SNMP) is the main management protocol for administrators to monitor their networking devices. In SNMP version 3, the protocol began to support encryption, a much-needed feature as previous versions were subject to all kinds of attacks with the clear-text protocol.

This latest Cisco PIX vulnerability revolves around the way the PIX firewall handles incoming SNMPv3 messages, or traps. The vulnerability was released on January 26, 2004, so by any standards this is a new attack. According to the Cisco advisory, this vulnerability affects versions of PIX OS 6.3.1, 6.2.2 and earlier, 6.1.4 and earlier, and 5.*x.x* and earlier.

Using SNMPv3 to Crash a PIX

The mere presence of this protocol targeted at the device will cause the firewall to crash and then reload itself, even if the given firewall does not have the SNMPv3 feature-set loaded. This exploit will cause a brief interruption of service and connectivity while the device recycles.

Detailed information is limited as to exactly why the PIX firewall module cannot handle the SNMPv3 message. Sending the SNMPv3 message or trap to a Cisco PIX device configured to accept SNMP messages will cause the machine to crash and then reload. The exploit can be performed from any number of SNMP tools and is easily repeatable, opening the doors to a potential automated worm or worse. In fact, it is quite astonishing how simple it is to use this attack, as there are no other requirements in the SNMPv3 payload, just the presence of the protocol is enough to cause the failure.

SNMPv3 Tools and Uses

Currently, there is no automated exploit code available on the Internet; however, we believe by the time this books prints we will see some automated proof-of-concept code in the wild. Even without a scripted attack on this vulnerability, the SNMPv3 DoS can be easily exploited through the use of SNMP tools such as SolarWinds or Castle Rock Computing's SNMPc software package.

To successfully exploit this vulnerability, all you will need to do is configure the software package to connect to the target firewall. Once the connection is established, the remote firewall will drop and recycle, causing the desired denial of service.

This is an extremely dangerous exploit, as it can be performed with very simple tools and a limited knowledge of networking devices and protocols. Should an easy-to-use, automated tool emerge in the wild, this could result in a pretty nasty threat for Cisco PIX administrators.

Defending against SNMPv3 Denial-of-Service Exploits

Fortunately, Cisco has provided us with three mitigating tactics to prevent successful exploitation of this vulnerability. It is important to note that this attack is only successful if the PIX firewall is running the SNMP server service. If the device is just sending SNMP traps to a SNMP monitoring agent, a much more common configuration, the exploit will fail. If the SNMP server is running and is not a necessary component of your firewall, you can disable it by using the following commands:

```
BrianPIX(config)# clear snmp-server
BrianPIX(config)# no snmp-server enable traps
BrianPIX(config)# no snmp-server [interface_name] [ip_addr]
```

The preceding commands will disable the SNMP server on the Cisco PIX device. If the SNMP server is required, another sanctioned Cisco workaround is available by limiting the devices that can connect via SNMP. By defining which IP addresses can connect to the device with SNMP, you limit the wide exposure of this being exploited by unknown hosts. This does not completely mitigate the vulnerability, though, as the approved IP addresses could send the SNMPv3 message, thereby resulting in the denial of service. Use the following command to define the allowable IP addresses:

```
BrianPIX(config)# snmp-server host [interface_name] [ip_addr]
```

Finally, the last mitigation technique would be to update your Cisco PIX installation to the latest software revision. According to Cisco, the correct and patched versions are 6.3.2 and later, 6.2.3 and later, and 6.1.5 and later.

Cisco PIX SSH Denial of Service

For many of us, Secure Shell (SSH) is the only trusted network management communication protocol, and is widely deployed throughout the enterprise. Administrators use SSH to remotely connect to networking devices and UNIX machines to perform remote management. Previously, protocols like Telnet were used, but given their clear-text nature, and the security risks inherent with it, many administrators moved away from the insecure protocol and began adopting the usage of SSH on critical devices.

Most networking devices now support the use of SSH, including the Cisco PIX family of firewalls. In late 2001, a vulnerability was released affecting the SSH protocol. Since the protocol itself was flawed, and not necessarily the vendor's implementation, multiple vendors were negatively affected, including Cisco. However, in Cisco's haste to release an updated revision on the PIX OS and IOS, they introduced a serious flaw in the SSH handler that causes a DoS vulnerability on all PIX firewalls that had the SSH server enabled.

Using SSH to Crash a PIX

As mentioned previously, SSH is the de facto standard for managing remote network devices. Network administrators rely on this protocol to make configuration changes and updates to the devices on their network. With this in mind, most Cisco networking devices, PIX especially, are running the SSH server and are thereby vulnerable to this exploit.

The Cisco SSH vulnerability was discovered and released in June 2002. The vulnerability was introduced after Cisco made an update to their software by patching a previous SSH vulnerability. This new exposure can be triggered by sending an overly large SSH packet to the device. Once the packet arrives, the SSH server attempts to perform a Cyclical Redundancy Check, or CRC, on the SSH packet. This CRC check commits far too much CPU processing and limits the ability for other functions to operate on the device, thereby causing the denial of service. The exploit can be repeatedly sent to the device, causing it to unexpectedly reload and introduce loss of connectivity. Typically, a reload on a Cisco PIX firewall can take several minutes; however, since the vulnerability can be exploited repeatedly, this reload loop could continue ad infinitum, or until you patch your system.

SSH Tools for Crashing the PIX

Currently, there is only one known public exploit for this vulnerability, although anyone crafty enough to use a packet generator and create his own malformed SSH packets can trigger this exploit. The public exploit is available through Rapid 7, Inc. and is called SSHredder. This tool is a collection of binary packets that can be sent to the vulnerable device through tools like Netcat. Complete with over 600 different binary packages, this tool is built to test the exploit on a variety of different vendor platforms.

To successfully trigger the exploit, you will need to run Netcat on your local machine and send the binary packet to the PIX firewall SSH server. Netcat is a networking utility used to read or write packets across network connections. It serves as a popular hacking tool, as it can be used to send traffic and set up TCP/IP listeners on a target machine. Netcat can be downloaded for Windows or Unix platforms from: http://www.atstake.com/research/tools/network_utilities/. Once Netcat is loaded on the local machine, you can download the SSHredder utility from Rapid 7 at http://www.rapid7.com/Product-Download.html.

To execute the exploit, use the following command:

```
F:\Tools\NT>nc -v 192.0.2.1 22 < 0000037.pdu
```

Dissecting the preceding line, you can see that we executed the Netcat program with the *nc* command. The *-v* option instantiates the "verbose" option for Netcat, detailing basic information once the connection is established. The IP address provided is our victim PIX firewall, and the number 22 is the port number for the SSH server. Finally, the < is used to send the file 0000037.pdu to the target device on port 22. This has successfully sent the malformed SSH packet that will cause the PIX firewall to crash. Obviously, this type of exploit can be easily scripted in Perl, or your other favorite shell scripting variant.

Advanced features of Netcat also allow you to spoof your source IP address to hide your identity a little better. Since only one packet needs to be sent to the target device to trigger the exploit, IP address spoofing will work. By spoofing your IP address, the administrator will have a much harder time tracking down the offending machine.

Defending against SSH Denial-of-Service Exploits

Cisco has provided many mechanisms to protect you from this basic vulnerability. It is important to note that SSH is not enabled by default on PIX firewalls, so unless you have configured the SSH server, you are most likely not vulnerable.

However, if you are performing remote device management, SSH will most likely be your one lifeline to the networking device; thus, disabling the service is probably not an attractive option. However, instead of disabling the server, it might be worthwhile to limit the IP addresses or devices that can connect to the firewall via SSH. This can be achieved through the use of ACLs. Cisco recommends blocking all SSH requests from the untrusted Internet segment, and only allowing specific IP addresses to connect. While this will not fully protect you from the vulnerability, as the approved IP addresses could still initiate the attack, it will mitigate you from most of the would-be attackers. To apply an access-list of this nature, follow this example:

```
BrianRouter(config)# access-list 25 permit host 192.0.2.32 22
BrianRouter(config)# access-list 25 permit host 192.0.2.195 22
BrianRouter(config)# access-list 25 deny any
BrianRouter(config)# interface Ethernet 0/1
BrianRouter(config-if)# ip access-group 25 in
BrianRouter(config-if)# ip access-group 25 out
BrianRouter(config-if)# exit
```

Additionally, since this particular exploit has been available for some time, Cisco has many updated versions of the PIX OS. Check with the Cisco Web site to find the most updated version for your PIX device. If you are running an older version of the PIX software, it might make sense to use this opportunity to upgrade.

Microsoft ISA Server Attacks and Solutions

Regardless of what the marketing documents might say, ISA Server is really nothing more than the old Microsoft Proxy Server with better wizards. Add to this the fact that Microsoft is certainly the "black sheep" of the security world and you end up with one disaster of a firewall product. Regardless of the lack of functionality and features within the product, early on, ISA server was targeted by many vulnerability researchers as their number-one task. Researchers and hackers were determined to find vulnerabilities and flaws within the firewall, thereby invalidating Microsoft's attempt at becoming a major security player. They achieved this goal in short order.

Since then, researchers have turned back to their favorite firewall vendors, such as Check Point Cisco and NetScreen, causing a lack of recent discoveries in the ISA Server product. Of course, it is always possible that Microsoft finally got their act together and put out an impenetrable firewall product. Okay, stop laughing, perhaps we were correct, and leading vulnerability researchers did move on to other targets. Nevertheless, while some of these exploits are old, they are equally damaging to those who are running various versions of ISA Server. In this section, we will describe some of the most damaging, and simple to run, exploits for the ISA Server product.

ISA Server Web Proxy Denial of Service

The very first vulnerability to be discovered in the product exploded on the scene in early April 2001. Of course, in pure Microsoft fashion, the first vulnerability was an exploitable DoS attack. This vulnerability resides in the Web Proxy service of the firewall, which is used to pass Web requests from internal resources to external Web servers. In other words, when an internal device requests content from a Web site outside the corporate network, the ISA Web Proxy service requests the content on behalf of the device and then relays the data once it is received from the Internet.

This vulnerability affects the Web Proxy service by creating a DoS condition that stops all processing of outgoing HTTP traffic. An administrator will need to manually restart the Web Proxy service on the ISA firewall to restore connectivity. The vulnerability affects Microsoft ISA Server version 1.0 on Windows 2000.

Using Web Requests to Crash ISA Server

The Web Proxy attack is easily scriptable and can be routinely initiated from internal resources. Inherently, ISA Server runs the Web Proxy service, so all ISA Server installations are vulnerable. The attack is mainly triggered by sending an elongated URL string to the target firewall. Regardless of the ultimate location, or whether the resource is available, once the ISA server begins to process the URL, the Web Proxy service will assume nearly 100 percent of CPU resources and stop passing all incoming or outgoing Web traffic. The attack can be performed by simply requesting a long URL resource, or by opening an HTML e-mail with this URL attack defined in the content. The latter attack is potentially more dangerous, as unsuspecting users might open unsolicited HTML from outside attackers that could initiate the exploit. This could be repeated several times, as once the firewall service is restarted, it is still vulnerable to the attack.

The Web Publishing service included with ISA Server processes HTTP proxy services from the Internet to internal Web servers. By default, the Web Publishing service is disabled and needs to be configured by an administrator prior to functioning. If the service is running, the same attack that can be instantiated from inside the network could potentially be performed from the Internet. From the Internet, the attacker would have to address a Web server currently available and protected behind the ISA server.

Web Proxy Tools for Crashing the ISA Server

To date, the only available exploit for this vulnerability is from SecureXpert labs: http://downloads.securityfocus.com/vulnerabilities/exploits/repeat.c. The scripted exploit can easily be executed from Linux machines. However, to show you the true power of this vulnerability, we will demonstrate the exploit without the scripted companion and just perform it through a Netcat session. Using the following command, you can overflow the Web Proxy service on your target ISA server:

```
F:\Tools\NT>nc -v www.stuckintheattic.com 80 < urlpush.txt
```

This is very similar to the Netcat command we provided in the previous Cisco attack. Essentially, we are opening a connection to the Web server stuckintheattic.com on port 80. Since the ISA server is proxying the request for us, it will handle all of the connection negotiation. Once the connection is opened, we send the contents of the text file urlpush, which contains our malicious payload. The contents in the text file are:

```
GET http://www.stuckintheattic.com/aaa(2997 more a's) HTTP/1.0
```

This single URL string is enough to overflow the Web Proxy service and cause the denial of service. In the text file, we have a simple HTTP 1.0 GET command, asking for the resource referenced in the URL. The actual URL reads "http://www.stuckintheattic.com/aaaaaaaaaaa.html," where there are a total of 3000 "a's" listed in the URL string. As you can see, this vulnerability is extremely easy to exploit.

The same type of exploit could be performed from the Internet if the Web Publishing service was running. The only exception being, where the fictional stuckintheattic.com domain is used from the inside, an Internet attack would actually need to use the real, and valid, address of a Web server behind the ISA server. The rest of the attack is identical and will cause the same result.

Defending against Web Proxy Exploits

Unfortunately, unlike the Web Publishing service, the Web Proxy service is a required component of ISA Server and must be running. This springs from the fact that ISA Server is a derivative of the old Microsoft Proxy Server application. With this being the case, the only remediation effort would be to update your installations of Microsoft ISA Server. This can be performed by installing the Microsoft hotfix MS01-021.

The Web Publishing service, while still vulnerable to this exploit, can be disabled if it is not needed. This will mitigate the risk of this attack being triggered from Internet intruders. The vulnerability to this service is also corrected with the MS01-021 hotfix.

ISA Server UDP Flood Denial of Service

ISA Server has a flaw in how the Winsock Proxy service handles fragmented UDP packets. The flaw can cause a DoS condition where the firewall is unable to process any traffic inbound or outbound. While it is common for most devices to suffer from "flood" attacks, this particular vulnerability revolves around how ISA Server handles the fragmented nature of the packets, requiring far fewer packets to be processed than most "flood" attacks.

Originally discovered by Tamer Sahin at Security Office, the vulnerability was released in November 2001. While this attack does take advantage of how ISA Server (more specifically, the Winsock Proxy service of ISA Server) processes the fragmented packets, the exploit does require that a significant amount of traffic be directed to the firewall. For the most part, this limits the success of the exploit from Internet attackers, pending bandwidth resources and Internet choke points. However, in respect to internal resources, this attack can be successful due to the increased bandwidth and resources on internal networks. The vulnerability affects all versions of ISA Server 2000.

Using UDP Floods to Crash ISA Server

Network flooding attacks are not new to the network security space. The original distributed denial-of-service (DDoS) attacks used to use these tactics to limit the accessibility of their victim's networks and resources. Additionally, this type of attack is not the most graceful; generally, they are easily tracked, and administrators can easily find the offending attacker.

The core of the attack results in the firewall processing a large amount of bogus traffic, thereby limiting the amount of processing available for legitimate traffic. This coupled with fixed resources on the firewall causes the denial of service, as there is only a finite amount of memory that can be consumed by a running application. In this instance, the Winsock Proxy service has a memory leak when presented with a large volume of fragmented UDP packets. In short, this causes a rapid consumption of system memory, which can cause substantial packet loss or an all-out loss of service. The loss of service typically requires a reboot on the part of the administrator.

UDP Floods Tools against ISA Server

A few days after the discovery of the vulnerability, Tamer Sahin released proof-of-concept code that sends a large amount of spoofed, fragmented UDP traffic to the target firewall. This exploit will certainly generate a large amount of network traffic and invariably set off any IDS sensors that are watching the wire. That being said, the exploit can successfully repeat and execute the vulnerability on target ISA firewalls, making this a real threat for your internal networks. The exploit code, named Opentear, is available from the Security Office Web site at http://www.securityoffice.net/articles/isa/index.php.

The exploit includes a simple-to-use interface; just ensure before you execute the program to have plenty of system resources on your machine and plenty of bandwidth between your machine and the target firewall. After executing the attack, the ISA firewall should be in a degraded state. For the best effect, you can run this exploit from multiple locations on the internal network, but by doing this, you are setting off every network monitoring alarm in the building.

Once compiled, simply run the exploit from a command prompt as follows:

```
#opentear 192.0.2.1
```

Once run, this simple command will begin to flood the provided IP address with the fragmented UDP packets. The exploit will spoof the source address of each packet sent with a false address, helping to obfuscate the attacker.

ISA Server UDP Flood Defenses

Microsoft released a hotfix that fixed this vulnerability, plus two others, prior to the discovery of the memory leak. MS01-045 fixed the Winsock Proxy service by correcting the way in which the service allocates and deallocates memory.

Applying this patch will remove the existence of the memory leak in the Winsock Proxy service; however, it does not fully mitigate you from flood attacks. UDP and TCP flooding attacks are written to occupy and allocate as much of the firewall resources as possible, thereby causing connection disruptions and degraded performance. In most cases, these attacks do not take advantage of a particular vulnerability (this attack excluded), but rather brute-force DoS condition. While ensuring your firewall is on the most current software revision will help mitigate most attacks, you cannot be fully protected from flooding types of assaults.

Some defense techniques will help you deal with network flooding attacks. First, the use of quality-of-service (QoS) or packet shapers will help remove the threat of large amounts of malicious traffic from being transmitted on your networks. Second, the use of active IDS can help reduce the amount of malicious traffic on network segments. These systems monitor traffic on your networks, and when abnormal or malicious traffic is encountered, they either block the traffic from progressing or make modifications to the firewall rule policy to block the unauthorized traffic. Using these techniques in concert with keeping up to date with firewall software revisions will help mitigate future and existing attacks from being successful on your devices and networks.

NetScreen Firewall Attacks and Mitigations

NetScreen has always been known for performance. Running on their own custom appliance, their high-end packet-filtering firewalls can process an insane 12 Gbps and have earned them the 2003 *Network Magazine* Product of the Year award (www.netscreen.com/company/news_room/new_releases/ pr_20030423_453.jsp). A strong market contender, this firewall manufacturer was just purchased by Juniper Networks for nearly $4 billion.

Even though the company has made promising firewall innovations, and continues to surprise the marketplace with new features and functionality, the security of their devices has been scrutinized by leading researchers worldwide. Over the past few years, several DoS vulnerabilities were found, as well as some information disclosure leaks within the core firewall product. In the next section, we will highlight a few of the more highly exploitable vulnerabilities within the NetScreen product suite

NetScreen Management and TCP Option Denial of Service

Administrators can manage the NetScreen firewall in a few different ways: through a command-line interface accessible via Telnet, SSH, or direct-connection through a console cable, or a WebUI that is available via standard HTTP or HTTPS. The firewall is capable of having an IP address for each active interface, as well as a "Management" IP address that administrators would use to configure the firewall via the methods mentioned previously. Firewall ACLs and permission can be set to allow or disallow certain hosts from connecting to the management IP address.

A flaw exists in a certain version of ScreenOS, NetScreen's proprietary operating system for their appliances, which can cause a system reboot if certain TCP options are set. In other words, users connecting to the management IP address with malformed TCP option settings can cause the firewall to assert and reboot, causing a loss of service and network interruption. Versions of ScreenOS 4.0.1r1 through 4.0.1r6, 4.0.3r1, and 4.0.3r2 are vulnerable to this attack.

Manipulating TCP Options to Crash ScreenOS

This vulnerability was discovered in July 2003 by the Papa Loves Mambo Research Group. The group found that Windows hosts that connect to the management interface of the NetScreen firewall with extremely large TCP window sizes would cause the device to crash. The TCP window size is used to determine the initial size of data that can be transferred during a normal TCP connection. In other words, one side of the TCP connection tells the other side how much data it can send before sending an acknowledgment packet. This type of TCP tweak is commonly used when you want to speed up transfer rates between hosts. The downside is that the increased data transmission consumes more memory in the process, as the IP stack needs to buffer the data before and after transmission.

The DoS condition exists when a Windows host with the increased TCP window size connects to either the Telnet or WebUI management interface. As soon as the connection is established with the firewall, the device sends invalid information to the onboard Application-Specific Integrated Circuits (ASIC), which cannot properly process the incoming data, thereby causing a reload of the entire device. This reload typically take a few moments to bring the device back to normal operating conditions, causing a loss of connectivity and dropped traffic.

Similar to many of the other exploits we have witnessed in this chapter, the attack can be triggered by an unauthorized user, as authentication does not need to take place for this exploit to be successful. This makes this attack open to anyone who knows the management interface of the device.

Registry Tweaks for TCP Options to Crash ScreenOS

Perhaps the most dangerous part of this attack is that there is zero need for any type of exploit code. A user can simply add a few tweaks to his Windows Registry and connect to the vulnerable device to cause the outage. The only saving grace here is if you have strong desktop policies that prohibit the average Windows users from making Registry modifications. If this is not the case, then anyone with knowledge of the firewall IP addresses could potentially launch the attack from the internal network.

To create the appropriate TCP window size to carry out the attack, the following Registry changes must be made. This information was provided by the Papa Loves Mambo Research Group

```
\HKEY_LOCAL_MACHINE\SYSTEM\CurrentControlSet\Services\Tcpip\Parameters
   Tcp1323Opts, HEX, 3
```

```
\HKEY_LOCAL_MACHINE\SYSTEM\CurrentControlSet\Services\Tcpip\Parameters
   TcpWindowSize, Decimal, 131400
```

With this information, the user will need to create two new DWORD values in the Registry. These new DWORDS should be named "TcpWindowSize" and "Tcp1323Opts." The TcpWindowSize value should be as a decimal value of 131400. The Tcp1323Opts DWORD should be set to a hexadecimal value of 3. These two values must be under the Parameters key in "Tcpip." Once these entries are added, the user must reboot the Windows machine

Now that the Registry entries are set, the user can connect to the firewall device to trigger the vulnerability. The user can perform this through a couple of methods, since both the Telnet and Web interface are vulnerable to this attack. To connect via Telnet use the following command:

```
F:\Tools>telnet 192.0.2.1
```

In this example, we are opening a Telnet session with the target host, 192.0.2.1, which is our NetScreen firewall. Once the initial TCP connection is established, the firewall should fall over.

To exploit this vulnerability through the Web interface, a user can simply open a Web browser and input the IP address into the address bar, such as http://192.0.2.1/. In addition, at a DOS prompt a user can start Internet Explorer by issuing the following command:

```
F:\Tools>start http://192.0.2.1/

F:\Tools>start https://192.0.2.1/
```

With either method, the firewall will crash once the TCP connection is established. Additionally, both of these tactics can be performed by using Netcat as follows:

```
F:\Tools>nc -v 192.0.2.1 23

F:\Tools>nc -v 192.0.2.1 80

F:\Tools>nc -v 192.0.2.1 443
```

In the preceding examples, Netcat will connect to the target device and cause the denial of service.

Defending ScreenOS against the TCP Option DoS

A couple of tactics can be employed to help protect against this attack. First, you can set the allowable devices that can connect to your management IP address within the NetScreen command-line interface. By using this command, only the specified hosts, or networks, will be allowed to open connections with the management interface. While this will protect you from untrusted attackers, the allowed hosts or networks could launch the attack and exploit your firewall. The following is the command necessary to define the allowable hosts or networks:

```
#set admin manager-ip 192.0.2.134 255.255.255.255
```

In this first example, we add a rule allowing only the IP address 192.0.2.134 to connect to the NetScreen management interface. This will prohibit anyone except the preceding IP address from accessing the management portion of the device.

```
#set admin manager-ip 192.0.2.1 255.255.255.0
```

In this second example, all users on the Class C subnet of 192.0.2.1-254 can connect to the management interface. This is a broader application of the first access control rule. This allows access to the potential 254 devices on the 192.0.2.x subnet.

Another remediation tactic, if you do not use the WebUI interface, would be to disable Telnet access to the device and only use SSH. Since SSH is not vulnerable to this attack, this protocol can be used to securely administer the device (a tactic you should have been using anyway). You can disable the WebUI or Telnet interface through the command-line interface.

Lastly, you have the option to upgrade to the latest version of ScreenOS. At the time of print, NetScreen firewalls are currently shipping with version 5.0 of ScreenOS. Therefore, if you are running one of the vulnerable versions, you can upgrade.

NetScreen Remote Reboot Denial of Service

While this is a somewhat older vulnerability, the possibility exists that an unauthorized user connecting to the WebUI management interface of a NetScreen firewall can cause a reboot of the device. As mentioned in the previous NetScreen vulnerability, the WebUI interface is designed to allow administrators the ability to make modifications to the firewall and firewall policies. While other options to manage the firewall are available, such as SSH, Telnet, and direct console connections, the WebUI is most commonly used among administrators and has a DoS flaw. The vulnerable only exists on the popular NetScreen 25 appliance and on versions 2.5 through 3.0.1r1.1 of ScreenOS. Other versions are not vulnerable.

Manipulating the WebUI to Crash ScreenOS

The NetScreen WebUI has a simple login display that provides access control to the main configuration sections of the interface. The user management system is proprietary to NetScreen, although third-party authentication mechanisms such as LDAP and SecueID are supported by the firewall. The vulnerability exists in the way the authentication is handled, specifically how the authentication mechanism handles the use of a long username. This vulnerability only exists when an authentication mechanism is being used.

The attack, once successfully applied, causes a general exception error and immediately reboots the appliance. This attack is extremely easy to initiate and does not require a legitimate username or login credentials. Furthermore, once the device reboots, and is properly functioning again, the vulnerability still exists, providing the evildoer an infinite loop of possible attacks.

Crafting the Long Username to Crash ScreenOS

As with many of our other examples, this attack does not require complicated exploit code, or any code for that matter. To trigger this attack, a user would only need to have a Web browser and the IP address of the WebUI, or management interface on hand. By opening a connection with a Web browser to the WebUI interface, the user is prompted for a username and password. Once the login page ·is loaded, the user can enter the letter "x" 257 times in the username login box and press Enter without providing a password.

The vulnerability exists since there is no boundary checking on the excessively long username. This overflows that amount of memory allocated for the field and causes the crash—and can be reproduced ad nauseum.

Defending ScreenOS against the Invalid Usernames

As with the previous vulnerability, the same mitigation and remediation steps can be followed to protect yourself from this vulnerability. First, you can set the allowable devices that can connect to your management IP address within the NetScreen command-line interface. By using this command, only the specified hosts, or networks, will be allowed to open connections with the management interface. While this will protect you from untrusted attackers, the allowed hosts or networks could launch the attack and exploit your firewall. The following is the command necessary to define the allowable hosts or networks:

```
#set admin manager-ip 192.0.2.134 255.255.255.255
```

In this first example, we add a rule allowing only the IP address 192.0.2.134 to connect to the NetScreen management interface.

```
#set admin manager-ip 192.0.2.1 255.255.255.0
```

In this second example, all users on the Class C subnet 192.0.2.1-254 can connect to the management interface.

Another remediation tactic would be to disable the use of the WebUI interface and only use SSH or Telnet to remotely administer the device. For security best practices, you should probably only use SSH as your administrative protocol. You can disable the WebUI through the command line.

Lastly, you have the option to upgrade to the latest version of ScreenOS. At the time of print, NetScreen firewalls are currently shipping with version 5.0 of ScreenOS. Therefore, if you are running one of the vulnerable versions, you can upgrade to the latest.

Novell BorderManager Attacks and Solutions

Novell, famous for the very successful NetWare network operating system and later the highly scalable NDS Directory service, also offers a firewall solution called BorderManager. We are not typically ones to pick on Novell, as they did a really good job with NetWare, but we bring up this vendor because there is a fairly obvious vulnerability within their firewall product. For those of you who remember and idolize IPX, this might bring back some fond memories. For us, we think that our descriptions of IPX in Chapter 7, "Network Switching," are most likely the last time that protocol will be written about for years to come, so you might want to take a few moments to skip ahead and enjoy Chapter 7. Don't worry; we will be here when you get back.

Novell BorderManager IP/IPX Gateway Denial of Service

A denial-of-service vulnerability was discovered in the BorderManager product in August 2002. This vulnerability resides in how the IP/IPX gateway handles large inputs of data on TCP port 8225. The IP/IPX gateway does exactly what it sounds like; it provides IP access to devices running the IPX protocol. In version 3.6 of BorderManager, the IP/IPX gateway is configurable through the NWADM32 utility. In this version, the listening ports are configurable; however, the standard port is TCP 8225. The vulnerability exists in version 3.6 SP1a of BorderManager.

Attacking the IP/IPX Gateway

Although configurable, most installations of BorderManager have the default listening ports of the IP/IPX gateway set. The DoS attack is triggered by sending over 2MB of data to the IP/IPX gateway listening port, typically TCP port 8225. The gateway receives that data and places the information in the buffer; once the buffer is filled, the module abends, causing the denial of service and ending all traffic flows, inbound or outbound.

This exploit, as with many of the previous examples, is extremely easy to perform, especially in the context of an internal network segment with increased bandwidth and relaxed network permissions. While it might be difficult to attack the IPX portion of the gateway since few people have IPX installed today, the IP portion is open and quite accessible.

Tools for Attacking the IP/IPX Gateway

While there is no current exploit available that can automatically trigger this denial of service, it is quite simple to perform with the Netcat utility we previously used in this chapter. The following command will send a file we have selected and cause the gateway to abend.

```
D:\Tools\Netware> nc -v 192.0.2.12 8225 < somethingcorporate.mp3
```

The previous command instantiated a Netcat session to our target BorderManager server on TCP port 8225. To trigger the condition, we needed to supply a file, or random data, that was larger than 2MB. Luckily, we found an MP3 file of my favorite band named *Something Corporate* performing a rendition of Dramarama's *Anything, Anything* that was around 2.5MB. We figured if that can't crash a Novell BorderManager server, nothing can.

Because of the manner in which the gateway crashes, we will never get confirmation that our attack was successful. However, if you are behind the BorderManager firewall and are on the inside of the network, you can simply try to connect to a resource on the Internet. You should find that the connection is dropped and you cannot connect to the site, demonstrating that you successfully took down your BorderManager server. Now you better go and dust off your old NetWare manuals, figure out what the equivalent to "Control-Alt-Delete" is in Novell, and then go find which one of the dusty, antiquated 386 machines in the wiring closet is the one you knocked over.

Defending against the IP/IPX Gateway DoS

Fortunately, there are a couple of workarounds to protect yourself from this basic attack. First, if you are afraid of disrupting the perfect balance your NetWare server has enjoyed for the last three years by installing a patch, then you can add some basic filters to protect yourself from this vulnerability. Make sure to drop all traffic destined to TCP port 8225, or whichever port you have the gateway configured to run on, for your BorderManager machine. In some cases, the use of Novell IP SOCKS clients necessitates the availability of TCP port 8225. If you support SOCKS clients in your environment, then you might not be able to install filtering for that port.

If TCP filtering is not an option for your environment, you can also install the BorderManager patch for version 3.6. The patch is available from the Novell site at http://support.novell.com/filefinder/12743/index.html. Detailed instructions are provided on how to install the patch.

Checklist

☑ Keep all firewall devices as up to date as possible with their software revisions.

☑ Lock down management interfaces by providing only the necessary hosts or networks access.

☑ Remove unnecessary components and services from your firewalls; if they are not being used, they do not need to be accessible.

☑ Periodically perform a full port scan of your firewall devices to determine if any unusual ports are open.

☑ Invest in Intrusion Detection technologies to help alert you when abnormal traffic is observed on your networks.

Summary

The firewall is usually seen as the chief security provider for your networks and resources; however, it is often overlooked that they might be the most vulnerable asset as well. Hopefully, this chapter helped demystify firewall technologies from being infallible networking devices to their true being: software developed by skilled humans. As we critique software vendors for sloppy development practices and shoddy releases, we too need to look at our firewall technologies in the same light. Many of the vulnerabilities demonstrated in this chapter were basic, and remarkably easy to exploit. While firewall vendors should most certainly be held to a higher standard for the services they provide, we too need to realize that anything created by human engineering is not perfect.

Through the course of this chapter, we examined the different types of attacks that are normally performed on firewall devices. Armed with this information you can begin to ask yourself questions similar to, "What damage could be done if my internal addressing scheme was compromised?" or "How much disruption would a DoS attack cause on my main Internet access points?" Having answers to these questions provides valuable data as to how you should construct your networks and what defense strategies you should employ to protect it.

The several critical vulnerabilities and their associated exploits were demonstrated to provide you with real-world examples of common attacks. These samples show that even the most dominant firewall vendors have serious flaws within their technology. These flaws could invariably cause you downtime, or much worse, provide inroads to your most protected assets on the internal networks.

Finally, while we touched on the major vendors, chances are you might be using a firewall technology that we did not discuss in this book. If this is the case, you should spend some time combing through security Web sites and your vendor's advisories to see if there are any significant vulnerabilities associated with your devices. Many of the mitigation tactics referred to in this chapter will apply, regardless of the vendor, and should be used when you cannot update the firewall software. Spend the time to protect your most critical security asset, without which, your networks will be nearly defenseless.

Solutions Fast Track

Firewall Attack Methods

☑ Information Disclosure attacks yield valuable information about firewall policies, network topologies, or IP address schemas.

☑ Denial-of-service (DoS) attacks are the most common firewall tactics and cause disruptions through loss of connectivity or degraded firewall performance.

☑ Remote Firewall Compromise attacks provide the most dangerous level of exploitation, allowing intruders to be able to manipulate the operating system or firewall policies.

Check Point Software Attacks and Solutions

☑ Check Point's ISAKMP implementation provides a powerful remote system compromise attack vector that could provide GUI access to the attacker.

☑ SecuRemote clients can disclose internal IP addresses for the firewall's interfaces through unauthenticated connections.

☑ Load the latest service or feature pack for your Check Point software to protect against these vulnerabilities.

☑ Version 4.1 has been placed on an end-of- life list by Check Point. Users will need to upgrade to NG soon.

Cisco PIX Attacks and Solutions

☑ Cisco PIX firewalls are susceptible to DoS conditions when SNMPv3 traps are sent to the device and when the device is configured to act as an SNMP server.

☑ PIX firewalls should either be patched to the latest revision or have the SNMP server functionality disabled to protect against the SNMPv3 DoS.

☑ Certain versions of the PIX OS are vulnerable to malformed SSH packets that could cause the device to reload, causing a denial of service.

☑ Upgrade to the latest PIX revision or limit hosts or devices that can connect to the firewall via SSH to defend against the SSH CRC vulnerability.

Microsoft ISA Server Attacks and Solutions

☑ Passing an elongated URL string through the ISA Web Proxy service will cause a service crash and all Web traffic will fail to traverse the firewall.

☑ Apply the Microsoft hotfix MS01-021 to defend against this vulnerability.

☑ ISA is vulnerable to UDP flooding attacks because of a memory leak in the Winsock service. This leak will ultimately lead to an interruption of service as system resources will be exhausted.

☑ Install Microsoft hotfix MS01-045 to mitigate the presence of this vulnerability.

NetScreen Firewall Attacks and Solutions

☑ NetScreen appliances will crash if a connection to a Telnet or Web administrative session is initiated with improper TCP options set.

☑ Limit the hosts or networks that can connect to the NetScreen management interface, or upgrade to the latest version of the ScreenOS to protect against the attack.

☑ The NetScreen WebUI authentication mechanism can be overflowed by providing an invalid username, which will ultimately cause the device to reload.

☑ Limit the hosts or networks that can connect to the NetScreen management interface, or upgrade to the latest version of the ScreenOS to protect against the attack.

Novell BorderManager Attacks and Solutions

☑ BorderManager has an overflow in the IP/IPX gateway, which will abend if more than 2MB of data is sent to the TCP listening port for the service.

☑ Either filter TCP port 8225 to mitigate the attempt or install the BorderManager update for version 3.6 to protect against this vulnerability.

☑ Some Novell installations require port 8225 for SOCKS connections and cannot have filtering enabled; if this is the case, download and install the Novell patch.

Links to Sites

■ **www.securityfocus.com** Great security resource for finding vendors' bugs and vulnerabilities.

■ **www.cisco.com/en/US/products/hw/vpndevc/ps2030/** The main Cisco PIX product page.

■ **www.cisco.com/en/US/products/prod_security_ advisories_list.html** Cisco Security Advisory page, detailing all public Cisco vulnerabilities.

■ **www.checkpoint.com/products/protect/firewall-1.html** Check Point's firewall product page.

■ **www.checkpoint.com/techsupport/alerts/index.html** Check Point's product security alerts and bulletins.

■ **www.netscreen.com/products/firewall/** NetScreen's product Web site.

■ **www.netscreen.com/services/security/security_notices.jsp** Security notices for NetScreen products.

■ **www.microsoft.com/ISAServer/** Microsoft ISA Server product page.

■ **www.microsoft.com/security/security_bulletins/** Security bulletins for MS products.

- **www.novell.com/products/bordermanager/** Novell's BorderManager site and details.

- **support.novell.com/filefinder/security/index.html** Novell specific security alerts.

- **www.atstake.com/research/tools/network_utilities/** @Stake's Web site and tools section.

- **www.rapid7.com/Product-Download.html** Rapid 7 Security site.

Mailing Lists

- **cust-security-announce@cisco.com** To subscribe, send a message to majordomo@cisco.com with a single line in the body "info cust-security-announce".

- **first-teams@first.org** A mailing list dedicated to security incidents and research. Subscribe at www.first.org.

- **bugtraq@netspace.org** A mailing list dedicated to vulnerabilities bugs. To subscribe to this, and a number of other mailing lists, go to www.securityfocus.com/archive.

- **cso@netscreen.com** A mailing list dedicated to NetScreen vulnerability and security alerts. Subscribe at http://www.netscreen.com/cso.

- **security@microsoft.com** Microsoft's security notification service. Subscribe at http://www.microsoft.com/technet/security/bulletin/notify.mspx.

Frequently Asked Questions

The following Frequently Asked Questions, answered by the authors of this book, are designed to both measure your understanding of the concepts presented in this chapter and to assist you with real-life implementation of these concepts. To have your questions about this chapter answered by the author, browse to **www.syngress.com/solutions** and click on the **"Ask the Author"** form. You will also gain access to thousands of other FAQs at ITFAQnet.com.

Q: If someone can attack the underlying operating system of a firewall, why would anyone install it on Windows or Linux instead of an appliance?

A: In the past, the price of firewall appliances like Check Point's Nokia IPSO were cost prohibitive to small companies. This lead to many administrators installing firewall products on beefy desktops of servers with common operating systems. The underlying security risks associated with the insecure OS was eventually addressed by each of the firewall vendors. Many vendors imbedded Intrusion Prevention Systems or process watching applications that made sure that the underlying OS could not be compromised, or if it was hacked, it would not start any unnecessary services, applications, or open any rogue ports. While these technologies still exist in firewalls, the cost of firewall appliances has dropped, making it more economical for smaller outfits.

Q: How can VPN technologies, like SecuRemote, have so many vulnerabilities?

A: SecuRemote has been the long-time "black sheep" of the VPN world. If you can successfully get Check Point's unsupported VPN client to install on your operating system without causing major IP stack damage, then you are well ahead of the game. Check Point's approach to this client is that it is a necessary evil in their industry, and not much attention has been paid in the development or QA efforts of this application. The only satisfaction we have is that Check Point is now starting to feel the pain of this, as other VPN technologies are becoming more prominent in the space, such as one from their appliance vendor Nokia. In short, many firewall vendors focus the bulk of their efforts on the core technology and do not give the necessary attention to ancillary features like VPN support. This ultimately opens many attack vectors for would-be hackers.

Q: What is the harm of having IP address disclosure of information leakage vulnerabilities?

A: While these seem to provide very little information and have seemingly low impact on your entire environment, for many attackers this provides the first steps in an all-out attack. If your firewall is openly providing the IP addresses of your internal interfaces, an attacker could take advantage of this information by leveraging one type of spoofing attack, where the hacker's source IP address is that of an internal segment. Default firewall configurations might allow any type of traffic to traverse the firewall if the network of the source IP address is defined on any of the firewall's interfaces. Many vendors have prevention mechanisms to prevent this, such as Check Point's Anti-Spoofing settings, where the firewall will drop traffic that has a network source address of interface one, and originates on interface two, or vice versa. These techniques are efficient at mitigating the attack; however, it requires administrative configuration that might not be present. So, while in many cases this information leakage might be rather benign, it could cause some serious damage if the firewall is not fully configured.

Q: Outside of patching my firewall, how else can I defend against DoS attacks from the inside or outside?

A: Most often, your firewall will have some type of routing device in front of it on the perimeter. This device can be tuned to drop fragmented packets, ICMP, or other types of unauthorized traffic through the router's access control lists (ACL). While this might substantially degrade the performance on the router for a period of time, most large perimeter routers can handle that type of usage for long durations. Conversely, on the inside of your network, routing devices or Layer 3 switches might not precede any of your firewall devices. To combat DoS style attacks on the inside, you can use network-based Intrusion Prevention Systems. These devices monitor all network traffic on the wire and drop malformed or unauthorized traffic prior to it reaching the target. Moreover, these systems are configured to look for a myriad of attacks and malformed traffic. Look at the NetScreen Intrusion Detection/Prevention product for a perfect example (www.netscreen.com/products/idp/index.jsp).

Chapter 5

Routing Devices and Protocols

Solutions in this Chapter:

- **Understanding the Roles of Routers on Perimeter Segments**
- **Securing Your Routers**
- **IP Routing Devices**
- **IP Routing Protocols**

Related Chapters:

- **Chapter 7 Network Switching**
- **Chapter 8 Defending Routers and Switches**
- **Chapter 11 Internal Network Design**

- ☑ **Summary**
- ☑ **Solutions Fast Track**
- ☑ **Frequently Asked Questions**

Introduction

Ask most networking professionals to create an analogy for routers and many would classify them as the "traffic cops" of your network infrastructure. This is because they guide and control the flow of network packets from source to destination. In our minds, we don't only think of routers as "traffic cops" because they are capable of so much more than simply directing traffic. We also think of routers as the sentinels patrolling and protecting your network's borders. Additionally, we think of them as the judges of your network because they can control the protocols used and thus define the laws of the land. To stretch this further, we often also consider them to be your ambassadors to the rest of the networking world by connecting your network to the Internet. As a matter of fact, in most organizations it wouldn't be difficult to think of core routers as the Presidents of the entire network, connected to everything and negotiating, facilitating communication, and keeping a watchful eye on the entire infrastructure. Routers have great capabilities, awesome strength, and are extremely important to your network. For these reasons, securing, maintaining, and properly configuring your network's routers is important to ensure that your network is as secure as it can be.

This chapter is designed to examine routing devices and their overall role in your network infrastructure. It is aimed at helping you understand why the security of your network's routers is one of the most important aspects in the overall security of your network. The chapter begins by examining the roles of routers on your network. We will discuss the roles of routers on the perimeter segments of your network, known as border routers. Border routers act as the sentinels at your network's boundaries and as your ambassadors to the rest of the networking world. This section also covers the major security considerations of border routers. Next, the chapter looks at routers on the internal segments of your network, the routers known as core routers. Core routers act as your network's judges, deciding the law of the land and as the Presidents of your entire infrastructure. This chapter also details the security concerns of core routers in these roles. The chapter then examines router security in general, covering physical router security, access controls, auditing, logging, and protocol security. Most of the contents of this chapter relate to Cisco routers running the Cisco Internetworking Operating System (IOS). However, this chapter also lists some of the other manufacturers and models of network devices that perform IP routing as of the time of this writing. It details some of the capabilities of those devices and shows what to consider when dealing with the security of each device classification. Finally, this chapter looks at the most important IP routing protocols and describes how those protocols are secured using industry best practices.

After completing this chapter, hopefully you will look at the routing devices in your infrastructure with a newfound respect. You will both understand the threats posed by unsecured and nonoptimally configured routers, and see how, when properly configured and secured, routers can be some of your biggest allies when it comes to securing and protecting your network.

Understanding the Roles of Routers on Your Network

It's true that routers form the basis for all modern internetworking, but what do routers really do? At the most basic level, routers direct packets of information across networks. In this most basic scenario, they unite multiple network segments and facilitate the communication between devices on those segments. Routers can connect many different types of media as well. A router might have Ethernet or Fast Ethernet interfaces, a CSU/DSU card for a T-1, a high-speed serial interface (HSSI), a fiber distributed data interface (FDDI), or maybe even interfaces for analog phone lines.

As this scenario gets more complex, with more network segments being added, different types of media being used in those segments, and many routers and other network devices in the picture, routers not only direct traffic but also work together to direct packets to destinations via the best paths. Routers also work together to maintain the accessibility of network segments by redirecting traffic around network failures. At this level, routers use protocols to exchange information about the status of the network. Routers then store this information in what is called a *routing table* and use that table to decide where to send packets based on the destination information each packet contains. Routers can use a variety of different protocols to communicate with each other, and we will examine some of the most commonly used protocols in the *IP Routing Protocols* section in this chapter.

Routers also play an important role in maintaining the security of your network. Given their positions, stationed between network segments, they have the perfect opportunity to deny unwanted traffic from traversing network boundaries. This type of security measure (commonly referred to as *packet filtering*) can be a very effective technique for preventing unauthorized network traffic from flowing freely on your network. Packet filtering, access lists, and other techniques for using your router to secure your network are discussed in greater detail in the *Securing Your Routers* section later in the chapter.

Routers can play many different roles in your network architecture. Some of the more common classifications for network routers are based on the function they provide the network and their location within the network architecture. Routers that are situated on external perimeter segments are called *border routers*, whereas routers that are situated on internal segments of your network are typically called *core routers* or *backbone routers*. Figure 5.1 shows examples of perimeter, internal, and DMZ networks.

Figure 5.1 Example Perimeter, Internal, and DMZ networks

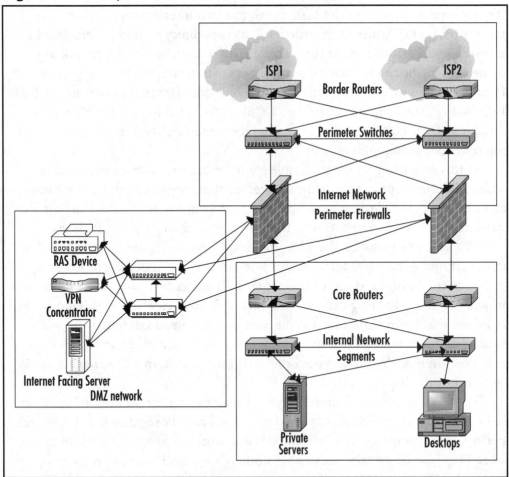

Understanding the Roles of Routers on Perimeter Segments

To begin to understand the roles of routers on perimeter segments, we want to be clear on the definition of the term *perimeter segment*. Perimeter segment refers to any network segment that is either located outside your corporate firewalls or to any network segment that connects an untrusted network to yours. As an example, the network segment between your firewalls and the rest of the Internet would be a perimeter segment. Your DMZ network (which is a network that contains your Internet-facing and publicly accessible servers and applications) or a network that connects your organization to business partners would also be classified as a perimeter segment.

Routers on these perimeter segments of your network would include border routers that might connect your network to the Internet, or border routers that might connect your organization to the untrusted networks of business or trading partners. Because of their responsibilities, border routers can be the some of the most important routers in your organization. Your border routers are usually responsible for your company's Internet access. Perhaps they are running BGP (described later in the chapter) and maintaining your organization's connection to the Internet via multiple providers. Your border router might even link your network to your manufacturing partner's network via a private leased line. In all cases, your border routers are responsible for directing packets from your network to untrusted networks (beyond your control), and a failure of these routers to perform their tasks would cause a major disruption in your organization's ability to do business.

Generally, routers on perimeter networks have interfaces on public networks or networks reachable via unfiltered Internet access. This makes them extremely vulnerable to attack attempts. For that reason, routers in the perimeter segments of your network are quite possibly the devices on your network that can benefit the most from increased security configuration. Moreover, because they are exposed, they can be the most difficult routers to secure. An unsecured border router can be an easy target for a denial-of-service (DoS) attack or might expose confidential information about your network configuration to potential attackers. An unsecured border router is also ineffective at filtering unwanted traffic, such as informational scans and attack attempts. However, a well-configured border router can prevent simple attacks, port scans, and can also serve as a valuable tool for detecting and monitoring attack attempts. Configuring routers for these jobs is discussed in the

Controlling What Your Routers Do section of the chapter. Because of the importance of border routers, and their relative vulnerability to the outside world, it is extremely important that extra time be spent securely configuring them.

Examining the Roles of Routers on Internal Segments

An internal segment of your network is any network segment on the inside of your organization's firewalls. Internal network segments are generally trusted networks. An example of an internal segment would be the network to which your company's file servers connect. The network segment that your workstations directly connect to would also be considered an internal network segment.

Internal routers are those that direct traffic between two or more networks within your organization. Your internal segment routers might be running OSPF, IGRP, EIGRP, RIP, or RIPv2, all of which are detailed later in the *IP Routing Protocols* section of the chapter. These routers might be connecting internal segments that span the different floors of your building or connecting your branch offices via some private communications medium like a point-to-point T-1 or a leased serial connection. In all cases, internal segments include the most important routers of all, your organization's core routers. In most network architectures, core routers are the routers through which all network traffic must eventually pass. Core routers are generally the largest and most powerful routers in your infrastructure. Wherever your internal segment routers are, they are undoubtedly a crucial piece of your network infrastructure.

A big difference between internal segment routers and border routers is that the former connects networks that share the same or very similar security contexts—there is a high level of trust between the networks. However, just because internal segment routers are located on fairly protected and trusted networks does not mean they can be neglected. In fact, core routers should be adequately secured based solely on their importance to your organization and your network infrastructure. Proper security will prevent attack attempts that might come from inside your network or might slip through all other means of network security.

Notes from the Underground…

Securing Your Internal Routers

Just because routers on your internal networks are protected from the rest of the network world by firewalls doesn't mean they are automatically protected. Intrusions can come from sources that you might not have considered. Picture this likely scenario: an e-mail worm is developed that exploits a known vulnerability in your router's operating system. Perhaps it's a vulnerability like the one discovered in July 2003 whereby certain types of packets sent directly to Cisco network devices can cause a DoS on those devices that can only be resolved by rebooting the device. You patch your border routers and make sure that no offending traffic can slip into your network. You have virus protection in place at all points of entry. Your mail server removes all offending attachments and your workstations all have the latest antivirus updates. You think you are fairly safe.

Unexpectedly, your network grinds to a halt. Your core routers are no longer routing packets. "How could this have happened?" you wonder. On your way to the server room, you walk past a conference room where a sales rep for some outside company has plugged in his laptop to check his Web-based e-mail account. He grabs you as you walk by. "Hey Buddy. Help me out for a second. Will ya? I just opened the weirdest e-mail, and now my system won't work. I didn't even know this person, but he claimed I needed to review this attached document. I opened the attachment and nothing happened. Now my computer is just sitting there." And thanks to this guy, that's exactly what your entire company is also doing. His "attachment" turned out to be the worm. His system wasn't patched against the vulnerability the worm was programmed to exploit, and when he executed the attachment, the worm quickly scanned your network for the devices it was programmed to exploit, found your core routers, and attacked.

As you can see, properly securing your internal routers is just as necessary as securing your border routers. As the saying goes, "an ounce of prevention is worth a pound of cure." It might not be possible to prevent a worm from entering your network via means such as this. However, with a good security configuration in place on your entire network infrastructure, including your interior routers, it is very possible to prevent any damage from occurring.

Securing Your Routers

So far, we have seen that your organization's routers are some of the most important devices on your network; unfortunately, we have also shown that because of their function they can also be some of the most vulnerable devices as well. So, how do you protect what is possibly your most valuable network asset? One technique is to begin by considering an overall security strategy for your routers. The security strategy we find most efficient and effective begins with the basics, starting outside the router and working inward, developing multiple layers of security. This strategy is similar to historical security strategies used in building castles, and in fact, you can think of your routers as the castles of your network kingdom. If you can imagine a castle floor plan, simplified, it might look something like Figure 5.2.

Figure 5.2 Think of Securing Your Routers in Terms of a Castle Architecture

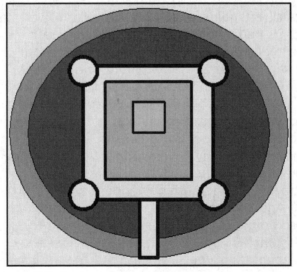

Think of securing your routers in terms of a castle floor plan. Beginning from the outside, we want to start with considering physical security. Much like a castle has a moat and walls to keep unwanted visitors out, we need to establish a physically secure location for your routers. After all, if one were to gain physical access to your router, he could simple unplug it and shut it down, or perform a password recovery on the unit to gain access. Next, progressing inward, we want to focus on configuration-level security. Much like a castle has a drawbridge and a gatehouse to control who is allowed entrance to the castle, we need to secure login access to your router for the same reason. Securing this access protects the router configuration, the router operating software, and the router's operating information. This level is also where we would consider logging and auditing. Just as the castle guards might have recorded all comings and goings, we must know when and what the users of your router are doing. Finally, at the center, we need to focus on your router's network security. We need to control what your router does, the protocols it routes, and the services it runs. Just as a castle has a keep, which is the most guarded section, your router's network security is the most important and guarded aspect of your network device.

Examining Possible Attacks on Your Routers

As previously mentioned, your routers can be the most vulnerable devices on your network. They can be the target of all types of malicious attacks and access attempts. Some of the most common threats to your routers include:

- **Attempts to gain access** These attempts are usually tried via known vulnerabilities in running services or through brute-force password guessing.

- **Hijacking sessions** An attacker might try to hijack a session after IP spoofing, predicting and altering sequence numbers, or some other means.

- **Re-routing** This attack is usually done by manipulating router updates and causing traffic to route to unwanted destinations.

- **DoS attacks** This type of attack can be tried with a number of methods such as circular redirects, Transmission Control Protocol – Synchronize (TCP SYN) attacks, and by attacking running services such as Simple Network Mail Protocol (SNMP).

- **Masquerading attacks** These attacks are preformed by altering IP address information within packets in an attempt to bypass packet filtering.

- **Vulnerability exploits** This type of attack attempts to exploit known vulnerabilities in the router's operating software or protocols.

Locking Down Your Routers

Locking down your router begins with physically securing your router. This includes considering the location where the router will be stored and the operating conditions inside that location. These measures are just the beginning steps to securing your router, but are the bases in which the rest of your routers security is built. This section looks at choosing and configuring the physical location where your router lives. It will examine the requirements for physical router security in terms of locks and personnel access control, and also touch on issues like climate control, fire suppression, and the means by which other harmful elements can be avoided.

Keeping Your Routers Physically Safe

At most organizations with a significant enough investment in technology, a room is created to house the delicate and expensive network and server infrastructure. These locations are called *data centers*, *server rooms*, or a *network operation center* (NOC). Hopefully, your organization has already established a data center for your entire network and server infrastructure ,or your organization leases data center space from a provider of data center services. In either case, knowing what to look for in a data center or in a space that will become the home for all of your network and server infrastructure, including your router, can always come in handy in the event that your organization decides to move data centers, or create one of its own. The two key components in most data centers are:

- Physical security
- Environmental control and monitoring

In the simplest terms, physical security means storing your router in a room with limited access. In more complex environments, physical security can mean biometric scanners, surveillance systems, and armed guards. The value and importance of your devices and your organization's budget will dictate which physical security solution is right for your situation, but the bare minimum necessary to maintain the physical security of your router is a data center room with locks on the doors that only authorized people can enter.

Another important component of your data center is environmental conditioning and monitoring. This means making sure that your router is protected from the elements. High temperatures, humidity, fire, and water can all damage your valuable equipment, and every care should be taken to prevent your router from coming in contact with these elements. The room in which you store you router should have an adequate air conditioning unit to ensure the proper temperature is maintained. Because the temperatures inside your components can be 15 to 25 degrees hotter than the temperature of the room in which they are stored, try to keep the temperature between 65° and 75°F. Again, depending on the value of your equipment and your organization's budget, air conditioning systems (sometimes called *air handlers*) can be anything from portable air conditioning units to complex air conditioning and climate control systems. The very minimum necessary for keeping your router in a stable temperature is an air conditioning unit that can be individually controlled and will function continuously.

The room in which your router is stored should also have a sufficient fire suppression system. With lots of electricity and continuously running devices, your data center is a fire risk. Depending on your budget, fire suppression can be anything from the minimum of smoke detectors and a fire extinguisher, to a sophisticated Very Early Smoke Detector and Alarm (VESDA) system with a fire suppression substance like FM-200, carbon dioxide, FE-13, or Inergen.

Finally, try to protect your routers from water. The room you choose for your data center should not have water pipes running through it or around it. It should not be located near any major water sources and optimally should not have exterior windows or skylights that can leak into the data center. If your HVAC uses chilled water to cool the room, make sure those pipes don't run right over your servers. In more complex data center installations, even the fire sprinkler system within the data center is drained and connected to a pre-action fire alarm that immediately pressurizes the sprinkler system with water should a fire be detected. If your data center has a fire sprinkler system, connecting the sprinkler system to an emergency power cutoff switch might prevent the worst of damage should the sprinkler system ever be set off.

Preventing Login Access to Your Routers

Preventing login access to your router means configuring access controls and securing all means of connecting to the router itself. Preventing unauthorized logins and attempted logins to the router will protect the router configuration, the router operating software, and the router's operating information. Configuring access controls include configuring some means of authentication and authorization, while securing the means of access includes securing all means that can be used to configure your device. This section looks at all the means of accessing your router and describes each. It also delves into the process by which those means are secured from unauthorized access.

There can be many ways to access your router, and it is important that each of these access points is secured or disabled. Many routers have all the means of accessing them enabled by default, and by disabling those means that are not in use we can focus on securing the means of access that are in use. For securing the means of access that are commonly used, there are various different types of access control methods, and it's important that we choose the right method for the situation. Let's begin by examining the means by which your router can be accessed.

Means of Accessing Your Router

There are six main means of accessing your router. Some use network connectivity and some do not. Some have default privileges while others are configurable. It is important to understand how a router can be accessed so that you can secure those access points.

- **The console port** This is the main access point and the only one enabled by default. The console port can be used for password recovery and requires a physical connection to the router.

- **Auxiliary port** A modem or terminal server can be connected to the auxiliary port for accessing the router should the network be unavailable. This port should be disabled and only used if a modem or serial device needs to be plugged in for access to the system.

- **The Virtual Teletype (VTY) or Virtual TTY ports** The VTY ports are virtual terminal ports that can be access via Telnet or Secure Shell (SSH) through the network. There are five VTY ports enabled by default on most Cisco routers.

- **SNMP** SNMP uses community strings to control read-only or read-write access to your router's configuration and information. SNMP is a very valuable service, but can be very dangerous to leave unprotected.

- **Trivial File Transfer Protocol (TFTP)** TFTP is a simple means of transferring files to and from your router. TFTP is usually used for uploading or downloading software versions or configuration files. TFTP can be dangerous because TFTP has no means of authentication. It can both run on your router and run on a server in your network.

- **HTTP or HTTPS** Most routers provide some means of configuring or monitoring through HTTP with a common browser. HTTP access should be disabled on routers. Even though it's convenient for quick configuration, the security risks are not worth the time saved.

Configuring Access Controls

There are various means of controlling access to your router, just as there are various means of accessing your router. Basic access control can be broken down into *authentication* and *authorization*. Authentication is basically identifying who can log in to the router, and authorization is controlling what they can do once they are logged in. There are various means of access control among different manufacturers of routers, but because Cisco controls 85 percent of the router market, they have set the standards for access control. On Cisco routers, the two main types of access control are those that are Authentication, Authorization, and Accounting (AAA) protocols and those that aren't. AAA incorporates access control protocols such as Terminal Access Control Access Control System Plus (TACACS+), Remote Access Dial-in User Service (RADIUS), and Kerberos. Other means of access control that aren't AAA protocols include simple authentication, TACACS, and extended TACACS. Cisco recommends using AAA methods for access control because of the protocol's superior capability to control, protect, and account for system access.

AAA Protocols	Non-AAA Protocols
TACAS +	Simple authentication
RADIUS	TACAS
KERBEROS	Extended TACAS

Non–AAA methods of access control can and still are used to secure access to routers even though it is not recommended. Simple authentication includes both line authentication and local username authentication. Line authentication comprises of setting up passwords that must be entered to connect to any of the VTY, auxiliary, or console ports. These passwords are generally set up on an access-point specific basis and the password is stored in the router configuration. Local username authentication gives us the ability to define username and password combinations to define different types of access. Again, the username and password combinations are stored in the router configuration. TACACS and extended TACACS are older protocols that allow centralized storage and maintenance of usernames and passwords. These protocols have been surpassed in functionality and security by newer protocols and are now generally unsupported by many router manufacturers.

AAA access control protocols are the best and most secure means of defining who can access your router. AAA services can use the TACACS+, RADIUS, and Kerberos protocols. TACACS+ is a proprietary Cisco protocol and despite its similar name is incompatible with TACACS and extended TACACS. RADIUS is generally compatible among equipment manufacturers and has many of the same features and advanced functionality of TACAS+. TACAS+ and RADIUS both use a central server to store username, passwords, and attributes that can be used to specifically define user privileges. Both protocols protect network traffic using a shared secret encryption algorithm as well. Kerberos is means of authenticating two users on an unprotected network and is generally set up on an organizational level and then incorporated into authentication for the network infrastructure. It uses secret-key cryptography and a trusted third party and would be a complicated and involved process to configure for a single or small group of routers. AAA services can use TACACS+ for authentication, authorization, and auditing, while Kerberos is a network authentication system only.

One final detail that is important in access control is configuring your router with login-warning banners. Login-warning banners don't really perform any technical security functions, but they are important for protecting your routers legally. A basic login-warning banner should include the following information:

- A "No trespassing" warning
- An unauthorized use warning stating that all use of equipment must be authorized by the owner
- A "No expectation of privacy" statement that alerts users to the fact that their use is being monitored

Things that should *not* be on a login-warning banner include:

- Location information on the router
- Router model or any configuration details
- A "Welcome" message

Configuring Logging and Auditing on Your Routers

Configuring logging and auditing on your routers is an important step in getting a handle on router security. Logging and auditing give us insight into what the router and its users are doing. Having accurate logging information is invaluable in diagnosing problems and detecting unauthorized access attempts. For this reason, it is extremely important to examine the output from your routers on a regular basis. The problem with logging is that, once configured, the output can be overwhelming and it can be difficult to differentiate important log entries from those that can be safely ignored. Therefore, it is important to be able to manage your log output with software that will sort and parse logs based on criteria that you can define. This section covers why log information is important and the different types of logging available on your router.

What Information Does Logging Capture?

We have said that logging is an invaluable resource, and that if correctly configured it can aid in the diagnosing of problems and the detection of unauthorized access. However, what information can be captured by logging, and how can that information help? At its most basic, logging captures events that occur on your router. Some events that are helpful in securing your router include:

- Router reboots and changes in interface status
- Configuration changes
- Traffic that violates access control lists (ACLs)
- Router login and command history

Logging also captures the time an event occurred, and it is crucial that the time on a logged event is accurate. For this reason, configuring your router with a Network Time Protocol (NTP) source is key for the accuracy of your logs.

Examining the Different Types of Logging

Most routers have many different types of logging. On Cisco routers, there are six different types of logging. Log messages can generally be sent to any combination of these log types:

- **Console logging** When the router sends log information directly to the console of the router. These logs are valuable only when you are logged in to the console because they are not stored or seen anywhere else.

- **Buffered logging** When the router sends logging information to a memory buffer that can be configured to store logged information. This buffer can only be viewed by logging in to the router and is cleared with each reboot.

- **Terminal logging** When any terminal line is configured to receive log messages. Like console logging, only the user logged in to the terminal at the time can see the log information. These logs are not stored anywhere on the router.

- **Syslog logging** When your router is configured to send its logging information to a syslog server. Syslog servers are processes that run on a server that listen for log messages and record those messages in a central log file. Some syslog services can also perform actions like alerting on the received logs.

- **SNMP trapping** When your router is set up to use SNMP and to send traps to a listening SNMP host.

- **AAA** If AAA is being used, the router can be configured to send detailed information to the authentication server.

Controlling What Your Routers Do

Controlling what you routers do is all about controlling the protocols being used and the default services being run on the router. These considerations are the core of your router security. Properly configuring the services your router runs, what protocols it uses, and the types of traffic it will accept and pass can prevent your router from being an easy target for attack or from being used to attack others. This section covers disabling unnecessary router services; what services are needed and which can safely be disabled. It also covers implementing ACLs to prevent your router from accepting and passing unwanted traffic. Rate limiting and packet filtering are also covered in this section. Finally, this section covers the configuration and security of the network protocols your router runs.

Disabling Unnecessary Router Services and Features

The default configuration of many routers includes services running on the router that are unnecessary. Sometimes, these services are there for legacy support and other services support special configurations. Disabling these unneeded services eliminates the risk that those services will be used to exploit the router or to gain information about the router. Doing this will not degrade the performance of the router, and in many cases will enhance your router's performance. In some cases, a service cannot be disabled or it is in use. In these circumstances, controlling access to the service is the best means to make those services as secure as possible.

Here are some of the most common services to be disabled:

- **Small Services for TCP and UDP** Small services are services that the TCP and UDP protocols recommend that a host should provide. These services are Echo, discard, daytime, and chargen. In some versions of the Cisco IOS, these services are enabled by default. These services are completely unnecessary on your router and should be disabled.

- **Cisco Discovery Protocol (CDP)** On Cisco routers, this protocol will provide you router information on other Cisco routers connected to it. Unfortunately, it can also provide information to would-be attackers. This service should be disabled.

- **Finger service** Finger is a service that allows remote users to query your router about the currently logged-on users. This protocol could reveal information about valid user accounts and should be disabled.

- **HTTP Service** The HTTP Service is a Web-based configuration and administration service that is provided by most router manufacturers. This service should be disabled on your router because the HTTP traffic is transmitted in the clear, including login and configuration information.

- **Bootp Server** Bootp is a protocol that allows other routers to boot from your router's configuration. This service should be disabled on your router to prevent unauthorized access to your router's operating system.

- **Configuration auto-loading** This feature allows your router to boot from a network location. This feature should be disabled on your router mainly because someone could exploit this feature to change your router's configuration.

- **IP source routing** This feature of IP allows packets to specify routes. This feature is generally enabled by default, but should be disabled due to its use in many different attacks.

- **Proxy Address Resolution Protocol (ARP)** ARP is used to translate network addresses like IP addresses into media or MAC addresses. Normally, ARP is confined to a single segment and does not traverse routers. However, the Proxy ARP service responds to ARP requests on an interface and effectively extends a segment across the interfaces upon which it is enabled. This service should be disabled on your router because of the danger it poses in leaking media addresses to untrusted networks.

- **IP Redirects, Mask Replies, and Unreachable messages** These are all specific message types of Internet Control Message Protocol (ICMP). ICMP is useful in determining information about your network, and it would almost be impossible to live without the commands *ping* and *traceroute* that use the protocol. However, these three types of ICMP messages are commonly used by attackers in gathering information about your network and should be disabled on your router.

- **Domain Name System (DNS) service** Most routers support DNS lookups, and if no DNS is configured will send DNS queries to the broadcast address 255.255.255.255. Unconfigured DNS servers can cause unnecessary broadcast traffic at the minimum, and in worst cases result in incorrect information being received by your router from rogue DNS servers. If not absolutely necessary, DNS should be disabled on your router.

- **Unused interfaces** All unused interfaces on your router should also be disabled. This prevents them from being used and also enforces the need for administration privileges when adding new interfaces.

Access Control Lists and Packet Filtering

Another important technique for securing your router is controlling the type of network traffic that reaches and passes through it This technique is called *packet filtering*, and the most common method of performing packet filtering is by configuring ACLs to prevent unwanted traffic from getting to and/or through your router. The process of creating ACLs to limit traffic can be complicated, so it is important to start with the following basic ACL ideals:

- Create ACLs that prohibit all unnecessary traffic.
- Create ACLs that filter both incoming and outgoing traffic.

- To prevent spoofing, create ACLs on untrusted interfaces that deny packets with source addresses of trusted and private networks.

- Create ACLs on trusted interfaces that only allow traffic with source addresses that are in your trusted network to pass.

- Create ACLs that restrict access to router services from external networks.

Securing Network Protocols

The final step in controlling what your router does is securely configuring the protocols it uses. The most common way to secure networking protocols is with the use of routing authentication. Unfortunately, only the newest protocols support authentication, and even some of those protocols don't protect the authentication password in transit. Another method for controlling routing protocols is by using protocol filtering. It is important to both filter the protocol information that is leaving your network and the protocol information that is entering your network. Configuring and securing the most common network protocols is discussed on a protocol-by-protocol basis later in the chapter.

Maintaining Your Routers for Optimal Security

Configuring optimal security on your routers is not just a one-time affair; it is a continual process that requires effort and diligence. The threats to your routers are constantly changing, and your security configuration should evolve to address those threats. As your router's configuration evolves it is important to maintain accurate records and archives of the changes and updates made. Equally important is keeping your router's operating system updated with the latest version from the manufacturer.

Performing Configuration Storage

An important consideration for maintaining the security and integrity of your routing infrastructure is the safe storage and archival of your router's configuration files. There is a method for storing the configuration of almost every router made, and this method should be used to store a copy of the configuration in a secure location every time there is a configuration change on the router and at specified intervals.

Your configuration files will contain information about how your router operates, including how it filters traffic, and the protocols in use. For this reason, these configuration files should be stored in a location that is secure from access by unauthorized individuals on a reliable storage medium. Because most of these files will be plain text, a protection mechanism such as encryption is also recommended to ensure that the configuration files don't fall into the wrong hands.

Keeping Up with Operating System Updates

Most manufacturers maintain the operating system that their devices use, periodically repairing any flaws that have been found and occasionally adding new features. In some cases, manufacturers charge a yearly maintenance fee for access to the latest operating system version that will include all fixes and updates. These services are extremely valuable and generally worth the price of admission. Most manufacturers also maintain a mailing list or Web site that alerts users to updates and version releases. Mailing lists are extremely beneficial because once joined, announcements are pushed out to all members as soon as they are available. With Web sites that maintain update information, you have to remember to schedule an appointment on your calendar to check for updates on a regular basis. As important as it is to keep current with the latest operating system updates, installing updates should be handled with care:

- Before installing any updates, remember to back up your current configuration and operating system so that you can roll back any upgrades that don't go exactly as planned.

- If possible, updates should be installed on test equipment first to try new features and ensure compatibility. If that is not possible, the updates should be applied and tested on your least important routers first before installation is attempted on your core router or border router.

Damage & Defense...

Vendors Move to a Secure-by-Default Strategy

In general, securing routers should be approached with a great deal of determination. It can be a tedious process of configuring, testing, and reconfiguring. Given this, it is no wonder that security configuration on routers doesn't happen as often as it should. To counteract this trend of insecure configurations, most network device and operating systems manufacturers are turning to a security mindset where devices are secure by default. Secure by default means that right out of the box, these device configurations will have the minimum of services and protocols enabled.

One major example of this trend is Cisco's new AutoSecure command that is available starting in IOS version 12.3(1). This feature is aimed at greatly simplifying router security configuration. Using the AutoSecure feature enables users to disable the less frequently used IP services that are often the targets of attack and to also enable IP services that can be beneficial in protecting a network from attack. Some of the IP services automatically disabled at the global level are the Finger service, PAD service (packet assembler and disassembler), Small-Servers Service, Bootp Server, HTTP server, Identification Service, Cisco Discovery Protocol Service, Network Time Protocol Service, and Source Routing. At each interface, AutoSecure also automatically disables ICMP redirects, ICMP unreachables, ICMP mask reply messages, Proxy-ARP, Directed broadcasts, and the Maintenance Operations Protocol Service.

In addition to disabling potential security threats, AutoSecure also enables features that enhance the overall security of the router. Primarily, AutoSecure globally enables commands such as service password-encryption, which protects passwords within the configuration from being visible, and service tcp-keepalives-in and service tcp-keepalives-out, which remove TCP sessions that aren't terminated properly. Auto secure also enables security on all access points to the router including the console port, vty, tty, and AUX ports and disables SNMP if its not being used or configured with default settings. AutoSecure also enables important security logging to internal buffers and all VTY and TTY ports, as well as securing the forwarding plane of the router.

Continued

> Unfortunately, the current version of AutoSecure provides no roll-back feature, so be sure to back up your existing running configuration before attempting to run this configuration.

IP Routing Devices

We have already discussed how, in a way, routers are the glue that connects the network world. This section covers the basics of all different types of IP routing devices. It examines the commonalties among the different types of IP routers and looks at the now common practice of including routing functionality into devices not typically responsible for that function. In each subsection, we examine various types of network devices that also perform IP routing, listing the top manufacturers of these devices and giving a quick overview of security considerations when dealing with these device types:

- IP routers
- Routing switches and network load-balancing devices
- Routing software and operating systems with routing level

IP Routers

When thinking of IP routing devices, the most obvious things that come to mind are routers themselves. Network devices classified as routers are dedicated to the purpose of IP routing. They are highly customized for this task, and because of that are faster and have more features and functions than the other types of IP routing devices covered in this section. Routers can be classified according to a number of different characteristics, but some of the most common characteristics used are their functionality and their capacity. While all routers can handle the basics of IP routing, it's how much traffic a particular router can process that separates it from the rest of the pack. The amount of data a router can process depends on its internal design and architecture and is generally measured by how much data can be processed by a router on a per-slot basis. To facilitate our further discussions of routers, we define the following categories:

- **Small office routers** These routers are generally stand-alone devices in a smaller than standard rack mount form factor. These routers might have a static architecture or have minimal upgrade and customization capacity. Routers in the small office routers category can handle less than 1 Gbps per slot of bandwidth.

- **Small to medium-sized** Small to medium-sized routers are generally a step above small office routers in form factor and functionality. These routers are generally housed in a standard form factor for rack mounting in a data center and generally have more than one slot for upgrades and customization. Routers in the small to medium-sized classification also have less that 1 Gbps per slot bandwidth capacity.

- **Medium- to large-sized** Medium- to large-sized routers are yet more advanced than their small to medium-sized brethren. They typically have more memory, better upgrade and customization capabilities, and are housed in a standard rack mount form factor. Routers in the medium- to large-sized classification have at least 1 Gbps of per-slot bandwidth and can have up to 2.5 Gbps of per-slot bandwidth.

- **Large- to extra-large-sized** Large- to extra-large-sized routers are the ultimate in IP routing technology. They are generally housed in a chassis-based form factor allowing for redundant and sometimes hot-swap upgrades and components. Routers in this classification have greater than 2.5 Gbps of per slot bandwidth to handle awesome levels of IP routing traffic.

There are many different manufacturers of IP routers. Some manufacturers focus on niche router markets while others make general IP router models that handle all levels of IP routing. Some of the more common router manufacturers include:

- **Cisco Systems** (www.cisco.com)

- **Lucent Networks** (www.lucent.com)

- **Juniper Networks** (www.juniper.net)

Cisco systems is said to have up to 85 percent of the IP router market. They design and sell all levels of IP routers. Table 5.1 lists their most common models.

Table 5.1 Cisco Router Models

Category	Model
Small office routers	Model 700 series, 1000 series, and 1600s
Small to medium-sized	Model 1700 series, 2500 and 2600 series, and Model 3810

Continued

Table 5.1 Cisco Router Models

Category	Model
Medium- to large-sized	Model 3600 and 3700 series, model 4000 series, and model 7202, 7204, and 7206
Large- to extra-large-sized	Model 7500 series, 7300 series, ESR 10000 series, and the 12000 and 12400 series

Lucent Networks also focuses on many levels of the IP routing market. It designs and sells routers all the way from the small office router category to the extra-large-sized router class. Table 5.2 lists some of the more common Lucent networks router models.

Table 5.2 Lucent Router Models

Category	Model
Small office routers	Pipeline models 25, 50, 75, 85, 130 and 220
Small to medium-sized	Office Router HS, LS, AccessPoint 300, and SuperPipe 155, 175
Medium- to large-sized	AccessPoint 450, 600, 1500
Large- to extra-large-sized	GRF 400, 1600, and NX64000 multi-terabit switch/router

Juniper Networks focuses on large, high-end routers. Juniper designs and sells routers in the medium to large and large to extra large classifications. Table 5.3 lists some of the more common models.

Table 5.3 Juniper Router Models

Category	Model
Medium- to large-sized	M5 and M10 series
Large- to extra-large- sized	M20, M40, M40e, J20 and M160 Internet backbone router, and the T320 and T640

Looking at Additional Router Functionality

In addition to routing packets, routers are versatile devices and can be integrators of diverse technologies in your network. As networks have increased in complexity, so have routers increased in functions. In many organizations, traditional data networks are being asked to handle telephone and video communications as well as data packets. Routers have become so flexible that it is very likely a manufacturer makes a model to accommodate just about any known media type and device. Some router models have even become application aware. They are able to direct packets based on the traffic type or information contained in the application layer of the packet.

There are vast arrays of router models that can accommodate virtually any type of network hardware available. Moreover, while all models can handle the basics of IP routing, the differentiation between router models is apparent in the types of devices the router can accommodate, the amount of data the router can handle, and the level of redundancy built into the router. Device compatibility and capacity are probably the biggest differentiators in IP routing devices. The most basic router models might have one or two Ethernet connections plus a serial interface for a WAN link and be able to perform the basic interior routing protocols, while higher-end routers might have many Ethernet interfaces, be able to handle ATM networks, and have the capacity for multiple fiber-optic links. Higher-end routers might also be able to handle more complicated routing protocols, including extended features like quality-of-service (QoS) prioritization, voice over IP (VoIP) protocols, video protocols, and extended security features like VPNs. In addition to these differences, another feature of higher-end routers is built-in redundancy and failover capabilities like multiple power supplies.

Routing Switches and Load Balancers

As network infrastructures have become more complex, it has become increasingly common for mid- and higher-end switches to include some level of routing functionality as a built-in feature. This trend has progressed to the point where even load balancing (Layer 4 through 7 traffic management) features have been integrated into some switch models as well. As a matter of fact, because of the increasing complexity of networks and continued consolidation of resources, many infrastructures are increasingly using mid-range switches for routing between small network segments, and in some cases consolidating core routing responsibilities into higher-end core switches. Many of these high-end enterprise class switches are used in large to extra large networks and are chassis-based switches. Chassis-based switches have a modular configuration, or chassis, that allows additional modules to be plugged directly into the switch backplane. Some chassis-based switches can even accommodate a complete router module inside the chassis. For more information on network switching, refer to Chapter 7, "Network Switching."

There are many manufacturers of network switches making a vast array of switch models. Using a similar categorization referenced in the previous section disregarding the slot–bandwidth measurement, let's look at some of the more common switch manufacturers:

- Cisco Systems (www.cisco.com)

- Extreme Networks (www.extremenetworks.com)

- Foundry Networks (www.foundrynetworks.com)

Cisco systems is said to have up to 70 percent of the network switch market. They design and sell switches for all levels of network infrastructure,; however, routing functionality begins with Catalyst 3000 series switches. Table 5.4 lists some of Cisco's most common models that support routing.

Table 5.4 Cisco Switch Models with Routing Functionality

Category	Model
Small office switches	Model Catalyst 3550 series
Small- to medium-sized	Model Catalyst 4000 series
Medium- to large-sized	Model Catalyst 4000 series and 6500 series
Large- to extra-large-sized	Model Catalyst 6500 series and 8500 series

In addition to Cisco's switch models that support routing, Cisco also has a number of switch models that support routing along with load balancing and extended traffic management. These features are able to direct traffic based on information in what is considered Layers 4 through 7 (the transport through application layers) of the OSI network model, like the actual protocol being used, or details about a particular session of network traffic. Table 5.5 lists some of Cisco's switch models that support both routing and load balancing.

Table 5.5 Cisco Switch Models with Routing and Load Balancing Functionality

Category	Model
Small office switches	Model Content Service Switch (CSS) 11501
Small to medium-sized	Model CSS 11501 and CSS 11503
Medium- to large-sized	Model CSS 11503 and CSS 11506 and Catalyst 6500 with content switching module

Extreme Networks also designs and sells network switches with built-in routing functionality. Table 5.6 lists some of the more common Extreme Networks switching models that include some level of routing feature set.

Table 5.6 Extreme Networks' Switch Models

Category	Model
Small office switches	Summit 1i, 5i, 7i, 24, and 24e3
Small to medium-sized	Summit 48, 48i, and 48si
Medium- to large-sized	Alpine series and BlackDiamond series
Large- to extra-large-sized	BlackDiamond Series

Extreme Networks' switches also support a server load-balancing feature set in most of its "i" series of switches. Foundry Networks is another popular manufacturer of network switches with routing feature sets. Table 5.7 lists some of the more common Foundry Networks models.

Table 5.7 Foundry Networks' Switch Models

Category	Model
Small to medium-sized	FastIron 4802, 400, and 800
Medium- to large-sized	FastIron 1500, and BigIron 4000 and 8000
Large- to extra-large-sized	BigIron 8000 and 15000

Foundry Networks also has a specific line of switch models that focuses on routing and load balancing. Table 5.8 lists some the ServerIron Foundry Network Line.

Table 5.8 Foundry Networks' ServerIron Switch Models

Category	Model
Small to medium-sized	ServerIron XL and ServerIron 100
Medium- to large-sized	ServerIron 400
Large- to extra-large-sized	ServerIron 800

Considering Security for Network Switches and Load Balancers

While most of the security measures discussed previously for routers directly apply to network switches, there are a few considerations unique to network switches operating as IP routing devices that you might want to consider when approaching the security of a network switch. Primarily, we must consider access control. While a router has very few ports, a network switch has multiple ports that are easily connected to. This could allow network sniffing and possible attack attempts should the network switch not be in a secure location. Another consideration is that network switches might have many networks of varying security levels all running on the same device segmented by VLANs. In these circumstances, all network management services and access control mechanisms should be secured completely for all VLANs, not just networks of a lower security zone. VLANs are not foolproof, and network hosts can create packets that traverse VLANs on some devices.

Routing at the Operating System and Application Level

Yet another means of performing IP routing is with your network operating system or with an additional application. Many network infrastructures use network servers with multiple network adapters as routers. Most network operating systems are able to perform basic routing features at the OS level, with some even able to participate in basic dynamic routing protocols. However, to support some of the more complicated dynamic routing protocols, additional applications are used.

Of the most common network operating systems, Microsoft Windows NT/2000/XP, Linux, SUN Solaris, FreeBSD, and UNIX all support basic IP routing functionality. Most versions of Linux, Solaris, FreeBSD, and UNIX come with a *route* command that allows static configuration of routes within an internal route table. Microsoft Windows NT/2000/XP also supports basic routing functionality with the *route* command. In addition to basic routing, Microsoft Windows NT with Service Pack 4 supports basic dynamic routing with RIP and RIPv2. Microsoft Windows 2000 Server supports dynamic routing with the Routing and Remote Access feature. It supports both basic RIP and OSPF routing protocols.

To begin to participate in complex dynamic routing protocols, additional routing applications have to be used. Some of the most common routing applications are GateD, ZebOS, and Zebra GateD. Now distributed commercially by Nexthop technologies (www.nexthop.com), Zebra GateD runs on Linux 2.4 or Sun Solaris 8 or 9. GateD supports RIPv1 and v2, OSPF, IS-IS, and BGPv4 dynamic routing protocols. The ZebOS product suite is made by IP Infusion (www.ipinfusion.com) and supports RIPv1 and v2, OSPF, and BGPv4, and runs on Red Hat Linux, SUN Solaris, and FreeBSD. Finally, Zebra (www.zebra.org) is an open-source routing application that is distributed under the GNU general public license (www.gnu.org). It runs on Linux 2.0.*x* and 2.2.*x*, FreeBSD, NetBSD, OpenBSD, and SUN Solaris 7. It supports RIPv1 and v2, OSPF, and BGP-4.

IP Routing Protocols

IP routing protocols are the languages that enable the dynamic IP routing process. Similar to languages, protocols facilitate information exchange. *Dynamic routing* is the process by which routers automatically discover the available paths within the network and the topology of the network itself. Protocols enable routers to communicate the information needed for this process to take place. With dynamic routing, routers must keep their routing tables up to date with the latest information about the routes on the network. This is the only way they are able to keep segments of the network reachable when links fail. Without routing protocols, all routes would have to be manually entered into each router on your network and then changed at each device when changes were made or failures occurred, which in most modern networks would be impossible.

Most modern routing protocols are one of two types:

- **Distance vector protocols** These are generally older and simpler protocols that work via broadcasts of all routing information between routers. Each router in a network broadcasts its routing table to its neighbors and then adds routes to its table from the broadcasts it receives. Deciding if a received route is inserted into the routing table depends on rules defined by the protocol.

- **Link-state protocols** These are the more complex and generally more modern protocols. Link-state protocols rely on each router to build a network topology map from any updates it receives from its neighbors. Each router then calculates the best path to each network using a common algorithm. Updates are only sent to neighbors when requested or when the state of a link in the network changes.

In addition to the two basic types of protocols, it is also possible to classify routing protocols as either Interior gateway protocols or Exterior gateway protocols.

- **Interior Gateway Protocols (IGPs)** IGPs are protocols designed to route within an organization or autonomous system (AS).

- **Exterior Gateway Protocols (EGPs)** EGPs are protocols designed to router information between organizations or autonomous systems.

Routing Information Protocol

The routing information protocol (RIP) is one of the oldest dynamic routing protocols still in wide use today. The first version of RIP was contained in BSD as *routed* when released in 1982, but some of the basic algorithms within the protocol were used on the ARPANET as early as 1969. RIP is a widely used protocol within small to medium-sized networks because it is relatively easy to set up and is generally compatible among different device manufacturers. RIP began as an EGP but is now almost exclusively used as an IGP. RIP is a distance vector protocol, which means that it compares routes mathematically using a value that represents distance, in hops, to a destination. *Hops* is a term used to describe how many networks a particular packet of data must traverse before arriving at the destination network. Some key pieces of information to remember about the RIP protocol include:

- RIP is a distance vector protocol.

- RIP is an open protocol described in RFC 1058.

- RIP updates use UDP on port 520.

- RIP updates are sent every 30 seconds by default.

- RIP allows a router to request updates from its neighbors when it comes online.

- The maximum size of a network that is using RIP is 15 hops.

How RIP Works

RIP defines the best route as the route having the shortest path to the destination network regardless of the specifications of your link or connection such as capacity or latency. RIP determines which path reaches a network via the shortest distance by comparing a distance metric, which is associated with each path in the route table. This distance metric is calculated by adding 1 for every hop between two routers along the path to a destination. To prevent routing loops, which are discussed later in this section, and other problems, the distance metric in the RIP protocol is limited to 15 hops. A distance metric of 16 denotes a network that is unreachable.

Routers using RIP exchange routing updates with their neighbors to build a complete table of all routes in the network. These routing updates are comprised of each router's entire routing table, which includes a list of networks and distance metrics for each of those networks. When a router receives an update, it must choose whether to enter each route in the update into its routing table. RIP uses the following rules to determine if received route updates should be kept or discarded. Using these rules, routers running RIP populate their route tables and are able to make routing decisions.

- The routes in updates will be entered into the route table if:

    - The network in the update is not currently in the routing table and the metric is less than 16.

    - The network in the update is currently in the routing table, but the metric is lower.

    - The network in the update is currently in the routing table, the metric is higher, but the update has come from the same neighbor from which the original update came.

- The routes contained in updates will be discarded if:

    - The network in the update is already in the route table, but the distance metric in the update is larger.

    - The network in the update is already in the route table, and the distance metric in the update is the same. (In some manufacturers' implementations of RIP, routes to the same destination with the same distance metric to different neighbors will be included in the route table and traffic will be load-balanced across up to four routes.)

Once RIP is running and all routers have populated their route tables, any changes or failures in the network mean that all routers must receive updates. This *convergence* process starts when a network change occurs, and ends when all routers have the correct network information. The time it takes for a network to recover from any change depends on timers that are a part of RIP and are generally a part of most distance vector protocols. These timers are associated to each individual route:

- **Update timer** The update timer is the amount of time to wait between sending updates. The default for this timer is 30 seconds.

- **Invalid timer** The invalid timer has a default limit of 180 seconds and is reset to 0 every time an update is received for a route. If the route has not been updated in 180 seconds, then the route is marked as invalid. This, however, doesn't mean that the router stops forwarding traffic to the next hop for that route.

- **Hold-down timer** The hold-down timer is also set at 180 by default and is set on a route when the invalid timer expires. When the hold-down timer expires, a route is put in a hold-down state and can't be updated. A route is also put into a hold-down state when an update is received for that route with a metric of 16, meaning that the route is unreachable.

- **Flush timer** The flush timer has a default of 240 seconds and is set each time an update for a route is received. If the timer expires, the route is flushed, even if the route is in a hold-down state.

RIP has built-in methods to speed convergence and help prevent routing problems like routing loops from creeping into the routing tables. Routing loops can occur when incorrect information gets into the routing table and gets updated throughout the network. One of the means by which a router speeds convergence is flushing all routes learned through an interface that it detects as down. This bypasses all timers and speeds convergence of the network. Routers also send updates to their neighbors immediately when they detect a change in metric for a route. This is called a *triggered update* and can dramatically speed convergence. *Poison reverse* is another method used by routers for speeding convergence. With poison reverse, if a router detects a downed link, it automatically sends an update with a metric of 16 for those routes to its neighbors. Its neighbors will automatically put those routes in hold-down and not propagate those routes to the rest of the network.

Routers also do not send updates back through interfaces from which they were received. *Split horizon*, as it is known, resolves the problem where if one router were to lose the connection to a network on one of its interfaces, its neighbor router could then send it an update for the same network. This would create a endless loop where each router would re-update its neighbors with the network it just learned from them with a higher metric. Each router would keep the route with the higher metric because the update is being received from the original router from which the update was originally received. Without split horizon, this routing loop would continue until the metric in the update reached 16 and the route update would no longer be accepted.

Along with providing methods for accelerating convergence, RIP also supports features that simplify configuration and ease protocol overhead. As a basic means of simplifying configurations within a RIP-enabled network, RIP supports the configuration of a default route. A default route simplifies configurations because it allows routers to forward traffic to a default next hop if a specific route to a destination can't be found. To reduce the amount of traffic used in route updates, RIP also supports *route summarization*. Route summarization is the process by which multiple routes are represented by a single more general route in route updates. In this way, updates representing multiple routes can be contained in a single update.

Another important thing to note about RIP updates is that route updates don't contain subnet mask information. The subnet mask to associate with a particular network in an update must be determined by the router receiving the update. If a router receiving an update has an interface on the network for which it receives an update, then the router will automatically assume the same subnet mask for the network in the update as it has on its own interface. If the router does not have an interface on the network for which it is receiving an update, the router will assume the subnet mask that is naturally associated with the network number. Because of this, networks using RIP cannot use variable-length subnet masks anywhere in their network. This means that all networks in an environment connected by routers running RIPv1 must use the same subnet masks. This might cause problems on some networks with segments of varying sizes and will likely result in IP address space not being used very economically.

Securing RIP

Even though RIP doesn't provide any type of security within the protocol or any authentication mechanism to protect communication between routers, there are still a couple of techniques that can be used to make your RIP protocol environment as secure as possible. At the very least, when implementing RIP, be sure to configure RIP networks and neighbors explicitly within your configuration. This will provide a basic control level over the interfaces that are able to exchange routing updates. In addition, configure access lists to prevent your router from receiving RIP traffic on interfaces that are not participating in the protocol. Finally, prevent your router from sending out routing updates on interfaces that don't need them by configuring those interfaces as passive interfaces.

When to Use RIP

RIP is a very reliable protocol, and is well suited to small and medium-sized networks. However, there are a couple of things to consider before deciding on RIP as the protocol for your network. The first consideration relates to the types of connections within your network. Are they all similar in capacity? Are all of your connections the same size in terms of bandwidth? What about latency and reliability? Are all of your connections a similar speed and similar media? If the answers to all these questions are yes, then RIP could be sufficient for your dynamic routing needs. If your network has disparities among its various connections, RIP might not be well suited for your network because RIP's distance metric does not consider any of a connection's attributes. To RIP, a 56k serial line is considered equal to a 1.54 Mbps T-1. Another consideration would network size. Does any path on your network contain more than 15 hops? If so, RIP is definitely not for you. RIP can only handle networks with paths less than 15 hops. Even if your network doesn't contain a path greater than 15 hops, in large networks, routing information updates every 30 seconds can mean network utilization at an unacceptable level and in some cases convergence can take too long.

Interior Gateway Routing Protocol

The Interior Gateway Routing Protocol (IGRP) was developed in the mid 1980s by Cisco systems. IGRP was designed specifically for routing within an autonomous system or within a network under a single entity's control and therefore is classified as an IGP. IGRP was also designed in an attempt to capture most the effectiveness of RIP while simultaneously extending its functionality and capabilities. Some fundamental details to remember about IGRP include:

- IGRP is a proprietary Cisco protocol.
- IGRP is a distance vector protocol.
- IGRP updates are sent using IP protocol 9 (IGP) IP datagrams.

- IGRP uses a metric that can represent a calculation of bandwidth, delay, reliability, load, MTU, and hop count.

- IGRP allows update requests from neighbor routers and are sent every 90 seconds by default.

- IGRP uses autonomous system numbers to segment routing domains.

- IGRP updates contain three types of routes: interior routes, system routes, and exterior routes.

How IGRP Works

Although in many respects IGRP is similar to RIP, it differs in fundamental features that extend upon the weaknesses in the RIP protocol. IGRP is a distance vector protocol, and as such determines the best route by mathematically evaluating routes using a metric value. IGRP also implements many of the convergence enhancing features that RIP contains, such as triggered updates, split horizon, poison reverse, and the flush, invalid, update, and hold-down timers. For the sake of brevity, we will not discuss any of the features that IGRP and RIP have in common; instead, we will focus on how IGRP differs from RIP and extends its functionality and usability.

A major improvement of IGRP over RIP is its capability to factor the specifications of a particular connection into the metric it uses to calculate best paths. The IGRP metric is a value that represents not only hop count as in RIP, but can also take into consideration bandwidth, delay, link reliability, load, and in some cases the maximum transfer units (MTUs) of a particular connection. The default configuration for the IGRP metric is to consider bandwidth and delay, but the metric can be customized to include weighted values for any of the link aspects discussed previously. The metric itself is calculated using constants that are combined with the link attribute values in an algorithm that provides a single value. It is possible to adjust IGRP's route selection by adjusting the value of the constants used in the metric calculation.

IGRP also implements autonomous system numbers and allows networks to be segmented into different routing domains. This practice can be helpful in limiting bad routes from propagating too far in your network. However, because different routing domains do not exchange information, segmenting your network should be done along obvious delineation points of region or organization.

Another unique feature of IGRP is route updates. IGRP route updates can contain three different types of routes. The updates also only include three octets of the network number but still do not contain subnet mask information. A route update can contain system routes, interior routes, and exterior routes. System routes are routes that contain networks that might have been summarized when crossing a network boundary. Interior routes are routes that contain information regarding the subnet for the network number of the interface to which the update is being sent. Exterior routes could be designated as the default route. Because IGRP route updates only contain three octets, the fourth is calculated based on if the route is an interior route, exterior route, or system route. If the route is an interior route, the first octet of the network number is assumed to be the same as the interface that received the update; the following three octets are filled in with the information from the update. For exterior and system routes, the first three octets are filled by the update, and the fourth octet is 0 because the routes have been summarized.

IGRP supports some unique features in routing that extend its capabilities beyond RIP:

- IGRP supports multipath routing and unequal cost load-balancing among routes.

- When a router running IGRP receives a route update that contains the same network it already has in its table from another neighbor, the router will install that route in the table as well and load balance traffic between multiple paths.

- IGRP can also be configured to load balance across unequal cost links, using a variance configuration.

- Links that fall within a configurable variance can be used in a load-balancing configuration.

Securing IGRP

Unfortunately, IGRP does not include any means of security within the protocol, and like RIP there are only a couple of different techniques to help make your IGRP environment as secure as it can be. The primary technique for securing IGRP would be to implement access lists that prevent IGRP traffic from unauthorized networks. Second, configuring IGRP correctly is the minimum you should do to protect your IGRP routers. Remember to configure IGRP neighbors explicitly and to configure the networks from which you plan to receive IGRP updates.

When to Use IGRP

IGRP is very well suited to small to medium-sized networks that contain many different types of links. However, IGRP (just as RIP) does not support VLSM, which can cause problems for complicated networks that are made up of many different types and sizes of networks. Networks using IGRP must be designed using contiguous blocks of natural networks. Finally, for larger networks, convergence times can be unacceptably long and the overhead of complete route table updates can be too high.

Enhanced IGRP

Enhanced IGRP (EIGRP) is an extensive improvement to the IGRP protocol. It is also a proprietary Cisco protocol that was designed for use as an IGP. EIGRP accommodates diverse network topologies and media, has fast convergence times, and a low network overhead. EIGRP has all the benefits of a link-state protocol even though it is an enhanced distance-vector protocol. Some fundamental facts to remember about EIGRP include:

- EIGRP is a proprietary Cisco protocol.

- EIGRP is an enhanced distance-vector protocol.

- EIGRP calculates routes using the Diffusing Update Algorithm (DUAL).

- EIGRP uses a metric that can represent a calculation of bandwidth, delay, reliability, load, MTU, and hop count.

- EIGRP supports VLSM.

- EIGRP only sends partial updates when the metric for a route changes, and it uses Reliable Transport Protocol (RTP) to send updates.

- EIGRP maintains three tables: a route table, a neighbor table, and a topology table.

How EIGRP Works

EIGRP is slightly different from the two protocols we have examined so far. It is classified as an enhanced distance-vector protocol because like all distance-vector protocols it relies on routing information provided by neighbors to create its routing table. However, unlike other distance-vector protocols, EIGRP does not send complete updates to all neighbor routers on a set timed basis. EIGRP only updates its neighbors when network changes occur, and then the routers only send the changed information. Because of this, EIGRP uses a lot less network bandwidth than RIP or IGRP do. This becomes important as your networks scale to larger sizes.

To find neighbors, routers using EIGRP use a neighbor discovery and recovery mechanism. Once identified, EIGRP sends only small hello packets to its neighbors to verify that they are still functioning. In addition, EIGRP uses a different means of calculating best paths than the other protocols we have examined so far. EIGRP uses a DUAL to make routing decisions. DUAL is a finite-state machine and is capable of storing the current router's route table and all its neighbors' route tables as well. This gives EIGRP the ability to converge very quickly, almost instantaneously. If a neighbor router were to fail, or a route were updated as unreachable, the router will already have a known second-best route that it can install in the routing table.

EIGRP relies on three tables to effectively make its routing decisions:

- Primarily, EIGRP maintains the *routing table*. Routes that are calculated as the best path based on route metrics are kept in this table.

- EIGRP also maintains a *neighbor table*. This table tracks all protocol interaction with the neighboring routers. Each neighbor router is entered into the table with its address and the interface on which it is reachable. EIGRP maintains contact with its neighbors via small hello packets, and the timers for these packets are also stored in the neighbor table along with packet sequence information used by RTP.

- Finally, EIGRP maintains a *topology table*, which enables EIGRP to converge extremely rapidly. The topology table contains all routes advertised by neighbors, whether they are the best paths or not.

Unlike RIP and IGRP, EIGRP updates contain subnet mask information. This allows EIGRP to do a number of things that RIP and IGRP cannot. Primarily, EIGRP supports VLSM. This allows network architects to use IP address space more efficiently and create non-natural subnet masks that more accurately reflect the size of a given network. The fact that EIGRP updates contain subnet mask information also allows the protocol to improve route summarization by allowing the summarization of routes based on any bit boundary. This in effect can reduce the route table size on all routers, thereby making the protocol more efficient.

Securing EIGRP

There are a couple of main techniques to help make your EIGRP routing domain as secure as it can be. The primary means of security within all protocols that support it is configuring authentication among routing neighbors. This technique can prevent unauthorized routers from participating in your EIGRP routing. EIGRP supports the use of MD5 authentication for neighbor routers exchanging updates.

It is also a good idea to prevent the sending and receiving of routing information on interfaces that don't need it or that are using another routing protocol. With EIGRP, you can prevent the router from sending route updates and receiving route updates by configuring the interface that you want to restrict as a passive interface. To do this on Cisco devices, use the *passive-interface* command with the interface-type and number.

Finally, you should also control what is contained in routing updates that are sent and received through your router. This is accomplished by configuring route filtering on the interfaces that are participating in EIGRP routing. Route filtering can generally be configured on a global level or on a per-interface level and can also be configured to filter incoming updates, outgoing updates, or both. Route filtering is configured by using ACLs.

When to Use EIGRP

EIGRP is a substantial improvement over RIP and IGRP for mid-sized networks. It's capability to converge quickly after network changes, its support for variable-length subnet masks, combined with its low network overhead make it an efficient alternative for RIP and IGRP networks. There are a couple of drawbacks to EIGRP, though. Primarily, DUAL is rather complex and can be difficult to troubleshoot. It can also become CPU intensive during periods of network instability when frequent recalculations are required. In addition, EIGRP also has a larger memory requirement than any of the previously discussed protocols because of the many tables it uses.

RIPv2

RIP version 2 or RIPv2 as its name suggests is essentially an update of its younger brother RIP. RIPv2 is a distance-vector protocol and is used primarily as an IGP. It was designed mainly to enhance RIP with additional functionality and was also specifically designed with backward compatibility in mind. Some basic details to remember about RIPv2 include:

- RIPv2 is an open protocol described by RFC 2453.
- RIPv2 is a distance-vector protocol.
- RIPv2 updates use UDP on port 520.
- RIPv2 updates carry subnet mask information.
- RIPv2 enables authentication between neighbors.
- RIPv2 is generally backward compatible with RIP.

How RIPv2 Works

RIPv2 essentially uses the same metric, calculation algorithm, and routing update process as RIP, so the means by which it populates its routing table and chooses optimal routes essentially remains the same. This has both good and bad implications for the protocol. On the plus side, RIPv2 is backward compatible with RIP. The extended information included in RIPv2 updates are positioned in parts of the update packet that RIP assumes to be empty, therefore allowing RIPv2 and RIP routers to communicate with each other. On the negative side, RIPv2 still broadcasts updates every 30 seconds, still uses a metric that does not account for any link attributes such as bandwidth or delay, and still suffers from long convergence times.

There are some enhancements in the RIPv2 protocol as well. The updated functionality of the protocol is worth a look. This updated functionality stems from the additional information carried in the RIPv2 routing update. One of the pieces of additional information that RIPv2 packets carry is subnet mask information. This allows RIPv2 to support variable-length subnet masks along with noncontiguous address space and classless inter-domain routing (CIDR). Another extremely valuable new feature that RIPv2 brings is authentication. Routers participating in RIPv2 routing can now protect updates by including authentication information, either as a plain-text password or MD5 authentication as supported by some manufacturers. Finally, RIPv2 updates carry a next-hop IP address, which becomes useful when routes are being redistributed between RIPv2 and another protocol, and they also carry a route tag for each entry, which while not used by RIP, can contain information on the source of the route.

Securing RIPv2

One of the substantial updates to RIPv2 over RIP is the addition of authenticated update exchanges between partners. When supported, authenticated updates should be the primary means of securing the routing protocol. Authenticating route updates from neighbor routers protects the router from accepting bogus routing updates that would then be propagated to the rest of the routers participating in the routing domain. The compromise of the routing tables could allow for re-routing of traffic, which could lead to either DoS attacks or allowing unauthorized access to your network. RIPv2 supports both simple authentication and MD5 authentication. Simple authentication includes a plain-text password with every route update. If the password in the update matches the configured password, the route update is accepted. While better than no authentication at all, simple authentication transmits the password without any protection across the network. This can leave the password vulnerable to eavesdropping. A better solution is to use the MD5 authentication scheme. MD5 includes with the update a hash that is generated from the update itself and a password or key. When an update is received, the hash is then compared to a hash that is computed by the router that received the update. If the hash matches, the update is accepted.

Along with authentication, it is important to configure the interfaces that are allowed to send and receive updates along with the networks that can be sent or received within those updates. To control which interfaces updates are sent from, it is possible to configure interfaces not participating in RIPv2 as passive interfaces. This will prevent updates from being sent on those interfaces, but unfortunately, it won't prevent updates received on those interfaces from being processed. Another level of security is controlling the networks that can be contained in route updates. A technique called *route filtering* can be employed at a global or per-interface level to filter the routes contained in updates. This filtering can be configured for route updates being sent, route updates being received, or for route updates both sent and received. Route filtering is accomplished by using ACLs to list networks that are explicitly allowed or denied. Those lists are then applied to incoming or outgoing route updates.

When to Use RIPv2

RIPv2 was designed to enhance the functionality and improve upon some of the original protocol's weaknesses. However, because RIPv2 still relies on the same metric information as RIP, still has problems with convergence times, and protocol overhead, it is still not suitable for larger networks. RIPv2 is a perfect upgrade for small networks still running RIP that don't foresee large growth but would like to take advantage of some of RIPv2's enhanced features like authentication and variable-length subnet masks.

Open Shortest Path First

In addition to being a dynamic routing protocol, Open Shortest Path First (OSPF) is the first link-state protocol we will look at. The *Open* in OSPF represents the fact that the protocol is an open standard developed by the Internet Engineering Task Force (IETF) and described in RFC 2328. It was designed as an IGP to route within a single autonomous system (AS), but with the Internet environment in mind. OSPF can tag routes that come into the AS from outside the network. The *Shortest Path First* in the name refers to the algorithm the protocol uses to compute the shortest path to every destination in the route table. OSPF can be an extremely complex protocol in very large networks, so in this section we will only examine the basics of the protocol functionality. Some basic details to remember about OSPF include:

- OSPF is an open protocol described by RFC 2328 and is generally compatible between devices from different vendors.

- OSPF is a link-state protocol.

- OSPF exchanges information with Link State Advertisements (LSAs). All information exchange is authenticated.

- OSPF updates are directly encapsulated in IP with the protocol field set to 89.

- OSPF is scalable. There is no hop count limit on the size of the network, and OSPF is designed hierarchically so that networks are divided into areas for easier management.

- OSPF supports VLSM.

- OSPF requires a lot of processor and memory resources on your router.

How OSPF Works

As mentioned earlier, OSPF is a link-state routing protocol. This means that OSPF determines the best path from itself to other destinations by maintaining a map of its network area in memory and computing the best path using that map. When a router is configured to run OSPF, it broadcasts hello packets from each interface configured with OSPF. It finds other OSPF routers by listening for OSPF hello packets. When another OSPF router is identified, the two routers authenticate and exchange configuration information before they exchange link-state advertisements (LSAs). Link-state databases are built by LSAs that are flooded to the entire network. LSAs describe each of the connections on a given router. LSAs contain information on each connection to a router, which includes a cost for each connection. This cost is a number based on details of the connection, including throughput, latency, and reliability. OSPF deals with network changes by flooding the network with LSAs whenever there is a status change within the network. When the link-state database is complete, the router can then calculate the best path from it to the rest of the network using the Shortest Path First (SPF) algorithm. In this way, routers using OSPF no longer have to rely on possibly bad routing information from other routers. They only have to ensure the accuracy of their own link-state databases to be able to find the best path to any destination on the network.

Because OSPF is a very processor-intensive protocol, OSPF is designed to simplify large networks by creating different areas. Routers within each area are then only responsible for maintaining a link-state database of the topology in their local area. In this way, OSPF can scale to accommodate extremely large networks. Each area then summarizes its routes into what is called a *backbone area*. This backbone area then summarizes routes to all areas attached to it. All traffic going from one area to another must go through the backbone area.

Securing OSPF

Two simple configuration changes can easily be made to help secure the OSPF protocol on your network. The first deals with changing the way in which OSPF finds and communicates with OSPF neighbors, and the second deals with authentication of the transmissions between OSPF routers. OSPF is an IGP and should never be seen outside your network; however, it is important to secure all aspects of your network, even your interior routing protocols.

In most installations, OSPF is configured in broadcast mode, meaning that any router on the network running OSPF with the appropriate configuration information can participate in OSPF routing. A more secure configuration would be to change the OSPF configuration from broadcast mode to directed mode. In directed mode, each OSPF neighbor must be explicitly defined in each router's OSPF configuration. This configuration provides a basic layer of protection against any misconfiguration because your router will only communicate with routers that have been configured to communicate with it.

Another configuration change that can be made to your OSPF configuration to increase security is to use the most secure authentication means possible. The

OSPF protocol supports authentication of all transmissions. However, the means for authentication can either be none, simple, or MD5. Simple authentication uses a password that is transmitted in clear text over the network. This leaves the password vulnerable to anyone capturing packets on your network. MD5 is the most secure authentication type and should be used. MD5 is the fifth generation of the message digest algorithm that allows messages to be converted into fingerprints or message digests. With this technique, the MD5 key is not transmitted over the network; instead, a message digest of the key known as a "hash" is sent instead.

When to Use OSPF

OSPF is great protocol for large to extra large networks. Because it is hierarchical, OSPF allows networks to grow by simply dividing large areas into smaller ones. However, OSPF can be very CPU and memory intensive; computing the shortest path first algorithm on a large link-state database can require a large amount of CPU resources, and the size of the link-state database can tax memory resources. OSPF is also a slightly complex protocol that can require extensive experience and training to design and operate properly.

BGP v4

BGP-4 or BGP version 4, is the latest revision of the Border Gateway Protocol (BGP). BGP is an exterior gateway protocol that manages routes between ASs. BGP is probably most commonly used among ISPs and enterprises with multiple Internet connections. In fact, BGP has been referred to as the protocol that glues the Internet together. BGP is an open protocol that was originally defined in RFC 1105 in 1989. Shortly after, in 1990 and 1991, BGP was updated to BGPv2 in RFC 1163 and BGPv3 in RFC 1287. BGPv4, which is the version in use today, was described by RFC 1771 in 1995. In this section, the terms *BGP* and *BGPv4* are interchangeable. BGP can be a fairly complex protocol and there are entire books devoted to it, so in this section we only look at the basics of the protocol. Some important details to remember about BGP include:

- BGP-4 is an open protocol described in RFC 1771.
- BGP-4 is an exterior gateway protocol (EGP) that manages routes between ASs.
- BGP-4 is a distance-vector protocol.

- BGP-4 uses TCP port 179 for communication between peers.
- BGP-4 neighbors must be set up explicitly; there is no neighbor auto-discovery process.

How BGPv4 Works

As mentioned earlier, BGP is an exterior gateway protocol that routes traffic between autonomous systems. An autonomous system can be thought of as a singular network entity or collection of networks that are under independent administrative control and share the same routing policies. For example, a large corporation's privately owned network would be an AS, as would an ISP's Internet network. Each of these networks operates independently of each other and is under the control of a single organization. These autonomous systems might have different routing policies and protocols running within them. BGP allows these autonomous systems to communicate with each other while still maintaining their independence.

Each AS that connects to the Internet using BGP must apply for and receive an autonomous system number (ASN) from the American Registry for Internet Numbers (ARIN). ASNs are then used by BGP to describe network prefixes. Network prefixes are groups of network addresses that are classless and can represent any number of network groups. BGPv4 manages routes by receiving BGP paths to network prefixes. These updates are called *prefix advertisements*. Prefix advertisements are the basic unit of information for BGPv4 and contain various details about the paths to other AS entities. One of the most important pieces of information in the prefix advertisement is the AS-PATH information. For each prefix advertisement, the AS_PATH information is a list of AS entities that traffic must pass through to reach the destination AS.

BGP is essentially a distance-vector protocol by design. BGP routers listen to their BGP neighbors for prefix advertisements and then use a distance-vector algorithm to compute the best path, which is then stored in the route table. BGP then advertises this best path to its neighbors. BGP, unlike other protocols, cannot build neighbor relationships on its own. Each neighbor relationship must be explicitly entered into the configuration manually. Given that BGP is a protocol that can connect two completely different entities, this is a feature, not a limitation. When a new neighbor is configured, every prefix is then sent to that neighbor; after that, only advertised prefixes are sent. Each AS is also able to customize BGP to enable their specific routing policies.

BGP actually takes two forms. I–BGP stands for Interior BGP and is used between BGP routers that connect to other autonomous systems but are located within the same AS. I–BGP allows all BGP routers within an AS to maintain the same routing table and communicate protocol information. E–BGP is the other form of BGP and stands for Exterior BGP. Routers belonging to different autonomous systems use E–BGP.

Securing BGPv4

BGPv4 is an exterior gateway protocol, which by definition means that the routing device running BGP will be communicating and exchanging information with a router that is outside your organization and not under your direct control. Of all the dynamic routing protocols, BGP's position as the protocol used on your network's boundary, outside your network's firewalls, makes it especially susceptible to attack attempts. This means that securing the protocol and its transmissions is extremely important.

There are a number of techniques to make your border router secure, which we discussed in the previous section *Securing Your Routers*. What we will discuss here is some of the things that can be done to secure your BGP routing environment. A couple of the most important techniques for securing BGP are implementing the strongest type of neighbor authentication and implementing access lists to prohibit BGP traffic from any source other than your BGP peers. BGP supports authentication of BGP peers or neighbors with the MD5 message digest algorithm. This feature should be implemented with all of your BGP peers, both external and internal. This will help protect your BGP routing process from unauthorized prefix advertisements. Additionally, the implementation of access lists to filter any BGP traffic that is not from your specified BGP peers will also add an additional level of security.

When to Use BGPv4

While BGP is an incredibly useful protocol for ISPs and large organizations with multiple Internet connections, it can be a bit much for small to medium-sized organizations to handle. The hardware requirements to handle BGP are substantial and the protocol can be tricky to configure properly.

Checklist

☑ Physical security

- Make sure the router location is secure.

- Make sure the router location is safe from the elements (fire, water, excessive heat).

☑ Secure access

- Configure access restrictions on VTYs, console, and AUX ports.

- Configure logging and auditing on all access attempts.

- Disable or protect SNMP, TFTP, and HTTP access mechanisms.

- Configure login banners.

☑ Secure the router configuration

- Make sure you have a secure backup of the latest router configuration.

- Disable unneeded services.

- Implement ACLs and packet filtering.

☑ Secure the routing protocols

- Choose the appropriate protocol for the situation.

- Use protocol authentication with the strongest level of secret key protection.

- Prevent unnecessary networks and devices from communicating with your router via your chosen protocol.

- Prevent the protocol from being run on unnecessary interfaces.

☑ Maintain good security practices

- Back up and secure router configuration whenever the device is changed.

- Maintain the latest patches and updates from the device manufacturer.

Summary

Routers are some of the most important devices in your network. More than likely, a router is responsible for your network's connection to the Internet, as well as for connecting remote office networks to yours. This chapter examined routing devices and their overall role in your network infrastructure. It aimed at helping you understand why securing your routers is one of the most important tasks to accomplish in securing your network. This chapter covered the roles of routers on your network and discussed the roles of border routers as well as routers on internal segments. It then covered general security considerations for your network's routers and talked about physical security, access controls, auditing logging, and protocol security. The chapter then looked at some of the most commonly used IP routing devices and finished with a discussion of some of the most commonly used routing protocols.

Routers within your network play different roles. Their basic function is to direct packets of information across networks, but they end up doing far more than just directing traffic. Routers actually work together to maintain direct traffic through the best paths on the network and to maintain the accessibility of network segments by redirecting traffic around network failures. Routers also play an important role in maintaining the security of your network. When properly configured, routers are able to prevent unwanted traffic from traversing network boundaries.

There are many different roles a router on your network can play, and these roles can generally be classified based on the location of the router within the network architecture. Most roles can be broken down into routers along the perimeter of your network and routers on interior segments of your network. Routers on the perimeter of your network are generally more accessible to the outside world than routers on your internal network are, making them more vulnerable to attack attempts. These routers can quite possibly benefit the most from increased security configuration. However, routers inside your network are possibly the most important devices in the entire network infrastructure. Any attack on a core router could prove devastating for your network, so it is equally important to secure routers on the interior of your network as well.

Although securing your networks routers is a difficult job, it is a very important task and should be handled with great care. It is important to view this task with an overall strategy in mind. It is always a good idea to develop layers of security that work together to form a complete security picture. You always want to consider the basic physical security primarily, as well as security of the router's configuration and access points. Logging and auditing are another level of security that plays an important role in maintaining your routers well being. Finally, the last but not least thing to consider is your router's network configuration, securing the protocols it uses, and the services it runs.

IP routing and the devices that support routing protocols allow for a significant amount of flexibility in order to facilitate diverse and unique network infrastructures/implementations. It is important to be familiar with the types and classifications of hardware devices that support routing. It also important to know what to consider when securing different types of routers or routing devices.

Dynamic routing protocols are the core of IP routing, and to begin to secure these protocols it is important to have a basic level of knowledge about the protocol itself. The six basic routing protocols in use today are RIPv1, IGRP, EIGRP, RIPv2, OSPF, and BGPv4. Each of these protocols has its strengths and weaknesses. Ensuring the security of the network protocols that your network uses is a major step toward accomplishing a secure network infrastructure..

Solutions Fast Track

Understanding the Roles of Routers on Your Network

☑ A very important part of an in-depth security strategy is securing and understanding the roles of routers on perimeter segments.

☑ It is equally important to secure and understand the roles of routers on internal segments.

Securing Your Routers

☑ To properly defend your networks routing devices, it is imperative to examine possible attacks on your routers.

☑ One of the first steps to take in securing your routing devices it to prevent login access to your routers.

☑ Another key component to an overall security strategy for your routing devices is to control what your routers do.

☑ Ongoing security requires diligent maintenance of your routers for optimal security.

IP Routing Devices

☑ Routers are the fundamental IP routing devices.

☑ Switches and load balancers can also include IP routing capabilities.

☑ Routing at the operating system and application levels is also an option for many networks.

IP Routing Protocols

☑ The oldest of the dynamic IP routing protocols, RIP is a distance-vector protocol that, although not secure, is suited to small networks and is still in use today.

☑ IGRP is a distance-vector Cisco protocol that is suited to small networks and implements features not handled by RIP.

☑ EIGRP is also a Cisco protocol that is a substantial improvement over IGRP and RIP. It is an enhanced distance-vector protocol that supports authentication and is commonly used in small to medium-sized networks.

☑ RIPv2 is an open protocol that implements some of the features lacking in RIP, such as variable-length subnet masks and authentication. It is also generally backward compatible with RIP, which makes it an easy upgrade.

☑ OSPF is a link-state protocol and is *open*, meaning that it is based on an open standard. It is a fairly complicated protocol with many features. It is extremely useful in large complex networks.

☑ BGP v4 is an exterior gateway protocol that is used to route data between different organizations' networks. ISPs and large organizations with multiple Internet connections most commonly use this protocol.

Links to Sites

- **www.ietf.org** The IETF Web site. This is the standards body for all of the open routing protocols used on the Internet, among many other things. Access to all of the RFCs mentioned in this chapter can be found on this site.

- **www.cisco.com** Cisco Systems is the leader in IP routing devices. This site has valuable information about IP routing, the latest IP routing devices, and Cisco proprietary routing protocols.

- **www.juniper.net** Juniper Networks is a manufacturer of high-end IP routers. This site has valuable information about IP routing and protocols.

- **www.extremenetworks.com** Extreme Networks is a manufacturer of network switches. This site has good information on network design, IP routing, and IP routing devices.

- **www.foundrynetworks.com** Foundry Networks is a manufacturer of network switches. This site has good information on the latest IP routing devices and IP routing protocols.

- **www.nsa.gov/snac/cisco** This NSA Web site contains valuable information on Cisco router security configuration.

- **www.cisecurity.org/bench_cisco.html** This Web site provides both a configuration guide and audit tool for your router configuration.

Mailing Lists

- **cust-security-announce@cisco.com** Cisco mailing list for security alerts.

- **www.ietf.org/maillist.html** Mailing lists for the IETF.

- **www.us-cert.gov/cas/index.html_** US-Cert security alert notification lists.

- **www.nanog.org** North American Network Operators Group (NANOG) mailing list.

Frequently Asked Questions

The following Frequently Asked Questions, answered by the authors of this book, are designed to both measure your understanding of the concepts presented in this chapter and to assist you with real-life implementation of these concepts. To have your questions about this chapter answered by the author, browse to **www.syngress.com/solutions** and click on the **"Ask the Author"** form. You will also gain access to thousands of other FAQs at ITFAQnet.com.

Q: Why is securing network routers so important?

A: Your network lives and dies by its routers. Without routers, network inter-connectivity would be impossible. Routers are most likely crucial in your everyday network functions such as Internet access and communications with business partners. Unsecured, your networks routers can be vulnerable to DoS attacks that could cripple their functions, or even worse, used against you to re-route traffic exposing confidential data.

Q: What are the benefits of a properly secured and configured network router?

A: A properly secured and configured router on your network not only functions properly with less maintenance required, but can be your biggest asset when it comes to securing your network as a whole. With routers' excellent position between network boundaries, they are able to prevent unwanted network traffic from roaming freely on your network.

Q: What is a basic strategy to consider when securing your router?

A: A basic strategy to consider when securing your routers is to develop multiple layers of security that all work together to form a complete security picture.

Q: What are dynamic routing protocols and why is it important to securely configure them?

A: Dynamic routing protocols are the core of IP routing. They are the language used between routers to communicate details of the network state around them. Securing the routing protocols running between your routers assures that incorrect information cannot be injected into the normal stream of protocol traffic to make unauthorized changes or cause a DoS to the network.

Q: Are routers the only devices that can perform IP routing?

A: No. Many different types of network devices support types of IP routing and even dynamic IP routing protocols. Purpose-built routers are designed to accommodate many different types of networks, protocols, and traffic levels.

Chapter 6

Secure Network Management

Solutions in this Chapter:

- Network Management and Security Principles
- Management Networks
- IPSec and VPNs
- Network Management Tools and Uses

Related Chapters:

Introduction

Throughout the preceding chapters, we described what an "internal" network segment really is, presented methods on how to assess the security of your network, document the network topology and aggregation points, presented information on the major firewall technologies and their associated products, how to attack those products using contemporary exploits, and we even talked about different ways to route information back and forth between our internal and external segments through your firewall. It won't be until the following chapters where we'll be presenting the wonders of network switching, internal segmentation, Intrusion Detection and Prevention Systems, and an in-depth look at applying the principles of this book in the Chapter 11. So, why would we stick the boring topic of network management right smack in the middle of all this excitement?

The answer is simple: before we dive head first, we need to make sure the lifeguard is on duty. Now is the time to discuss management of the network, *before* you spend a bunch of time designing an unmanageable beast of a network. Most people will tell you that network management is a boring task relegated to caffeine-addicted network operations center (NOC) drones who just wait for the big red button to light up—not true! The true bragging rights of the network engineer come from being able to measure your successes in bar graphs and pie charts, suitable for board-room meetings. What we discuss in this chapter will allow you to quantify all the late hours that you spend in the wiring closets and data centers, and prove to the budget steering committee that it really *was* worth the extra $100k to outfit all floors with managed switches instead of dumb hubs (see Chapter 7 for more information on managed switches—but not before you finish this chapter!).

In the next section, we present five basic network management principles that will guide us through setting up our "Mission Control" center (space helmet optional). As a glimpse into the segmentation discussion in Chapter 11, we are going to discuss the concept of a management network and how to best keep things segregated on that network. No management network is complete without some form of transport layer encryption (this is the one network that will have far-reaching control over your entire infrastructure, so you're going to be highly motivated to keep prying eyes away). We will present IPSec and other VPN technologies as a way of maintaining the integrity and confidentiality of your management tools. Then, we will see those five network management principles applied in a sampling of popular tools, running the full gamut from free open-source tools, to high-end five-figure enterprise management suites of applications. At the end of the day, you'll have a room full of blinking lights that would bring a tear to any NASA scientist's heart.

Network Management and Security Principles

Like any good chapter with the word *management* in the title (be it Business, Sewage Treatment, or Network Management), you have come to expect the body of knowledge boiled down into a handy wallet-sized version that can serve to guide us throughout the rest of the chapter. Well, we certainly don't like to disappoint, so we have summarized all you'll ever need to know about network management into five very broad security principles that we will refer back to throughout the rest of this chapter. In addition, if you are one of the first 1000 readers to turn the page, we will even throw in a diagram at no extra charge

Figure 6.1 Network Management Principle Pentagon

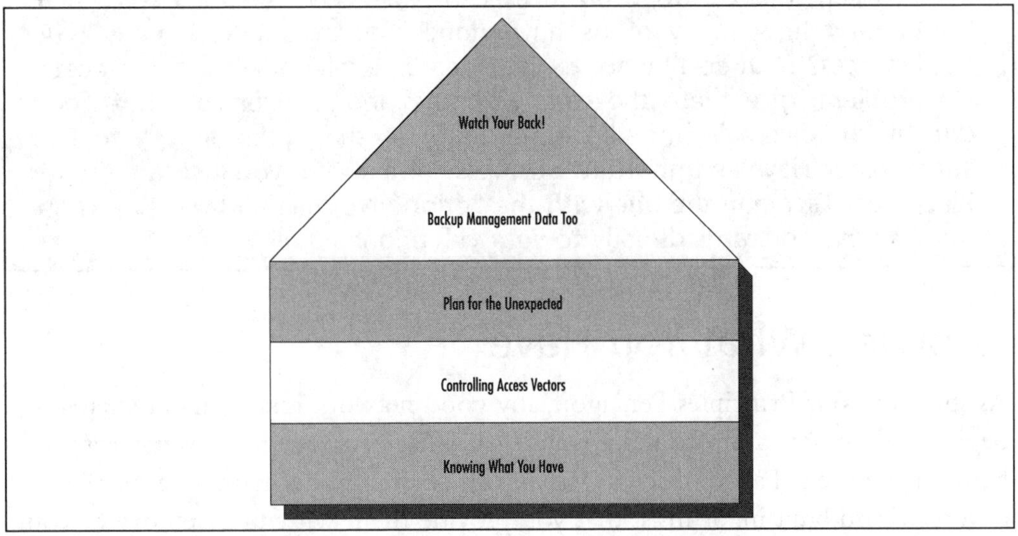

As you can see from Figure 6.1, after you have a solid foundation with Knowing What You Have, Controlling Access Vectors, and Planning for the Unexpected, you are ready to build on that with intelligent backups of your most critical management data. The pinnacle of our diagram is Watching Your

Back, where we introduce prudent security measures that can dramatically decrease your exposure to electronic eavesdropping, and with any luck turn you into an appropriately fearful, paranoid security engineer who encrypts everything, including your business cards.

Notes from the Underground…

Specially Coded Business Cards

While it might seem insane to encrypt your business cards that you hand out to people, there is something to be said for *encoding* them. We're not going to confess to any of our tricks, but let's just say that some people have different versions of business cards printed at work, all with different extension numbers for our telephone, as well as slight variations in e-mail addresses (sandres@securitysageguide.com versus stevea@securitysageguide.com versus steve.andres@securitysageguide.com).

Need to drop off a business card to receive a cool T-shirt at a booth (and how many of us have done that at one too many RSA Conferences?), but don't want to get listed on a telemarketer's call sheet? No problem; give them the card with the phone extension that goes directly to voicemail, and the e-mail address that goes directly to the spam folder. Have an important business contact that you just ran into at Black Hat? Give him the one with the "priority" e-mail and the extension number that forwards directly to your cell phone.

Knowing What You Have

As shown in our Principles Pentagon, any good network management strategy begins with an inventory to get a handle on what you have in your environment. Most of the tools that we discuss later in this chapter either have a network discovery wizard built in, or insist that you provide them with an inventory of your networking devices as part of their initial setup. If you've been reading along with us, we covered the importance of network asset inventory back in Chapter 2. We also covered a number of great tools to make this (sometimes dreaded) task a lot more manageable (pun intended).

The importance of an asset inventory cannot be overstated. Without a detailed list, you will not know where to spend most of your dollars and most of your time. If you have relatively few Windows machines, there hardly seems to be a reason to invest money in a Microsoft SMS solution. By the same token, if you have very few UNIX servers, using a management system based on *rshell* and *rexec* commands would be impractical at best.

Controlling Access Vectors

Once you have a snazzy-looking network map and a detailed asset inventory in front of you, it becomes a lot easier to see all of the access vectors to your information resources. An access vector is any conduit or method with which an unauthorized or authorized user can view, manipulate, or erase sensitive data. The most common access vectors are summarized in Table 6.1.

Table 6.1 Common Access Vectors

Name	Method/Conduit
Console	Direct access to the file server's keyboard, or the firewall/router's serial configuration port.
Shoulder-Surf	Peering over one's shoulder to watch keystrokes.
Local Subnet	Computers within same collision domain might eavesdrop or attack.
Local Network	Computers within the same network might be able to attack information resource.
Wireless	Often overlooked, this includes both authorized and hostile wireless connections.
Dial-Up Modem	Legacy dial-up modem pools can be a dangerous vector if not managed correctly.
VPN	Virtual private network (VPN) connections that come through the firewall should watched.
Internet	Anything that your firewall does not block can become an access vector.
Malicious Outbound	Don't forget that sensitive data transmissions can originate inside and be destined for malicious hosts beyond your firewall.

While you certainly can't annotate every variation of an access vector on your network map, it can be beneficial to call special attention to VPN, dial-up, and wireless connections, since those are so easily ignored during security planning. Contemporary wisdom brings us to conclude that everything in the big cloud labeled "Internet" is bad (or potentially hostile), and everything on this side of the firewall is good. However, that's not always the case. While every network is different and you must craft your own strategy using the constraints placed before you, we will attempt to provide some guidance on minimizing your risk exposure for these attack vectors. This isn't a "How To" chapter; it is about guidance and principles and tips to get you started.

Console

While it is undoubtedly the most damaging access vector, *console* access is also the easiest to mitigate. This access vector can, by definition, only be used if there is direct, physical access to the hardware in question (router, firewall, file server, database, etc.). If the attacker can actually walk right up to the device and touch it, then you know you're in trouble. The best password policy in the world won't stop the attacker from popping open the case and walking out the door with your hard drives. With your data safely at home, she can spend days or weeks with password-cracking programs to try to get at your data. In reality, there are backdoor methods to avoid password protections altogether that take less than an hour. Or, the attacker could not even care about the data for herself, but instead just use it to extort money from the victim (perhaps resulting in a public relations backlash should this incident be reported to the mainstream media).

Make absolutely sure that you have appropriate physical access controls in place wherever there is in information storage device. This includes not only your nicely chilled "showcase" NOC with the smoked glass windows and the multimillion-dollar fire suppression system, but also each and every one of your wiring closest and server rooms. Now, notice that we said *appropriate* physical access controls; while you might need a state-of-the-art proximity card system for your NOC, your wiring closets might be okay with just a good, solid deadbolt lock. The point is to have something—anything—to prevent a casual tinkerer or a determined attacker from laying their hands on your information. If all he has to do is reach under the receptionist's desk to find your HR database—and don't tell me you haven't heard of *that* urban legend—you have not exercised proper controls. If the attacker has to saw through a deadbolt (and thus making quite a ruckus) to get to your hubs and switches, you have succeeded.

NOTE

More information about physical access controls can be found toward the end of Chapter 2, as well as the Network Management Tools section later in this chapter.

Shoulder-Surf

We've all seen the "shoulder-surfer" in action. The login prompt comes up on the screen, and the coworker next to you leans in uncomfortably close so that he can watch your keystrokes as you type them, hoping to capture your password. The usual mitigation technique for this is to either type ridiculously fast, such that your coworker can't keep up, or give him a menacing stare and tell him to back off. Both are troublesome. We even know some people who will make mistakes on purpose in their passwords and use the backspace key frequently while typing, so that the potential shoulder-surfer gets confused in the process.

We're going to stop short of embarrassing ourselves by telling you about cultural etiquette and proper personal space issues; anyone who has seen either of us eating lunch can tell you that etiquette is something we do not list on our résumés. However, besides the obvious mitigation step of having others turn their heads, another (more techie) method is to employ two-factor authentication. In this strategy, the user only has a short PIN to enter, and the rest of the "password" is made up of a short-lived numerical sequence (the "token code") that appears on a key fob, credit card-sized device, or Palm Pilot applet. If the annoying individual next to you leans in for a peek, chances are he will spy your token code and not your PIN, since it is more easily read. The look on his face when he realizes that the number is only valid for the next 59 seconds is quite priceless!

Notes from the Underground…

Take My Token… Please!

I'm definitely anything but tactful when it comes to personal-space issues. I'll either ask someone to move out of the way and turn their head, or I will just move them out of my way and turn their head. That being said, I must confess that I did lose my patience with a particular shoulder-surfer back when I was working for the University of California. We will call him "Tim" (since that was his name). UCLA had invested heavily in the SecurID two-factor authentication system for their centralized billing and campus authentication project, and all staff members were issued big 3- x 5-inch token cards and instructed to never put them in their wallet (although they were wallet sized). Eager to learn about all the access privileges that he did not possess on the IBM ES9000 Supercomputer that ran the Bruins' über-database, Tim would always get especially close and intimate with you as you went to log in. It became so bad that at one point, I just handed him my token and asked him to read the "password" off to me! Little did he know that I used the diversion to enter in my PIN without observation, before sliding the keyboard over to him and having him enter the token code (which would expire in a matter of seconds). Shortly after this little stunt (about 10 seconds after, with time still ticking down on the SecurID), Tim excused himself to rush to the "bathroom" and apparently made a pit stop at his desk to attempt a login using my credentials.

Not only did Tim not have my PIN (only my token code, which was invalidated as soon as I used it no matter how much time was left), he also received a call from Academic Information Services, the campus' authentication police. After a four-hour "tutorial" on the punishments associated with California Penal Code section 500 (unauthorized access to a State-owned computer system), Tim was relocated to a Circuit City nearby, where he now enjoys snooping on credit-card numbers and pestering senior citizens with extended warranty sales pitches.

If you're interested in learning more about two-factor authentication, a number of white papers at vendor Web sites are definitely worth reading. The major player in this market is RSA Security, with their SecurID tokens, but you can also find similar token solutions from ActivCard, Authenex, CryptoCard, and Rainbow. Links to vendor Web sites are listed at the end of this chapter.

Tools & Traps…

A SecurID by Any Other Name

Although there are a number of vendors out there sporting two-factor authentication options (a recent search on Google revealed 31,400 hits), our favorite is still the original: the SecurID token from Security Dynamics, which later purchased RSA Security and adopted the acquired name. Many newer vendors have tokens in the form of USB keys, but we prefer the rugged design and simplicity of the RSA SecurID key fob. Newer models even employ the *Rijndael* cipher, also known as the Advanced Encryption Standard (AES), newly certified from the U.S. Government.

Notes from the Underground…

Alien Technology?

DES (the data encryption standard), which was the encryption standard for over 20 years, was replaced in 2000 by AES (Advanced Encryption Standard). AES is based upon the *Rijndael* block cipher written by Joan Daemen and Vincent Rijmen, two Flemish gentlemen from Belgium. Since the 70's, the United States had very strict regulations governing the export of crypto outside of the United States. These regulations were 'relaxed' in 1999 and quickly afterward, the encryption standard adopted by NIST and the US Government was a 'foreign' one that could not have legally moved across US borders just months before…

Local Subnet

Machines that are located within the same *collision domain* of one another will, by definition, be able to see each other's network traffic. This is usually the case when you are using hubs; with network switches, each port becomes its own collision domain and these issues are not present. Note that at aggregation points, again by definition, all the traffic will be aggregated into one stream, which can lend itself to eavesdropping. However, the point of this access vector is the ease with which machines, within the same collision domain of the information resource, can eavesdrop on data bound for the file server, and requests being ful-filled back out to workstations.

The easiest mitigation step for this attack vector is also one that will greatly increase network performance; replace all of your hubs with manageable switches and you can (practically) cross this attack vector right off your list. See Chapter 7 for an extended discussion on collision domains, broadcast domains, hubs, switches, and beef jerky (we're not kidding).

Local Network

The access vector that we're calling *local network* is your run-of-the-mill network-based attack, with an emphasis on ones originating within the "trusted" part of your network infrastructure. These are the ones that can surprise you at 3 A.M. on any given Sunday because you assume (perhaps incorrectly) that anyone within your organization would have no reason to maliciously pilfer information from your databases. Even the world's largest Internet service provider, America Online (AOL), fell victim to this attack vector.

Notes from the Underground…

AOL SecurID Bypass

With your personal bias for or against AOL aside, you have to admit that they do have a pretty amazing user membership. Accordingly, their internal customer information systems must have high security. One such system (which has since been replaced) was the Customer Records Information System (CRIS), which held sensitive information on more than 23 million subscribers. The system was engineered with two-factor

Continued

authentication (using RSA SecurID tokens), but was set to implicitly trust all "on campus" connections from within the AOL headquarters.

Some former AOL employees knew the architecture of CRIS and knew that it was much too difficult to try to hack the SecurID system to access CRIS remotely. Instead, they just needed to compromise an internal machine, and redirect all requests via that workstation. Sadly for AOL Customer Service, this was not very difficult. In June 2000, through the normal coercion that happens in every spam message we all receive, a particularly non-savvy customer service representative clicked on a link that launched a malicious Web site (www.computerworld.com/security-topics/security/story/0,10801,46090,00.html). Therein, an ActiveX control was loaded and (thanks to the user clicking "YES") executed on the internal AOL computer. From there, it was quite easy for the attacker to route requests via this workstation. Since the CRIS security architects made the assumption that internal requests were always valid (and thus ignoring the *local network* attack vector), millions of subscribers were affected.

Since that time, AOL has changed their authentication methods to always use SecurID two-factor authentication regardless of internal or external connections, and has since rewritten their internal systems (calling the new system "Merlin"). Sadly, once again an AOL customer service rep was tricked into accepting (and executing) a file transfer via instant messaging in February 2003 (www.wired.com/news/infostructure/0,1377,57753,00.html). Although the new Merlin application required a username, two passwords, and a SecurID token, using elementary social engineering and spoofed e-mails from AOL Operations, attackers were able to gain access to the Merlin database of 35 million subscribers!

We don't mean to beat up on the AOL security engineers—we're sure they're kept quite busy and we would probably have just as difficult a time securing a network that big across an employee community of very differing skill levels. However, if nothing else, it makes you consider the local network attack vector in an entirely new light, as well as ponder the wisdom in allowing these customer service workstations to access the Internet at all.

And if that doesn't get you thinking, just sit back and consider that their customer database went from 23 million to 35 million in just three years! Guess all those CDs by mail really do have an effect.

Wireless

The time might soon come when all of us feel completely safe in deploying a wireless segment of our networks. As of our publication date, that level of comfort is still not there. From a corporate security engineer's point of view, there simply isn't enough benefit to outweigh the potential security costs introduced by wireless networks. Unfortunately, sometimes other parts of the company (Sales, Marketing, Executives) have more pull in IT efforts than those in security, and the convenience of a wireless local area network (WLAN) is demanded by many these days.

If you are one of the many who have been forced to (or perhaps willingly) install a wireless network, you should definitely pay close attention to these attack vectors and note them with some ridiculously bright yellow highlighting in your network map. Some mapping tools mentioned in Chapter 2 even use a different icon for wireless access points (WAPs) to make your job of identifying them easier. After documenting all of the WAPs throughout your network, it wouldn't be a bad idea to hire an outside firm to "sweep" through your building(s) to make sure that no unauthorized WAPs have found their way on your network. With the price point of these devices going south of $50, don't be surprised to find a WAP right next to the chewing gum and tabloids in the "impulse buy" section of your supermarket.

Make sure to consider the attack vectors introduced by both unauthorized and authorized wireless workstations. The unauthorized threat is pretty obvious: someone can park across the street, point a Pringles can at your building, and get to your HR intranet—even the U.S. Secret Service is using the popular potato chip receptacle as part of their regular security sweeps (www.computerworld.com/mobiletopics/mobile/story/0,10801,74806,00.html).

What you might not consider at first is the danger posed by *authorized* wireless connections. All too often, these connections are not encrypted, or the machines themselves are subject to compromise because they lack some form of personal firewall software installed. A study performed by AirDefense (a WLAN security vendor) in April 2003 showed that 88 percent of wireless connections at a Boston trade show are unencrypted. Additionally, some WLAN workstations were configured to connect to *any* WAP available, putting your corporate workstation (and any information on it) at risk if it were to connect with a WAP run by an attacker (referred to as a "rogue access point"). Without a personal firewall and by associating with these rogue access points, an attacker could compromise the security of your sales executive's laptop using any number of common exploits, install a Trojan program to record keystrokes, and then sit back and wait for the laptop to wander back to your access point. Even with encryption enabled, the Trojan would be able to piggyback on the authorized wireless connection, retrieve sensitive information, and transmit it back to the attacker. Make sure you are aware of both authorized and rogue access points operating within or near your building.

Dial-Up Modem

Some of you reading this might never have heard of a "Shiva" before, but those who have will know it is synonymous with dial-up modem pools that were popular before broadband Internet access was made available to most U.S. homes. If your company does have these legacy dial-up modem pools, you should definitely run—not walk—to your nearest VPN vendor and plan a strategy to phase them out. With high-speed Internet access down to $30/month in some areas, there just isn't much sense in having a dozen phone lines (each with minimum telco charges, usage charges, and perhaps even toll-free surcharges if your company provides that) waiting to accept connections.

If you used that yellow highlighter we talked about in the previous section for the wireless segments, you should use a red marker to circle any leftover dial-up modem pools. These usually sit behind the firewall, and aren't heavily guarded. Anyone in the world with a dial tone can reach your modem pool and attempt to log in. While brute-forcing a VPN password over a few weeks will definitely be noted in the firewall logs and the IDS logs, it would be quite believable to hear that the dial-up pool either performs no logging, or that logs are almost never reviewed, since the connections are assumed to be trusted.

Tools & Traps...

Who Is Shiva?

Many vendors exist (or existed) for dial-up networking services, but the name Shiva stands out among the rest of them. Their LANrover series of connectivity products was quite popular, and we've come across it on a number of engagements. Luckily for us on the attack and penetration team, these devices almost always have single-factor (password) authentication, which is easily brute-forced (set password = username, or try a blank password). Worse yet, the default administrator password of "shiva" is almost never changed.

The Shiva LANrover was an excellent product, don't get us wrong. It's just a technology that has come and gone, and now needs to take its place on the shelf along with eight-track tapes and laser discs.

Virtual Private Networks

VPN connections are a difficult attack vector to visualize. Often times, your VPN device is also your border firewall. In some large installations, dedicated VPN concentrators such as the Cisco 3005 VPN Concentrator (formerly the Altiga 3005) perform all the encryption services and offload the number crunching from the main firewall. In both cases, you must consider the authentication methods used as well as the authorization to use network resources.

If your firewall is performing VPN services, you at least have one thing going for you: your firewall definitely has knowledge of the VPN traffic. If you run a separate VPN concentrator, this might not be the case. Most times, dedicated VPN concentrators are installed "next to" the corporate firewall (meaning they have one interface on the Internet and the other interface connected to the internal network), rather than being in-line with the corporate firewall. This means that while an attacker might not be able to attempt too many telnet connections to your firewall's outside interface without your IDS becoming suspicious, you might be ignoring the same type of probing on the VPN concentrator.

Once a workstation makes a connection to the VPN concentrator (or VPN services running on your firewall), what authentication methods are used? Again, more is better in this case, and we like to see two-factor strong authentication used in conjunction with these devices. The good news is that the integration between VPN concentrators and back-end authentication systems running RADIUS (discussed later in this chapter) is quite mature. You should be able to add two-factor authentication to your VPN deployment without too much configuration hassle (there will, of course, be a hefty price tag).

After successfully authenticating to the VPN concentrator or firewall, the big question is, *just what is that remote user authorized to connect to?* It's not enough to be satisfied with authentication; you must consider the dangers involved in providing remote users with unrestricted authorization throughout your internal network. Because these remote connections are likely from machines that are outside of your control (home computers) or that your IT team only maintains infrequently (a traveling salesperson with months' old anti-virus signatures is a common occurrence), you must have a healthy amount of distrust for these machines. Most VPN installations we have seen on our customer engagements are architected such that once a user is connected, he is on the local network and is able to do anything and contact any machine he pleases.

This is quite dangerous! Imagine if your vice president's young son was able to reach the keyboard during a currently logged-in session. In the process of downloading the latest Jennifer Garner movie from an illegal warez site, his son was also able to infect that laptop and spread—via the *authorized* and *authenticated* VPN connection—to the rest of the internal network.

It is for this reason that we suggest quarantining VPN connections so that they are only allowed to connect to essential servers, and that they are given IP address assignments from a completely different DHCP pool than normal users, so you can easily identify them. In Figure 6.2, we see a suggested topology where the VPN users have a dedicated network segment for their connections, apart from normal internal workstations. Furthermore, the VPN service network is only connected to the resource network (housing directory services, e-mail, etc.). Even if someone were to compromise a VPN session or even one of your remote users' computers, she would not be able to connect to the HR database or any Accounting data stores.

Figure 6.2 Sample Topology Showing Dedicated VPN, Resource, Management, and DMZ Service Networks

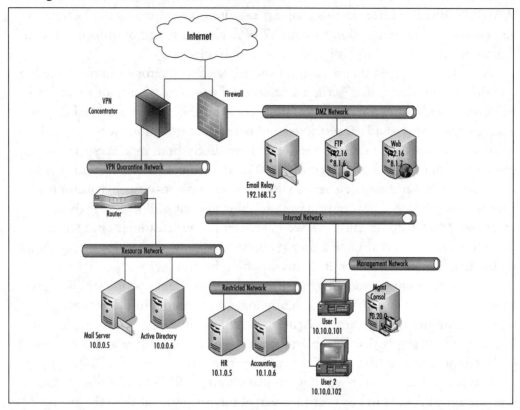

Figure 6.2 illustrates the concept of a highly segmented network, and we will showcase the benefits to a dedicated management network later in this chapter. Don't let the complexity of the diagram distract you from the concept behind it; the more you can segment your network and classify the traffic that traverses it, the easier your management task becomes.

Internet

At last, we arrive at the one access vector that you knew you had all along: the big wide world of the Internet. If you are living in the 21st century and your network doesn't have some form of connection to the Internet, you probably have a good reason for it (perhaps a military network with an "air gap" defense). For the other 99 percent of us, we must treat the Internet very seriously when we consider attack vectors. By just sliding in one rather small RJ45 cable into your firewall, you have now allowed the 6.4 billion inhabitants of Earth (or, more accurately, the small percentage of those Earthlings who have Internet access) an opportunity to invade your network. We all knew that this was an important attack vector, so there's no sense in convincing you of it now. The fear of Internet-based attacks is inherent in any modern network, and should continue to be feared and respected for many years to come.

Malicious Outbound

A malicious outbound attack vector is one where the "attack" is usually invited (whether it should be is another story) and the damage is in the opposite direction in which most of your equipment is designed to detect. Much like the example of the AOL customer service rep that we presented earlier, it is quite easy to convince a less-savvy computer user at an organization to click on a URL within an e-mail, open an e-mail attachment, or accept a file transfer from an unknown person on instant messaging (IM). The process is illustrated succinctly in Figure 6.3.

Figure 6.3 Malicious Outbound Connections Can Lead to Information

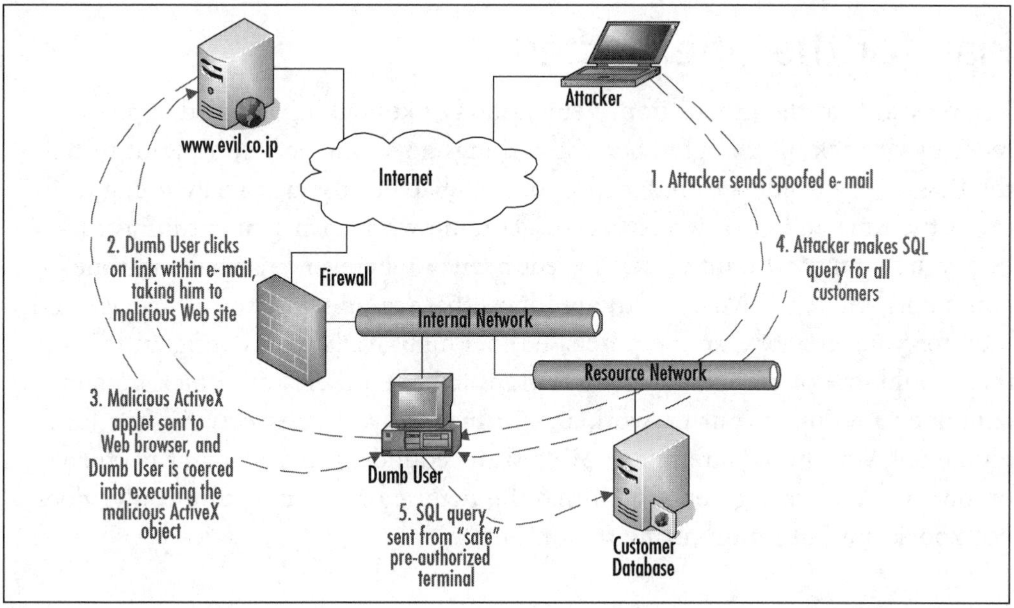

The attack begins with a spoofed e-mail from the organization's IT team or upper management, usually sent to a wide distribution of employees (just to make

sure the attack works). The next phase involves convincing the user to click on the link, execute the attachment, or save the files sent via IM. Once this Trojan software installs itself, the attacker has remote control over the victim's machine. The attacker wastes no time, and runs a query of the customer database, but routed via the victim's computer, so that the database server believes that (and logs as such) the request is coming from the (assumed to be genuine) workstation. This, as you can imagine, can lead to a great deal of information disclosure and a huge public relations blemish should the newspapers find out about this.

So, what can be done about this and where do you use the highlighter on the topology map? You can put the highlighter away. There isn't just one conduit that might have malicious intentions; there is a potential for hundreds of attack vectors (one for each computer that sits on your internal, trusted segment). The key to mitigating this attack vector is employee education and a strongly enforced, written security policy for your network. If there is no business reason to be accepting file transfers from a stranger during business hours, make sure that this is not being done! If you have outsourced call centers to other countries, make sure they uphold the same high standards as you do at corporate headquarters. Stay vigilant!

Plan for the Unexpected

Yes, we can hear the groans from here: nobody likes talking about disaster recovery or backup strategies, but when things go south, you don't want to tell the boss that you skipped that section of the chapter. If you're really going to invest the time and energy to create a secure network management infrastructure, you're going to want to add in redundancy wherever financial and time constraints will allow. Many of the products that we present later to manage and monitor your network can be purchased in a high-availability configuration, so that should one of the management stations fail, the other would pick up and continue to monitor your network and/or manage your network. As shown in Figure 6.4, you should attempt to place your redundant management platforms on diverse network segments, such that the demise of one upstream router does not knock out both monitoring stations.

Figure 6.4 Redundant Management Stations on Diverse Network Segments

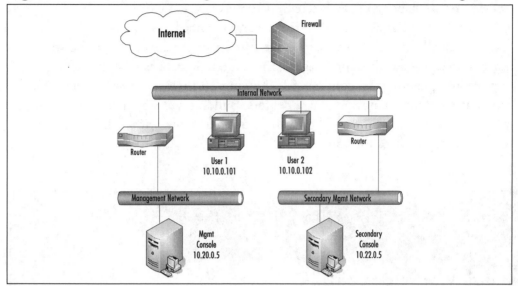

For more demanding monitoring needs, your organization can contract with third-party monitoring services (such as those provided by Keynote, www.keynote.com) that can check on the status of your externally facing equipment (such as Web servers, mail servers, and FTP sites) several times per minute and from different parts of the world. While your local management station might claim that your Web site is online, it might have different latency characteristics depending on your originating IP address. The real benefit here is if you are, for example, a multinational swimsuit company with Web order placement; it might be of interest to you that your site loads extremely slow from Thailand and is completely offline if you're in Australia. If you run a secure corporate network, it is much more important to know about some internal distribution-layer switch or router that failed. Third-party monitoring services will never be able to give you that level of detail because the devices are tucked away behind your border firewall.

Depending on how mission-critical your network management activities become, you might also want to invest in a secondary NOC, sometimes referred to as a "hot site" because it can be activated at a moment's notice and you can start managing your entire network from that location. If you were a nationwide insurance company with a centralized NOC that controls thousands of branch offices, you would definitely be interested in a secondary base of operations. If you are like most network administrators, with important but *not mission-critical* network operations, you will be quite happy with some off-site data backup storage, and perhaps some drills to simulate network outages.

After the 9/11 attacks in New York, many financial customers of ours immediately began "hot site" projects, to make sure that they are ready should something of that magnitude happen again. In fact, one large financial institution is even running nationwide commercials showing off their multi-site operations center and redundant-powered data centers. Building your own "hot site" can be quite expensive, and you should probably consider going with a third party that provides these services for you.

Tools & Traps…

Hot, Warm, or Cold?

A "hot site" is named that for the same reasons why "hot swappable" hard drives have that designation. The hard drives can be changed at a moment's notice and without rebooting. A hot site can be placed into operation in a matter of minutes, which is very comforting to the board of directors and shareholders. However, for this level of comfort, there is a great deal of cost. All information resources must be duplicated, and any database records that are updated need to be synchronized to the hot site almost instantaneously.

A "cold site" is one that has most of the infrastructure to take over network operations, but perhaps not any of the real high-ticket items (like large database servers). This is the least costly solution and works great when you just need a second base of operations online within a couple of days. This allows enough time for you to order off-site backup tapes to be delivered to the cold site, new equipment to be purchased, and network routing rules to change.

A nice middle ground to both of these options is a "warm site," which can come online within hours. As you can expect, the costs lay somewhere between the hot and cold sites, but the benefits are great. You can't just flick a switch and have all of your network operations move from New York to Iowa, but with a good deal of coordination, some courier-delivered backup tapes, and a lot of coffee, you should be able to pull off a company-saving miracle before dawn.

Continued

> The costs involved in doing this yourself are rather high (unless you're of the Fortune 500 variety). Don't try to reinvent the wheel; seek the help of third-party companies that specialize in disaster recovery, such as VeriCenter (www.vericenter.com/products/disasterrecovery). They offer hot, warm, and cold sites, as well as other managed services.

In addition, the most mundane but often overlooked measure of redundancy is to make sure that any notification procedures used by your notification and network monitoring tools have multiple paths. This means that notifications shouldn't be e-mail only (what if the e-mail server is down?). Make sure that your notification options include telephone, alphanumeric pager, SMS cellular, FAX, and print-out options.

Back Up Your Management, Too

While this is the least glamorous of the network management principles, it definitely has its place among the other four. Many times, we are aware of the sensitive nature of our customer database, our financial records, and other company-specific information stores. All of these will likely have a backup method and rotation that is far outside the scope of this book. However, what is often overlooked is the value—and indeed, the importance—of your network management systems. In case of disaster, you will certainly worry about your customers and other revenue-generating databases first. However, after the initial shock wears off, you will likely lament the loss of your network management system if you have failed to include it in your normal backup procedures.

Perhaps nightly backups are too cumbersome, but certainly monthly backups of your network management and monitoring systems are in order. The costs involved in adding your management stations to your existing backup jobs are nearly nonexistent. Even if you don't want to add the management systems to your regular backup, burning everything (system Registry settings and *init* scripts included) to a CD-R and taking it home with you certainly isn't an enormous amount of effort. This management principle is satisfied if you employ the use of hot/warm/cold sites, which practically require the backup of management systems along with the data-centric devices.

Watch Your Back

The final suggestion, and the pinnacle of our principle pentagon (try to say that 10 times fast!), is a caution to "Watch Your Back!" At each stage in designing your network management solution, consider a healthy dose of paranoia as your best yardstick. Your network management console will be able to monitor bandwidth as well as deactivate routes. With a flick of the mouse, you could quite easily (and hopefully accidentally) bring your network to a screeching halt. Therefore, you need to take an ounce of prevention in everything that you do regarding your management network. There's definitely a reason why we called the chapter "*Secure* Network Management."

Authentication

The first part of a healthy paranoia is finding out whom you can trust. Put in network management terms, this means who are your authorized managers? If you're reading this chapter, certainly you probably fit into this short list, but who else should be allowed to control your network resources? Make sure to include people who can fill in for you when you are sick or away on vacation (okay, that last part was a joke; we know that you don't actually take vacation).

Once you have compiled this list, you have to determine how these people can be authenticated and how this authentication is embodied in the myriad of network management equipment available. As discussed previously, two-factor authentication is very attractive because it is hard to compromise. You not only need to know a username and a PIN, but also a temporary, ever-changing code that can only be obtained by physical possession of a key fob or calculator-sized token. The two-factor authentication server (in the case of the RSA SecurID system, the back-end is referred to as the "ACE Authentication Server") will make the determination as to whether the username + PIN + token code is genuine, but that is all it will do. Authentication is just a matter of saying you are who you say you are, but it does not allow you to do anything. That is the function of the *authorization* method you choose.

Even if you don't choose a two-factor system and decide to use password-based authentication instead, you still need a centralized server to store all this information. You're definitely not going to enjoy setting up (or removing) user accounts from all your managed devices, and you certainly don't want to use general-purpose accounts that are shared among a number of people. All managers should have their own login credentials so that audit trails and activity logs can actually have some meaning behind them, and so that we know who to point the finger at when things mysteriously stop working in the middle of the night. So, what's the best way to centralize all this information?

Most authentication vendors (be it the RSA ACE Authentication Server, or otherwise) will have a service or daemon that you can run on one of your less-used servers. This will accept the authentication requests and respond with a thumbs-up or a thumbs-down. Almost all of the solutions on the market today will support the RADIUS protocol, which allows for cross-vendor (and cross-platform) integration of billing technologies (and was originally developed for the big phone company in the early 1970s) and authentication. Using a RADIUS server (or more likely, a proprietary authentication server that speaks the RADIUS protocol), your individual network devices will be able to inter-communicate and decide on access to configuration functions. A similar, but incompatible, authentication protocol is TACACS+ (Terminal Access Controller Access Control System Plus), developed in June 1993 and documented in RFC 1492 (www.faqs.org/rfcs/rfc1492.html). TACACS+ (and its predecessor, TACACS without the +) has been all but replaced by RADIUS in most networks, with Cisco being the most notable hardware vendor that still has strong roots in TACACS+.

To use this centralized user authentication system, it's just a matter of configuring your network devices to forego their internal database of users and instead consult the local RADIUS or TACACS+ server for user logon requests. To enable TACACS+ on a Cisco 1720 router and have it consult the authentication server located at 192.2.0.22, the appropriate commands issued in configuration mode would be:

```
Router(config)# aaa new-model
Router(config)# aaa authentication login default tacacs+ enable
Router(config)# aaa authentication enable default tacacs+ enable
Router(config)# tacacs-server host 192.2.0.22
Router(config)# ip tacacs source-interface loopback0
```

This would instruct the router to contact the TACACS+ server at 192.2.0.22 for authentication duties during initial login (line two) as well as for entering privileged mode (line three, also called "enable mode"). If the TACACS+ server cannot be located, the authentication method will fall back on the standard Cisco IOS "enable" password.

RADIUS servers are available on almost all flavors of UNIX, Novell NetWare, and Microsoft Windows. You can even use some tools to integrate directly with your Novell NDS (now called eDirectory) or Microsoft Active Directory directory services, thus eliminating the need to have separate accounts at all, and giving users the added benefit of single-sign-on (and no reason to forget their network management password).

Tools & Traps…

And Liberty and RADIUS for All

It's not too hard to find a RADIUS server that will slip right into your existing network architecture without breaking the bank. If you are a Novell-centric organization, check out Novell BorderManager Authentication Services, which is a souped-up version of the Novell RADIUS Service for NDS announced in September 1997. Microsoft bundles a RADIUS server with its Internet Authentication Service, available in their Windows 2000 and Windows Server 2003 server products. And when in doubt, you can visit Funk Software and read up on Steel Belted RADIUS, their humorously named authentication server. They've been around since 1992 and have some very educational white papers available on their site, www.funksoftware.com.

Authorization

Once someone has established his identity to the satisfaction of your authentication server, the process of authorization begins. This is usually very simple and can be summarized succinctly: you're here, now what do you want? In most cases, such as the Cisco router configuration noted previously, the thumbs-up signal from the authentication server will just authorize the user to connect to the network device. Other times, the authentication server itself plays a bit of the authorization role, by storing certain access-level information and providing that to network devices when asked.

It is important to remember that it is the network device that is performing the authorization (in other words, allowing itself to be placed in configuration mode, etc.). The authentication server might provide hints as to the users' access levels, but it does not dictate them. The authorizing device must be willing to accept and enforce those hints. Using the Cisco Secure Access Control Server

(ACS), shown in Figure 6.5,you can set a user's privilege level 7, (for instance, 15 is the default, signifying full administrator, and 1 is the guest level of access) and thus restrict which commands he/she may issue on the router.

Figure 6.5 Configuring Network Devices Using Secure ACS

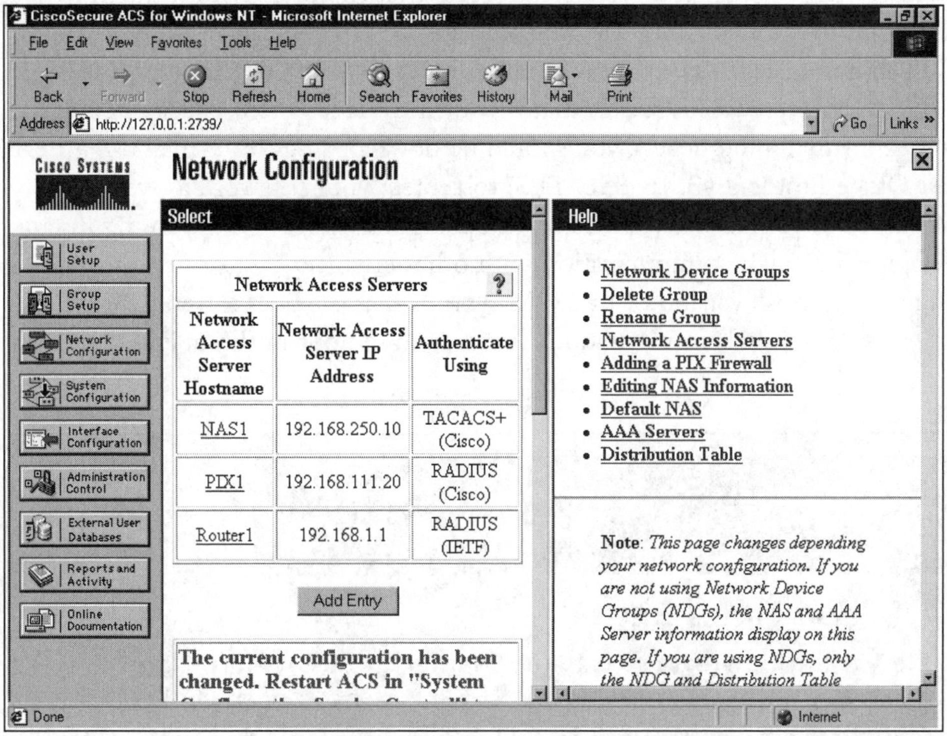

Encryption

The easiest piece of paranoia-avoidance to employ is also the most powerful. Encryption is so very critical to a network management strategy. We saw in Chapter 2 how easy it is to sniff packets off the network wire. What if, while you were using a network management tool to log in to a remote router, someone on your local subnet was able to intercept that password being transmitted during that telnet login session? Certainly, all the authentication and authorization schemes that you have worked so hard on will now be useless.

Nothing on your management network should be transmitted in clear text, if possible. You should never use telnet to log in to a router, firewall, or managed switch. Insist on using Secure Shell (SSH) for your management logins. If your network equipment doesn't support an encrypted management method, you should demand this feature from your vendor. SSH should be used whenever telnet would have been used previously. Any management tasks that are performed using Simple Network Management Protocol (SNMP) should use a nondefault community string (in other words, not "public"), and you should strive to use SNMPv3, which includes encryption. If you are unable to use the newer SNMPv3, you should disable all read-write abilities within the SNMP agents, and use SNMP only for monitoring.

Even nonmanagement network traffic that traverses your management segment should be encrypted. This means that if your help desk system checks a POP mailbox for incoming tickets, you should be downloading this e-mail using POP3S (Post Office Protocol v3, via SSL/TLS) to protect your password as well as the contents of the e-mails. If your network operations team is fond of using instant messaging for quick communication with other engineers, make sure that they are using an enterprise version of these IM systems that provides for encryption, so that sensitive network configurations aren't discussed out in the open.

Tools & Traps...

A Trillion Times Better

After seeing how easy it was (in Chapter 2) to eavesdrop on your network's data packets zooming by, you might be concerned that your IM software is also leaking valuable company information. In fact, it is, but not for the reasons you are thinking. While most folks know that e-mails can be read, inspected, or manipulated in transit, they seem to have made an assumption that IM messages are private (owing to the fact that there is no one central scary IT director to stand in their way). In reality, the network manager can easily read an IM session and perhaps capture more damaging information about the employee's love life, car troubles, and so forth.

If you must use IM products at work, you owe it to yourself to check out Cerulean Studios' Trillian product (www.ceruleanstudios.com). The intent of the software is to bring all your IM protocols together in one utility, to avoid running three sets of IM software. However, the best feature of Trillian is the ability to encrypt all AOL Instant Messenger (AIM) conversations, using what they refer to as SecureIM and 128-bit key

Continued

> lengths. Using Trillian, you are free to comment to your network engineer across the country about network vulnerabilities that you have found, as well as transmit passwords (it's more secure than using the phone!).

Management Networks

In Chapter 3, "Selecting the Correct Firewall," you were introduced to the concept of a demilitarized zone (DMZ) or service network. This is where you should provision all of your servers that are going to need outside access. The reasoning is sound and simple: provide limited external access to a small segment of your network, rather than allowing potentially hostile traffic to enter the "inner sanctum" of your network fortress. In this fashion, any externally launched attacks can only be targeted toward DMZ machines, and any compromised machines in the DMZ will only be able to attack others in this screened subnet (assuming no access from the DMZ to the internal segment). Your external Web-browsing customers can still get to your content, but they can't *ping* the vice president's laptop.

The need to segment your network is paramount. If you are to provide proper management to the rest of the network, this special "control" network segment must be subject to very different rules than other segments are. As we learned in the previous section, encryption on the management network is very important. To be thorough, you would want to make sure to encrypt anything and everything on this network segment, preferably at the network transport layer. This means that you wouldn't have to worry about using telnet or other clear-text protocols because everything on that network would be encrypted. Not only will segmentation aid in defining the boundaries of this "encrypt everything" security policy, it will also greatly ease the creation of access control lists (ACLs) within routers at the edge of the management network.

The firewall (if possible) or router that you place between the internal network and the management network should be configured to only pass a discreet set of management protocols (SNMP, ICMP, etc.) to your management console(s) and only from predetermined management agents. Figure 6.6 depicts a properly filtered management network segment, blocking commonly used (and abused) file-sharing services, but allowing management data to flow to the consoles.

Figure 6.6 Management Network with Firewall Blocking Nonessential Traffic

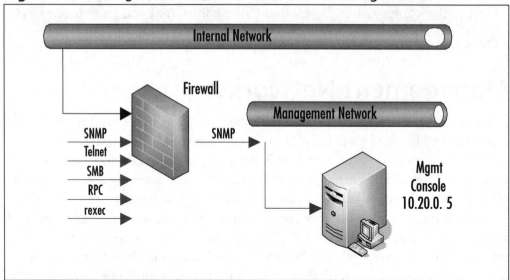

It is recommended to keep your management stations as dedicated consoles, and not used additionally as normal computers (for word processing, e-mail, or web-browsing activities). This also means keeping these machines off your Microsoft domain or Novell NDS tree. These machines should be pure network management and not dependant on your normal IT infrastructure. As stand-alone workstations, you can effectively close off all Microsoft SMB ports (135, 137, 139, 445) and really lock down that firewall policy to ensure security.

IPSec and VPNs

The need for network-level security and encryption on your management segment is essential. The traffic on this network is sensitive by nature, so we must treat it with a different level of care than our usual internal network traffic. As mentioned in previous sections, encrypting the entire contents of this management network segment would be ideal. One way to achieve this goal is to use purpose-built commercial solutions that can divert all traffic through an encrypted tunnel, thus protecting the contents inside. Another solution, somewhat preferred due to the low costs involved, involves using the IP Security (IPSec) suite of protocols to ensure confidentiality and authenticity of network packets.

By performing its functionality at the network layer, IPSec is able to protect data transmissions without any modification to applications or clear-text protocols that lie above the transport layer, and without any changes in the users' functionality. This flexibility is due to the fact that IPSec is an end-to-end encryption strategy; only the two endpoint computers need to be IPSec-aware. The routers, firewalls, and other devices that are along the path between the two do not need to understand (and preferably cannot) the IPSec traffic that is traversing through them. This allows IPSec to be run across very diverse network infrastructures—even over the Internet. You could use IPSec on your management station in California sending traffic to a DNS server in Hong Kong, and the routers and satellite signal relays between the two endpoints (including the ones that are under your control as well as the ones that belong to the ISP) would not have to be reconfigured, as shown in Figure 6.7.

Figure 6.7 IPSec Tunnels Across Diverse Networks

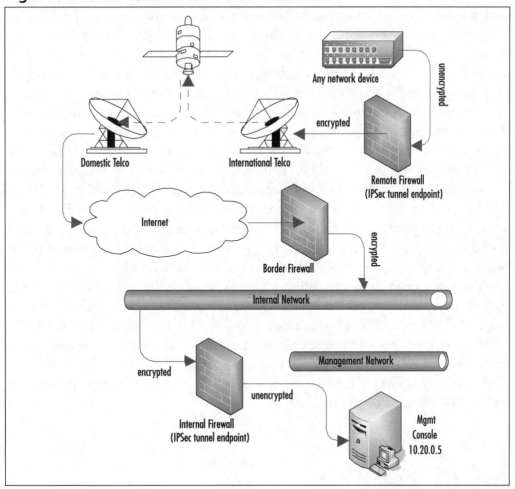

IPSec Modes and Protocols

This use for IPSec is called *transport mode*, in which two endpoints use TCP/IP and the data is secure from the originating machine all the way to the destination device. Another mode for IPSec is *tunnel mode*, in which the IPSec security is performed by the gateway devices nearest the endpoints, but not by the actual endpoints themselves. This is useful sometimes when the end devices are not intelligent enough to speak IPSec, but you still want to provide encryption services. There's no big mystery why it's called "tunnel mode"; the IPSec services on the gateway construct a virtual tunnel between itself and the other gateway, allowing client-to-client communications to flow in the tunnel away from eavesdropping.

As an added bonus, IPSec also allows for a rich set of message authentication, which means you can trust that the source machine identified in the TCP/IP headers is genuine and not spoofed. This is performed by the Authentication Header (AH) protocol, one of two protocols that implement the core IPSec encryption services. AH ensures the integrity of the header data by performing a cryptographic hash on the entire header block. On the receiving end, the same cryptographic hash is computed and compared to the one stored within the AH datagram, to detect if anything has changed in transit. If nobody has changed the headers, the message is genuine and can be trusted. Note that if you are behind a firewall performing NAT for your endpoints, the firewall will *by definition* change the source IP address (in other words, not maliciously), and that will make the AH hash fail. In that case, you would define the IPSec services in tunnel mode, terminating at your firewall (or not use AH). AH does not encrypt any data and thus does not provide confidentiality of your messages. The whole point of AH is proving that the message headers have not been tampered with.

The other major protocol is Encapsulating Security Payload (ESP), which can provide authentication and encryption services. The difference here is that the original TCP header is not authenticated (like in AH). Instead, the ESP header in transport mode is placed between the original header and the TCP header, thus protecting the data payload without fussing with the TCP header. This makes ESP especially useful for NAT-based networks, where the exterior header can and will be changed by the firewalls on either side.

IPSec Configuration Examples

We could spend the better part of an evening discussing the myriad ways to configure and deploy IPSec (trust us—we're a ton of fun at parties!), but we're going to concentrate on two examples that will present a good example on IPSec deployments. Consult your particular hardware vendor's documentation for more specific configuration steps.

Windows 2000 Server

For Windows 2000 Server, an IPSec Policy Agent is built in to the operating system, making IPSec deployments quick and painless. Well, perhaps a little pain, but more of a paper cut than a knife wound. You can make light work of the IPSec configuration process by using one of the three built-in IPSec policies, or you can be really thorough and create your own. Begin by starting the Microsoft Management Console (MMC) named **Local Security Policy**, located under the **Administrative Tools** section of your Start menu. Along the left-hand side, you'll see the **IP Security Policies on Local Machine**. Once that is selected, you will see three built-in IPSec policies in the right pane of the window, as depicted in Figure 6.8.

Figure 6.8 Windows 2000 Built-In IPSec Policies

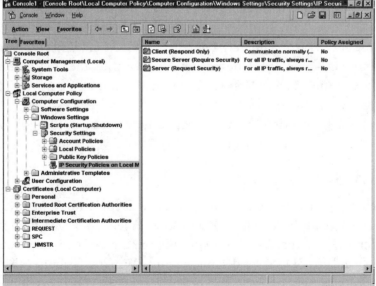

Although you could start from scratch and roll your own policies, the three that are provided are more than enough to get you started. These predefined policies are bidirectional; if you attempt to connect to a non-IPSec machine after enabling one of these policies, the connection will fail. Make sure you troubleshoot all of your connectivity issues prior to tinkering with IPSec. Next, we will briefly examine all three policies.

- **Client (Respond Only)** This policy is used when you want your workstation to be willing to establish an IPSec connection, but only if the other machine requires it. This might come in handy if you are setting up a regular user's workstation. You could safely leave all the users at "Respond Only" and then just enable the file server to require IPSec. For our purposes in network management, we won't be using this policy extensively.

- **Secure Server (Require Security)** This policy is a lot more our style: forceful and demanding. If the other machine does not respond to the IPSec request or is too old to know what IPSec is, the connection will fail. In other words, this policy rigorously enforces encryption with the other network devices at all times. This is going to be the policy that we *want* to use, but it might not be the policy that we are *able* to use, depending on the rest of the network.

- **Server (Request Security)** The final built-in policy is (as you could have guessed) a compromise between the other two. This policy will cause the server to politely request an IPSec tunnel negotiation from the remote machine. If the negotiations fail or the other machine is not IPSec aware (such as Windows NT or Windows 95), an unsecured network session is established. This allows for greater flexibility while you're building up your secure management network and before all of your devices are IPSec capable.

Windows Server 2003

Much of what was said in the previous section will apply for Windows Server 2003, which has virtually the same IPSec Policy Agent packaged with it. Some notable differences are that Win2003 will support the newer Triple Data Encryption Standard (3DES) by default, whereas Win2000 requires the High Encryption Pack or Service Pack 2 in order to support 3DES. Additionally, Win2000 only allows for Diffie-Hellman Group 1 and Group 2 key strengths, which correspond to 768-bit and 1024-bit lengths, respectively. Win2003 adds the ability to use a 2048-bit key length.

> **NOTE**
>
> For more in-depth information on Microsoft Windows Server 2003, you will enjoy reading another book in the *Security Sage* series (and even if you don't enjoy books, you should buy this one anyway). *Security Sage's Guide to Attacking and Defending Windows Server 2003* by Erik Pace Birkholz, Joshua Leewarner, and Eric Schultze (ISBN: 1931836027) is an excellent resource for the busy CISO who needs more than just the basic installation and configuration information. If you have questions about the changes to the underlying OS security and how to best protect your Windows Server 2003 installations from compromise, this is the book for you.

Cisco IOS Routers

With Cisco routers, there are no nicely predefined IPSec policies. All configuration must be done manually. However, the configuration itself is pretty straightforward, and the ability to configure and monitor absolutely everything involved with the IPSec tunnel setup, negotiation, and tear-down makes the IOS configuration tools very versatile. Although your exact configuration might vary from the example provided here, all of the steps that we will discuss will have to be performed regardless of individual IP addressing, and so forth.

The first step is to define the Internet Key Exchange (IKE) policy that the router will be using. IKE policies are the set of values that this network device is willing to use with another system. It helps to remember that this is a *list* of all the acceptable values on this router; when the remove device connects to the router, the negotiation occurs across this set of possibilities. In the following example, we set the encryption type to 3DES and the hash type to use the Secure Hash Algorithm (SHA). Then, we inform the router that the encryption will be based on a pre-shared secret (a common password that is used on both ends), and that the security association (SA) for this tunnel should last for one day (86,400 seconds):

```
router(config)# crypto isakmp policy 10
router(config-isakmp)# encryption 3des
router(config-isakmp)# hash sha
router(config-isakmp)# authentication pre-share
router(config-isakmp)# lifetime 86400
router(config-isakmp)# end
```

The next step is to actually specify that pre-shared secret that we're going to use on both endpoints of the IPSec tunnel. With these commands, you must specify the IP address of the remote router so that the correct pre-shared password can be used for encryption (here we specify passwords for two remote routers at two different branch offices):

```
router(config)# crypto isakmp identity address
router(config)# crypto isakmp key UCLAbruins address 192.2.231.12
router(config)# crypto isakmp key LAlakers address 192.2.112.3
```

So far, we've just done preparatory work. Now, the actual IPSec tunnel must be created. First, we need to define just *what* traffic should be encrypted. For our purposes, we want to encrypt everything flowing from the management network depicted in Figure 6.2 to our remote Los Angeles branch office:

```
router(config)# access-list 110 permit ip 10.20.0.0 0.0.0.255 host
192.2.231.0 0.0.0.255
```

Now we come to the final configuration step, which is very difficult to read and understand. The first group of commands is the "transform set," which defines the IPSec mode (tunnel) as well as the algorithms to be used with AH and ESP:

```
router(config)# crypto ipsec transform-set MyTransformSet ah-sha-hmac
esp-3des
router(config-ctypto-trans)# mode tunnel
router(config-ctypto-trans)# exit
```

Now that we have the encryption settings defined by the transform set, we need to make a set of attributes by linking a particular transform set with the appropriate remote network device and the address list (previously defined as ACL 110) that will trigger the IPSec tunnel to begin encryption:

```
router(config)# crypto map TheBigMapping 10 ipsec-isakmp
router(config-crypto-map)# match address 110
```

```
router(config-crypto-map)# set peer 192.2.231.12
router(config-crypto-map)# set transform-set MyTransformSet
router(config-crypto-map)# exit
```

Just when you thought you were done, there's just one more thing you have to do: assign this newly created crypto-map to one of the interfaces, hopefully the interface that will see all of the encrypted traffic:

```
router(config)# interface ethernet 0
router(config-if)# crypto map TheBigMapping
router(config-if)# exit
```

Whew, now that was a mouthful. Other network device vendors make this IPSec configuration process easier, so don't be scared away just because of the complexities involved in the Cisco IOS configuration steps. Whatever encryption solution you end up creating, make sure that you leave yourself some backdoor access to manage the IPSec settings. There is nothing more frustrating (trust us on this) than spending hours crafting a wonderful IPSec security architecture, and then locking yourself out of the remote branch office due to some silly error. Since you specified strict IPSec settings, the remote servers will not listen to you since you are unencrypted. Make sure to have an extra pair of hands near the remote machines while you are configuring the servers.

Network Management Tools and Uses

And now, for our feature presentation: Bring out the tools! The heart of any good management network is the monitoring and management tools that you use. The mark of a good network management tool is one that has three out of the following four qualities:

- Reliability
- Ease of Use
- Flexibility/Configurability
- Reliability

And yes, we're not mistaken when we list reliability in there twice. If your management software can't be relied upon, then you might as well just not have it. The ideal solution is software where you just "set it and forget it" (much like the popular chicken rotisserie oven) and it provides you with timely alerts, easy management, and rock-solid stability.

Secondly, the ease of use for the software package that you decide on must be there. With other enterprise software deployments (like some CRM packages that we have endured), there is an extremely high learning curve, but they say that it's worth it in the end. The difference is that with network management software, there can be no learning curve. If it's going to take you 45 minutes to figure out how to get a detailed uptime report for a router that just lost its upstream connection, this software is of absolutely no value at all.

Lastly, the flexibility and configurability of your management solution should also factor into your selection. While any tool (even a DOS batch file) will work if you just want to PING a bunch of addresses, for those with more demanding needs, you're going to need a software package that will have the scalability to grow with your company. It must also have a rich feature set that is ready for tomorrow's management needs. You'll want to look "under the hood" and see if the particular software package that you're investigating stores data in a readily accessible database (MySQL, Microsoft SQL, Oracle) or if it uses a proprietary data format (or even worse—plain text flat file). Additionally, you want to note how many different methods the software package has to monitor your networks' health. While a simple ICMP PING is nice, it's hardly useful in today's locked-down networks. Make sure you can perform TCP port scanning, response time monitoring, custom HTTP query string checks, etc. If your budget allows for it, environmental monitoring would be a great thing to invest in now, and plug-in to the monitoring platform that you purchase.

Big Brother

As with our other chapters, we like to start listing out the free or open-source tools first, so that you can try them out without getting a big budget approval process going. One of the perennial favorites in any discussion of network monitoring is Big Brother, now owned by Quest Software. Spending many years as a community-supported monitoring tool, Big Brother enjoys quite a following with over 2000 subscribers to their mailing list and over 200 custom monitoring plug-ins written by passionate users. Now, Quest Software supporting the product, a new version dubbed Big Brother Professional Edition has been released with the Professional Edition has enhanced diagnostics and a simplified installation routine. Much like other open-source software, sometimes getting the right version of the software for your particular CPU can be difficult. The Professional Edition includes a no-hassle installer, automatic configuration, and best of all, the comfort of telephone-based technical support in case you run into trouble.

While the user interface may be a bit simplistic (see Figure 6.9), it is also incredibly easy to understand. With its color-coded HTML display, it's hard to find a reason not to install Big Brother, at least at first. If you find that it fits your needs, great—continue on to chapter 7. If you still want some more features or configurability, continue onward to the following pages.

Figure 6.9 Big Brother HTML status display

Big Sister

Borrowing its name from the success of the Big Brother network monitor, Thomas Aeby from Switzerland wrote the Big Sister software to also provide basic network monitoring functionality in an open-source format. Version 0.99b1 was the most recent as of our publication date, and it has both a Windows binary as well as Unix distributions. For each item in its HTML output, you may drill-down into the details and see statistics and status down to the partition level for a monitored server. Changes in status (up and down) are maintained in a log for service-level agreement (SLA) monitoring. And, if you're a real Big Brother fan, you can even apply a stylesheet to Big Sister to make the entire interface appear like Big Brother.

Figure 6.10 Big Sister Network Monitoring with Graphical Map

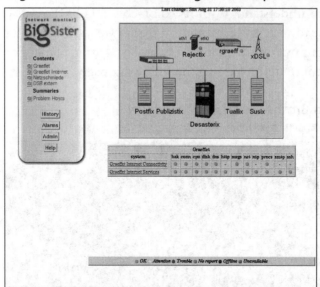

MRTG

MRTG is one of the most versatile statistics graphing packages on the market. You can't walk into a network operators' group meeting without someone trying to show off their impressive connectivity backbone by using MRTG statistics and graphs. Chances are, even your ISP uses MRTG to monitor your dedicated Internet connection. There are certainly more expensive solutions, but MRTG is such a well-focused solution for basic monitoring and historical performance logging reasons, it is no wonder it has thousands of happy companies on its user list.

MRTG is based entirely on a PERL script that performs the SNMP polling of traffic counters. MRTG marries the real-time data from the SNMP requests to trending information on what has happened within the past day, week, month, and year. A lightweight C program logs all information, performs the trending calculations, and generates beautiful (at least in our mind) graphs that can be embedded in HTML for presentation to management or geeks alike.

Anything with an SNMP addressable counter can be used as an input for MRTG, so don't feel like you have to limit yourself to monitoring the outbound traffic on your company's Internet link (the most common use for MRTG). There have been some creative people that have turned MRTG into an early warning system for DDoS attacks on their IIS web farm, but just graphing the amount of web requests per second that the IIS web servers were taking.

Figure 6.11 MRTG HTML Output showing router utilization statistics

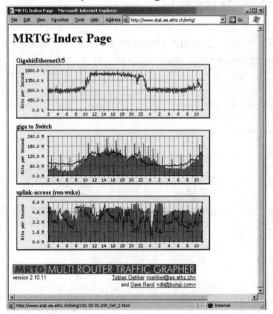

Paessler PRTG

Borrowing on the same logic that Big Sister used with its Big Brother analog, the PRTG product from Paessler provides much the same functionality as MRTG, but with an easier installation process and a much simplified configuration interface. If you are installing on a Windows-based machine, PRTG is a better bet for you than MRTG because the former can install as an NT service under Windows NT 4.0, Windows 2000, Windows XP, and Windows Server 2003. Combine this with the fact that you don't need to install your own PERL interpreter and PRTG starts sounding pretty good.

A free version of PRTG is available for non-commercial use and will do most of what any normal user could want in terms of monitoring and graphics. A Professional version of PRTG is available for only $49.95, and offers the ability to monitor unlimited amounts of devices and can customize the HTML reports that are presented to the user. PRTG maintains trending and statistics for up to one year, and can present hourly, daily, and weekly reports. Additionally, an automatic e-mail can be sent out nightly to keep the entire IT team abreast of the sensor usage statistics. Notifications can also be sent out when a certain threshold of usage (daily or monthly) has been exceeded. This is very useful for ISPs and

Web Hosting companies that sell their services under contract not to exceed a certain number of bytes transferred.

Figure 6.12 PRTG HTML Output showing network utilization

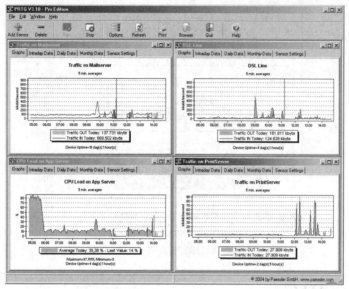

IPCheck Server Monitor

Paessler also makes IPCheck Server Monitor, which does more than PRTG can do in terms of monitoring. Furthermore, IPCheck has an advanced notification engine which PRTG itself lacks. IPCheck lacks the strong accounting features of PRTG, but it makes up for that in a very slick web-based user interface that is extremely easy to configure.

IPsentry

A small step above open-source software is the realm of shareware software. IPSentry, by RGE Inc., is a simple network monitoring tool that concentrates more on notification than on a graphical user interface with network maps. In fact, most of the IPsentry system is text-based. As you can see from Figure 6.13, the software will run through a battery of "checks" to run against predefined machines at a predefined schedule. For debugging purposes (as well as just plain nerdy fun), you can see exactly at what stage of the monitoring process the program is in, and the outcome of the monitored machines.

IPsentry is able to perform not only ICMP PINGs to determine if a remote host is alive, but also TCP open port monitoring, drive space monitoring, ODBC data source monitoring, NT event log monitoring, File content monitoring (looking for keywords in log files), and even third-party temperature probes to report environmental conditions. In terms of notification options, IPsentry does not disappoint. Along with standard e-mail messages, IPsentry is able to perform an audible notification using a pre-recorded .WAV file, SMS messaging on your cellular phone, launch an external application (presumably for further notification features), send an error report to your centralized SYSLOG server, restart the machine or the service, transmit an HTTP POST command, or even control the lights in the office (provided the lights are part of an existing X10 home management system). Through the use of plug-ins, IPsentry is able to quickly respond to the emerging needs of the small-to-medium business which cannot afford Unicenter, but are still willing to pay some money for software that is a cinch to install, configure, and use.

Figure 6.13 IPSentry Shown Modeling Different Devices

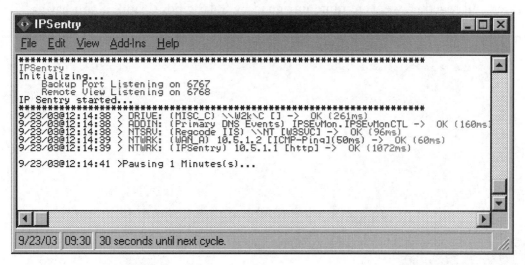

SolarWinds Orion

Many network engineers have become familiar with SolarWinds by downloading the company's free Advanced Subnet Calculator and free TFTP server. Beyond their free products, SolarWinds offers a slew of networking tools that they've divided into nine separate categories, which they bundle into five different packages. Each package targets a different position, ranging from the system administrator to a ISP network engineer. For our purposes, we want to look at the "Orion" suite of utilities for network monitoring.

This powerful set of web-based monitoring tools definitely does not disappoint. While more pricey than the open-source alternatives (currently $2370 to monitor up to 100 devices), the money is well worth it in terms of a rich user interface and detailed reporting—down to the raw SNMP data that it is capturing. Network Computing magazine awarded Orion their Editor's Choice award for its "…uncluttered and flexible display show[ing] network status, diagnostic direction, and trends clearly and without requiring customization." Out of the box, Orion is able to perform PING as well as TCP sweeps of your network, and can report on bandwidth, CPU, Memory, and Disk Space utilization. With a completely customizable report writer interface, you can customize Orion to product details service level agreement (SLA) justification documents for your customers or management. You can also create an entire role-based access control system, so that you can give your more trusted IT employees the ability to login and view certain areas of the network, while not being able to edit some other areas. All together, we were quite intrigued by Solarwinds Orion. If you have a couple thousand dollars lying around, I think it would definitely be a wise purchasing decision.

Figure 6.14 Solarwinds Orion Details Location Monitoring

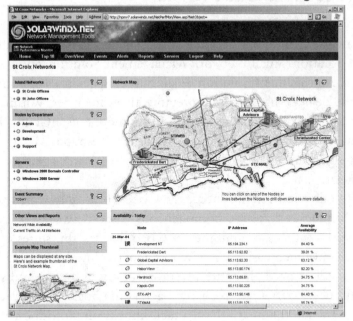

IPSwitch WhatsUp Gold

IPSwitch gained recognition by offering quality shareware before the Internet grew into a household word. Educational professionals and students probably recognize the name since IPSwitch produces the freeware FTP client program WS_FTP LE. WhatsUp Gold grew from an earlier IPSwitch offering, WS_Ping, a shareware utility that allowed network administrators to graphically map their network resources for scheduled ping sweeps or telnet access. Since its humble beginnings, IPSwitch has added a laundry list of features to the product that make it a logical choice for monitoring small to medium sized networks for which Computer Associates Unicenter or Hewlett-Packard OpenView would be overkill.

The original version of the product from 1996 monitored devices at the network layer of the OSI model, but the current version has monitoring abilities at the application layer for some popular databases and groupware applications. A powerful network profiling function can detect and create a map of all the TCP, NetBIOS, and IPX services (yes, even IPX) detected on the wire. As expected, WhatsUp Gold can produce all of the expected real-time alerts that we all hate to receive at 2 AM in the morning. With their most recent version 8.01, WhatsUp Gold has added a failover option, which automatically switches monitoring control to a secondary machine should the primary machine fail.

Cisco Systems CiscoWorks

Cisco actually produces five versions of its CiscoWorks management software: IP Telephone Environment Monitor, LAN Management Solution, Routed WAN Management Solution, Small Network Management Solution, and VPN/Security Management Solution. Each bundle specializes in configuring and monitoring the devices in one of the previous five categories. Within the LAN Management Solution alone, there are six sub-components: nGenius Real Time Monitor, Device Fault Manager, Campus Manager, Resource Manager Essentials, CiscoView, and Common Services. This isn't a network management system for the faint of heart.

Unlike the other tools mentioned here, CiscoWorks only works with Cisco products. For campuses that have homogeneous Cisco networks, or even heterogeneous networks with a large number of Cisco devices, this suites of products make management much easier. CiscoWorks allows administrators to backup device configurations on their entire inventory of Cisco routers and switches, as well as roll out new configuration changes across the board. This sweeping power comes in handy when the next DDoS attack knocks on your door, and you need to apply very particular access control list (ACL) filters to all of your perimeter routers.

CiscoWorks also provides a wealth of statistics and health-monitoring functions for your Cisco devices and presents them in a way that is more easily digestible than a *show counters* command within the IOS software. Naturally, CiscoWorks provides real-time alerts in case we're sleeping during some of the really exciting network attacks.

Computer Associates Unicenter

Computer Associates' Unicenter calls itself an Enterprise Management solution based on its capability. Since no network will contain everything that Unicenter can monitor, you purchase the core product and then purchase individual modules based on your network needs. For instance, Unicenter has Lotus Notes, Microsoft Exchange, and DB2 modules. Many of these modules do more than just monitor the health of systems. The Exchange module, for example, includes backup capabilities in addition to a full barrage of statistic monitoring.

Unicenter allows the IT Director to run the department as if it were a completely separate service business, mapping IT needs directly to Business costs and benefits. This helps immensely with the "business side" of justifying a server upgrade to the C-level management. Decisions can be made using a stack of historical performance metrics and TCO trending. If something happens on the network, Unicenter has numerous ways to get your attention in real-time. The real power, however, is in an intelligent event correlation engine, that can tell you whether the blast of a hundred SNMP failure alerts the NOC just received from retail stores all over Australia is really due to the single event of a distribution switch in Buenos Aires being restarted. Because of its support for industry-based standards such as SOAP, XML, and UDDI, Unicenter can be as extensible as you have the patience for it to be. IT can link to your custom point-of-sale cash registers in rural Minnesota, as well as your home-grown payroll software, with just the need for a lightweight API between them.

Microsoft Systems Management Server

The Microsoft entry into the world of management and monitoring is more of a server-based management tool, than a network-centric one. Coming a long way from the version 2.0 release in May 1999, Microsoft Systems Management Server (SMS) 2003 has a massive amount of fixes and new features built in to the November 2003 release. SMS 2003 has an entirely re-worked GUI client, new *server roles* for easy one-click deployment, integrated reporting, and a healthy dose of stability (remember how we harped on reliability a few page ago?). While, sadly, Microsoft has now removed support for Novell NetWare (along with eight others) in the list of OSes that SMS will attempt to manage, we still think that this is a solid management tool for networks that are mostly Windows-based.

SMS allows you to perform true asset-based management of your large enterprise network, collecting a bunch of inventory data in one place to bring smiles to the faces of your auditors. Using Windows Management Instrumentation (WMI), you can drill down to a crazy amount of detail for each managed resource, including BIOS chip revision and chassis enclosure data (if supported by your CMOS). SMS allows for detailed software metering, to ensure that not only are you not exceeding your software licenses, but that you also don't over-purchase licenses for software that is underutilized.

Notes from the Underground...

Microsoft System Center 2005

Still in development, Microsoft is definitely positioning all of its enterprise management tools and software to end up being plug-ins to the Microsoft System Center 2005, to be released sometime during 2005 (we hope). As part of their Dynamic Systems Initiative, Microsoft hopes that System Center 2005 can bring together all of your management resources into one view, "reduce the total cost of ownership for IT investments", and virtually eliminate the manual operational tasks that contribute to configuration errors, "...the underlying cause of failure more than 50% of the time."

The behemoth that will be named System Center 2005 will be comprised of SMS 2003, the OS Feature Pack, the Device Management Feature Pack, the Administration Feature Pack, Microsoft Operating Manager (MOM) 2005, and the System Center Reporting Server. They will also have a lighter version called MOM 2005 Express, which has most of the functionality of MOM but targeted for smaller environments.

Hewlett-Packard OpenView

OPenView is the management product that needs no introduction. Arguably, HP OpenView sets the standard for network management with plug-ins for virtually

on the entire network segment is not a bad idea either. With dedicated management consoles on the management network, you will be able to parade the venture capitalists through the room without worrying about the impression it may make on them.

IPSec is a great tool that helps hide the contents of your message while they are in transit. The pre-defined policies in Windows 2000 or 2003 are most definitely preferred, as they are less prone to error and likely to be a good fit. For those network devices that can perform the IPSec encryption themselves, attempt to perform encryption from the originating management console to the remote network device. Cisco has a step-by-step discussion of their IPSec implementation, so help is available.

Once your network infrastructure is in place, you're ready to install all the exciting network monitoring and management software that your wallet can afford. Starting out with something small, inexpensive, and uncomplicated is a good strategy. As you find yourself bumping up against the limits of the software's capabilities, you need to purchase one of the more expensive and robust application product suites. Your choice in network monitoring software should consider the support structure in place behind some of these open-source companies. You want to make sure the same company is going to be around next month when your network goes down and you need to track down an old router configuration. Back up all of your network management data just like your customer data, but you can feel free to do it less frequently. A good rule of thumb is to take a backup image whenever a router configuration or other critical monitoring device is changed, and then just store that CD off-site.

Intermission is over! Now onwards to the wonderful world of Network Switching in Chapter 7.

Solutions Fast Track

Network Management and Security Principles

- ☑ **Knowing What You Have** Without a good idea of what you're in charge of managing, you have little hope of effectively controlling.

- ☑ **Control Access Vectors** Know where your enemy will strike from, and fortify those locations.

- ☑ **Plan for the Unexpected** If you have the ability to afford redundant networks and management consoles, implement them! When the downtime hits (and you know it will), you will at least prove due diligence.

☑ **Backup Management Data** Remember to backup your valuable management information; in case there is tragic loss of building or property, you'll be able to land on your feet at a different location.

☑ **Watch Your Back** There are malicious people out there and there are casual sniffers, but both groups are out to get your passwords. Make them work for it; encrypt all your network management communications.

Management Networks

☑ Segregate your network management activities on to its very own segment

☑ You will be able to keep an eye on network health without worrying about internally initiated attacks

IPSec and VPNs

☑ **IPSec Purpose in a Management Network** Not only does IPSec assist in providing confidentiality to your clear-text protocol traffic, it also allows you to mask any open port activity by hiding everything within the tunnel.

☑ **IPSec Modes and Protocols** Depending on the capabilities of your network devices, you can either perform end-to-end encryption (preferred) or have the gateways nearest to the devices perform the encryption on behalf of the devices.

☑ **IPSec Configuration Examples** Windows 2000 and 2003 make the IPSec task simple with predefined policies. Cisco is much more configurable, but has a much steeper learning curve.

Network Management Tools and Uses

☑ **Reliability** If you have to spend time monitoring your management software, it just isn't useful anymore.

☑ **Ease of Use** Spending hours to figure out the user interface of a complex management system completely ruins your ability to respond to network outages in a timely fashion.

☑ **Flexibility/Configuratbility** Your network management software needs to grow along with your organziation

Links to Sites

- **http://nsa2.www.conxion.com/win2k/guides/w2k-20.pdf**
National Security Agency guide to setting up and properly configuring Windows 2000 IPSec services.

- **www.microsoft.com/windows2000/techinfo/planning/security/ipsecsteps.asp** Microsoft's step-by-step guide to IPSec (including planning and deployment methodologies).

- **www.blueridgenetworks.com** Blue Ridge Networks makes commercial end-to-end encryption tunneling products, like their CryptoServer.

- **www.openview.hp.com** HP OpenView network management suite.

- **www.ca.com/etrust** Computer Associates eTrust Security Command Center.

- **www.ipsentry.com** RGE, Inc. IPSentry network monitoring software.

- **www.bb4.com** Big Brother flexible network monitoring.

- **http://bigsister.graeff.com** Big Sister network monitoring.

- **http://people.ee.ethz.ch/~oetiker/webtools/mrtg/** Multi Router Traffic Grapher (MRTG).

- **www.paessler.com/prtg** Paessler Router Traffic Grapher.

- **www.paessler.com/ipcheck** Paessler IP Check Server Monitor.

- **www.solarwinds.net/Orion/** Solarwinds Network Monitoring software.

- **www.cisco.com/en/US/products/sw/netmgtsw/** CiscoWorks Network Management software

- **www.cai.com/unicenter/** Computer Associates Unicenter

- **www.microsoft.com/smserver** Microsoft Systems Management Server (SMS) 2003

- **http://csrc.nist.gov/CryptoToolkit/aes/rijndael/** Advanced Encryption Standard (AES); Rjindael.

- **www.rsasecurity.com/products/securid/** RSA SecurID two-factor authentication.

- **www.cryptocard.com** Cryptocard two-factor authentication.

- **www.authenex.com** Authenex two-factor authentication.

- **www.activcard.com/products/tokens.html** ActivCard two-factor authentication.

- **www.wardriving.com** Information on wireless local area network (WLAN) eavesdropping.

- **www.shiva.com** Legacy dial-up modem pools.

- **www.vericenter.com/products/disasterrecovery** Disaster Recovery "hot sites."

- **www.netbotz.com** NetBotz WallBotz server room monitoring devices

- **www.solarwinds.net** Solarwindws Network Management suite of applications

Mailing Lists

- **www.nanog.org/mailinglist.html** North American Network Operators' Group

- **www.canog.org** Canadian Network Operators' Group

- **www.swinog.ch** Swiss Network Operators' Group

- **www.frnog.org** French Network Operators' Group

- **www.sanog.org** South Asian Network Operators' Group

- **www.afnog.org** African Network Operators' Group

- **http://list.waikato.ac.nz/mailman/listinfo/nznog** New Zealand Network Operators' Group

- **www.mplsrc.com/mplsops.shtml** Great resource for people involved in large, MPLS networks

- **http://listserv.nd.edu/cgi-bin/wa?SUBED1=resnet-l&A=1** Must-read information for anyone in charge of a University's Residential Housing Network

Frequently Asked Questions

The following Frequently Asked Questions, answered by the authors of this book, are designed to both measure your understanding of the concepts presented in this chapter and to assist you with real-life implementation of these concepts. To have your questions about this chapter answered by the author, browse to **www.syngress.com/solutions** and click on the **"Ask the Author"** form. You will also gain access to thousands of other FAQs at ITFAQnet.com.

Q: It seems like a ton of work to setup dedicated management networks (in some cases you even recommend redundant management networks) and dedicated management consoles. I can just load up my trusty Sam Spade utility and troubleshoot whatever I need on my laptop. What's the point?

A: Listen, we're not going to pretend that everyone reading this book is going to run out and implement all of the suggestions. Moreover, a management network when your "enterprise" consists of about 20 machines is complete overkill. But once you get to the point where you need to worry about multiple internal routers, multiple internal segments, several Class–C blocks' worth of user workstations, and some site-to-site VPN connections, you really owe it to yourself to invest in a management infrastructure that begins with a separate network and a dedicated console.

Q: Okay, you've sold me on the management network, but I don't see why I need to waste money on a dedicated management console. Why can't I just have my Network Engineer's computer be designated as the management console?

A: Well, one reason is because we told you not to, but that answer never worked real well with your parents either. The main reason is for separation of duties. While your network engineer might be primarily responsible for the uptime of the network, what happens when he/she steps out to lunch and locks their workstation (as all good security-conscious users should do)? A router went down in Duluth and instead of fixing the problem, you're trying to crowbar your way past the engineer's workstation lock. Then what happens when the engineer goes on Jury Duty? Are you going to make that person change their password before they leave, and change it back? Should they just write their password on a sticky-note and put it on the screen? You can see where we're going with this one, and you should really consider that with prices for reliable desktop computers sliding well south of $1000, it's a no-brainer.

Q: How often should I backup my Management Network data?

A: Excellent question with an easy answer: as often as the data changes. In most networks, the router configurations, topology layout, and routing tables are fairly static over several months. If this describes your network, I would just backup each time you had a change in configuration or routing or anything else that has a material effect on your ability to manage and monitor your network. If the only thing that changes about your network management is your log files, we would suggest moving those logs onto a dedicated SYSLOG server, and backing up that server nightly along with the rest of your dynamic data.

Q: Should I place my wireless access points in front of, behind, or parallel with my corporate firewall? I've heard arguments for all three, but since you're the experts I'm going to ask you.

A: Although it sounds tempting and is very convenient, we're going to strongly urge that you do *not* put your wireless access points behind your firewall. You just don't want to invite that level of risk into your sphere of influence. Treat your wireless segments just like hotel broadband access; allow people to connect and receive a DHCP address, but they can only access the Internet after agreeing to a boilerplate end-user license agreement and entering in their employee ID and password. This just gets them on to the Internet, however. If they want access to their network file share, they need to use their VPN client just as if they were connecting from home or a hotel room. In this manner, you protect yourself from wardrivers that just want to use you for free Internet, plus, you stop people from inadvertently creating a conduit from the airwaves directly to your Oracle Financials server.

Q: The IPSec section of the chapter frightens me; is this level of encryption really necessary is all I want to do is monitor the bandwidth pumping through our core routers?

A: Absolutely! Do you think we would write all of this if it were optional? Okay, you're right—we probably would, but you should still implement IPSec. Even when you are using encrypted protocols such as SSH, you still give away information to a potential attacker about the methods in which you manage the network. If they see a lot of port 22 activity from you machine to a router, they can safely assume that the router has an SSH daemon listening. In contrast, IPSec tunnels all the communication such that anyone sniffing on the wire would only be able to see the tunnel itself and not any data inside.

Chapter 7

Network Switching

Solutions in this Chapter:

- **Understanding the Open Systems Interconnect (OSI) Reference Model**
- **The Origin of Switching**
- **Evaluating Switching Standards and Features**
- **Moving Switching beyond Layer 2**
- **Using Switching to Improve Security**
- **Choosing the Right Switch**

Related Chapters:

Introduction

Welcome to the wonderful world of switching. No other component better defines an organization's network than the switches that it uses. Without the switch, you don't have a network; you have a bunch of disconnected workstations working at a fraction of their potential. This chapter will tell you why you need a switch instead of a hub, and how to pick the right switches for your organization. Many readers right now probably think they already know this, but these same readers probably buy their networking equipment in one of two ways:

- They check out what's on special at the local computer superstore.
- They ask for as much money as they can get out of the CFO and buy whatever they can afford.

Both of these techniques will produce a network, but what do you tell the CFO when he or she asks, "Why do you want $100,000.00 for a switch when I just saw an advertisement for a $20.00 switch?" Let's flip it around and see how you answer this question: "The IT director of my last company requested $100,000.00 for our network infrastructure and you can do the same thing for $20.00? I know how much I'm saving, but what am I losing?"

At the end of this chapter, you still won't know what switch to buy or how much it costs. It is not our intent to recommend a specific vendor or brand of switch over another. You will, however, know the proper questions to ask when you're shopping for a switch, and more importantly, you will know how to defend your decision. A prepared consumer is an informed consumer. Moreover, if you read carefully, you'll find a few helpful hints on securely configuring your switches regardless of whom you buy them from.

Understanding the Open Systems Interconnect Reference Model

Switching is designed to work within the confines of the Open Systems Interconnect (OSI) model. Unless you've been operating your network from beneath a bridge (this will seem funnier later in the chapter), or under a rock, you should already be familiar with this concept. However, although the mechanics of the OSI model might not be foreign, the origins of the OSI model might.

The International Standards Organization (ISO) created the seven-layer OSI model to explain how data travels across a network so that engineers could create their products with a common framework. The model divides all network information into seven discrete layers. Every node on the network has a component responsible for a specific layer of this model. Each node allows the appropriate component to code/decode the data, generically called a *protocol data unit* (PDU), intended for that layer. This allows the component responsible for a specific layer of the source computer to communicate directly with the component responsible for that same layer on the destination computer. This compartmentalizes the design process so that multiple engineers can successfully work on different pieces of the same product and allow for complete interoperability of that product with other products engineered to the same standard. Figure 7.1 presents a simplified view of the model.

Figure 7.1 Simplified View of the OSI Reference Model

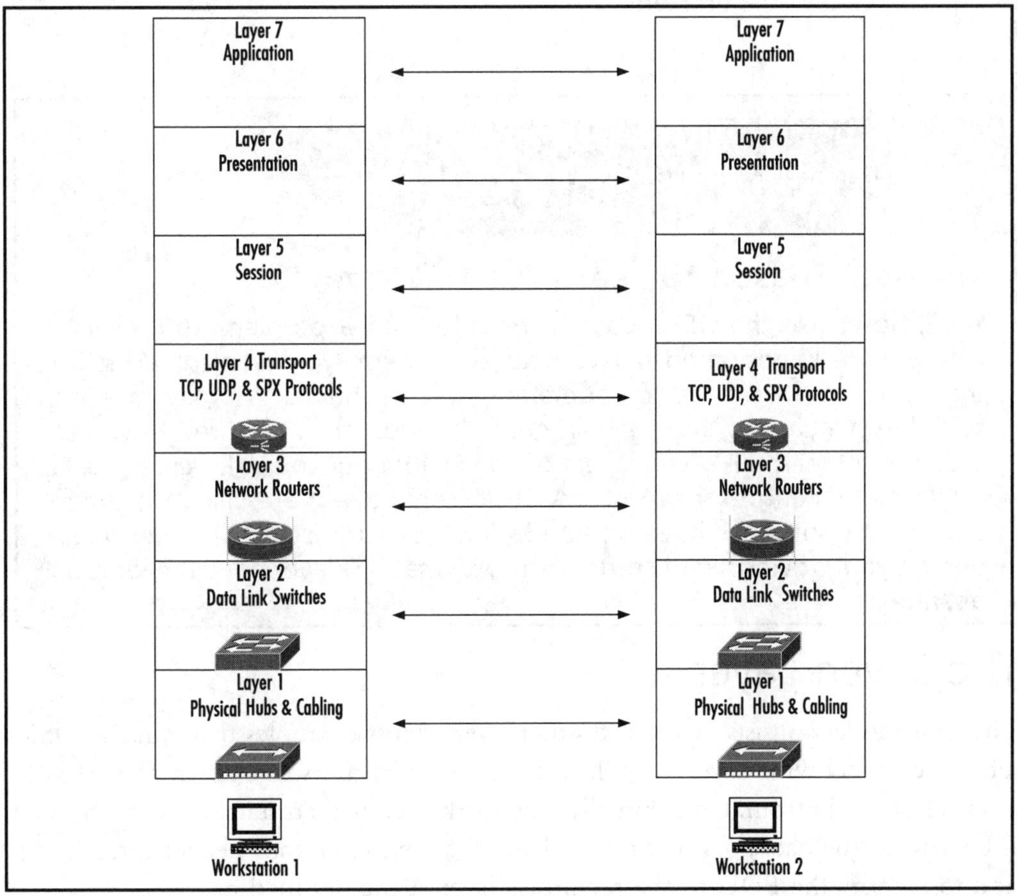

The OSI model mainly serves as a guide for the advisory bodies that really create the standards. Much of the networking hardware and software that exists today can fit nicely into the model, but not quite everything. The two most common networking protocol suites, Transmission Control Protocol/Internet Protocol (TCP/IP) and Internetwork Packet Exchange/Sequenced Packet Exchange (IPX/SPX), existed well before the ISO created the OSI and both suites still get the job done, although IPX/SPX is approaching retirement. Since they pre-date the standard, they don't fit the model perfectly, but they come close.

The OSI model also helps network engineers understand some of the complexities of the networks that they create and maintain. During a network crisis, a network engineer can apply his knowledge of the OSI model to determine the layer at which the problem is occurring. Then, the network engineer can closely examine the components responsible for that layer and only that layer so that he can quickly resolve the problem.

Notes from the Underground…

The Real Reason to Learn the OSI Model

You'll never use the OSI model to troubleshoot a problem and, even if you're actually designing networking equipment, you won't need it for that either. You *will* need to understand at least the first four layers when selecting switches so that you can properly assess their features. However, if you don't learn all seven layers of the OSI model you will never pass a single networking exam. And now that cars have more silicon in them than plastic surgeons have on hand, don't be surprised if the first question on your driving exam starts with, "At what OSI layer does the ignition operate?"

The Seven Layers

The OSI model consists of seven distinct layers. Most examples diagram the OSI reference model with Layer 7, application, at the top, and work down to Layer 1, physical, at the bottom. Conceptually, this works better than starting with Layer 1, because as the data goes down the chain, the next layer adds header information to identify the PDU to the reciprocal layer at the destination.

Let's take a look at a very simple network (see Figure 7.2). This sample network consists of an end user using a Web browser to access content from a single Web server. The end user physically connects to the Web server using four segments of category (CAT) 5e cable, two switches, and a router. We will refer back to this network in steps as we discuss the OSI model. The OSI model consists of seven layers as follows:

1. Physical

2. Data link

3. Network

4. Transport

5. Session

6. Presentation

7. Application

Figure 7.2 Sample Network

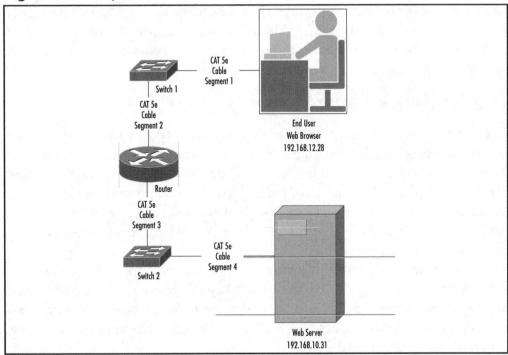

Switches generally operate on Layer 2; however, more advanced switches can also operate on Layers 3 and 4. With the exception of niche products and load balancers, switching seldom takes place above Layer 4; therefore, we will stop our discussion at Layer 4, the transport layer.

The Physical Link Layer: Layer 1

Layer 1 prescribes the nuts-and-bolts hardware used in networking. Examples of this include network cables and hubs. In our sample network, the CAT 5e cable links the end-user workstation to Switch 1, the switches to the router, and the Web server to Switch 2, all at the physical layer of the OSI model.

The Data Link Layer: Layer 2

Traditional switching occurs at the data link layer. Data link layer functions include examination of MAC addresses for end-to-end delivery of frames and Logical Link Correction (LLC). Switches serve as the best example of a component for this layer. PDUs at this layer are called *frames*. The frames travel across Layer 1 of our sample network on the CAT 5e cabling until they reach Switch 1, which then uses the frames' MAC addresses to move the data out the proper port of the switch. Since the switch has to use the MAC addresses of the frames, this part of the trip happens at Layer 2 of the OSI model.

The Network Layer: Layer 3

The network layer users networking protocols, such as IP (Internet Protocol) and IPX (Internetwork Packet Exchange) to provide communication between nodes. Routing occurs at this layer, so the traditional network device responsible for this is a router, but that's changing. PDUs at this layer are called *packets* or *datagrams*. In our sample network, the end-user Web browser sends a simple PDU over the CAT 5e cabling at Layer 1. Switch 1 gets the PDU and encodes it for the next part of its journey, transforming the PDU into a frame at Layer 2 of the OSI model. Since the Web browser is on the 192.168.12.0 network and the Web server listens on the 192.168.10.0 network, a Layer 2 device cannot transmit the data to the Web server. Instead, the router sees the frame, encodes it for transmission as a packet, and then sends it to Switch 2. This leg of the journey takes place at Layer 3 of the OSI model.

The Transport Layer: Layer 4

The transport layer includes the higher-level protocols such as TCP from the TCP/IP suite and Sequenced Packet Exchange (SPX) from the IPX/SPX protocol suite. In the real world, this is the layer that transports Web and e-mail traffic. PDUs at this layer are called *segments*. In our sample network, the data goes from a humble collection of 0s and 1s from the end-user workstation to Switch 1. Here, the switch encodes the data at Layer 2 as a frame, and then sends that frame to the router. The router realizes that the frame needs to go to another network, so the router encodes the frame as a packet at Layer 3 of the OSI reference model. Since the router has to send the PDU to Switch 2, a Layer 2 device, the router adds the necessary Layer 2 header, and then passes the frame onto the switch. The switch then sends the frame to the Web server. The Web server receives the electrical signal at Layer 1. The network interface card (NIC) drivers remove the Layer 2 header information while the TCP/IP protocol stack unpacks the Layer 3 header information. Now the Web server has a segment to examine. The segment tells the computer what type of traffic it has. In this case, the segment contains a Web server request using HTTP. Now, the upper layers of the OSI model take this information so that the Web server can then return the requested information. Now that you understand the networking niche that switches must fill, we can examine their evolution.

The Origin of Switching

Switching lends itself to many topologies, such as Token Ring and Fiber Distributed Data Interface (FDDI), but most network administrators consider switching as an advanced descendent of Ethernet networking. Ethernet started with Robert Metcalfe of Xerox's Palo Alto Research Center (PARC) in the 1970s. Two other companies, Digital Equipment Corporation and Intel, realized the potential of Ethernet, and together these three companies established DIX (Digital Intel Xerox) Ethernet in 1980. For Ethernet to emerge as a mature technology, it required the blessing of organizations that could anoint it as a standard. The Institute of Electrical and Electronics Engineers, Inc. (IEEE) transformed DIX Ethernet into the IEEE 802.3 standard officially on June 23, 1983, which the American National Standards Institute (ANSI) approved on December 31, 1984. Most networking professionals now consider Ethernet a synonym for IEEE 802.3.

Notes from the Underground…

Novell and Ethernet Frame Types

Novell divides Ethernet into four different frame types:

- 802.2
- 802.3
- Ethernet II
- Subnetwork Access Protocol (SNAP)

Novell NetWare used what Novell called 802.3 as the frame type for Sequenced Packet Exchange/Internetwork Packet Exchange (SPX/IPX), Novell's proprietary protocol suite, in version 3.11. The rest of the industry calls this "802.3 RAW" because Novell introduced the product before the IEEE ratified the standard, so it's not quite 802.3. When Novell introduced NetWare 3.12, they switched the default frame type to what they called 802.2, which they explained was 802.3 with Logical Link Correction (LLC). The rest of the industry calls this "802.3." Any NetWare administrator needed to know this (and still does in some instances) because NetWare servers using different frame types cannot communicate with each other even though they're using the same protocol. Therefore, by default, any administrator who installed a new server with the default settings had a server that could not see any of the other servers, and more importantly, the clients configured to use those other servers. Fortunately, NetWare servers could bind all four frame types to a single NIC, so properly configured NetWare servers could communicate with the rest of the installed base.

What about the other two frame types? Novell TCP/IP traffic uses Ethernet II, and AppleTalk uses the SNAP frame. The IEEE designed the SNAP frame so that vendors could run multiple protocols—any protocol—simultaneously. Switches really don't care what the frame type is; they just pass the traffic. Routers, however, need to know what frame types to route, so this really becomes more of an issue for routers than for Layer 2 switches. This used to be a big deal on Novell networks that spanned wide area networks (WANs), because Cisco called the frames one thing and Novell called them another, so the people configuring these things had to make a couple of passes at the configuration. In many medium to large

Continued

companies, one group configures the servers and another group configures the routers, so, when coupled with the inconsistent frame names, this can make routing NetWare problematic. Now, since Novell uses native TCP/IP, there's no point in routing IPX at all for most companies using NetWare. Even if you want to use IPX on the LAN side, it still makes more sense to use TCP/IP for WAN connections. Some folks will try encapsulating IPX in TCP/IP, which again doesn't make much sense unless you really need to use a version of NetWare more than six years old. Moreover, all current versions of NetWare support Macs natively over TCP/IP, so NetWare shops don't need to worry about AppleTalk, either.

Ethernet transmits data across a physical medium in the form of a linear bus. Most administrators familiar with the current look of Ethernet probably don't see the architecture as a bus, but rather a star or, in the case of a large network, a star cluster. Originally, a thick coax cable, known appropriately enough as Thicknet, snaked its way from workstation to workstation creating the original Ethernet networks. Eventually, Thicknet gave way to a less ponderous grade of coaxial cable that most engineers called Thinnet. Thinnet made it easier to link computers, but network engineers still had to deal with the limitations of the bus architecture. Creating a network of computers from a single cable, or multiple cables patched together to create the equivalent of a single cable, presented its own special challenges, especially when connecting computers between floors. If one station malfunctioned or if an end user carelessly kicked the wire loose on his computer, the entire network could crash. Network engineers demanded an easier method of building a network. Enter the hub.

Notes from the Underground...

Types of Ethernet

Ethernet comes in multiple physical flavors. All of the current forms of Ethernet evolved from 10Base-T. The "10" indicates that data flows over this network at 10 Mbps. The "T" means that this network architecture uses twisted pair cable. Specifically, it uses unshielded twisted pair (UTP) cable, similar to telephone cable.

Continued

- 10Base5 predates 10BASE-T. The "10" here still refers to the speed, but the "5" stands for the maximum length of the network, which can measure 500 meters. 10Base5 uses Thinnet.

- 10Base2 predates 10Base5 and even predates using the metric system. This form of Ethernet uses thick coaxial trunk cable (Thicknet) and can transmit data a maximum of 185 meters, or just slightly over 200 yards. This accounts for the "2" in its name.

UTP isn't the only game in town, though. Replace the "T" with an "F" and now we're using fiber. Fiber comes in multiple grades and connection types, so manufacturers usually talk about these connections as "FX," where the "X" can stand for any type of connector or grade of fiber. We call Ethernet that transmits data at 10 Mbps over fiber 10Base-FX. If the data moves at 100 Mbps, this is 100Base-FX.

For additional information on this, please see the "Network Speed" and "Distance Limitations" subsections of "Evaluating Switching Standards and Features."

Hubs

Many novice system administrators confuse switches and hubs, so before we examine switches, we should understand the switches' closest ancestor, the hub. The invention of the Ethernet hub allowed network engineers to organize the network in the now-familiar star topology. Network designers could now place a hub in central wiring closets and then run a wire from each port of the hub to a terminal. A hub is network concentrator with multiple ports that connects end stations or other concentrators to each other. The hub, the simplest type of medium attachment unit (MAU), operates at Layer 1 (physical) of the OSI model, acting as a switchboard that, in essence, transforms the star topology into a linear bus from an electrical perspective. From a visual perspective, it looks like a star, but from the data's perspective, it looks like a straight line connecting all of the terminals. Network engineers can easily increase the size of the network by daisy chaining hubs together to create even larger local area network (LAN) segments. However, the ease of adding stations proves to be a double-edged sword.

NOTE

Even though each terminal connects to a hub with a unique *segment* of cable, this is not what network engineers mean when they discuss a *network segment*. All terminals plugged into a hub and even a daisy chained collection of hubs share a common segment in network-speak.

Carrier Sense Multiple Access/Collision Detection

Ethernet transmits data using a mechanism known as Carrier Sense Multiple Access/Collision Detection (CSMA/CD). The phrase *multiple access* seems simple enough: multiple machines can use the network. However, only one station at a time can transmit data on the bus. Ethernet uses *carrier sense* to see if the network will accept its data before sending, but carrier sense can only tell the station that the network has availability at this exact instant. By the time the terminal acts on this information, the situation could have changed, and if two or more stations transmit data on the same segment at the same time—regardless of the data's destination—this will cause a collision. Any data involved in a collision do not reach their destination. This leaves us the last part of the term, *collision detection*. The terminals learn of the collision, reset for a random time period, and then repeat the procedure, much like the instructions on a bottle of shampoo (lather, rinse, repeat translates into send, collision, repeat). If the resend window were fixed as opposed to random, each station involved in the collision would wait the exact same time to resend its data, which of course would force collision after collision in perpetuity, creating a never-ending cycle of failed transmissions: lather, rinse, repeat at its worse. All of the terminals on a network segment form a *collision domain*. Figure 7.3 demonstrates a single collision domain.

Figure 7.3 Single Collision Domain

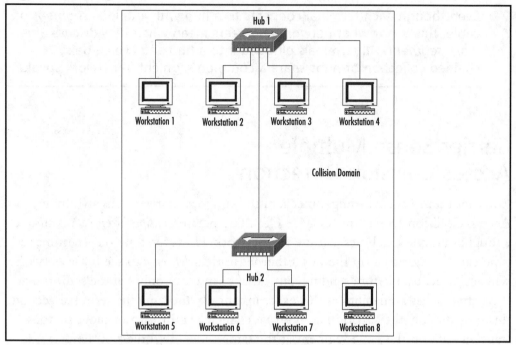

As the number of stations increases on the segment, the number of collisions will increase as each station fights for its share of bandwidth. Not only do collisions decrease the speed at which data make it to their destination, collisions clog the segment, which can cause additional collisions. End users will see their network access speeds slow to a crawl and might even believe that their computers have crashed again. With enough workstations, this can create a condition in which only collisions occur and no useful data is transmitted. Further slowing data, Ethernet is a shared medium, so every node on a segment must examine all the information on that segment to determine if the information is destined for it. If the information is really intended for that station, the station will act on it. If not, the station will ignore it, but only after wasting some processor cycles determining the relevance of the data. To correct this condition, a network designer will have to reduce the number of collisions without reducing the number of workstations.

If we restate the problem in still another way, the new network design must decrease the size of the collision domain without decreasing the number of nodes on the network. This creates the logical choice of creating multiple collision domains. Switches help with this, but, as with the old joke says, "You can't get there from here." CSMA/CD makes Ethernet possible, but it also makes switching necessary. However, we need to make one more stop before we get to switches.

Bridging

Each segment functions as a unique collision domain, so proper network design must split the LAN into multiple segments, while allowing each station on all of the segments to communicate with each other. Network engineers originally used a device known as a *bridge* to segment the network. A bridge consists of little more than a computer with multiple network ports, a central processing unit (CPU), and a set of instructions that tell the unit how to transfer data. The IEEE 802.3 specification divides data that travels over the network segments as *frames*. Ethernet divides the frame into nine discrete fields. The third field contains the 6-byte Media Access Control (MAC) address of the frame's destination, and the fourth field contains the 6-byte MAC address of the frame's source. If the source machine does not know the MAC address of the machine to which it wants to send data, the source machine creates a frame with a destination address of FFFFFFFFFFFF. This is called a *broadcast address* and forces all machines on the local area network (LAN) to examine the frame. Usually, a frame has a specific machine as its source; this type of frame is a *unicast*.

If the destination address belongs to a node on the same segment as the source, the bridge will ignore the frame since it will get to its destination without any intervention from the bridge. If the bridge determines that the frame's destination will take it to another segment from its source, the bridge will forward the frame to the correct port. Only the stations on the originating segment and the correct destination segment will see this frame. If the bridge does not know to which port it should send the frame, it will flood all of the ports except the port on which it received the frame with a broadcast to request the location of the destination node. If the machine exists on the network, it will reply to the bridge. The bridge will now forward that unicast frame to the port on which it received the reply, and it will remember the location of that node for as long as it can so that it can forward future frames to that node without having to re-learn its location. This accomplishes the original task of segmenting the network while maintaining complete connectivity, but the process of examining each frame comes at a cost of speed. Examining all of the frames with a CPU takes time, so the frames take longer to reach their destination. We call the amount of time that a bridge takes to examine a frame before forwarding it *latency*. High latency not only decreases the total transmission speed, but it can make some applications such as Voice over IP (VoIP) and video conferencing worthless. High latency will make everyone on a VoIP call sound like robots from a bad 1960s sci-fi movie. The network now has collisions under control, but at the cost of increased latency. The increased complexity of this system also raises the OSI layer from one to two.

Tools & Traps…

Media Access Control (MAC) Address

The MAC address is a unique 12-digit hexadecimal identification number given to every network device by its manufacturer. This has nothing to with Apple Computers and their Macintosh product. To avoid confusion, network engineers will alternately call this number the *hardware address*. Despite its name, most NICs allow you to change the MAC address, which you should *never* do without an excellent reason and full understanding of the ramifications of your decision.

The first six hex digits are known as the organizational unique identifier (OUI), which the IEEE grants to hardware manufacturers. For additional information and a complete list of OUIs, see http://standards. ieee.org/regauth/oui/index.shtml. Do you have a guess as to the owner of the first entry on the list? You guessed it—Xerox.

And Then Came the Switch

If an engineer could design a multiport bridge that could use a chip specifically designed for forwarding packets, frames could flow across the network without any latency (or as the kids call it these days) at *wire speed*, the maximum rate at which the specification will allow data to travel on a given topology. Well, the engineers at Kalpana did just this in 1990 with their invention of the *Etherswitch*. The Etherswitch can transparently (in other words, does not change the data in any way) bridge the data from one segment to another segment. The silicon responsible for the frame forwarding is an Application-Specific Integrated Circuit (ASIC). Each port on the switch is its own collision domain. Network engineers can use the switch ports to attach hubs, limiting the collision domain just to that hub, or attach nodes directly to a switch port for even greater bandwidth to the station. (See Figure 7.4).

Figure 7.4 Collision Domains with Switches

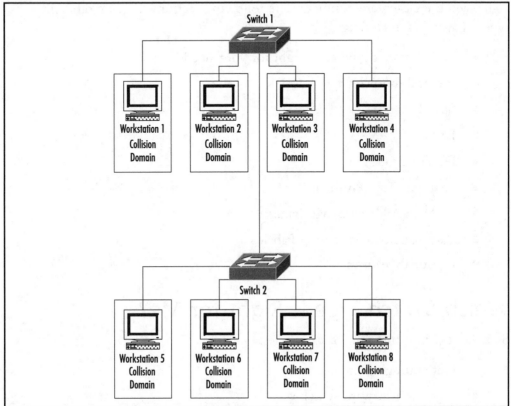

Evaluating Switching Standards and Features

Many companies offer a variety of switches, while other companies make a wide range of NICs. Despite these obstacles, almost all of the Ethernet switches work with each other, as do the Ethernet NICs. Why? They work together because they all have to (at a minimum) conform to the IEEE 802.3 specification. The switch manufacturer can add additional features once the switch meets minimum requirements—as long as the new features do not cause any of the mandatory features to stop working. Since switches all work minimally at Layer 2, any switch will offer improved security over a hub. Whereas a hub sends traffic to all workstations regardless of the intended recipient, switches only send data where they need to go. This makes sniffing a switched network much harder than sniffing a nonswitched network. Once we accept this one-switch commonality, we then need to look at what makes each different so that we can choose the right switch for each environment. The following sections describe different types of switches, including:

- Which type of switch is right for your needs?
- Physical footprint
- Speed
- Distance
- Duplex mode
- Spanning Tree Protocol
- Content Addressing Mechanism
- Backplane and Switching Fabric
- Optional Features

Which Switch Type Is Right for Me?

Switches fall into three major categories:

- Cut-through switches
- Store-and-forward switches
- Combination switches

Cut-through switches take the least amount of engineering, while a high-quality store-and-forward switch takes the most engineering. Since an Ethernet switch must stay IEEE 802.3 compliant, each of the three types produces the same result, although the speed and latency will vary.

Cut-Through Switches

Efficient switches need to keep latency to a minimum. Cut-through switches do this by forwarding frames as soon as the switch reads the destination address. This saves time since the switch does not have to read the entire frame. The drawback is that this method prevents the switch from determining if it's sending a valid frame to an end station. If the switch does forward an invalid frame, this will cause a complete retransmission from the source machine. This can cause an unacceptable level of performance on a network with a high number of errors. This type of switching takes the least amount of processing power, so most of the less expensive switches will use this method. You will generally find this type of switch only at the access layer of the network.

Store-and-Forward Switches

Every Ethernet frame without an optional extension ends with a 4-byte frame check sequence (FCS) field. Network devices can run a cyclic redundancy check (CRC) on this field to determine the validity of a frame. If the frame fails its CRC, the destination device requests that the source device resend the frame. A store-and-forward switch reads the entire frame by storing it in memory. Once the switch stores the frame, it can then run a CRC on the frame. If the frame passes the CRC, the switch forwards it to its destination; hence the name "store-and-forward."

If the frame fails the CRC, the switch reports this to the source device and requests that it resend the frame. This limits the failed traffic to the local collision domain, greatly reducing the impact of invalid frames on the entire network. This process requires significant processing power, which could increase the latency of the transmission, but most of the current switches that employ this technique have extremely powerful processors that can perform these checks at wire speed so that they do not add to the latency of transmission.

Combination/Other Switches

Switch vendors don't exclusively have to use either of the previously described methods. Some use a combination of both. For example, Cisco has a switching methodology called "FragmentFree" in which the switch waits until it has enough data to qualify as a full Ethernet frame before forwarding it. This doesn't eliminate all frame problems, but it does prevent a common frame error, called a *runt*. You could encounter other proprietary methods from different vendors, but each vendor should be able to compare its method to either cut-through or store-and-forward.

Evaluating the Physical Footprint

Switches have mass, and by definition, anything with mass occupies space. In the world of computers, we refer to the amount of space that equipment consumes as its *footprint*. Lower-end networking equipment will rest on shelves, but all of the professional equipment will provide a mechanism for mounting inside of a rack. Network engineers measure the amount of rack space that equipment occupies in *rack units*. When it comes to the physical dimensions, switches fall into two basic categories: stackable and chassis. Usually, stackable switches take up less space but also have fewer ports than chassis switches do.

Notes from the Underground...

Racks and Rack Units

Most vendors design their equipment to fit into a 19-inch-wide rack. Vendors use *rack units* to measure the vertical distance that rack-mounted equipment occupies, with 1U being the least amount of vertical space that any rack-mounted device can occupy. One rack unit measures approximately 1.75 inches.

Mountable equipment with considerable depth and/or weight will require a four-post rack or cabinet so that the device can get support from the front and back.

Stackable Switches

Stackable switches get their name from their low height, allowing engineers to "stack" multiple switches vertically in a small amount of space and then chain them together as a cohesive unit, or "stack." Generally, any switch in this category will only occupy one or two rack units.

One vendor, Xylan, used to describe its stackable switches as "pizza boxes" because of their close resemblance to the genuine article. Stackable switches fit snugly into 19-inch racks and usually occupy no more than four rack units of space. Stackable switches rarely exceed 50 ports, configured as 48 normal ports and two high-speed uplinks.

Stackable switches come in fixed configurations with very little expandability. Some modules will have one or two slots that can accept various uplink modules, such as fiber connectors for Gigabit Ethernet or 100Base-FX. Don't expect too much more expandability than this. Some stackable switches, such as the early 3Com SuperStack models, use proprietary cables to connect to each other to give the illusion of one large switch. The cables act as the backplane for this configuration. Other switches use standard CAT 5 cable to interconnect with other switches.

Stackable switches come in the managed and unmanaged varieties. Some high-end managed varieties even have redundant power supplies, Layer 3 switching and VLANs, although you will probably not find a stackable switch any fancier than this. Most of these features will be covered shortly, so don't worry if you don't recognize some of these terms; you will come to love them soon enough.

Chassis Switches

Chassis switches consist of a large frame, or chassis, into which a network engineer installs modular components, such as port blades, management modules, power supplies, memory, PCMCIA cards, and other miscellaneous pieces of hardware. Chassis allow for the greatest flexibility and the greatest port density over other configurations. Xylan, an early switch manufacturer (now part of Alcatel), heavily advertised its ability of "any-to-any" switching. An engineer could configure a single Xylan OmniSwitch with Ethernet, Fast Ethernet, FDDI, Copper Distributed Data Interface (CDDI), Token Ring, and ATM, thus enabling disparate OSI Layer 1 technologies to coexist.

Chassis switches usually need some type of configuration, so these always are of the managed variety and either come with a redundant power supply or the option to add one. Vendors usually reserve their top features for their chassis solutions, so anything that a vendor has will usually make it into these models. Some chassis switches can take as little space as a large stackable, but most come with a much larger footprint and a price to match. Not any room can take every chassis. Some chassis switches can require 20amp or larger circuits, while some might completely monopolize three 15amp circuits simultaneously. Sucking down all of the power can create a huge heat buildup, so some switches might generate up to 7500 Btu/hr, requiring adequate ventilation.

Tools & Traps…

Inadequate Ventilation and Power Can Harm Your Security!

Network engineers often neglect the environmental factors surrounding the installation of network equipment. Often, a network engineer has earmarked a locked cabling closet for a switch without thinking about the heat that the switch will generate. Once the switch gets in there, the room heats up like a convection oven. The equipment will burn out at those temperatures, so the network engineer will then keep the closet door open so that the heat can vent into the rest of the building. This keeps the temperature lower, but it completely negates all of the security. Any slightly knowledgeable hacker in the building now has free reign to run password recovery routines on the switch, allowing him to hijack it and any data that flows through it.

A similar situation occurs when the switch room doesn't have enough power to run the switch. Switches have minimum power requirements, and if the switch doesn't get this minimum amount of power, it won't run. This doesn't sound like a security problem, but after spending $50,000.00 or more on a large chassis switch, some network engineers don't want to go back to the CFO and ask for a few hundred dollars more to run additional circuits into the room. Instead, they'll just crack the door open and run a few extension cords from around the corner. There goes the security.

In short, if you can't meet the minimum environmental needs for a given switch, get another switch.

Network Speed

The IEEE set the speed of Ethernet at 10 Mbps over coax with the original specification 802.3-1985, and then later revised the standard in 1990 to allow this same speed over unshielded twisted pair (UTP) CAT 5 cable. The 802.3u -1995 standard increased the speed to 100 Mbps over CAT 5 UTP; the industry commonly refers to this networking topology as *Fast Ethernet*. The 802.3U specification also covers Ethernet and Fast Ethernet using fiber. Still, even over fiber, the speed needs to stay at 10 Mbps and 100 Mbps, respectively, to maintain adherence to IEEE 802.3.

Tools & Traps...

How to Know Your Bits from Your Bytes

Is there any difference between "Mbps" and "MBps?" They look almost the same. However, as Mark Twain once noted, "The difference between the almost right word and the right word is the difference between the lightning bug and the lightning."

The uppercase "M" means "Millions" using the standard convention of the metric system, while a lowercase "M" means "milli," or "thousandths." Using a lowercase "b," The abbreviation "bps" stands for "bits per second." An uppercase "B" changes the meaning to "bytes per second." As there are 8 bits to a byte, using an uppercase "B" instead of a lowercase "b" gives an error of nearly a magnitude. Is that big? In California, a magnitude five earthquake destroys your nerves, but a magnitude six earthquake destroys your house. One magnitude matters.

Remember: you always measure network transfer speeds in "bits per second."

In 1998, the IEEE set a standard for Ethernet transmissions at 1000 Mbps, which the industry calls Gigabit Ethernet, or 1000Base-X. Gigabit Ethernet has multiple standard revisions based on the medium over which the signal will travel, typically either copper or fiber. Fiber cabling comes in many different cable types and termination types, but the data must operate at 1000 Mbps to conform to the Gigabit Ethernet standards. The IEEE ratified standard 802.3ae for Ethernet running at 10 Gbps (10 GE) in June 2002, but the products at this level have not yet fully matured, so this chapter will not spend too much time discussing this standard.

Distance Limitations

Unlike speed, the type of cabling will affect the distance that all varieties of Ethernet can transmit data. In all cases, all switches must reliably transmit frames 100 meters using CAT 5 cable. Ethernet, Fast Ethernet, and Gigabit Ethernet using CAT 5 cable are called 10Base-T, 100Base-T, and 1000Base-T, respectively. Fiber dramatically increases the distance that frames can travel. Most network engineers call Ethernet over fiber 10Base-FX, and Fast Ethernet over fiber

100Base-FX. The more common implementations of 10Base-FX—10Base-FB and 10 Base-FL—can transmit frames 2 km. The less common 10Base-FP has a 500-meter limitation. 100Base-FX can transmit frames up to 2 km using multimode fiber, but some instances of the specification can be as short as 300 meters. Gigabit Ethernet over fiber can have multiple names depending on the type of fiber used, such as 1000Base-LX (Long Wavelength Laser), 1000Base-SX (Short Wavelength Laser), and 1000Base-LH (Long Haul). Gigabit Ethernet can extend a network anywhere from 220 meters up to 5 km, and even well beyond that using the latest technology. The distance not only varies with the type of fiber but also with the type of laser that the manufacturer chooses to employ.

Damage & Defense...

Cabling, Cabling, Cabling

Bad cabling will haunt you more than refinancing telemarketers will. The reason? Most network administrators do not have the proper tools to troubleshoot CAT 5 cabling, much less fiber. The faster the data travels, the more likely improper cabling will affect your network. Symptoms can include stations connecting at low speeds, but not high speeds; a high number of frames with errors; or a link indication without the ability to transmit data. The definition of "bad" in this instance does not just refer to physical defects. You must take into account distance and termination.

If you have the opportunity to run new cabling, get a company that actually knows how to do it! Many administrators and consultants think that they can run CAT 5, but many of these people have not seen the EIA/TIA 568A & 568B Standards for terminating CAT 5 cabling. Simple test: quiz your cable installer on the differences between the 568A and the 568B specifications. If he doesn't grumble something about colors and instead rolls his eyes, you know you should be investing your money elsewhere.

Don't try to save money by pulling less expensive cabling, because the cost of the materials represents a small portion of the total cost of the job. When using copper, always pull at least CAT 5e four-pair cabling. Even though Ethernet and Fast Ethernet only use pins 1, 2, 3, and 6 (one pair for sending and one pair for receiving), 1000Base-T uses all four pairs. Although it might be tempting, never use the extra pairs to transmit voice

Continued

or other traffic because you might need those extra pairs later for data. Run dedicated cable for your telephone extensions. We've even seen networks where they split a four-pair cable into two Ethernet drops. As you can imagine, poor network quality was rampant at this company.

Finally, and most importantly, fiber connections use a real laser to transmit data. Never stare into a strand of fiber or the fiber interface on a switch—you can do serious damage to your eyes. What if the switch is turned off? Cemeteries are filled with people killed by "unloaded" guns. Don't take a chance, and keep unused fiber ports covered at all times.

Duplex Mode

Duplex mode controls whether a switch can send and receive information simultaneously or only perform one action at a time. Half duplex mode resembles a telephone conversation; one person listens while the other person speaks, and then they switch. A switch in full duplex mode can transmit and receive data at the same time. The duplex mode can vary by port, so that some ports can work in half duplex mode while others can operate in full duplex mode. In addition, for a switch port to function at full duplex the device attached to that port must also function at full duplex. Full duplex mode can only work in an environment free from collisions. A hub cannot guarantee a collision-free connection, so all hubs work in half duplex mode only. The specification insists that a switch autosense the mode, but that does not preclude vendors from adding options to select the mode manually. Whenever possible, don't rely too heavily on auto-negotiation, as it can sometimes fail, leaving you with puzzling results. If you manually adjust your settings, make sure that everyone on the networking team understands this. This will save a lot of debugging time when a station fails to access the network.

Spanning Tree Protocol

Unlike routers, switches can only have one path to a node. What happens if someone plugs in two cables to the same switch, causing a loop? Spanning Tree Protocol (STP) takes over. Figure 7.5 gives an example of a network loop. If Workstation 1 wants to send data to Workstation 2, Workstation 1 must first send the data to Switch 1, and Switch 1 must get the data to Switch 4. Switch 1 has learned through the network that it can reach Switch 4 by sending frames either through Switch 2 or Switch 3. If Switch 1 sends the data to Switch 2, Switch 2 must now make a decision to where to send the data. Switch 2 has learned through network discovery that it can reach Switch 4 directly or it can send it to Switch 1, which can send it to Switch 3, which can then send it to Switch 4. If Switch 2 decides to take the latter path, this throws the network into a loop. Switch 1 receives data that it already sent and the entire process repeats indefinitely.

Figure 7.5 Network Paths without STP

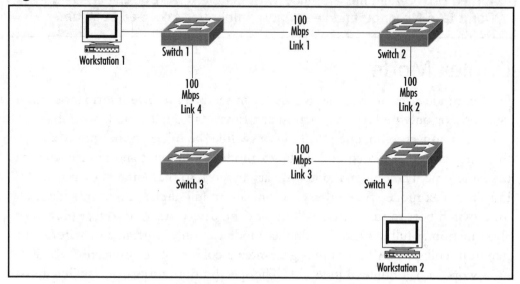

When STP senses a loop as in Figure 7.5, it immediately takes steps to deactivate one of the redundant links. STP cannot physically unplug the cables, but it can put ports in *blocking* mode instead of *forwarding* mode so that they cannot send data. Once STP has dealt with the offending ports, each switch can now learn the correct paths to each station. Even though the physical network will look similar to Figure 7.5, the data will see something similar to Figure 7.6. In this diagram, STP has removed Link 3 from the network. However, what if Link 1 were to die? If it weren't for the network loop, Link 3 added redundancy, but it also appears that STP has killed that. Fortunately, that isn't the case.

Figure 7.6 Network Paths with STP

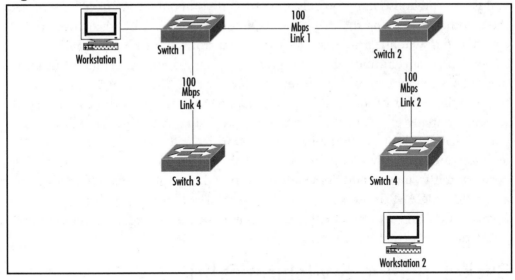

STP has the intelligence to sense a malfunctioning link and then reactivate a redundant link so that the data flow can continue. In many implementations, it can take about 50 seconds for a port to change states from blocking to forwarding once it receives information about a topology change. In a very large network, this can cause a disruption of several minutes while the switches *converge*, or change their port configuration based on the topology change.

Network engineers should monitor Spanning Tree changes closely. A stable network should only see changes with the addition or deletion of switch links. An STP change can indicate a fault or the unauthorized addition of network equipment into the environment. A savvy hacker with access to a couple of live network ports onsite could even purposely cause an STP change that forces traffic across a switch that he controls.

Content Addressable Memory

Switches need to forward frames, and to forward frames they need to know where to deliver them. Each frame contains a 6-byte MAC address of the station to which the frame needs to go. The MAC address acts similarly to a house address. Once we know the address of a house, we can eventually get there. If we've never gone to that house, we'll probably have to look it up on a map or ask for directions. A switch has to do the same thing. It asks directions by flooding all ports with a request for the MAC address. If the machine with that MAC address hears the call, it responds with directions.

Just like looking up an address on a map, this takes a lot of time. Couldn't you get to the house more quickly next time if you could remember how to get there without checking the map again? Of course you could, and so could the data. Once a switch learns a path to a station, it stores the path in its memory. The Ethernet specification does not prescribe how manufacturers hold this information, but many use content addressable memory (CAM). Generally, you can measure the power of the CAM by how many MAC addresses the switch can remember at any given time. If a switch cannot maintain a large enough CAM table to handle all of the traffic in your network, it will constantly have to re-learn the location of MAC addresses that it should already know. This increases network traffic and latency. Some advanced switches might use a different mechanism than a CAM or use another component in conjunction with the CAM, so if you cannot find statistics for this component ask the vendor what replaces the CAM on that particular switch.

Backplane and Switching Fabric

Once a frame enters a switch port, the switch must now move this frame to another port. Depending on the type of switch, this journey can take the frame across the switch's backplane, or, as some manufacturers call it, the *switching fabric*. The ports on some switches are on cards that slide into slots in the switch framework, or chassis. If the destination port is on the same card as the source port, the frame never travels across the switch's backplane; instead it travels across the card's fabric, freeing the switch's backplane to move other frames.

The capacity of a backplane is measured by how much data can move across it in a given time, the same way we measure port speeds. Usually, you will see these speeds reported in Mbps or gigabits per second (Gbps). If the backplane of a switch can handle all of the traffic that the ports can send its way, the switch is known as "non blocking." This is a good thing. If the aggregate bandwidth of all the ports exceeds the capacity of the backplane, the switch will have to refuse the excess traffic by blocking it. This will cause the network to slow down as devices must re-transmit data or throttle back their speeds.

The IEEE does not set a standard for the speed of the fabric, so each vendor has a large amount of latitude in this category. As such, this category easily differentiates cheap switches from their faster cousins. We'll return to this when we discuss choosing the right switch.

Optional Features

The 802.3 specification provides for a consistent platform so that Ethernet devices can interoperate. Manufacturers must meet these minimums if they want to boast IEEE 802.3 compliance. However, the IEEE 802.3 standard also describes the parameters for optional Ethernet features. Some of these features even have their own specifications, such as IEEE 802.1Q for VLAN trunking, which we'll discuss in the *VLAN* subsection. A switch doesn't need to meet the IEEE 802.1Q standard to be an Ethernet switch, but if the manufacturer says that the switch is compliant to this standard, you know that you'll be able to create VLANs using this switch and switches from other manufacturers' products that make the same claim.

Switch Management

The management feature quickly divides switches into two camps. Switches that do not allow administrators to perform any configuration are called, appropriately enough, *unmanaged*. Configuring an unmanaged switch is simple: plug in the power and then attach the computers—you're done! Most don't even have a power switch, so they come up automatically when you plug in the power. It doesn't get much simpler than that. Why would you want to manage a switch when you can get one that doesn't need it? There are quite a few reasons.

Every switch will have its own list of features that you can use through the management console, but most will allow you to change port parameters, such as the speed and duplex; monitor performance metrics on your network; send alerts when errors occur through Simple Network Management Protocol (SNMP) messages; and allow the implementation of advanced features. Oddly enough, it is the powerful management features that make these switches targets for attack (see Chapter 8). Unmanaged switches cannot be attacked because the higher-level intelligence is just not there.

Although each switch can implement management in its own way, most managed switches will have a console port to which you can make a serial connection.

Notes from the Underground...

Common Serial Port Settings

There's no law or standard that dictates the serial settings, but this will cover 95 percent of the managed devices on the market today:

- **Speed** 9600 bits per second
- **Parity** None
- **Data Bits** 8
- **Stop Bits** 1
- **Flow Control** None

The first four settings abbreviate to *9600, N, 8,* and *1*.

Once you've connected to the console port, most switches will allow you to put an IP address and gateway on the switch for management through telnet, secure telnet (SSH), SNMP, or a Web browser. The IP address on the switch exists for management only. A common Layer 2 switch will never use an IP address for moving data.

Remote management using one of the IP protocols makes it possible to finish configuring the switch from the comfort of your office instead of standing in a cramped wiring closet balancing your notebook in one hand while you try to type with the other. Most modern switches even have advanced Web interfaces that make most common tasks as easy as pointing and clicking, so even if the switch sits on a box next to your desk, you'll still want to put an IP address on it so that you don't have to do everything through the command-line interface (CLI).

Virtual Local Area Networks

Switches already segment networks, but virtual local area networks (VLANs) take segmentation to the next level. VLANs allow you to designate which ports can directly communicate with each other and which ones need the assistance of a router. For example, a hypothetical company has two departments, Finance and Sales. Neither department shares data, but all of the company's computers connect through a single switch. To make sure that network traffic from each department doesn't interfere with the other department (or to keep certain data away from prying eyes), you could create a group of ports that belong to the Finance department's LAN and another set of ports that belongs to the Sales department's LAN. VLANs can even extend past the boundaries of a single switch.

In the previous example, the Finance and Sales departments could have workstations that connect to multiple switches within the company's LAN. In this case, the Finance and Sales VLANs can also extend across all of these switches. The IEEE 802.3 standard has specifications for manufacturers who want to include VLANs as a standards-based feature. The IEEE 802.1Q standard deals with VLANs; therefore, VLANs created on one vendor's switch that conforms to the 802.1Q standard will work with VLANs on any other vendor's switch that complies with the 802.1Q standard.

Vendors often find that strictly adhering to standards stifles their ability to provide superior solutions and differentiate their offerings from the rest of the pack, or a vendor might need a solution prior to the ratification of a standard. For example, Cisco engineered the Inter-Switch Link (ISL) protocol as a proprietary trunking protocol similar to the 802.1Q standard. ISL gives Cisco switches additional VLAN functionality, but it can only work with other Cisco devices, so Cisco now opts for 802.1Q on its newer products instead of its proprietary ISL.

Some advanced switches can form VLANs dynamically based on a wide range of information, such as IP addresses or user logins. These abilities will vary by manufacturer and even by product lines from the same company. Obviously, VLANs don't set themselves up out of the box, so only managed switches will have VLAN capabilities. We'll see in later chapters how the security provided by VLANs can be subverted, but at a minimum they do provide features that make them worth the time needed to configure them.

Port Aggregation

Port aggregation allows a switch to combine, or aggregate, multiple connections that act as single pipe to transfer data. This increases the total bandwidth, and adds fault-tolerance in case one of the links in the bundle dies. Port aggregation takes more than just plugging in multiple connections between switches. As you learned in the section on STP, this will just cause a network loop. On switches that support this feature, the network administrator can manage the switch and create the aggregate. The 802.3 standard has provisions for vendors who want to enable this feature and make it interoperable with port aggregation from other vendors who also conform to the specification.

Moving Switching beyond Layer 2

Conventional switching uses MAC addresses to move traffic to the correct switch ports at Layer 2 of the OSI model. Networks have grown far more complex since the first switch entered the market, and as such, network engineers now require switches that can move data based on more than just MAC addresses. These advanced switches can now use information from higher layers of the OSI model. As such, we say that these switches can perform multilayer switching.

Understanding the Need for Layer 3 Switching

Switches do an excellent job of eliminating collisions from the network, allowing LANs to grow much larger than with hubs. This does not mean, however, that a switched network can grow indefinitely. Switches deal with the garbage and congestion from Layer 1 and Layer 2 of the OSI model, but there are five more layers above those, and each of these layers can add its own special problems to the network. Layer 3, the network layer, creates protocol-based connections between network devices. Most administrators will recognize IP, IPX, AppleTalk, and NetBEUI as common protocols at this layer. Instead of the MAC addresses that Layer 2 uses, Layer 3 uses protocol addresses configured through software.

Protocols at this layer fall roughly into three categories: routable, unroutable, and routing. A routable protocol by definition can transmit packets between multiple networks or subnets; an unroutable network cannot. Routable protocols use routing protocols to find the routes that they need to get from network to network. Common routable protocols include IP, IPX, and AppleTalk. NetBEUI is a common unroutable protocol. Routing Information Protocol (RIP) for IP and IPX and Open Shortest Path First (OSPF) are common routing protocols. Does this mean that unroutable traffic can never cross a WAN? No. Some routers, for example, can bridge NetBEUI traffic, which allows it to transverse a WAN. Therefore, some administrators would argue that NetBEUI is routable, since a router is moving the packets. The individuals who create networking exams usually do not agree with this argument.

IP uses its familiar 32-bit address to connect devices across the LAN and across the world. IPX uses an 80-bit address. Routers can move these packets between networks because part of each address represents the network and part of the address represents the host. Think of the host address as your street address and think of the network address as your city and state. If someone tried to send mail to your home address of 123 Main Street from the same city as you, the local postmaster could probably find you. If the mail came from another city, however, the post office wouldn't have any idea where to send the mail. Even when the mail does make it properly between cities, it takes more time than when sending mail within the city, just as switching moves data much faster than routing.

Figure 7.7 Comparing IP Addresses to House Numbers

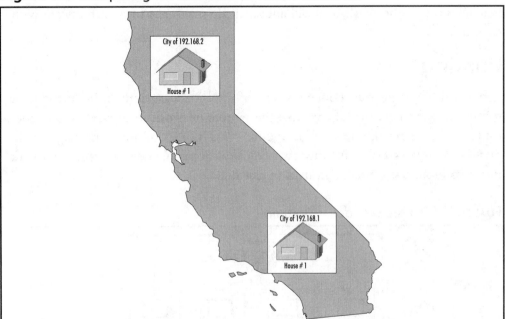

Let's take a look at two houses in the hypothetical state of Taxilvania. The first house is in the city of "192.168.1," and the second house is in the city of "192.168.2." Both of these houses have the identification of "#1." If someone in the southern city wants to send a letter to House #1 in the northern city, that person will need more information than just the house address. In this example, the person would have to address the letter to House #1 in the city of 192.168.2. Using a real TCP/IP address, this would look like "192.168.2.1."

Just as with Layer 2, Layer 3 uses both unicasts and broadcasts. When a station knows the destination for its data, it uses a unicast packet, but when it doesn't know, it floods the network with a request. Examples of these requests include IP Address Resolution Protocol (ARP) requests and IPX Get Nearest Server (GNS) requests. This works well on a small network, but what happens when thousands of stations on the same network send these requests? Unlike Layer 2 collisions,

Layer 3 broadcasts extend beyond each segment to the entire network. Therefore, all of the network devices on a single network or subnet comprise a *broadcast domain*. With enough stations on a network, broadcasts can choke out real data and bring the network to its knees. This condition is called a *broadcast storm*.

Sound familiar? We've effectively recreated the same Layer 2 problem (collisions) as a more colossal problem at Layer 3. Clearly, the network engineer needs to reduce the size of the broadcast domain without reducing the number of machines on the network, and still allow all the machines to communicate with each other.

Routing

A network engineer can reduce the size of the broadcast domain by introducing routers into the network. If we take the sample network in Figure 7.8 and add a router to it, we get the network in Figure 7.9. This second network diagram divides each workstation into its own collision domain, and divides the network into two broadcast domains instead of just one.

Figure 7.8 Single Broadcast Domain

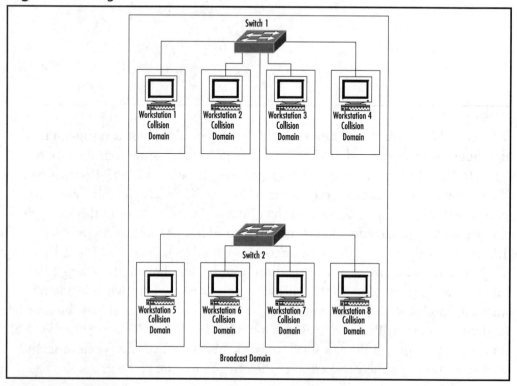

Routers divide broadcast domains as effectively as switches divide collision domains. Routers squelch broadcasts. A broadcast storm on one side of a router has no effect on network devices on the other side of the router. This seems so easy, why wouldn't a network engineer just replace all of the switches with routers?

Figure 7.9 Multiple Broadcast Domains Using Routers

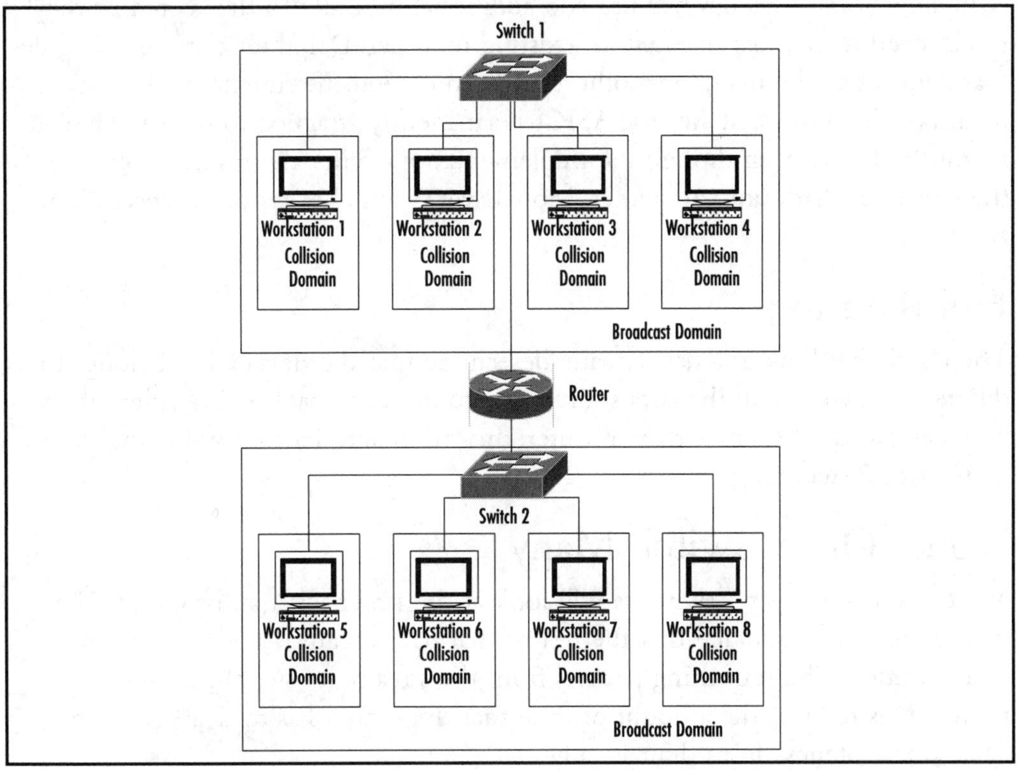

There are many reasons not to do this. First, routers cost extremely more than even high-end switches on a price-per-port basis. Second, the amount of work that it takes a router to manipulate packets takes so much more processing power that routers can introduce a great deal of latency into a network. Therefore, network engineers have to balance the need to logically divide a network with the monetary cost and packet latency associated with a router "hop."

Layer 3 Switching in Action

The venerable network engineer, remembering how much switches improved over bridging, tried to do the same thing with routing. By adding routing processors to switches, engineers allowed the switches to route packets in addition to just forwarding frames. Moving the routing to the switch lowers the cost and reduces the latency. However, many mechanisms exist for accomplishing Layer 3 switching. Some switches need to add additional modules to the switch or they might need to add *daughter cards* to existing modules. Daughter cards are modules that connect to the main, or motherboards, to extend the functionality of the main boards. Some switches use ASICs permanently attached to the switch. You might think that even though the implementations differ the results should be the same, but that's not true either. Most Layer 3 switches move packets one of two ways.

Full Routing

These switches look at a data stream, determine that the destination belongs to a different network than the data source, and routes each packet. Even though switches can do this faster than a router, this still makes Layer 3 switching slower than Layer 2 switching.

Route Once, Switch Many

More advanced Layer 3 switches will look at the first packet and route it. The switch will then conclude that the rest of that data stream needs to go to the same location. The remaining packets from the stream are switched rather than routed. This reduces the amount of time that the switch has to deal with the data, so the latency drops dramatically.

Layer 3 Switching and VLANs

As you might recall from earlier in the chapter, VLANs allow network engineers to isolate traffic on the network. This does isolate the traffic, but at some point, the stations from one VLAN might need to talk to a station on another VLAN. More importantly, stations from two different VLANs might need to reach a connection on a third VLAN, perhaps to get to the Internet. Network engineers can use these VLANs to create multiple networks or subnets in the same switch or in multiple switches installed throughout the campus. Switches with Layer 3 functionality now allow the multiple VLANs to communicate with each other quickly and efficiently. Without the Layer 3 functionality, the switches would have to access an external router to move packets between the VLANs. This could greatly reduce performance and increase latency on the network.

Understanding Multilayer Switching

Multilayer switching refers to moving data based on OSI layers beyond Layer 2 without using an external router. Some vendors will call "Route Once, Switch Many" at Layer 3 multilayer switching and leave it at that. Other vendors will actually use information at the higher levels to make additional switching decisions. Most vendors who go beyond Layer 3 to make switching decisions usually only go one level higher. Switches with Layer 2 and Layer 3 functionality give us transparent bridging and routing, respectively, at high speeds. What happens at Layer 4?

Just as when playing "Name That Tune," a collection of individual notes finally resembles a song, at Layer 4 data starts to resemble protocols that people can recognize. From the TCP/IP world, Layer 4 defines such protocols as HyperText Transfer Protocol (HTTP), HyperText Transfer Protocol Secure (HTTPS), and Simple Mail Transfer Protocol (SMTP). A network engineer could, as an example, use Layer 4 information to route all SMTP traffic to a particular switch port. From a security standpoint, a network engineer can use Layer 4 switching to make sure that only SMTP traffic reaches a mail server, thereby eliminating potential hacking. A firewall can serve the same function, but a firewall does not have the same performance as a switch.

MLS can also provide Quality of Service (QoS). For example, if a campus network carries both voice and data, the switch can assign a higher priority to voice traffic to reduce choppy conversations caused by congestion of other data traffic or high latency. Data traffic can typically survive higher latency than voice or video streams can, due to all of the built-in error-correcting mechanisms.

Only the highest-end switches can perform MLS. It requires additional memory and processing power that your average switch will never hope to have. As such, these switches cost more money and take more expertise to configure. You'll usually only find these switches at Fortune 1000 companies, large government installations, or other organizations that have large networks and even larger budgets.

Using Switching to Improve Security

Locking the door to the wiring closet doesn't cut it as high security anymore; the savvy network engineer has to take a few more precautions. Most network engineers don't give switch security a second thought because switches don't store any data. However, they do transfer data (and potentially confidential data), and that's all the motivation a talented hacker needs.

Patching the Switch

Many switches allow for firmware upgrades to fix known problems. Usually, this only applies to managed switches, but unmanaged switches might have a big enough problem that the vendor will release updated chips for the switch. Anyone who has ever "flashed" a switch can attest to how nerve-racking it is. If anything goes wrong, that could be it for the switch, and you've just ruined your evening. Given that, why flash them?

Depending on the nature of the patch (and prevailing indecency laws in your state), you can elect not to install the patch. Some patches directly affect the security of the switch, and if this is the case, no matter what else you do, you will always have this security hole until you fix this. When it comes to security, you cannot keep your head in the sand. Make it part of your routine to regularly check your vendor's Web site for code updates, or better yet, if you're low on SPAM, see if you can sign up for your switch manufacturer's proactive notification mailing list.

Damage & Defense…

Flashing a Switch

Many things can go wrong upgrading a switch image or firmware, but you can avoid most of these by preparing for the upgrade. This is not the type of thing that you do off-the-cuff.

- **Prepare a back-out plan** You need to have a specific plan to correct the condition or work around it before things go south because you won't be thinking clearly after the fact.

Continued

- **RTFM** No vendor wants its helpdesk flooded with frantic calls about dead switches, so all vendors go out of their way to list the steps in excruciating detail (usually). You need to read the instructions at least twice—once before you start and once as you're performing the upgrade. If you don't understand a step, call the vendor for clarification. This is not a good time for improv.

- **Know your equipment** Is the patch that you just down-loaded really intended for the product and particular model that you're trying to flash? If it is, does the switch meet the minimum specifications, such as memory or storage space? If the answer is "No" or "I don't know," do *not* continue!

- **Gather your materials** If you need more memory, different cables, or anything else, make sure that you have all of these handy before you begin.

- **Back up the configuration** A switch will sometimes lose its configuration after a firmware upgrade. If you have a compli-cated configuration, you don't want to recreate it from memory at 2 A.M.

- **Use a UPS** The switch and the station pushing the update need to be on an uninterruptible power supply (UPS) during the procedure, because even a minor power fluctuation at the wrong moment could lead to a weekend you'll never get back. The switch should always connect to a UPS at all times anyway, so this step shouldn't inconvenience you too much.

- **Choose the right time** Flashing a switch will probably require a reboot, so you don't want to do it in the middle of the day when everyone should be working. Avoid the temptation of loading the switch early with the hope of just rebooting it on your way out the door, because you could get a lockup in the middle and kill the switch. Warn your users well ahead of time whenever possible and keep abreast of important company events so that you can schedule around them.

- **Verify the update** After you've followed all of the vendor's instructions, confirm that the firmware did upgrade, and make sure that the switch is working. If everything looks good, you're done. Congratulations!

Securing Unused Ports

Do you know where all your ports are? Administrators will often light up unused jacks in case they need to plug in a station there in the future. This can make sense if the administrator has extra switch ports, but consider the location of the empty, hot jack. Is it in a conference room frequented by numerous, unmonitored visitors? Is it next to an open loading dock in a warehouse that's never had a computer? Scenarios such as these and similar ones present quick entry points for a fast hacker with a light notebook. Boom! DHCP kicked the hacker an address, and now he has the "My Documents" subdirectory from every Windows 2000 workstation with a blank password. However, all your users save all their work on the servers, so you don't have to worry, right? Honestly, beyond physical security, this is all that you can do for an unmanaged switch. The rest of the safeguards rely on configuration options only available on managed switches.

Adding Passwords to the Switch

Most managed switches will allow a password for viewing mode and a password for configuration. Some switches might use different passwords for direct (console) access and another set of passwords for remote access (Telnet, SSH, HTTP, and so forth). Determine which ones your switch supports and set all of them with hard-to-crack passwords. Many administrators don't see a need to password the switch, especially a Layer 2 switch without VLANs, since the worst thing that could happen is that someone could shut it down and then lock everyone else out with a password. A quick reset in the wiring closet will fix this. The company suffers some downtime, and the administrator gets annoyed. This doesn't seem like much, but if you add up how much productivity this little stunt just cost the company and put some salary numbers behind it, you come up with a substantial cost. Unfortunately, it gets worse from here.

Port Mirroring

One of the best traditional tools in a network engineer's arsenal is a capturing device, or *sniffer*. Traditional Ethernet transmits data over a shared medium, so every station on the wire sees all of the traffic. Usually, stations ignore data that the sender did not mean for them to see. However, a network sniffer operates in *promiscuous* mode, which means that it acts as if every frame that it sees belongs to it. A network engineer can find a lot of problems this way, but a hacker can steal all of a company's data this way, too. Switches don't use a shared medium, which is how they avoid collisions. This also prevents sniffing from all but the best hackers who can actively fake MAC addresses, discussed in Chapters 6 and 8. This also prevents network engineers from diagnosing problems on a network.

Computer engineers took this into account when they designed switches. What should a network engineer do if he needs to see all of the traffic going to and from a server on a particular port? Many switches have a feature called *port mirroring* that allows a network engineer to send all of the activity from one port to another port without affecting the traffic of the original port. The network engineer can now attach his sniffer to the second port to look for irregularities. If the switch doesn't have a password, a hacker can easily do the same thing, and capture everything going to and from that server. Most data travels across the network unencrypted, so it becomes trivial for the hacker to reassemble the data stream into usable files. Most POP3 mail passwords go across the network unencrypted, also, so the hacker can continue to download user mail from home if the company uses POP3 mail and has remote access to its mail system.

Remote Management

Most managed switches allow users to configure them or to check the network status from a workstation using Telnet, SSH, HTTP, HTTPS, or some other protocol. Consider the limitations of each protocol. Most administrators will use HTTP if available because the graphical interface makes it easier to configure the switch. The drawback is that HTTP has no encryption, so consider the path that you take to the switch. Is it secure? Could someone put a sniffer between you and the switch and get the switch password? If this seems like a likely scenario in your shop, using a Web browser from your desk might not be an option. Does the switch support management using HTTPS, which is also known as Secure Socket Layer (SSL)? If so, this provides a much safer management platform. What if you need to use a text interface to make changes with the CLI? Telnet suffers from the same security problems as HTTP. SSH gives access to a CLI, plus it uses encryption. Check to see if your switch can use SSH, and use that instead of Telnet. Some administrators feel safe enough by not configuring an IP address on a switch, thereby eliminating all remote access functions. Some switches come preconfigured from the factory to use DHCP to obtain an IP address, so the switch might get an address despite your best efforts.

> **NOTE**
>
> No version of Windows has a built-in SSH client, so you can wait for Bill Gates to write one, or you can download PuTTY for free from www.chiark.greenend.org.uk/~sgtatham/putty/.

Some switches will allow administrators to restrict remote management to specific IP addresses. If your switch has this feature, determine from which stations you need to access the switch, and then enable the restrictions accordingly.

Remote Monitoring

A network engineer cannot be everywhere in the organization, but he does have to know what every piece of equipment is doing all of the time. Fortunately, most managed network devices allow network engineers to monitor these devices from a central, remote location.

Simple Network Management Protocol

Many managed switches allow administrators to monitor status through SNMP. SNMP is a powerful, standards-based protocol that can monitor any aspect of a switch that a vendor allows. Vendors create special files called Management Information Bases (MIBs) that contain all of the SNMP functionality unique to their devices. This allows the protocol to work for devices from multiple vendors, while still giving each vendor enough flexibility to account for all of the features in each unique device. Unfortunately, most SNMP messages travel in clear text over the network, which makes them subject to sniffing on nonsecure links. On February 12, 2002, the CERT Coordination Center issued an SNMP advisory, which was updated as recently as May 14, 2003. The advisory (www.cert.org/advisories/CA-2002-03.html) lists specific security issues with this protocol and lists vendors affected by it. If you need to use SNMP, check to see if your product made it to the advisory. If it has, check with your vendor to see if a patch exists, and if it does, apply it. If no patch exists, carefully weigh the benefits versus the risks before implementing SNMP. The advisory also gives a piece of common-sense advice: if you don't need SNMP, turn it off. This applies to most features in the world of computing.

After all of this, if you've decided that you do need SNMP, remember that SNMP "passwords" are called *community strings*, and most implementations have a read-only community string and a read-write community string. The defaults are usually "Public" and "Private." You should change these immediately.

The Internet Engineering Task Force (IETF), the organization responsible for maintaining Internet standards through Requests for Comment (RFC), has created a second revision to SNMP called SNMPv3. RFC 3414 (www.ietf.org/rfc/rfc3414.txt?number=3414) deals specifically with security for SNMPv3. Examination of this protocol shows that the IETF has included provisions for user authentication and encryption, making SNMPv3 much more secure than earlier versions. This standard has only existed in its present form since December 2002, so only very new devices will support all the features of this standard.

Damage & Defense...

Do You Need the Read-Write Community?

SNMP not only has the power to monitor a switch, but vendors can also write MIBs to configure the switch. Most administrators who use SNMP to proactively monitor the condition of their switches never use it to reconfigure the switches. If you fall into this category, deactivate the SNMP read-write features of the switch if possible. Remember: before version 3, SNMP stood for "Security's Not My Problem."

Other Protocols

Some vendors use proprietary protocols for monitoring or configuring their switches. For example, Cisco switches and routers use Cisco Discovery Protocol (CDP), a Layer 2 protocol, to exchange network topology information. This information floats across the network unencrypted without a password. Depending on the configuration of your network, this information might even get transmitted across the Internet. Given the huge prevalence of Cisco equipment, other vendors, such as Hewlett-Packard, have started supporting CDP. Even if a particular vendor doesn't support CDP, this does not preclude that vendor from having a similar feature using a different protocol.. Check the documentation thoroughly and turn off any features that you don't plan to use. Vendors usually brag about these features, so you shouldn't have much of a problem learning about these features, and that's half the battle.

Setting the Time

Many switches log activity that could prove vital if you have to investigate a possible security breach. If this happens, you will need to know that the time logged for each event is accurate or you won't be able to correlate these logs with the logs from any other machines. Most current switches allow administrators to configure automatic time synchronization via Network Time Protocol (NTP). This will give your switch accurate time, but be careful when you configure this option: some equipment will allow you to configure it as a time server as well as a client, which could inadvertently give away information about your network. In addition, either configure all of your devices to use the same time source or, better yet, if you have one device capable of acting as an NTP server, configure that device to synch its time with a reliable time source and then configure the rest of your internal devices to get their time from your internal time server. This will decrease your amount of Internet traffic and increase security since you can close the NTP port on your firewall for all of the other devices. The less traffic that can leave your network, the better.

Using VLANs for Security

VLANs can effectively divide LANs into multiple subnets that administrators connect through routing or Layer 3 switching. However, as an administrator, if you have a group of computers to which most users should not have access, some switches with a VLAN feature will allow you to create a VLAN that most other users cannot access. In some cases, an administrator can create a VLAN for the management interfaces of the switches themselves and create another VLAN for user traffic. In this way, the administrator can limit who can get to the management functions of the switches.

Some switches will allow you to create VLANs limited to certain protocols. For example, if all of your network services rely strictly on TCP/IP, you could create VLANs that filter out the other protocols to prevent possible security breaches.

Using Multilayer Switching (MLS) for Security

MLS can switch traffic based on the content of that traffic. For example, an administrator could configure an MLS switch to send all of the campus' SMTP traffic to the only port where the administrator has set up the company's SMTP server. This can prevent pirate mail servers or mail-enabled viruses from operating inside the network where the firewall can't stop this type of activity.

Choosing the Right Switch

Now that you know what features differentiate switches, how do you know what switch you should purchase? Buying a switch with features that you don't need will drain your budget of money that you could spend elsewhere, while under-buying could force you to upgrade earlier than you should. In most campuses, you'll need to purchase more than one switch. Should you only purchase the same, exact switch no matter where you place it in the campus? You probably don't want to do this.

Vendors divide campus networks into multiple layers. 3Com uses the terms "desktop," "workgroup," and "core," while Cisco uses "access," "distribution," and "core." Other vendors have their own terms for each layer. For example, most vendors will use "backbone" synonymously with "core" and "edge" instead of "access." As Cisco has created a business training administrators, let's discuss the campus network using their terms.

Understanding the Layers of the Campus Network

Designing a large network might seem to be a daunting task, but it becomes much more manageable if you split it into smaller pieces. Most large networks will have three distinct layers: access, distribution, and core. Each layer serves a specific function in the campus network, and as such, each layer will use different devices. Even small networks will still have these three layers at a functional level, although multiple layers could get combined into the same piece of equipment.

Access Layer

Switches at this layer of the campus connect directly to workstations. High port density and low price per port differentiate switches at this layer from the other layers. Switches at this layer might provide for more aggregate bandwidth from the ports than the backplane can handle to deliver the lowest price per port. These switches seldom do more than Layer 2 switching and will often even lack management functions.

Distribution Layer

Switches at this layer aggregate traffic from the access layer before passing it up to the core layer. Most of the special features, such as VLANs, MLS, and access policies get set at this layer. These switches need to have high bandwidth, fast processors, and enough ports to accept all of the switches from the access layer. These switches also need to have high-speed uplinks to the core. If the campus has topologies other than Ethernet, such as Token Ring or Fiber Distributed Data Interface (FDDI), switches at this level should provide the translations.

Core Layer

This layer meshes all of the traffic from the distribution layer, controlling traffic at an enterprise level. This level cares about nothing except speed. Although most switching involves Ethernet, Asynchronous Transfer Mode (ATM) still plays a huge part at this layer, especially in the telecommunications industry. Legacy FDDI continues to survive in this space due to its reliability, but at a high cost and only 100 Mbps transfer speeds, don't expect to see any new installations.

The "Grab Bag"

Those of us older than dirt should remember Pierce Brosnan's pre-007 days when, hawking soda with his proper British accent, he declared, "Ours is not a perfect world." Your needs might not perfectly fall into any of the previous three categories. Cisco calls a combination of the distribution layer and the core layer a *collapsed backbone*, so admittedly, even Cisco realizes that all networks do not contain each layer as a separate entity. Some networks might find it necessary to collapse the backbone even further and combine all three layers into a single switch or a group of switches acting as peers. Don't let a preconceived notion of "layers" lock you into a structure that doesn't work for your company.

Assessing Your Needs

This is the point where you combine your knowledge of what's available with what you can use. To do this, we need to examine the entire campus environment and understand how the company works.

Mapping the Campus

You don't need an elaborate map of your campus, but you do need an accurate one that you can read. If you haven't used a diagramming tool like Microsoft Visio in the past, you should consider it now. The campus map needs to show all of the wiring closets, server rooms, user and printer locations, and any other wiring drops that have special significance. The map need not be to scale, but you should indicate any cable runs that could approach or exceed 100 meters. Remember: you have to consider the length of the cable between two locations and not the actual distance; meandering conduits can greatly increase distance. This distance also includes drop cable lengths, and not just the cabling in the wall.

On your second pass through the network, concentrate on the rooms where you need to place the switches. Make a note of the available power, air conditioning/heating, racks, cabinets, and data drops. Contact facilities if necessary to get this information. Note any equipment already in these locations so that you can estimate the power and environmental control resources left for the switches.

Understanding the Data

Believe it or not, many network engineers and administrators know surprisingly little about what their company does. If the company halted its normal operations and started to make widgets, these administrators probably wouldn't notice any difference. However, to design a network you have to understand what the users need it to do. You need to understand how much data the users move and how often. You also need to know the location of the users in relation to their data. All of this will make a big difference in designing your network.

Assembling the Pieces

Now, you have a good idea of your environment. Let's look at a few example networks to see where we would use each type of switch.

Single-Floor Office Building with a Central Server Room and Wiring Closet

The network doesn't get any simpler than this. You might think that any switch might do here, but we haven't analyzed all of the data. We need to factor into the equation how many users we have and what they do. First, let's consider 24 users, six network attached printers, a single fileserver, and a single mail server. All of these connections could easily fit into a single 36 or 48 port 10/100 stackable, unmanaged switch. If this switch has two Gigabit Ethernet uplinks, the servers will find a high-speed home. If you need to track network performance, you could look for the same type of switch with management capabilities. A network this small doesn't require more than fast Layer 2 switching. If the users work with large files, the switch should be nonblocking, which means that the total aggregate bandwidth of all of the ports will not exceed the capacity of the backplane. What if the office grows to 100 users?

Most stackable switches don't have more than 48 standard ports, so this scenario requires at least three stackable switches. Assuming that each switch has two Gigabit Ethernet uplinks, you could use one Gigabit uplink between each switch to form a chain, or designate one switch as the core and use it to uplink to the other two switches. Either scenario leaves one Gigabit Ethernet uplink for each server, with a Gigabit uplink remaining. Computer usage should dictate which you use. Look for the heaviest users of the file server, and put these people in the same switch as the file server. Try to do the same with the mail server. Users who need equal access to both servers can go into the core switch of the second configuration.

If you take this same scenario, but with a chassis switch, you can configure the box with enough 10/100 blades for all of the workstations and printers, and a Gigabit Ethernet card for the servers. Provided that the switch is nonblocking, all workstations have equal access to the servers. If you need additional speed and flexibility, you could replace all of the Ethernet blades with 10/100/1000 blades. Switch blades with Gigabit ports have a lower port density than 10/100 blades, so this will take more slots in the switch, limiting future upgrades. You could add Layer 3 functionality to this network to divide departments, but given only 100 workstations, you would probably not see much of an improvement in performance.

Multifloor, Multibuilding Campus with Distributed Wiring Closets

Now, let's imagine the same network, but concentrate on just one floor in just one skyscraper of a large, multibuilding campus. Each floor has 200 users and about 20 printers. Each floor has its own wiring closet, but there's only one central server room in the complex. We would probably start with high-density stackable switches for the workstations or a single chassis loaded with 10/100 blades on each floor. The floor switches would uplink to a high-end switch in the ground floor wiring closet of each building. If we use a single chassis on each floor, we could aggregate up to four 1000Base-LX links between the ground floor switch and each of the other switches on the floor. Aggregate links will provide increased bandwidth and fault tolerance in case of a cable or port issue. In the case of stackable switches, each stackable switch will get a single 1000Base-LX connection to the ground floor chassis. All inter-floor connections will use fiber due to distance restrictions.

Regardless of whether we use stackable switches or a chassis, we'll create a VLAN on each floor with its own subnet. If we use a chassis on the floors, the floor switches will provide the Layer 3 switching functionality; otherwise, we'll use the Layer 3 functionality in the ground floor switch. The ground floor switches from each building will connect to a central chassis in the server room using aggregated 1000Base-LX connections for increased throughput and fault tolerance. All chassis will have dual power supplies, but the central switch will also have a dual management card for fault tolerance. All servers will plug directly into the core switch, with the intranet server using two aggregated 1000Base-T connections for throughput and fault tolerance.

One of the servers belongs exclusively to Accounting, but the Accounting department has users all over the campus on every floor. After studying the department's data usage, you discover that all Accounting users regularly access a specialty finance package on the Accounting server that uses port 1678 TCP. Since your distribution switches at the bottom of each floor have Layer 4 switching features, you create a dynamic VLAN based on port 1678 TCP that connects Accounting directly to their server, while limiting everyone else's visibility to it.

Finally, the core switch attaches to the company WAN using ATM OC-3 to connect this site to the company's second campus at the other end of the country. Now, the company has all of the resources necessary to get its job done.

Living in the Real World

Imagining the perfect network is a lot of fun, but we live in a world of budgets and legacy equipment. Don't limit your network design based on your perception of the budget; let the CFO worry about that. Your job is to present the best network that you can with a price estimate. Map the network and indicate the type of switch and features that you want in each location. Now, check with the vendors to see what they have that matches what you want. If they don't have exactly what you imagined, ask one of their sales engineers what their equivalent is and see how that works into your design. If the CFO can't afford this design, repeat the process until you have one that the CFO will approve, but with each new design, highlight features that you had to omit to make the price point; that's the CYA feature of network design. While you're practicing CYA techniques, don't forget to add annual maintenance into your budget request for equipment that needs it.

Most of this chapter has stayed vendor neutral, but now you need to pick a vendor. The 802.3 standard provides for a lot of interoperability, but the truth is that most of the top name vendors have used proprietary techniques to improve upon the standard. Mixing vendors forces you to stick with a strict standard and not use the features that you probably paid for when you bought the switch. Moreover, vendors have tested their equipment the heaviest with their own equipment. A bug from one vendor might cause another switch to malfunction, which will take you forever to diagnose because the malfunctioning piece of equipment really isn't the problem. You can usually exclude unmanaged access layer switches from this dogged brand loyalty since they don't have any special features about which to worry; however, cross-platform bugs are still an issue.

Unfortunately, not every network engineer has the luxury of upgrading an entire network at once. Often, infrastructure can get upgraded one switch at a time, which means that the network might temporarily have a mix of vendors at the distribution layer or even core layer. In this case, you have to carefully consider the equipment that you're proposing and check with each vendor to see if they know about any potential problems. Then, adjust your plan accordingly. Even though a multivendor network makes it hard for you to diagnose problems, it makes it easier for the vendors. As soon as you call one of them with a problem, they won't hesitate to tell you that it's the other vendor's fault!

Choosing an Established Vendor

How should you choose your vendor? In the late 1980s, IT professionals often joked, "Nobody ever got fired for buying IBM." You can never overlook the 800-pound gorilla in any industry. Consider the reputation of each vendor. When you see the vendor's name with a product review, which way do most of the reviews go? How long has the company been in business? Using an established, stable company usually means that they will still be in business long enough to honor the full warranty of your equipment. Established companies usually have a large client base, which means that if a problem does exist with a particular product, you probably won't be the first one to encounter it, and the company might have a patch for it by the time it affects you. Many established companies stay in business by using a conservative strategy; they rarely release the first-of-its-kind products, but they usually aren't too far behind the company that did. These veterans of networking have learned the difference between the cutting edge and the bleeding edge. When these companies do fall too far behind the curve, they simply buy a startup leading the pack, which puts them back on top.

Gambling on a Startup

At the other end of the spectrum, you have startups, the best of which are usually formed from the top engineers from the big companies. These small companies usually enter the market with a superior product at a low price and a lot of enthusiasm. If possible, you want to meet with representatives from these companies at trade shows such as NetWorld+Interop. These trade shows allow you to see the products, and more importantly, the people behind them. Startups often can't afford a large sales force to attend these shows, so you get to talk to the actual systems engineers (SEs) who will help you when you encounter a problem. SEs have trained so hard to learn their product lines that they've had to lose all other skills, including the ability to lie. Pump these people for as much information as you can. Find out how many support staff they have, the hours they work, and how long it takes for them to get back to you, and where they have a physical presence. Equipment from startups can sometimes require an onsite visit from the regional SE. The first time you find out that your region includes 10 other states, with your SE living at the far end of your region, shouldn't be when your network has stopped passing traffic.

You expect to find SEs tired, especially at a Las Vegas trade show, but if it looks like they're one step short of asking you to put them out of their misery, there's a good chance that their product has a lot of bugs and it will take a long time before they answer your support call. If the SEs look well rested and knowledgeable, you could have a winner on your hands. If the company has a decent staff, but hasn't sold very many units, you can usually expect personal attention. If you buy enough of the vendor's products and have a clean shop, the vendor might even offer you a discount on the condition that you tour potential customers through your facility so they can see the switch in action. Not only does this save you some money and get you a little recognition from your peers, it also puts you on the fast track for technical support. The last things a startup needs are a disgruntled reference and a malfunctioning demonstration network. Finally, get all contracts and Service Level Agreements (SLAs) in writing, but always remember that these are just pieces of paper, and they can't bring a failed company back to life. Warranties by themselves don't fix networks.

Looking at the Brand Names

In networking, Cisco is the 800-pound gorilla. Cisco has an established reputation in the industry and has either built or bought technology for every level of your enterprise. Cisco started as a router manufacturer, but now derives more revenue from switches than from routers. Cisco's recent acquisition of LinkSys even gives them a significant stake in the Small Office/Home Office (SOHO) market. Cisco's size also means that you will probably find more people familiar with Cisco equipment than from any other manufacturer, so hiring staff to work with your network becomes much easier. Cisco products usually come with a 90-day or one-year warranty, depending on the product. Cisco has various support plans (SmartNet) to extend the warranty for at least three years beyond the date that they discontinue the product. Cisco technical support will usually not disappoint you, which is good considering how much the support contracts cost.

3Com occupies the same market space as Cisco, although 3Com gets far less attention these days. Like Cisco, 3Com has a product for every level of most enterprises, including some of the best NICs on the market. You won't see any bleeding-edge products from 3Com, but you will see stable products that perform well. 3Com usually has good technical support, and depending on the product, longer warranties than Cisco. 3Com core products usually have a one-year warranty, while access layer products can have five-year or lifetime warranties. Review the warranty on each product carefully before you buy it. If you're considering a simple, unmanaged switch, you'll never have to apologize for any of the 3Com SuperStack 3 Baseline models.

Notes from the Underground…

Getting System Engineers to Help Design Your Network

On a personal note, years ago, I scribbled out some requirements for my new network and then I visited various vendors at NetWorld+Interop. I invited a sales engineer from each to build a quick diagram of my requirements using their products. I had a nice collection of diagrams by the time I hit the 3Com booth. When I gave my requirements to the 3Com sales engineer, he considered my list and said, "You don't need a chassis switch, you need stackable switches."

"No, I need a chassis. Please design the network around that parameter."

"No, this type of network only needs stackable switches. I can design this whole thing in just a minute," he insisted.

Continued

> "I've spent a year talking to my users to understand how they use the network, I've built the servers, and I know where and what type of cabling I have available. I used to work for a company that makes switches. I really, really want chassis switches in this design."
>
> He and I discussed this for a few minutes, until he decided to stop arguing with me and draw me a network design—with stackable switches. I thanked him, and dropped his card and his design in the trashcan on my way out of the booth.
>
> Over the next two years my company purchased almost a half million dollars from a startup that we first saw that day at the trade show; the ones that drew me a network with chassis switches.

Hewlett-Packard figures prominently in this category also. Their performance and warranties closely parallel 3Com, and the folks at technical support do their best to help you even with products well beyond their salad days. HP offers both managed and unmanaged, stackable and chassis solutions. HP also offers a 10G switch (made by Foundry). If you run a shop heavy with HP servers and printers, looking at HP switches makes a lot of sense.

IBM has stopped selling all switches except Token Ring—which it invented—since it formed a strategic alliance with Cisco. If you have legacy Token Ring that you need to integrate into a modern LAN, try Alcatel. Their acquisition of Xylan allows them to build switches with Token Ring, Ethernet, ATM, and WAN ports all in the same chassis.

This certainly does not complete the list of established networking companies. If you want to be thorough, you should also examine offerings from Nortel (Bay) and Enterasys (Cabletron).

Moving from the familiar to the startups, let's begin with Extreme Networks. Founded in the mid 1990s, Extreme barely qualifies as a startup anymore. Their products start at the core layer and then get faster. The company isn't venerable by normal business standards, but those standards don't really apply to the IT sector. Unlike older networking companies, Extreme doesn't have a product at each layer. Their lowest-end switch, if you can call it "low," comes with a ton of high-end features pounded into a 16-Gbps backplane. Their high-end switch can hold up to 1,440 10/100 ports on a 768 Gbps backplane, and the firmware runs a feature set that pushes the envelope well past Layer 3 switching to include load balancing and transparent Web cache redirection. If you normally buy your switches from the same store where you buy beef jerky, prepare yourself for sticker shock; however, when you start comparing the prices to other high-end switches, you'll realize that you have a real contender here.

Next comes Foundry, which like Extreme, should really come out of the startup category. Foundry produces high-end switches and load balancers. Your CFO might not know the name "Foundry," which had its initial public offering (IPO) in 1999, but anyone familiar with the equipment at major co-location facilities will recognize it. Unlike Extreme, Foundry does have a product line for the access layer, if you need high performance at the network edge.

A more traditional startup, Force10 Networks, founded in 1999, did very well in a series of tests reported in the February 3, 2003 issue of *Network World* magazine (www.nwfusion.com/reviews/2003/020310gbe.html). Force10 only has 10 GE products, so you won't see it at the network edge anytime soon, but you will see it at the core of any company that needs the highest throughput possible and doesn't mind betting on a newcomer.

In the final category, we want to mention SOHO vendors, but not by name. You know these companies because you install their products every time one of your friends wants you to split his DSL connection. If your company's business network has the same importance as the network your friend's son uses to download cheat codes for his latest video game, feel free to install these switches. If you do install these, don't forget to get some double-stick tape for the bottom of the switch so the weight of the CAT 5 cables doesn't pull it off the shelf. And while you're at your favorite hardware vendor getting the switches, pick us up a pack of beef jerky.

Checklist

☑ Only patch ports as necessary.

☑ Update the switch firmware whenever possible to remove possible bugs.

☑ Password-protect the switch whenever possible.

☑ Use secure protocols, such as HTTPS and SSH, whenever possible, or better yet, perform all of your configuration from the console.

☑ Limit remote management of the switch to only the stations that you need, if possible. If the switch allows for this, turn off remote management if you're not using it.

☑ Disable unnecessary monitoring/reporting protocols on the switch. Learn how to properly configure the ones that you do use to avoid security holes. In most cases, make sure you disable SNMP read–write abilities.

☑ Consider using VLANs to give special stations extra security when possible.

☑ Create at least one extra VLAN, if possible, for most of your workstations, so that the primary VLAN remains as an administration-only VLAN for extra security. Many vendors use VLAN1 as a default administrative VLAN1 with special access privileges, so you'll want to move your end users to another VLAN for this reason alone.

☑ Use MLS to configure static or dynamic VLANs to provide extra security for single-function servers, such as mail and Web servers.

☑ Keep a backup of managed switch configurations in case of emergency.

☑ Diagram and document your network to aid in troubleshooting. Include warranty support phone numbers, contract numbers, serial numbers, and other information that will help you quickly resolve a problem if you need to call technical support.

☑ Baseline your network performance. Lower than usual performance can indicate tampering or an intrusion. This also gives you an opportunity to learn to use your diagnostic tools in a nonemergency situation.

Summary

Switching grew out of the need for increased network bandwidth. Various network topologies exist today, but Ethernet, as defined by the various IEEE 802.3 standards, accounts for the vast majority of current LANs. The original Ethernet installations required snaking cables between computers in a bus topology. The introduction of Ethernet hubs allows for installations that look like a star topology, but actually still act as a linear bus. This allowed network engineers to increase the size of the networks.

Ethernet works on CSMA/CD, which means that too many stations connected with hubs will adversely affect the performance of the entire network since they all belong to the same collision domain. The invention of the switch allows network engineers to split the network into multiple segments, with each segment acting as an individual collision domain.

The first switches were little more than ASICs acting as transparent bridges. Traditional switches work entirely on Layer 2 of the OSI Reference Model, using MAC addresses to forward frames between network devices. Even though switches eliminate collisions, they do not eliminate broadcasts. Broadcasts, whether at Layer 2 or Layer 3, generally consist of service requests flooded over an entire network. All machines participating in this exchange of flooded frames and packets belong to a single broadcast domain. A network experiences a broadcast storm when the sheer volume of broadcasts prevents other information from passing between the devices.

Routers, working at Layer 3 of the OSI model, kill broadcasts by splitting a LAN into multiple networks or subnets. Each subnet works as its own broadcast domain. The expense and latency that routers add to the design of the network curtail their use. Layer 3 switching moves the routing function into a less expensive, faster device so that networks can more easily reap the advantages of routing.

Some switches can even use more extensive measures for moving data by examining Layer 4 of the OSI model. At this layer, switches can examine the common protocols, such as HTTP and SMTP, to make their switching decisions. Switches that work at this layer need high-level hardware to perform these functions without increasing the latency of the network.

Switches vary greatly in features and price. A small, stackable switch can take as little as a couple of inches in a rack, while a large chassis switch could monopolize the entire rack. All switches fall into two categories: unmanaged and managed. Unmanaged switches come in fixed configurations and allow for little more except Layer 2 switching. Managed switches could add nothing more than simple monitoring functions, or include high-end features, such as VLANs, Layer 3 or Layer 4 functionality, remote monitoring, port aggregation, redundant power, or other propriety functions. Depending on the capabilities of the switch, some switches operate as cut-through, which means that they forward frames immediately after reading the frame's destination. Store-and-forward switches wait for the entire frame and then forward it. Usually, very fast switches opt for the store-and-forward approach since they can process the frames quickly and reduce the number of runts on the network.

Whether managed or unmanaged, switches can vary greatly in performance. High-performance switches have fast backplanes so that even when all of the ports send the maximum amount of data at once, the switch does not have to block any data. High-performance switches also have large CAMs so that they can maintain very large switching tables.

When choosing a switch, consider where in the network the switch will go. Campus network models often contain three layers: the access or edge layer, the distribution layer, and the core or backbone layer. Simple, inexpensive switches usually go at the edge to connect workstations. Extremely fast, powerful switches sit at the core to control traffic for the enterprise. In between, network engineers usually use high-performance, feature-rich switches to provide policy-based switching and aggregate the access layer traffic for transmission to the core.

Switches come from multiple vendors. The established vendors, such as Cisco and 3Com, provide a full line of switches for all layers of your network and have the reliability that comes from longevity in the field. Often, startups can provide a better price per performance ratio, have bleeding-edge features that established companies do not have, or fill a niche ignored by the sector giants. Of course, these companies have little or no track record, which means that you assume some risk when purchasing from these companies. Regardless of the vendor you choose, sticking with a single vendor as much as possible—especially at the core—makes sense so that you can avoid incompatibility problems and leverage proprietary features.

Solutions Fast Track

Understanding the Open Systems (OSI) Reference Model

☑ Hubs work at Layer 1, switches work at Layer 2, routers work at Layer 3, and TCP works at Layer 4 of the OSI Reference Model.

☑ Starting with Layer 7, the OSI model layers are: application, presentation, session, transport, network, data link, and physical.

☑ The generic term for data encapsulated at each level is a Protocol Data Unit (PDU). The PDU at Layer 2 (such as from a switch) is a *frame*. The PDU at Layer 3 (such as from a router) is a *datagram*. The PDU at Layer 4 (such as from HTTP traffic) is a *segment*.

☑ The OSI model allows engineers to compartmentalize their designs so their work can easily integrate with the work of other engineers.

The Origin of Switching

☑ Most switches are flavors of Ethernet based on IEEE 802.3.

☑ Switches bridge data using ASICs instead of slower processors.

☑ Transparent bridging and switching are generally used interchangeably.

☑ Switches segment network traffic into separate collision domains.

Switching Standards and Features

☑ Switches vary from each other by their speed, management, size, performance, memory, multilayer switching abilities, port aggregation, VLAN abilities, and other special features.

☑ All switches must meet certain interoperability standards before they can claim IEEE 802.3 compatibility.

☑ In most cases, you can connect switches with CAT 5e cable up to 100 meters. Beyond that distance, you should use fiber.

☑ Manufacturers can add proprietary features to their switches and still achieve IEEE 802.3 compatibility.

Moving Switching beyond Layer 2

☑ Multilayer switching looks at Layer 3 and sometimes all the way to Layer 7 to make switching decisions to better segment the network.

☑ Multilayer switches can route traffic faster than external routers can.

☑ Multilayer switches increase the efficiency of VLANs by adding routing within the switch.

☑ Multilayer switches can add firewall features inside your network without sacrificing performance.

Using Switching to Improve Security

☑ Switches, like servers, need a proper configuration to maintain security.

☑ Turn off all unnecessary features.

☑ Password-protect managed switches.

☑ Every feature a switch adds could also add a security hole, so read the documentation carefully.

☑ Beware of protocols that transmit too much information, such as CDP and SNMP.

☑ Check any log files often to look for security violations.

Choosing the Right Switch

☑ Choosing the right switch involves understanding your networking needs and examining the product lines from the various vendors.

☑ The Campus Network model divides the network into three layers: access, distribution, and core.

☑ Make sure that the switch you buy is right for the network layer where you plan to use it.

☑ Make sure that your plan can accommodate necessary growth.

☑ Use presales engineers from different vendors to help you design your network, and then examine their designs carefully to see if the plans meet your requirements.

☑ Compare the offerings of multiple vendors before making a final decision.

Links to Sites

- **www.chiark.greenend.org.uk/~sgtatham/putty/** Download site for PuTTY, a freeware SSH client.

- **http://standards.ieee.org/regauth/oui/index.shtml** Index of IEEE OUIs.

- **www.cert.org/advisories/CA-2002-03.html** CERT Advisory for SNMP.

- **www.nwfusion.com/reviews/2003/020310gbe.html** *Network World* review of 10GE switches.

- **www.sniffer.com** Information on protocol analyzer from Network Associates, Inc.

- **www.tamos.com/products/commview** Information on CommView protocol analyzer from TamoSoft.

- **www.ietf.org/rfc/rfc2273.txt?number=2273** IETF specification for SNMPv3 Applications.

- **www.ietf.org/rfc/rfc3414.txt?number=3414** IETF specification for SNMPv3 Security.

- **www.wildpackets.com** Information on protocol analyzer from WildPackets.

- **http://standards.ieee.org/getieee802/portfolio.html** IEEE download site for 802 standards and links to other IEEE download groups. IEEE makes any of their standards that are at least six months old free for download. New standards require a subscription.

- **www.iso.ch/iso/en/ittf/PubliclyAvailableStandards/ s020269_ISO_IEC_7498-1_1994(E).zip** OSI Reference Model part

1 standard. The links on the main page are broken, but this link modified from their general page works.

- **www.iso.ch/iso/en/ittf/PubliclyAvailableStandards/ s025022_ISO_IEC_7498-3_1997(E).zip** OSI Reference Model part 3 standard. The links on the main page are broken, but this link modified from their general page works. There does not appear to be a part 2 link on their page.

- **www.iso.ch/iso/en/ittf/PubliclyAvailableStandards/ s014258_ISO_IEC_7498-4_1989(E).zip** OSI Reference Model part 4 standard. The links on the main page are broken, but this link modified from their general page works.

- **http://download.microsoft.com/download/VisioStandard2002/ vviewer/2002/W98NT42KMeXP/EN-US/vviewer.exe** Link for free Microsoft Visio reader so you can share your network diagram with other users, even if they don't have Visio.

Most established manufacturers, such as Cisco and 3Com, have intuitive homepages that we will not list here. The following are for harder-to-find companies.

- **www.extremenetworks.com** Extreme Network's homepage. This startup specializes in high-performance, feature-rich switches.

- **www.foundrynetworks.com** Foundry Network's homepage. This startup specializes in high-performance switches and load balancers. It has enough of a reputation in the industry that many no longer consider this a startup.

- **www.ind.alcatel.com/technologies/index.cfm?cnt=index** Alcatel's infrastructure homepage.

- **www.force10networks.com** Force10 Network's homepage. This startup only makes 10 GE products.

Mailing Lists

- **www.extremenetworks.com/apps/Subscribe/GetEmail.asp** Sign up for the *Extreme Velocity Newsletter*. This newsletter provides information on the latest products from Extreme Networks and informative How-To articles.

- **www.eweek.com/newsletter_manage**   *eWEEK Product Update Newsletter.* This newsletter gives you the latest information on products tested by eWEEK for Ziff-Davis.

- **http://infosecuritymag.bellevue.com**   *Security Wire Digest.* A newsletter specifically for security alerts.

- **www.submag.com/sub/nc?wp=wpdly2**   *Network Computing Newsletters.* This link allows you to sign up for multiple industry newsletters geared toward networking.

- **www.cisco.com/tac/newsletter/signup**   *Cisco Technical Assistance Center Newsletter.* This mailing list provides the latest information from Cisco's technical support team. Cisco uses this mailing list to inform subscribers about security problems relating to Cisco equipment.

Frequently Asked Questions

The following Frequently Asked Questions, answered by the authors of this book, are designed to both measure your understanding of the concepts presented in this chapter and to assist you with real-life implementation of these concepts. To have your questions about this chapter answered by the author, browse to **www.syngress.com/solutions** and click on the **"Ask the Author"** form. You will also gain access to thousands of other FAQs at ITFAQnet.com.

Q: What are common examples from the first four layers of the OSI model?

A: Hubs and cabling from Layer 1; switches from Layer 2; routers from Layer 3; TCP protocols, such as HTTP, and SMTP at Layer 4.

Q: What is the difference between a collision domain and a broadcast domain?

A: Collision domains include all of the network devices on a single segment, while a broadcast domain consists of all of the devices on a single network or subnet. Usually, all devices connected to a single switch port comprise a collision domain, while routers demark the boundaries of a broadcast domain.

Q: What is the maximum number of network devices that I should have in a single broadcast domain?

A: A single TCP/IP subnet allows a maximum of 16,777,214 ($2^{24}-2$) network devices; your network should never approach this maximum. A typical network will generally support up to 254 devices on high-quality switches. Networks running multiple protocols (TCP/IP, IPX, AppleTalk, DLC, NetBEUI, and so forth), low-end switches, or bandwidth-intensive applications should consider reducing this number. Some vendors claim that their equipment can handle up to 2000 machines, but most network engineers would recommend implementing VLANs and/or Layer 3 solutions well before you hit this number.

Q: Since switches work at Layer 2, below the network protocol layer, does the number of protocols that I run on my network really affect switch performance?

A: Yes. All traffic consumes bandwidth. You should eliminate unneeded traffic from the network to reduce the total volume moving over the switches. Workstations configured with IPX/SPX will still send out requests for data via this protocol, even if the network lacks the servers to respond. Extending the example, if all of your servers only run TCP/IP, uninstall or unbind all other protocols from all of your workstations. Check all of your network attached printers; many of these automatically run TCP/IP, IPX/SPX, DLC, and AppleTalk, creating unnecessary broadcasts. Most Apple Macintosh computers run on TCP/IP natively, so you can usually disable AppleTalk on the Macs without adversely affecting them. Limiting your number of protocols also improves security since you don't have to examine extra traffic for security problems.

Q: Can a network analyzer help diagnose problems on a fully switched network?

A: Although a switched network prevents a network analyzer (sniffer) from seeing every frame, the analyzer can still quickly discover broadcast storms, a common network problem. Port mirroring allows sniffers to dig deeper into specific problems without affecting network access. Network engineers can examine port traffic on switched ports without port mirroring by temporarily connecting a hub to the port in question and then connecting the sniffer and the other network device into the hub. If you don't have a protocol analyzer, you should get one. Check out Chapter 2 for a detailed description of the most popular protocol analyzers on the market.

Q: Should I get all of my switches from the same vendor?

A: Unmanaged, Layer 2 switches almost always interoperate well. If your network has more complexity than that, you should stick to a single vendor, especially at the core. Working with a single vendor will allow you to leverage all of the switches' proprietary features and reduce the amount of "finger pointing" when a problem arises.

Chapter 8

Defending Routers and Switches

Solutions in this Chapter:

- **Attacking and Defending Your Network Devices**

- **Cisco IPv4 Denial of Service**

- **Cisco HTTP Get Buffer Overflow**

- **Cisco Discovery Protocol Denial of Service**

- **Confusing the Enemy**

- **Breaking Out of Jail**

- **Attacking Simple Network Management Protocol**

Related Chapters:

Introduction

Even with today's heavy concentration on protecting the internal segments, networking devices rarely get their share of attention. Administrators have been focusing on end-point security, or securing the desktop—efforts geared to stop the next SQL Slammer or Blaster worm. Virus scanners, patch management, and vulnerability assessment systems continue to be purchased by IT and security teams to ensure that their internal networks will not be devastated by the next virus or worm outbreak. The IT mindset continues to be that Microsoft products pose the biggest security risk to their enterprise.

While the validity of that last statement will be argued for many years to come, the fact is that while administrators are focusing on securing those vulnerable systems, the devices they use to segment and protect their networks could pose just as serious a risk. Tell us if these statements sound familiar:

- Don't fix what isn't broken.

- Our routers and switches are doing their job, no reason to make any changes there.

- The core router uses a non-Microsoft operating system, so it is secure by default.

- I've never had to reboot my router, so it must be doing its job securely, right?

- There's a new slew of Microsoft patches every month! Thankfully, our routers aren't like that at all!

While it might be true that your network infrastructure has been working flawlessly for many months, it does not necessarily mean that you can neglect those devices. Network devices need just as much attention, if not more, than any Microsoft operating system or application. By the end of this chapter, you should be able to answer your co-workers quips as follows:

- Don't fix what isn't broken.

  - If it were broken, how would you really know? How often do you log in to the routers? How often do you examine the log files?

- Our routers and switches are doing their job, no reason to make any changes there.

- How are you measuring the performance of your routers and switches? Do you know how many dropped packets or network input queue overruns you've had lately?

- The core router uses a non–Microsoft operating system, so it is secure by default.

  - While a vendor can claim that their operating system might be *more* secure, it's an entirely different story to be secure by default. The only thing that routers do by default is to route packets. Whether that is a packet of confidential data routed out to the Internet or not is up to the configuration.

- I've never had to reboot my router, so it must be doing its job securely, right?

  - Out of sight, out of mind, right? In fact, with many of the vulnerabilities listed throughout this chapter, denial-of-service (DoS) of the router isn't the goal. Silently reading your configuration (or worse, your traffic) is the goal—and all without a reboot!

- There's a new slew of Microsoft patches every month! Thankfully, our routers aren't like that at all!

  - You're right, most router vendors aren't like that at all. By that we mean that you aren't going to get the latest router vulnerability notification in e-mail, in the system tray, on your favorite newsgroup, and on CNN.com. You'll have to visit the vendor's site and figure it out yourself. Does that mean there aren't as many patches? No, it means you aren't being notified of them.

This chapter highlights some of the most common and damaging attacks that focus on the core of your network. These attacks take advantage of protocols and devices running at Layer 2 (switches) and Layer 3 (routers) within your enterprise. After completing this chapter, we wouldn't be surprised to see the look on your face when you realize that the latest Cisco IOS version is a double-digit number. Before you move on to other chapters, it might be a good idea to take a few minutes and check each of your network devices' current operating system revision.

Attacking and Defending Your Network Devices

A quick search on SecuirtyFocus.com, or your favorite security site, will surely detail thousands of potential network device vulnerabilities. While we set out to offer a comprehensive guide to network infrastructure security, drowning you in hundreds of attack techniques and exploits would neither benefit you, or us. Instead, we have set the following criteria to decide which attacks to demonstrate:

- Ease of exploit (How easy is it to accomplish?)

- Popularity (How common is this?)

- Impact (How dangerous is this exploit?)

While most of the attacks shown here focus primarily on Cisco devices, they are not the only vendor susceptible to these techniques. We choose to focus on Cisco primarily because of their market dominance and prevalence in the industry. Furthermore, because some of the attacks described here revolve around the protocol, and not necessarily the vendor's implementation of the protocol, the attack might work on other vendors' devices.

Notes from the Underground...

Why Only Cisco?

This is just one of many examples where market dominance and pervasiveness in the industry can have some negative repercussions. Cisco Systems has been blessed with the ability to consistently deliver quality products to the networking world and therefore are revered in the industry as being the best at what they do—developing cutting-edge networking devices. However, their industry prominence also places a very large "Bulls-Eye" on their devices, motivating researchers and hackers around the world to find and compromise vulnerabilities on their appliances and their underlying operating system, the Cisco IOS.

Prominent security research groups such as Phenoelit have been focusing much of their time and effort on Cisco devices, resulting in significant vulnerability findings and exploits. Many of these vulnerabilities

Continued

have major ramifications on the security of your network, such as remote packet sniffing and DoS characteristics (detailed in depth later in this chapter). Why do these researchers spend most of their time inspecting the Cisco line of devices? Quite simply, it's much cooler to write exploits that affect 85 percent of the Internet, rather than only 5 percent. For these reasons, we spend the majority of this chapter covering these vulnerabilities and various exploit tools.

It is important to note, though, that this does not mean that non-Cisco related networking devices are vulnerability free. In fact, many of the lesser-used networking devices, such as 3Com, have had vulnerabilities discovered. Most often these vulnerabilities are of a very low-risk nature (low-risk exposure is similar to information disclosure types of attacks), and do not present the clear and present danger as those depicted later in the chapter. Moreover, many of these researchers find flaws in an underlying protocol the network device uses, such as SNMP, expanding the impact to any networking vendor that supports SNMP communication. While many of these vulnerabilities affect numerous vendors, many of the exploit tools are written solely to work on Cisco devices, simply because it will have the largest affect and wreak the most havoc.

If you would like to perform further research as to whether your networking devices have any known vulnerabilities or flaws, you can use www.securityfocus.com/bid.

Simply select your vendor from the drop-down box provided and look through the results set to find your particular device or hardware revision. Other security-related Web sites can be found at the end of this chapter and can be useful for vulnerability research.

Cisco IPv4 Denial of Service

The Cisco Ipv4 DoS vulnerability was originally released on July 16, 2003. This Cisco vulnerability was the most publicized network infrastructure vulnerability in recent times. While the worldwide impact of this attack was much less than security experts expected, the potential damage to networks was nearly catastrophic given the proliferation of Cisco routers and switches on internal and Internet networks.

This DoS attack revolves around Cisco's implementation of an input queue. In other words, the malicious traffic inappropriately marks the input queue on the Cisco device as full. Once the input queue is marked as full, it causes the device to stop processing traffic on the affected interfaces. To make matters worse, once the device is affected by this DoS attack it does not self correct by reloading or clearing the input queue. Administrators need to manually reload the Cisco device in order to restore operation. Furthermore, without any corrective action or performing any workarounds, once the device is reloaded it is continually susceptible to the attack, potentially causing further DoS conditions. At the time of the release, nearly all Cisco routers and switches that were configured to handle IPv4 packets were vulnerable to this attack.

According to Cisco, a specific sequence of IPv4 packets could initiate the DoS condition on all of the Cisco devices. The protocols necessary to trigger the attack were IP 53, better known for SWIPE and most commonly used for IP encryption; IP 55, known as IP Mobility, and was used to support mobile nodes connected to the Internet; IP 77, known as SUN-ND, was used for Sun Network disks prior to NFS; and IP 103, or Protocol Independent Multicast, was used for routing. Sending each of those IP packets to the victim device with a Time to Live (TTL) of 1 or 0 would cause the DoS condition.

Exploiting the IPv4 DoS

There are multiple exploits available for this DoS vulnerability now, and most are written for the Linux platform. You can find exploits at: www.hackingspirits.com/eth-hac/exploits/exploits.html. While most of these exploits need to be compiled and then run, it is possible to inflict this condition on a given Cisco device with just the use of *Hping*, available at www.hping.org.

Hping is a common command-line packet assembler for Linux, FreeBSD, NetBSD, OpenBSD, Solaris, and MacOs X. The following is an excerpt of how you would use *Hping* to flood the input queue on a Cisco device:

```
#hping (routerip) --rawip --ttl X --ipproto 53 --count 76 --data 26
```

In the preceding command, we used the *Hping* utility to send an IP 53 packet to the router IP address. We used the *rawip* setting to send the raw IP header and data. The TTL was set to *X*, because it would change for each host we were targeting. To define the TTL, complete the following steps:

1. Ping or traceroute the host to determine the TTL.

2. Subtract the number provided from the traceroute or ping from 255.

If you recall, the TTL must be 0 or 1 by the time it reaches the target IP. The *ipproto* setting is used to define which of the IP protocols to use. The *count* setting determines how many packets to send or receive. The *data* switch dictates how big the payload should be. In this scenario, it will be 20 bytes for the header, plus 26 bytes for the payload. The exploit code currently circulating on the Internet uses variations of this very same *Hping* command to carry out its attacks.

Defending Your Router against the IPv4 DoS

As with many vulnerabilities, the best way to defend against this attack is to update the device's software to the latest revision. At the time of the release, Cisco made available updates to all their versions of IOS, the main Cisco router OS, and CatOS, the main Cisco Catalyst OS. The latest version of the operating systems all have fixes for this particular DoS vulnerability.

In many scenarios, it is not always practical to think that you can quickly and correctly update all of your networking devices with the latest software revision. Change control procedures are sometimes implemented to help ensure that patches or updates to a system do not cause outages or other problematic behavior on a production network. While these procedures do provide account-ability and protect the core network from failures, they can also add a substantial amount of time for testing and approval prior to rolling out your update pack-ages. For this particular vulnerability, Cisco supplied device-level workarounds in the form of access lists to provide the necessary protection to mitigate this attack. These workarounds can often be implemented much quicker and easier than a full IOS update, allowing administrators to react more efficiently to the vulnera-bility. The following are some examples:

```
BrianRouter(config)# access-list 125 deny 53 any any
BrianRouter(config)# access-list 125 deny 55 any any
BrianRouter(config)# access-list 125 deny 77 any any
BrianRouter(config)# access-list 125 deny 103 any any
BrianRouter(config)# interface Ethernet 0/1
BrianRouter(config-if)# ip access-group 125 in
BrianRouter(config-if)# ip access-group 125 out
BrianRouter(config-if)# exit
```

In the preceding example, you can see that we disallow IP traffic 53, 55, 77, and 103 to all devices. We then apply the access list to *interface Ethernet 0/1* for bidirectional traffic (denoted by the *in* and *out*). Theoretically, we should apply this access list to all interfaces that are currently active on the device. It is also important to note that while this is a fairly straightforward access list, if you are currently using any of the protocols listed for production reasons, then this will negatively affect your enterprise network. While it would be uncommon to use these protocols in today's networks, prior to implementing these rules you should use a packet capture application and examine to see if they are currently being used on your network. This will help ensure that you will not cause any degradation of service to your internal users.

Cisco HTTP Get Buffer Overflow and UDP Memory Disclosure

As if July weren't a tough enough month for Cisco, the talented hacker called "FX" of the Phenoelit group discovered another bug in the IOS code. FX discovered that the HTTP server, usually used for configuration and control, is susceptible to a buffer overflow that can result in remote command execution. Furthermore, they discovered that using an existing UDP memory leak vulnerability in the Cisco IOS in conjunction with the HTTP overflow resulted in an extremely high success rate of exploitation. We will first discuss these two vulnerabilities separately, but the true power comes from taking these two medium-risk exploits and combining them into one, extremely high-risk vulnerability.

In August 2003, Cisco released the UDP Memory Disclosure vulnerability. On nearly all versions of IOS, routers running the "UDP small-servers" service were vulnerable to this information disclosure attack. Through expert analysis, Phenoelit discovered that a specially crafted UDP echo packet destined to the victim router could result in a response from the affected router that contained actual packet data. Using the leak in the memory IO blocks, it was possible then to remotely sniff actual traffic on a remote Cisco router. As a proof of concept, Phenoelit created the application IOSniff, available at www.phenoelit.de/fr/tools.html.

Almost simultaneously, Phenoelit discovered a buffer overflow in the HTTP server on Cisco routers. Nearly all versions of the IOS were vulnerable to this. The overflow occurred when 2GB of data was passed in a URL string to a victim router. The overflow allowed for the execution of arbitrary code, meaning that this exploit code returned a remote shell from the victim router. While 2GB of data is a significant amount to send over the Internet, it is quite feasible when you think about the high-speed networks on the internal corporate segment. Therefore, this exploit has particularly far-reaching consequences when you think about your internal Cisco routers.

As previously mentioned, while these two vulnerabilities seem to have very little in common, using them in concert provides a near perfect exploit of remote Cisco routers. The HTTP exploit code from Phenoelit uses parts of the IOSniff code that relies on the UDP small-servers, causing the need for both vulnerabilities to exist on the same router. The HTTP exploit first sends its 2GB of data within the URL to begin the process. The UDP echo memory leak process is then initiated, sending the UDP echo packets to the victim router repeatedly to pull known IO memory addresses. The IO memory addresses collected from the UDP vulnerability provide the logic that the Phenoelit exploit will then use to determine which memory address to send the shell code to.

Notes from the Underground...

Beware the Low-Risk Vulnerabilities

This is just one of many examples where two (or more) low-risk vulnerabilities can be strung together by a savvy attacker to create one very large and very high-risk vulnerability. The same can be said about a number of low-risk information disclosure vulnerabilities marked "low" or "informational" in most Vulnerability Assessment software packages (see Chapter 2 for more information). When united, these little pieces of information can focus the attacker with laser-like precision on the task at hand, without wasting any time on nonexploitable attack vectors.

For most exploits, addressing the right block of memory is the trickiest process. Many exploits require an intimate knowledge of the operating system or application where the overflow exists to successfully exploit it. By using the UDP memory disclosure bug, the guessing is removed from the equation as we can reliable determine how best to send our exploit code.

Once the shell code is sent to the remote router, and the HTTP server has been successfully overflowed, the result will be a remote shell to the affected router. The shell code returns a command-line interface to the router, disables all of the VTY, or virtual interfaces, and removes the *Enable* password verification, which is used to obtain the highest level of privilege on the router. Thus, you are left with complete backdoor access to all of the router's configurations and debug capabilities. In short, you now own this remote router.

Exploiting 2-for-1

It's no difficult task to figure out the most damaging or well-known exploit of this vulnerability. Yes, you guessed it—our friends at Phenoelit have a handy tool just waiting to exploit both the HTTP and the UDP vulnerabilities. They're the 2-for-1 special at the router vulnerability supermarket.

Phenoelit has cornered the market on Cisco IOS research and development and is revered in the industry for providing proof-of-concept code. The exploit used to pull off this security coup is called "CISCO CASUM EST" and is available at www.phenoelit.de/fr/tools.html. For those of you who are curious, that exploit tool is loosely translated (thanks to the Internet translation Web sites and our ninth-grade Latin teacher) into "Cisco is destroyed" or "Cisco has a violent death."

The proof-of-concept code provided primarily works on Cisco 1600 and 2500 series routers running UDP small-servers and the HTTP server and version 11.*x* of Cisco IOS. It is important to note that most internal routers used in enterprise networks will be these smaller series routers that are vulnerable. In short, this exploit could cause major outages on most internal network segments. Written for most UNIX platforms, once compiled the actual use of the exploit is extremely easy.

```
BrianRouter # ./CiscoCasumEst -i <interfaceid> -d <targetrouterIP>
```

While there are a few options available in the command, such as -*v* for verbose and -*T* for Test-Mode only, you can see that actual usage is quite straightforward. Phenoelit did an outstanding job on this exploit, as it performs many different tasks behind the scenes. Of particular note is that the IOS remains fully functioning throughout the entire exploit and that the configuration is preserved. In fact, without serious IDS monitoring or tight router controls, the only way to know that the exploit took place would be the error messages that pop up on the router console during the exploit.

Defending against the HTTP and UDP Vulnerabilities (*Cisco Renatus Est*)

The title for this section either means "Cisco is born again" or I've insulted your parents accidentally (if you are reading this chapter, Sister Ann Marie, I'm sorry I didn't pay more attention in class). Like most of the other Cisco vulnerabilities discussed in this chapter, there are a number of ways to protect yourself from this vulnerability. For starters, there are very few reasons why you would need the UDP small-servers service running. In many Cisco hardening guides, this service is seen as unnecessary and it is often recommended that it be disabled. Disabling this service not only removes the possibility of this exploit working, but also mitigates the UDP memory leakage vulnerability. To disable the service, simply type this command on a Cisco router:

```
BrianRouter(config)# no service udp-small-servers
```

The next step in mitigating this attack would be to disable the HTTP server on the router. To disable the service, simply use this command:

```
BrianRouter(config)# no ip http server
```

If the HTTP service is an integral part of your IT processes, then access control lists (ACLs) should be used to prevent unauthorized access to the service.

```
BrianRouter(config)# ip http access-class 25
BrianRouter(config)# access-list 25 permit host 192.168.1.32
BrianRouter(config)# access-list 25 permit host 192.168.1.195
BrianRouter(config)# access-list 25 deny any
BrianRouter(config)# interface Ethernet 0/1
BrianRouter(config-if)# ip http access-class 25 in
BrianRouter(config-if)# ip http access-class 25 out
BrianRouter(config-if)# exit
```

In this example, we are only allowing the HTTP traffic from the hosts 192.168.1.32 and .195. The rest of the HTTP traffic to the router is dropped, thereby eliminating the chance of the vulnerability being exploited from other remote systems. However, it is important to note that the two hosts referenced in the preceding code still could take advantage of the vulnerability in the service since HTTP traffic is permitted for their IP addresses.

Lastly, unless certain processes and controls prohibit it, you should update the version of IOS on your routers. Updated versions have fixes already present that will mitigate these attacks on your devices.

Cisco Discovery Protocol Denial of Service

Cisco Discovery Protocol (CDP) is an administrative protocol that works at Layer 2 of the IP stack and is used on Cisco routers to share information with neighboring routers. Information disclosed in these transmissions include Cisco IOS version, IP address, and other management information such as management

IP address, duplexes, device capabilities (router or switch), and native VLANs. While this information is dangerous enough in the hands of an attacker, there are more serious consequences with this protocol.

The vulnerability, also first discovered by FX at Phenoelit, can cause any of the three symptoms to your Cisco device:

- A device reboot after 3–5 CDP frames are received.

- Device will stop functioning after 1000+ frames are received.

- Use all available device memory to hold CDP neighbor information.

In all of these circumstances, this attack will cause a DoS on your Cisco device.

Exploiting the CDP Denial of Service

To make matters worse, a simple tool is in the wild from the crew at Phenoelit. This tool, when used, will effectively cause a DoS condition on all vulnerable Cisco devices on your network. The tool is called Phenoelit IRPAS and can be downloaded from Phenoelit at: www.phenoelit.de/irpas. The tool currently only works on Linux-based machines. The following is some sample usage, taken from the Phenoelit Web site, which will cause the DoS condition on your Cisco devices:

```
BrianRouter# ./cdp -i eth0 -m0 -n 100000 -l 1480 -r -v
```

This command will send the maximum-sized CDP frame with random data link addresses to all hosts within your multicast domain. Nothing else is needed to potentially cause a large outage on your network segments.

Preventing CDP Attacks

Mitigating your risk against this attack is quite simple: disable CDP on all of your Cisco routers and switches, or update to the latest version of Cisco IOS. The vulnerability was first fixed in version 12.0 of the IOS. However, if you are still running a version of IOS prior to 12.0, then the command to disable this feature is:

```
BrianRouter(config)# no cdp run
```

This will disable CDP on your device and protect against this attack. Remember, however, that CDP is used in some applications, such as CiscoWorks 2000, so there might be a use for the protocol in your environment. If this is the case, weigh the risks versus the rewards of running this protocol and determine what your ultimate goals are.

More information on this vulnerability can be found at the Phenoelit Web site and the Cisco Web site:

- www.phenoelit.de/stuff/CiscoCDP.txt
- www.cisco.com/warp/public/707/cdp_issue.shtml

Confusing the Enemy

The primary goal for an attacker once he or she has compromised a system or network is to make the decision of where to go next. Attackers plot their moves by footprinting the networks and computers around them. This data collection can be as simple as a port scan on the local subnet or sniffing the local traffic on the compromised system. Both techniques are useful, but watching the traffic as it goes by will give the attacker a chance to see clear-text passwords and other useful information. By confusing the enemy using a flood of information, it is possible to bypass certain security or management features in high-end and low-end products alike.

MAC Flooding

In the past it was believed that being on a switched network would prevent users from listening to other traffic. In today's world this is no longer true; even though your networks are switched, a malicious user can still sniff traffic through Media Access Control (MAC) flooding and turn your expensive switches into 10-dollar hubs.

The following example gives a brief review of the importance of MAC addresses and how this attack can cause large problems.

Assume Computer A wants to send some data to Computer B and both nodes are physically located on the same switch. Computer A transmits the data to Computer B via a switch to which both computers are connected. When data is received at the switch, the OS on the switch looks at the MAC address of the destination node to determine the port to which to send the traffic. The switch then references the Content Addressable Memory (CAM) table, which houses the MAC addresses of each node physically connected to a port on the switch. The switch then determines that the MAC address for Computer B is located on port 2 and forwards the traffic to the host.

CAM tables have the capability to learn what MAC addresses are on a particular physical switch port. When a host becomes live on the network, the MAC address is entered into the CAM table and stored so that traffic can be forwarded to and from the computer. Understanding this, we can exploit the CAM by forcing it to learn incorrect MAC entries. Furthermore, when a switch does not have an entry for a host in its CAM table, the traffic is broadcasted to each port to help find the host. When the destination computer responds, the MAC address is then entered into the table and all subsequent traffic is only forwarded to the correct port. In addition, since CAM tables are fixed size (size depends on the manufacturer and type of switch) we can flood the table with incorrect entries, thereby allowing us to see all of the traffic. For example, suppose that as Computer A, an attacker wants to see all traffic that is destined for Computer C. Using DSniff (a tool that is explained in the next section) he can flood the CAM table with entries that are incorrect. By his filling this table, the switch will not know the physical location of Computer C and will broadcast all of the traffic to that host to each of the physical ports. This will allow the attacker to see some of the traffic on the subnet.

On a grander scale you can see how quickly someone would be able to see what is going on with the network. Assume that a 48-port switch suddenly has to broadcast all of the traffic to all of the ports. If you are sniffing the wire when this happens, you will see a lot of traffic.

Flooding the CAM Tables

The original tool used to exploit this vulnerability was known as *macof*, written by Ian Vitneck. Today, the more widely used tool, DSniff, written by Dug Song accomplishes the MAC flooding attacks and a few other Layer 2 exploits in a simple interface. DSniff can be downloaded from Dug Song's site at http://monkey.org/~dugsong/dsniff. It is written for just a few platforms, including Linux, OpenBSD, and Solaris; however, older versions of the tool that were ported for Windows can be found at www.datanerds.net/~mike/dsniff.html.

This tool is quite easy to use and very powerful. It has the capability to fill even the largest CAM tables within a matter of seconds. There are many other uses for the tool as well, including password sniffing, and launching man-in-the-middle attacks. The primary use of the tool has been for sniffing traffic and pulling passwords on a switched environment; however, there are a few other great tool bundles with it, such as mailsnarf, urlsnarf, and webspy. mailsnarf is great at decoding mail messages

Preventing the CAM Flood

Since MAC flooding convinces the switch that all of the MAC addresses for a particular subnet are located on a single port, the easy defense for this uses port security. Port security for this exploit means allowing the switch to only associate or learn a particular number of MAC addresses for a specific port. In other words, you could limit the switch to learn only one MAC address per port. This would mean that only one computer could be connected to a specific port, disabling the ability for DSniff to incorrectly fill the CAM table with erroneous entries. Furthermore, depending on the vendor implementation, a port might be able to be shut down if a large number of MAC addresses are requesting entry into the CAM table for the port (much like how DSniff would work).

The downside to this security measure is that you would have to be cautious of how many computers or devices would reside on a specific port. In our example, we said that only one MAC address could be present on a port. If we add another switch or hub to that port, and connect multiple computers, then the port might shut down since you have more MAC addresses present on the port than the permitted one address. To accommodate this, you would have to change the security on the port to allow more than one MAC address. It is easy to see the administrative overhead that would occur; however, this is a relatively easy solution for such a severe problem.

ARP Spoofing

Another simple way for our unfriendly attacker to footprint the network is through the use of Address Resolution Protocol (ARP) spoofing. This technique is somewhat similar to the MAC flooding where all traffic is transmitted so that the attacker can listen; however, it has a few more devious effects. This type of attack is also known as a *man-in-the-middle attack*.

When a computer wants to transmit on the network, it must know the destination's MAC address. Assume Computer A wants to send data to Computer B. Computer A knows the IP address for B (10.10.10.2), but doesn't know the MAC address. Therefore, Computer A broadcasts an ARP message asking "Hey, 10.10.10.2, what is your MAC address, I have some data for you." Each computer on the subnet will receive this message; however, only Computer B, with the correct IP address, will answer—the rest will disregard the ARP packet. When Computer B receives the ARP message it will respond with the correct MAC address. When Computer A received the ARP response from Computer B it will send the data, and the switch will forward it on to the correct port (refer to the CAM table example in the previous section).

An ARP attack exists when, in this example, an illegitimate computer, say Computer X, responds, impersonating Computer B before the real Computer B has the opportunity. Computer A then sends the data unknowingly to the wrong computer. Once Computer X has the data, it can then hold on to it and do nothing, or send it on to the original recipient, Computer B. This process can also work in reverse where Computer B sends the data back to Computer X, and then Computer X forwards the data back to Computer A.

The result of this is that Computer A completed the transmission, but had no idea that the data was passed through another computer on the network. Figure 8.1 illustrates the attack in more detail.

Figure 8.1 Normal and Attack ARP Communication

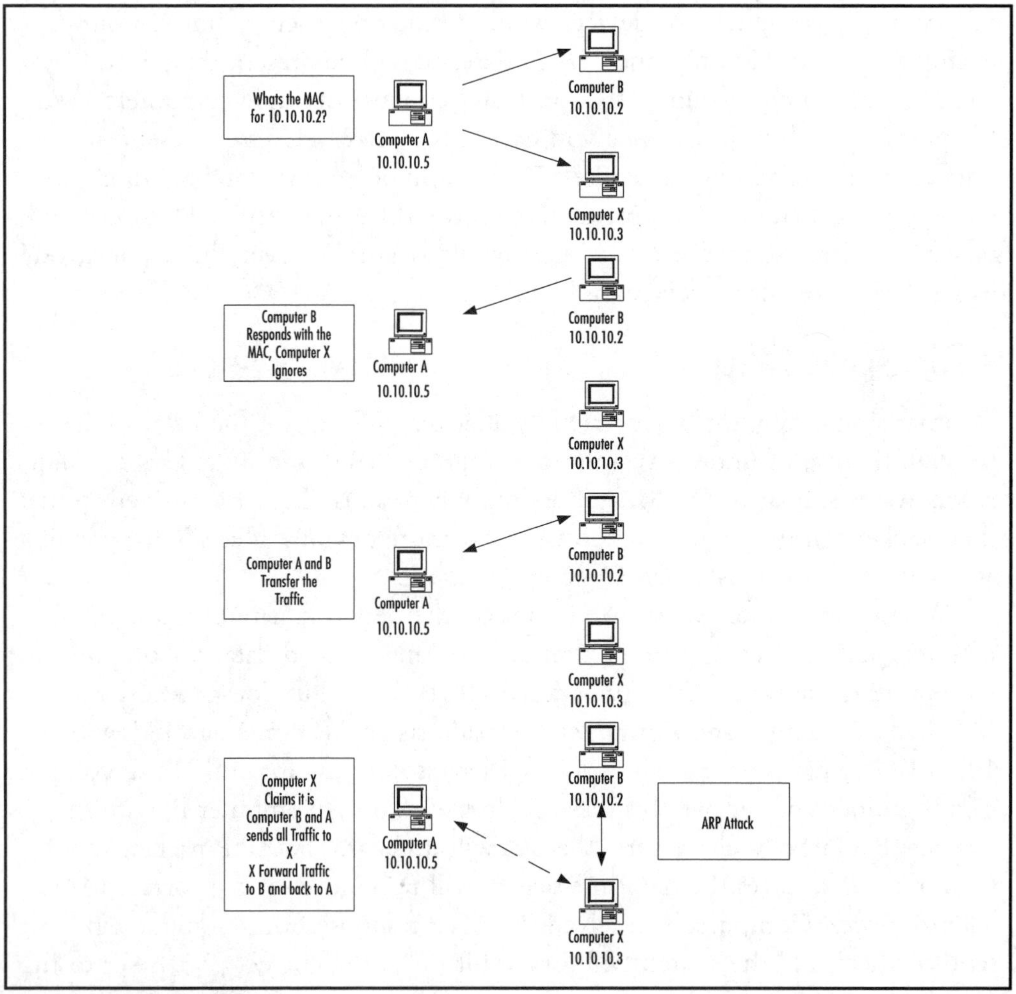

On a grander scale, you can see how this could be quite disruptive on your network. Imagine an end user getting a hold of one of these tools and initiating this attack against the CEO of your company. The end user would be able to see much of the traffic the CEO transmitted during the course of the day. Traffic that could be viewed would be HTTP, FTP, SMTP, SNMP, and many others. Therefore, as you can see, this could be a huge problem on your network. Furthermore, this is only exacerbated when you see how easy the following tools are to use.

Tools and Their Use

DSniff has the functionality for this type of attack built in also. Additionally, a newer tool known as *Ettercap* can provide the same results with an even simpler interface (http://ettercap.sourceforge.net).

Written for many platforms, including Windows, Ettercap is an easy-to-use tool that has almost all of the features of DSniff. Inherently, Ettercap can collect passwords for Telnet, FTP, POP, HTTP, SMB, SSH, and many others. It also has the capability to sniff HTTPS encrypted traffic.

The graphical interface Ettercap uses makes it all that much easier for networking novices to execute on your network. Figure 8.2 depicts a simple ARP-based sniff of two hosts on a switched network.

Figure 8.2 Ettercap ARP Sniff

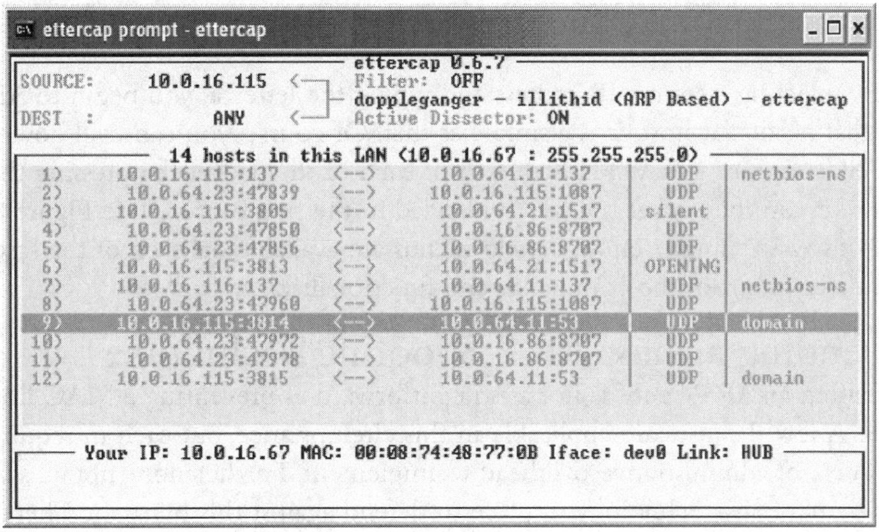

In this example we are using ARP-based sniffing on the host address 10.0.16.115 with destination traffic going anywhere on the network. While there are far too many commands to include, we will detail how to begin this sniff.

Upon launching Ettercap, the application probes to find all of the devices and MAC addresses on the local subnet and attempts name resolution on each. In Figure 8.3 you can see all of the available IP addresses and possible destination addresses.

Figure 8.3 Ettercap Startup Screen

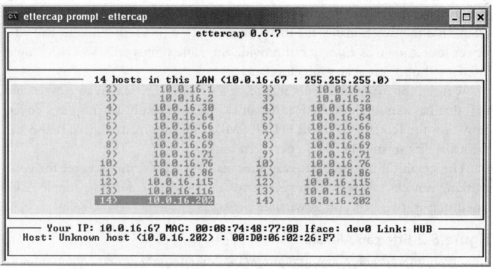

By selecting a source IP address and typing the letter **a**, you begin to ARP sniff that particular host. It is a simple as that. Of course, you can drill down into the ASCII output or raw HEX output of each of the packets by pressing the **Enter** key on the packet trace as evidenced in the first capture (see Figure 8.2). As if this wasn't simple enough, help menus are available on each of the screens with descriptions of the commands and functionality.

Defending against ARP Spoofing Techniques

Preventing an ARP spoof is not as straightforward as preventing a MAC flooding attack. A few defenses are applicable in this circumstance, but each m requires a good deal of administrative overhead to implement. Furthermore, not all switch vendors have any technology in place to defend against this behavior. Therefore, our recommendation is to use a combination of the following solutions:

- **Tuning IDSs for large amounts of ARP**   IDS sensors can be tuned to look for large amounts of ARP traffic on local subnets. This could be a good way to keep an eye on the possibility of one of these attacks being launched. To our knowledge, there isn't currently a signature for this type of attack, so the sensor will be ineffective in determining an actual ARP spoofing attack. While this limited information can be helpful in hunting down possibilities, many false positives will be realized under this configuration.

- **Placing static ARP entries on critical devices**   Placing static ARP entries on critical devices, such as router and servers, is also a possible solution in the prevention of this attack. Since the entries will be statically placed on each device, the host will not have to query the network to find the MAC address of the device to which it wants to transmit. Without this ARP request, the attacker will never have the ability to spoof the host. The downside to this is the obvious administrative overhead.

- **Using private VLANs**   Private VLANs can be a possible solution to this problem as well. Private VLANs create communities within a given VLAN to limit the amount of ARP traffic that exists. There are many downsides to this solution. First, private VLANs are not supported by every switch vendor, which might make this solution difficult to deploy in many organizations. Second, the use of communities limits the amount of interhost communications. Many hosts will not be able to communicate with devices outside their communities.

As mentioned, ARP spoofing attacks will be difficult to defend. It is best to keep this in mind as you start to develop VLANs and subnets—all the more reason to keep critical systems and users on their own segments.

Breaking Out of Jail

As you might have learned already in Chapter 7, VLAN technology is a great way to segment your network without the hassle of running new physical cabling. While this gives security-conscious network admins an advantage in terms of segmenting, the foolish network admin will assume that segmentation means security. In fact, VLANs are not a security measure, but rather a segmentation tool that happens to (accidentally) aid in security by removing the ability to access certain resources. However, remember: the walls that separate nodes in a VLAN'ed switch are made of silicon, and they will always be easier to topple than an air-gapped physically segmented network.

VLAN Jumping

This attack is a little more sophisticated than the others mentioned thus far. Thankfully, our friends have not automated this through a simple interface yet, so the use of this exploit in the wild has only occurred on a minimal basis. The goal of this attack is for the user to see all the traffic from each of the different VLANs and subnets. The malicious user will try to convince the upstream switch that his workstation is also a switch with trunking enabled. This will work on several different brands of switches, but can easily be mitigated.

There are a couple methods for a user to jump from one VLAN to another. Starting with the most basic, the user will need to convince the switch that his workstation is a switch through the use of the Dynamic Trunk Protocol (DTP). Trunking and DTP are used to pass all VLAN traffic and information to other connected switches.

Previously, we talked about using VLANs to separate users and department subnets. We also mentioned that while users might be in the same department, they might be physically located in another building. Consequently, the use of VLANs would have to span many switches. Trunking and DTP are the method in which this is done.

In this basic attack, a malicious user will need to craft a packet that makes the upstream switch think that the device is another switch with trunking enabled. When this happens, all traffic from various VLANs will be transferred through the link to this host, giving the user access to all the traffic on that switch. While this attack is basic in nature, it can easily provide access to all the data on the network.

The slightly more complicated attack is a variation on this theme. A malicious user will insert/use two headers of 802.1q encapsulation within his packet to fool the switch. When the packet is transmitted to the first switch, the switch will peel off the 802.1q header and pass it on to the next upstream switch. The second switch will receive what looks like an 802.1q trunk packet from the downstream switch (because of the second 802.1q header) and pass it on to the destination address. In this manner, the malicious user can send illegitimate traffic through multiple VLANs to the target host. Two switches have to be in use for this to work.

Dot One Queue

For more information about the VLAN trunking described here, you can download the IEEE specification file at http://standards.ieee.org/getieee802/download/802.1Q-2003.pdf. Pay close attention to section 8, which explains the principles of operations that would make this type of attack even feasible. If you're still a bit cloudy on the whole trunking concept, visit Annex D of the IEEE 802.1q standard, which gives a concise history of VLANs.

Hop through VLANs in a Single Leap

Currently, there are no known tools that can automate these attacks; however, it is possible to modify the packet contents to achieve the hack. Given the amount of work it would take to accomplish this, it does not seem feasible that a large attack could be used on a network. However, understand that new tools come out every day for automating attacks like these, and it probably won't be too long before someone finds a way to accomplish this.

Building a Stronger Wall around VLANs

The easiest way to mitigate the basic VLAN attack is to set all user and server ports to *DTP Off*. This will disable the ability for a normal user to trick the switch into becoming a trunk on that particular port. Second, you will want to make sure that all of your legitimate trunking ports are in their own VLAN and are not part of any of the departmental subnets you have set up.

Damage & Defense...

Better VLANs

Think securing your VLANs against a VLAN jumping attack is difficult? It's just a matter of changing your switch ports from the defaults (which are likely "auto-negotiate") to "off." Witness the degree of difficulty in the Cisco Catalyst CatOS family:

```
CoreSwitch> (enable)  set trunk 1/1-1/24 off
Port(s) 1/1-1/24 trunk mode set to off.
```

Attacking Simple Network Management Protocol

Simple Network Management Protocol (SNMP) is the most-used network management mechanism in place. Almost all vendors include SNMP Management Information Bases, or MIBS, for their devices. These MIBSs collect the data that will be polled by the SNMP agent. Given that SNMP is such a widely used tool, it should come as no surprise that most versions of the protocol are completely insecure. In versions 1 and 2, the only authentication that exists is the community strings for the SNMP read and write permissions. These community strings, although they have a catchy name, are still pass-phrases that are stored on most network devices in clear text. Furthermore, these community strings, unless encrypted with a different technology, are passed on the wire in clear text, making it quite easy for someone sniffing your network to pull the pass-phrases. Recently, SNMP worms have been released that look for devices with null read and write strings, or with devices that have "public" as their read string, which is generally a device's default configuration.

Securing the protocol isn't as tough as you can imagine. Some vendors have begun to implement version 3 of the protocol. Inherently, this new version supports encryption and authentication, two huge advances from the previous implementations. Because not all vendors have support for the new version, it becomes difficult to use it as a standard within your environment. Borrowing from a joke found in a previous chapter (can you find it?), some have said that earlier versions of SNMP used to be an acronym for "Security's Not My Problem!"

Notes from the Underground…

Can You Be Too Managed?

Additionally, take a look at the devices that you currently monitor via SNMP. Do all of them have to be monitored? Some devices rarely need to be polled and can easily have SNMP disabled on them. Furthermore, even if a device has to be monitored with SNMP read access, you need to ask yourself, "do I need to be able to change the setting or modify the record and therefore necessitate SNMP 'write' permissions?" If not, disable the Read-Write level of access and use only SNMP Read-Only. You'd be surprised at just how many oddball devices on your network (printers, newer copiers, fax machines) have SNMP enabled by default with default passwords. Although it might be fascinating to be able to poll the paper tray capacities of all those devices from the HQ office in Fort Lauderdale, sometimes you have to know where to draw the line on SNMP.

Sniffing the Management… Protocol

The following is an example of how dangerous community strings can be in clear text. In this example, we used Snort to sniff some SNMP traffic and pulled the clear-text community string (Figure 8.4). We used the Snort application to prove that no advanced decoding capabilities were required to pull the passphrase. In Figure 8.5 you'll see that we used SolarWinds to download the Cisco router running configuration. Obviously, this information is deadly in the hands of an attacker, as it shows all of the configuration settings of the Cisco router. What's worse, in Figure 8.6, we use the built-in Cisco Password Decoder utility in SolarWinds to crack the Telnet password for the router. Consequently, by simply capturing and using the SNMP community string, we now have a legitimate login to the router.

As mentioned previously, our first step in this multifaceted attack will be to use a common freeware sniffer to watch passing traffic pull SNMP community strings from the wire. SNMP version 1, the most commonly implemented version, is completely in clear text and without any form of encryption, thereby allowing us to easily pull the password off the network.

Figure 8.4 Snort Capture of SNMP Community String

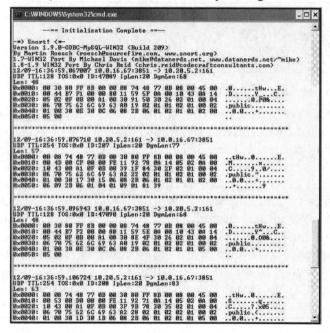

As you can see from Figure 8.4, the trace shows our computer sending SNMP requests to the router, IP address 10.20.5.2, via port 161. On the right-hand side you can see in clear text the community string used— "public." The next step will demonstrate the use of IP Network Browser in SolarWinds to enumerate the router.

Using our recently discovered SNMP community string, we now will use the application to connect to the router. SolarWinds is a sophisticated Windows application that allows administrators to connect to their networking devices and perform remote management. In the wrong hands, this application can provide a treasure trove of information. Simply launching the application and providing the IP address of the router and the community string will unlock the keys to the kingdom.

Figure 8.5 IP Network Browser Router Enumeration

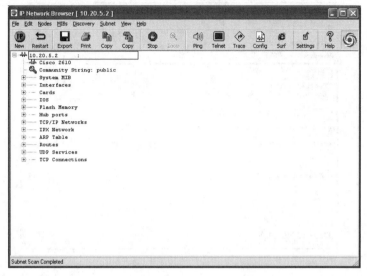

Figure 8.5 is a full view of all the information the router provided via SNMP. Immediately, we have access to information showing the router interfaces, IOS, ARP tables, and routes. While on the surface this information seems fairly benign, it can provide the necessary network topology and routing details to an attacker. While access to this data can be dangerous enough, we are going to use more of the advanced features in the SolarWinds product to further compromise the device.

Once we have enumerated the device, we will then move on to our next step, which will be to download the running configuration of the router. The running configuration contains all of the instructions and information the router needs to perform its job. It also contains all the necessary information we need to "own" the router (yep, you guessed it, router passwords).

By clicking the **Config** button on the toolbar, we will be able to download the running Cisco configuration.

Figure 8.6 IP Network Browser Router Enumeration

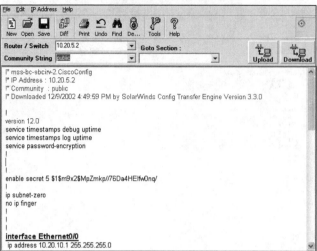

Figure 8.6 shows the first page of our router's configuration file. As you can see, the file shows the encrypted enable password in the file, as well as the IOS version (12.0). At the bottom of the screen you can see the first Ethernet interface and some of the corresponding IP information. While the IP information is exciting, it really doesn't help us further compromise the device. To really take this to the next level, we will need some passwords.

In Figure 8.7, we scroll down the configuration file toward the bottom. There we find the XOR'ed password for the console and Telnet connections—the gold mine we were looking for.

Figure 8.7 Router Configuration with Weak Encrypted Passwords

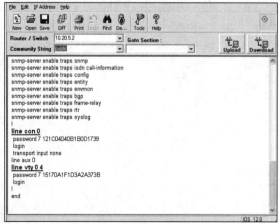

In Figure 8.7, you can see the XOR'ed passwords and more information regarding the console and Telnet (listed as VTY, or virtual) interfaces.

The next step is to click the **Decode** button on the SolarWinds tool bar. This will launch the SolarWinds Cisco password decoder. It is important to note that the decoder will only be able to decode the Telnet or console passwords. The enable secret password (shown in Figure 8.6 as "1m9x2$MpZmkp//76Da4HE") uses a different, more advanced encryption algorithm, as opposed to the enable password or console/Telnet password that uses a weak XOR encryption.

Figure 8.8 SolarWinds Cisco Password Decoder Used

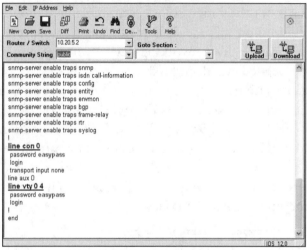

Figure 8.8 depicts the running configuration once the magical "decode" functionality is used. Voilà! the passwords appear to us in clear text. Now we have two methods to gain access to these boxes:

- We can Telnet to them and use the decoded telnet password, "easypass" (shown in Figure 8.8 under the "Line VTY" section).

- If we are an employee with physical access to the router, we can use a console cable and use the Line Con 0 password (in this example they both happen to be the same; in the real world, this should not be the case).

This example demonstrates the ease in hacking a router and gathering information when SNMP information is out on the wire in clear text. While many external factors exist that would make this example slightly more difficult in a true, enterprise network, the theory is the same. Internal attackers will chain vulnerabilities or misconfigurations together to gain more information on your network and your network devices.

Defending against Inherent SNMP Weaknesses

The easiest and most fitting solution to this clear-text password (excuse us, "community string") issue would be to employ SNMP v3 on all of your networking devices. In the cases where the use of SNMPv3 is not achievable, the use of IP Security (IPSec) might be. Many hardware vendors, including Cisco, support the use of IPSec as a secure transfer of SNMP information to a management station. This is not the easiest solution to implement; however, it does provide a reliable transmission method. It is worth further note to add that IPSec can add some overhead to the networking device you are monitoring, as all the packets must be processed and decrypted.

The first step in setting up IPSec to run on a Cisco router, or any Cisco device, is to create extended access lists that will permit the IP traffic through. IPSec uses protocols IP 50 and 51 as well as UDP 500 for communication. Using the example in the ACL section you can see how to create these ACLs. The next step is to create our ISAKMP Policy. Policies define the use of authentication (pre-shared secrets), encryption, and hash information. The following is an example of setting up an ISAKMP Policy:

```
BrianRouter(config)# crypto isakmp policy 5
BrianRouter(config-isakmp)# authentication pre-share
BrianRouter(config-isakmp)# encryption 3des
BrianRouter(config-isakmp)# group 2
BrianRouter(config-isakmp)# exit
```

In this example, we have used pre-shared secrets as our authentication method with triple-des encryption for communication. The next step is to set the authentication pass-phrase. This password should use a combination of letters, numbers, and symbols.

```
BrianRouter(config)# crypto isakmp key str0ngp4$$w0rd address 192.168.1.100
```

Here we have set the password to the preceding key and tied it to our management station at 192.168.1.100. Next, we create our transform mode and set the values for protecting our traffic; in this case, triple-des with SHA hash. We will also use the transport mode instead of tunnel.

```
BrianRouter(config)# crypto ipsec transport-set 3des-sha-xport esp-3des esp-
sha-hmac
BrianRouter(cfg-crypto-trans)# mode transport
BrianRouter(cfg-crypto-trans)# exit
```

Since we have already have included our extended ACLs to allow the traffic, we must now create a crypto map and install the newly created policy to an interface (ideally a separate management interface).

```
BrianRouter(config)# crypto map snmp 5 ipsec-isakmp
BrianRouter(config-crypto-map)# set peer 192.168.1.100
BrianRouter(config-crypto-map)# set transport-set 3des-sha-xport
BrianRouter(config-crytpo-map)# exit
BrianRouter(config)# interface Ethernet 1/1
BrianRouter(config-if)# crypto map snmp
BrianRouter(config-if)# exit
```

For further information on how to lock down your management networks, or the best ways to securely manage you network infrastructure, refer to Chapter 6.

Vulnerability Chaining

From the experienced attacker's perspective, what is more valuable: one high-risk vulnerability, or two medium- to low-risk vulnerabilities? Well, we suppose the answer would vary, but for the most part attackers like to be armed with many medium- to low-risk vulnerabilities when they start to pick through a network's defenses. Why would this be true? Simply stated, attackers like to chain their vulnerabilities together. As the level of sophistication of network engineers increases, it might become harder and harder to find blatant, high-risk vulnerabilities open and Internet accessible. However, it is completely conceivable to have a number of low-risk vulnerabilities on a router that the engineer just hasn't had a chance to tend to yet.

Just as we witnessed in the Cisco HTTP and UDP vulnerabilities, and the SNMP weaknesses (as alluded to in previous sidebars), having multiple exploits in your arsenal can sometimes be significantly more dangerous than having a high-risk vulnerability. Attackers will often use information garnered from one system, or a particular vulnerability, to attack another.

For example, if we compromise a router on the perimeter and discover a weak Telnet password in the running configuration, we might try to use that Telnet password on each of the subsequent routers and switches we encounter. While no vulnerability might be present on the other devices, we are using the information we culled from our previous attacks to try to compromise devices further into the network.

Yet another example would be where a Microsoft IIS server is set up with the default script mappings enabled and is set with the default file permissions enabled. While medium-risk vulnerabilities exist within the mapped applications in IIS, there are also inherent low-risk vulnerabilities associated with the file-system permissions. However, when these two scenarios are coupled, the result is one, serious, high-risk exploit. Being able to exploit the script mappings, and then having very loose file permissions on the server, provides the attacker any number of options to "own" the server.

Administrators are usually overburdened with too many systems to look after and way too many users to support. This is why we commonly see reused passwords and misconfigured systems. To combat these types of attacks, varying methods of defense need to be deployed throughout the enterprise; this is commonly referred to as a "Defense in Depth" strategy. In our previous IIS example, even though the vulnerabilities would still exist, a host-based intrusion prevention system would not allow the compromise of the server. Furthermore, in our earlier SNMP example, the use of IPSec and tunneling would have removed the clear-text community string retrieval from the realm of possibility. While the burden of an administrator isn't likely to decrease in years to come, it has become more important to leverage differing types of security technologies to provide your "Defense in Depth" strategy.

Checklist

☑ Take a complete asset inventory of all your network devices.

☑ Assess the criticality of each device in regard to your business continuity.

☑ Audit each device and determine the critical services necessary for each.

☑ Disable all unnecessary services and use ACLs to limit access.

☑ Make sure security technologies are used whenever possible, including SSH instead of Telnet and IPSec instead of clear-text management techniques.

Summary

Networking devices are designed to pass traffic from one node to another, one network to many. In theory, these devices should be invisible to attackers, but as we learned from this chapter, unfortunately they are often naked to even the most novice of attackers. Given that these devices are the core to our networks, one would think that they would get the appropriate amount of attention and care, but we have come to learn that this is just not the case. Apparently, since routers and switches do not have a nice little graphic located in their "System Tray" to remind us of updating them, they rarely get updated.

Next time you talk to your network administrator, or routing team, ask them what version of IOS a particular router is running, and wait to see the dumb-founded expression. It is not that they are to blame; networking devices just often can easily be forgotten about because they do their job: route and pass traffic. Now, when these devices fail, well, then it is a different story. Many of the attacks demonstrated here can be the cause of these devices failing. The Cisco IPv4 and CDP DoS exploits can easily bring the highest-end routers to their knees, and with an easy, command-line utility to boot. Just because your high-end router cost $65,000 doesn't mean that the $25,000/yr office assistant cannot render it useless with some simple tools downloaded from the Internet.

If you take away nothing else from this chapter, remember the simple mitigation techniques used to defend against most of these attacks. The use of ACLs and disabling unnecessary services have limited investments in time and resources, but they certainly pay off when compared with the consequences. With the proper ACLs and router hardening, updating the version of your IOS is almost a secondary or tertiary level of defense.

Solutions Fast Track

Cisco IPv4 Denial of Service

☑ Using a special sequence of packets, the router believes that the input queue is filled and stops accepting new traffic.

☑ Use ACLs to prohibit unauthorized traffic from reaching the router.

☑ Filter out and disable unneeded and exotic functionality (such as IP Protocol 53, which is SWIPE, and Protocol 77, which is SUN-ND).

☑ Stay updated on the latest versions of IOS.

☑ Use an IDS (covered more in Chapter 9) to look for suspicious traffic.

Cisco HTTP Get Buffer Overflow

☑ Specially crafted UDP packets can cause an information disclosure of actual packet data.

☑ Unusually large HTTP requests can cause the built-in Web server to return a shell prompt to the remote attacker.

☑ Disable UDP Small-Servers and HTTP Services—they are hardly ever needed.

☑ Use ACLs to limit access to the router's HTTP interface.

☑ Stay updated on the latest versions of IOS.

Cisco Discovery Protocol Denial of Service

☑ If not configured properly (or disabled), CDP can provide valuable infrastructure information to your potential attacker.

☑ Disable CDP on all routers where it is unnecessary.

☑ When absolutely necessary (for management consoles such as CiscoWorks), only enable CDP on the interfaces that absolutely need it.

☑ Use ACLs to control the CDP traffic coming in to and going out of your internal network segment.

MAC Flooding

☑ MAC flooding can happen by overloading the switch's CAM table with enough phony MAC addresses appearing on all ports that it doesn't get a chance to catch up.

☑ Enable port security on all switches. This should stop the problem dead in its tracks.

☑ Move all critical assets to a secured VLAN.

☑ Tune IDS systems to look for irregular traffic.

ARP Spoofing

- ☑ An easy attack that is still hard to track down, ARP spoofing simply involves taking over another node's identity and convincing surrounding network devices that you should receive all network traffic that once belonged to the other machine.

- ☑ Apply static ARP entries on all critical devices.

- ☑ Move all critical assets to a secured private VLAN.

- ☑ Tune IDS systems to look for irregular traffic.

Breaking Out of Jail

- ☑ Although difficult to reproduce, it is possible to jump from one VLAN to another.

- ☑ Turn off Dynamic Trunking Protocol (DTP) on all ports on all switches.

- ☑ Statically set all trunking ports.

- ☑ Move all trunking ports to a single VLAN.

Attacking Simple Network Management Protocol

- ☑ Because SNMP versions prior to 3 did not support username/password authentication or encrypted tunnels, it is quite easy to sniff the wire for important (and damaging) information about the inner workings of your company.

- ☑ Use SNMP v3 for encryption wherever possible.

- ☑ Disable SNMP on unnecessary devices.

- ☑ Use IPSec where SNMP v3 is not applicable.

- ☑ Medium and low-risk exploits can be used together to form a high-risk vulnerability.

- ☑ Be conscious of the low-risk vulnerabilities present on your network and the exposure they cause.

☑ Deploy preventative technologies like IPSec or Host-Based Intrusion Prevention Systems to reduce your exposure and lessen the likelihood of a successful attack.

☑ Do not use common passwords on critical networking devices.

Links to Sites

- **www.phenoelit.de** The absolute authority on all Cisco vulnerabilities. Expert research and analysis.

- **www.cisco.com/warp/public/707/advisory.html#advisories** All Cisco advisories and security-related information.

- **www.securityfocus.com/bid/** Great security resources for multi-vendor bugs and vulnerabilities.

- **http://monkey.org/~dugsong/dsniff** The main site for downloading Dug Song's DSniff application. Site also includes documentation and articles on the value of using DSniff to help secure your enterprise.

- **www.datanerds.net/~mike/dsniff.html** More information regarding DSniff and its many uses. It is also the main distribution for Windows ports of famous tools and utilities such as WinPcap.

- **http://ettercap.sourceforge.net** This site houses all of the Ettercap releases and documentation for download. Also present are FAQs and Ettercap history.

Mailing Lists

- **cust-security-announce@cisco.com** To subscribe, send a message to majordomo@cisco.com with a single line in the body "info cust-security-announce."

- **first-teams@first.org** A mailing list dedicated to security incidents and research. Subscribe at www.first.org.

- **bugtraq@netspace.org** A mailing list dedicated to vulnerabilities bugs. To subscribe to this, and a number of other mailing lists, go to www.securityfocus.com/archive.

Frequently Asked Questions

The following Frequently Asked Questions, answered by the authors of this book, are designed to both measure your understanding of the concepts presented in this chapter and to assist you with real-life implementation of these concepts. To have your questions about this chapter answered by the author, browse to **www.syngress.com/solutions** and click on the **"Ask the Author"** form. You will also gain access to thousands of other FAQs at ITFAQnet.com.

Q: What is the best way to make my network devices invisible to attackers?

A: The use of access control lists (ACLs) is the best way to accomplish this. There are very few reasons why an IP would need to connect directly to your device; mostly this is used for management purposes. Allow the specific IPs that need access and deny the rest.

Q: How should I react to 0-day exploits affecting my core network devices?

A: Depending on the nature of your business, making changes to core devices could be a no-no during normal business hours (especially if you are a bank). The proper use of ACLs and keeping your IOS revision updated during maintenance windows will go a long way in protecting you. In cases where you have done all of the preventative maintenance possible and you are still vulnerable, we would have all of our IDS systems listening and watching for illegitimate traffic destined for our hardware network devices. You cannot prevent the attack, but at least you will know what is happening.

Q: Should I use TFTP (Trivial File Transfer Protocol) to manage my network device configurations?

A: TFTP does serve a great purpose in network administration. In large networks it is very difficult to keep track of configurations and changes. Keep in mind, however, that TFTP is not a secure network transfer and should be used with extreme caution. Consider placing ACLs on routers or switches that have TFTP configured. In addition, consider an implementation of TFTP with IPSec to encrypt the data on the wire.

Q: Where can I find more information on hardening Cisco routers?

A: A great hardening guide is available at: http://nsa2.www.conxion.com/ cisco/. This is a National Security Agency Guide on how to configure Cisco routers securely. It provides information and tips on various Cisco security features.

Chapter 9

Implementing Intrusion Detection Systems

Solutions in this Chapter:

- **Understanding Intrusion System Basics**
- **Comparing IDS/IPS Vendors**
- **Subverting an IDS/IPS**

Related Chapters:

- Chapter 1 Understanding Perimeter and Internal Segments
- Chapter 2 Assessing your Current Network
- Chapter 3 Selecting the Correct Firewall
- Chapter 6 Secure Network Management
- Chapter 10 Perimeter Network Design
- Chapter 11 Internal Network Design

Introduction

Protecting a corporate network is a game of sorts—administrators pitted against hackers. Unfortunately, security administrators must always play defense. You don't know when or from where the opponent will attack. It could be a stampede or a precision strike. Your job is to prevent the attack from happening or, as a worst-case scenario, clean up afterward.

One thing that you do know is *what* will be attacked—every resource that is accessible from the Internet and everything to which those resources connect, internal and external. Ideally, you would want to prevent these attacks from even happening. That is where firewalls (see Chapter 3, "Selecting the Correct Firewall") and proper network segmentation (see Chapter 11, "Internal Network Design") come into play. However, inevitably, some packets will creep past your defenses. What then?

Let's imagine that your house has been or is in the process of being burglarized. Your firewall (deadbolt lock) should have prevented this, but you forgot that you left the side window open (unprotected VPN connection). What is next? Well, at the very least you would want to know what happened, what was stolen, or what was damaged. Proper logging (insurance photos) can take care of what is missing, but that gives you little comfort. What if you could have been notified while the burglary was taking place? A home burglar alarm (your Intrusion Detection System, or IDS) will watch for suspicious activity (signature/trigger strings), and when something odd happens, it should notify the authorities (send an e-mail or an alphanumeric page to your belt).

You're doing well so far, but you still worry about someone being able to break into the house and steal your wife's jewelry before the authorities arrive. If there were a way to prevent the jewelry box from opening, you would feel safer. A special monitoring device (an Intrusion Prevention System, or IPS) where any attempts at opening the jewelry box are met with the lid slamming closed would be excellent.

And while you're at it, you can make the game more interesting; add decoys, divert the burglar's attention. Hide the street address (using Network Address Translation, or NAT) to confuse the burglar. You can even go as far as diverting the front walkway from reaching your front door, and instead lead to a fake front door (honeypot). If someone walks right up to the fake front door and tries to force it open, it must be a burglar, because all of your friends and family know to use the side door.

This chapter guides you through an understanding of IDS basics and types of components within intrusion detection systems. It presents comparisons of just some of the many IDS solutions available. You will also be shown how attackers fool IDS systems and navigate around them. In addition, a new breed of IPS is introduced, with their benefits and detractors, and using honeypots and honeynets to divert an attacker's attention. When you've finished this chapter, you will be able to decide what type of IDS solution (whether a mix of IDS, IPS, and honeynets, or just a simple signature-based router trigger) will work well in your environment.

Understanding Intrusion Detection and Prevention Basics

The National Institute for Standards and Technology (NIST) Special Publication SP800-31 aptly describes intrusion detection as "the process of monitoring the events occurring in a computer system or network and analyzing them for signs of intrusions, defined as attempts to compromise the confidentiality, integrity, availability, or to bypass the security mechanisms of a computer or network." Understanding the different types of IDS components and where they fit best allows you to build a solid protective mechanism for your network.

IDSs fall into two basic categories:

- Host Intrusion Detection Systems (HIDSs)
- Network Intrusion Detection Systems (NIDSs)

HIDSs usually take the form of software agents that install on important hosts to report and prevent unauthorized activity back to a central console. This management station usually has a very large database of known attack signatures (the clues that show someone is trying to break in) and a reporting mechanism to notify the network administrator. The software agents are usually highly OS-specific because they hook into the operating system at a very low level. This is necessary because they need to monitor all threads and system call activities, to make sure there is no suspicious activity. Because of this, a HIDS agent will almost always have a performance impact on the machine on which it is installed.

NIDSs are often network appliances or hardened servers with special software that attaches to the network and monitors traffic looking for attacks. NIDSs can be further subdivided into passive devices (which simply monitor the traffic that flows past them) and inline devices (which actually inspect traffic as it flows through the machine, using two or more NICs).

A new wrinkle to the market has been the introduction of a new breed of device that is essentially a souped-up IDS. An IPS will make automated changes to a system under attack or actively endeavor to prevent those same attacks. Some can directly modify firewall rules to filter out future packets from the same attacker or—when in an inline configuration—drop the offending packets before they even reach the target device. This is a vast improvement over an IDS, that will usually only detect an attack; its only response mechanism is to send an alert to an administrator (via e-mail, pager, etc.).

An important distinction to make here is the two roles that IDS and IPS play in a modern network. While many vendors might have (mistakenly) touted IDS as the watchdog for your network, it is hardly a one-click installation. Neglected IDS servers are usually quickly located to be the scapegoat of network intrusions, when it was really the lack of tuning an IDS that was at fault. Rather than consider the IDS the night watchman of the network, you should think of it more as the closed-circuit cameras that are sometimes installed; they won't prevent an attack on their own, but if a skilled technician is watching them (or the IDS logs), you can learn a great deal about your attackers and potential adversaries. In much the same way that packet sniffers (see Chapter 2 for more information on the vast array of protocol analyzers on the market today) allow a skilled network engineer to diagnose a routing problem, a well-tuned IDS can allow a security engineer to improve security in other prevention devices. Gary Golomb, an IDS expert and noted speaker at conferences such as CanSecWest, remarked in October 2003 that "The IDS serves the single purpose of sitting back and watching over everything to see if people are still getting though." He goes on to say, "Whether it's because of vulnerabilities in network designs, application vulnerabilities, or unknowingly misconfigured devices, they [attackers] do get through."

So, do you need an IDS or an IPS? What about both? Which product is which? And as if the concepts weren't muddled and confusing to begin with, many vendors' marketing departments are having an identity crisis over what to label their product. Some products marketed as IDS are really more IPS in nature, and the reverse is often true as well. Industry pundits have gone so far as to announce the death of IDS in favor of IPS in 2003. More people still recognize the term *IDS* over *IPS* so the burial ceremony might be a bit premature. Most vendors will likely incorporate IPS features into their IDSs to make them viable long after the bagpipes stop playing.

Intrusion Detection System Sensors

In the September/October 2000 issue of *IEEE Software*, members of CERT discussed the role of IDS in a "defense in depth" strategy. They mention it is to "positively identify attacks without falsely identifying non-attacks." Another role is to issue warnings to "help users alter their installation's defensive posture to increase resistance to attack." A successful IDS implementation should take into account:

- **Network inventory** The IDS should know if it is located amongst a gaggle of Windows Web servers, versus strictly UNIX-based FTP servers. This will greatly reduce the amount of false positives when a misguided attacker attempts an IIS attack on your UNIX machine. The event should be noted, but not as severe as an IIS attack on your Windows Web servers.

- **Sensor deployment** The sensors (also called intrusion detectors) that make up an IDS must be placed in the optimal locations to provide relevant results to the security team. Just like you wouldn't put your burglar alarm's motion sensor in the hall closet, you should also make sure that your sensors are positioned so they can "see" a great deal of your traffic.

Sensors come in one of three main categories, with a fourth emerging category sure to make a strong showing in years to come:

- **Network-based** Network-based IDS (NIDS) sensors monitor network traffic at a collection point, like the internal and/or external interface of a firewall. They allow passive responses to events (an e-mail alert), and they may capture all packets involved in the detected attack for later analysis. Some allow sending TCP RST (reset packets) back to attacking hosts, which forces existing connections to disconnect. This will not keep an attacker from coming back later and trying again, and it will inform the attacker that he is dealing with an automated system, which might be more information than you're willing to give away.

- **Host-based** Host-based IDS (HIDS) sensors are software packages installed locally on a machine you want to monitor. The sensor watches for events involving local system attack patterns, like account creation, password changes, system file changes, and so forth. They usually report their findings back to a central management console, which then can send an e-mail alert or other notification mechanisms.

- **Hybrids** Hybrids are host-based sensors that also watch network traffic to and from the monitored host. They watch for system-level events like a host-based sensor, but also watch for "suspicious" network activity aimed at the host they are protecting.

- **Honeypots** Honeypots and honeynets are a bit different from other sensor categories. They can detect known attacks, but are much better suited to detecting and recording as-yet-unknown attack patterns (the so-called Zero Day attacks). They are vulnerable systems or virtual systems that emulate vulnerable systems. Since they are not and should not be used for legitimate services, any activity at all on these systems should raise an alarm. Initial reports of the worm that would eventually be named MS Blaster came from people who had set up honeypots. They noticed a change in the normal scans of their network and used the honeypot logs to determine that a new worm was circulating.

Sensors are passive by design, although we will see in later sections that some inline IDS solutions and most IPSs are active by definition. IDS sensors will typically monitor all the activity on a particular network segment, sitting and listening quietly without altering any of the information. All activity is analyzed for a match to what the sensor has been told is bad. The sensor can use a number of methods to determine this. See Table 9.1 for a list of the methods and a description of each.

Table 9.1 Methods Used by Intrusion Detection Sensors to Differentiate Good and Bad Traffic

Method	Mechanism	Pros	Cons
Pattern matching	Scans incoming packets for specific byte sequences (the signatures) stored in a database of known attacks.	Identifies known attacks. Provides specific information for analysis and response.	May trigger false positives. Requires frequent updates of signature tables. Attacks can be modified to avoid detection.

Continued

Table 9.1 Methods Used by Intrusion Detection Sensors to Differentiate Good and Bad Traffic

Method	Mechanism	Pros	Cons
Stateful matching	Scans for attack signatures in the context of a traffic stream rather than individual packets.	Identifies known attacks. Detects signatures spread across multiple packets. Provides specific information for analysis and response.	May trigger false positives. Requires frequent updates of signature tables. Attacks can be modified to avoid detection.
Protocol anomaly	Looks for deviations from standards set forth in RFCs.	Can identify attacks without a signature. Reduces false positives with well-understood protocols.	May lead to false positives and false negatives with poorly understood or complex protocols. Protocol analysis modules take longer to deploy to customers than signatures do.
Traffic anomaly	Watches for unusual traffic activities, such as a flood of UDP packets or a new service appearing on the network.	Can identify unknown attacks and DoS floods.	Can be difficult to tune properly. Must have a clear understanding of "normal" traffic environment.
Statistical anomaly	Develops baselines of normal traffic activity and throughput, and alerts on deviations from those baselines.	Can identify unknown attacks and DoS floods.	Can be difficult to tune properly. Must have a clear understanding of "normal" traffic environment.

NIDS placement is an important part of its effectiveness. If the sensors are monitoring a small portion of your total network traffic, you might miss an attack and leave yourself exposed. NIDSs should be placed at all traffic concentration points. In a switched network, you will not be able to monitor all traffic at first because a switch will only transmit packets to your particular port if they are destined to that port. This can be easily overcome by enabling "port mirroring" features on the ports where your IDS sensors live. In Chapter 2, we discuss this in greater detail, but port mirroring (or "SPAN" ports as Cisco refers to it) changes your expensive managed switch into a low-end hub that repeats all packets to the SPAN port. This is horrible for performance but fantastic for monitoring. Figure 9.1 shows where NIDS sensors could be placed in a typical WAN topology.

Figure 9.1 NIDS Placement in a Typical WAN Topology

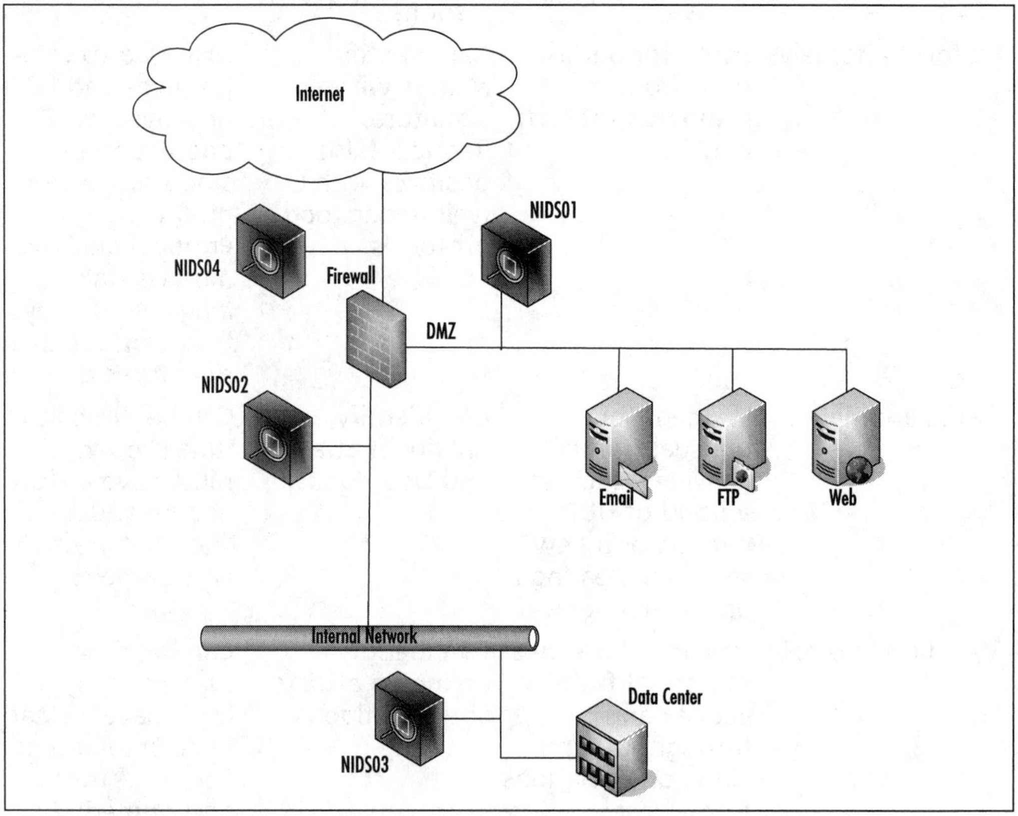

Notice that each network segment has its own sensor. Some would consider this excessive: Why would you need both NIDS02 and NIDS04? Isn't that redundant? In fact, it is not. NIDS04 will most certainly experience the most traffic of all the sensors, but that doesn't mean that NIDS02 is useless. In fact, having NIDS04 as a baseline is extremely useful for finding where your firewall has leaks. If an attack sequence is detected in NIDS04 and then also in NIDS02, you know that your firewall allowed malicious traffic through. You can correlate this with the firewall's log file as well (although during an attack this might be compromised). Now let's say that you notice an attack sequence in the NIDS02 log file, with a source IP address of 192.0.2.94. Of course, you will assume that this is an external attack by the IP address. However, what if the source IP address was spoofed (many modern worms do just this)? A quick scan of the NIDS04 log will show that the packet was never seen outside the firewall. This leads us to believe that the attack was launched from inside the firewall and with a spoofed source IP address. Watch out—you might have a talented and angry IT employee on your hands!

Notes from the Underground...

Poo-Pooing the Honeypot

A number of people have been researching ways to demonstrate the limitations of honeypot technology, as well as proof-of-concept tools. The whole premise of honeypots is to covertly monitor the activities of a target audience, who are technically skilled and are likely able to manipulate and query any resources attached to the honeypot itself. One article references www.antihoney.net, but as this book is heading to press, no site exists at this address.

Intrusion Prevention System Sensors

A new acronym to toss into your (already crowded) techie vocabulary is Intrusion Prevention Systems (IPS). While many analysts and some over-zealous sales managers will attempt to sell you on the fact that it is a revolution in computer security, it's more of an *evolution* from a monitor-and-report system, to a monitor-and-do-something system. The clear call to action for many security teams has been the recent (perceived) failures of firewalls in stopping the Code Red and NIMDA attacks of a few years ago. The uninformed scream, "But we have a firewall? Isn't it supposed to block the bad stuff?"

How Did We Get Here?

Indeed, the firewall should block the "bad stuff" and block it does—but limited to the rule base that is defined. Certainly, a decade ago, when the NCSA Mosaic Web browser was just hitting the streets, nobody ever worried about HTTP being a vehicle for an attacker; go back just five years and you would still find people who believed Web traffic to be "safe." So, we all go about our lives, setting our firewalls to fiercely defend against attempts to reach the unencrypted Telnet port, the collection of Microsoft Networking ports, and prevent unauthorized remote procedure calls on our Sun workstations. Want someone to connect to our Apache Web site to view the latest press releases—sure, what's the harm in that?

As soon as the attackers-at-large realized that they weren't getting anywhere running head-on into the firewall, they started investigating what they could do with the few ports that *were* left open. The HTTP port was not only inviting, but due to the constant stream of traffic going to today's Web servers, a small attack packet mixed in with thousands of legitimate requests would be hard to detect manually.

This Darwinian evolution should have been pretty obvious to any of us. When someone wants to break into a company, he studies the layout of the building. Soon, he learns that the side door leading to the lunch area is never locked (no firewall at all). Consequently, the attacker walks in, steals a laptop, and goes home. Next week, the CEO orders that all doors be locked at all times (firewall put into service). However, of course, the front door is still open during business hours for customers to walk in (akin to the HTTP port being left open), right? Therefore, the attacker now just pretends to be a customer, walks in, and when nobody is looking, swipes another laptop. The following week, the CEO orders that closed-circuit cameras be mounted at all doors to prevent further loss. This time, the attacker returns at night, with a mask, and fetches yet another laptop. It's only the day after when the videotape is reviewed that the loss is detected.

No matter what countermeasure we put into place, there will always be a method to get around it. In that last example, the company's IDS solution was represented by the cameras. They monitor the intrusion points but do little more than notify the owner *after* the theft has occurred. What's the next logical step for the CEO and his laptops? Hiring a security guard wouldn't be a bad idea. The nice part is that the guard will be able to stop and question people who show up knocking on the doors (ports) of the building. No longer is it a reaction to the videotapes; it is instead a proactive security move. In much the same way, the evolution from IDS to IPS is natural and expected. To stay ahead of the attackers, we must move from reacting to being proactive about our network security.

Where Are We Now?

Modern IPS solutions go further than IDS systems by actively attempting to stop an in-progress attack. In June 2003, the *Gartner CIO Update* defined this new evolution of technology as follows:

> Intrusion prevention must block malicious actions using multiple algorithms. Intrusion prevention systems must provide blocking capabilities that include signature-based blocking of known attacks. However, intrusion prevention systems must also move beyond simple signature-based approaches—such as those used by antivirus and intrusion detection systems—to at least support policy, behavior, and anomaly-based detection algorithms. These algorithms must operate at the application level in addition to standard, network-level firewall processing. It must also have the wisdom to know the difference (between attack events and normal events).

The real risk with IPS sensors is that there is very little difference between attack events and normal events (the "false-positives"). If legitimate traffic or system functions are falsely deemed "bad" by the sensor, blocking the legitimate event might shut down a business process without human intervention. Because of the powerful blocking features in these IPS solutions, a degree of caution must be used before "flipping the switch." John Dias, security analyst at Lawrence Livermore National Laboratory, quips that "For those using IPS, by the time they've mastered the subject of blocking, they're being blamed for everything." Lloyd Hession, chief security officer for Radianz, agrees: "These devices become a lightning rod inside an organization, and it's typical to blame the IPS for any problem."

After evaluating your IPS strategy in a test lab, factor in a few weeks of "baseline" testing before activating the IPS blocking mode. During this time, you can teach the IPS what is good and what is bad. During this all-important learning period, it is imperative that all possible valid activities are performed on the monitored system. Make sure your weekly patch update procedure or data backup routine is allowed by the IPS. Otherwise, the IPS will block the very beneficial activity of updating your machine, because it is an unknown system activity. This is extremely important, so let's all read that again: Make absolutely sure that your IPS rules allow for legitimate patch updates and data backup routines! Your baseline testing should last longer than just a few days because some automated update routines only run once per week. Maybe you only back up your servers weekly—whatever the case, you want to make sure that all of your well-crafted disaster recovery and data backup plans aren't blocked by your shiny new IPS.

There are three main delivery formats for IPSs, summarized as follows:

- **Network-based** Network-based IPS (NIPS) sensors use a different architecture than network-based IDS sensors do. The traffic is analyzed for known attack patterns. When a pattern is matched, the configured reaction (alert, log, send reset, etc.) is performed. Unlike IDS sensors, they can also take action to prevent the attack from happening again. By either modifying firewall rules or blocking the traffic themselves, IPS sensors can make a response to an event happen almost immediately. Network-based IPS sensors act very similar to network-based IDS sensors. They monitor network traffic at a collection point, like the internal and/or external interface of a firewall. Usually, they are inline and have traffic flow between two or more network interfaces. They allow passive responses to events as well, but their true power is in their capability to dynamically block the offending traffic.

- **Host-based** Host-based IPS (HIPS) sensors are similar host-based IDS systems with one major difference. HIPS sensors have teeth. They have the capabilities to respond to an attack instead of just report that one is happening. They can prevent malicious access to system resources and intercept malicious actions before any damage is done. This type of sensor is particularly useful on publicly exposed high-profile Web servers. Should an attacker manage to get through your security layers, he will still not be able to change the content of your homepage (defacement) because any disk writing activity will be prevented.

- **Tarpits** A network that responds to an attacker's probe packets with the slowest possible response is a *tarpit* (a term borrowed from geologists, and the dinosaurs that eventually died in the pools of tar just south of Los Angeles). With most modern (and rapidly spreading) worms, a probe packet for reconnaissance precedes the attack packet. Capitalizing on this knowledge, a tarpit will slow the initial probe by responding very slowly and forcing the attacking computer to retransmit the probe packet many times. More information on tarpits can be found later in this chapter.

Like NIDSs, the placement of your NIPS devices directly affects their effectiveness. In network-based IDS or IPS systems (such as those represented by Figure 9.1), you usually place a sensor on each network segment; in a host-based system, there would be a small software agent on each machine that reports back to a central management console. This IDS or IPS console would hopefully be located in a secure management segment of your network (see Chapter 6 for more information on designing dedicated monitoring and management VLANs).

Comparing IDS/IPS Vendors

This section lists various IDS packages as well as several honeypot and tarpit products—both commercial and open source. While the aim of this chapter is not to definitively recommend a product for your organization, it is our sincere hope that we can present a representative cross-section of the IDS and IPS market that will aid you in your eventual purchase decision. Evaluation versions of these products are (usually) readily accessible and should be installed in a test network before making any final determinations. Most of the products listed in the following IDS section have really evolved in the past couple of years into a blended IDS/IPS system. Rather than split hairs by shoehorning them into either the IDS or the IPS bucket, we present them here as a combined section. We had hoped to invent a new acronym (IDAPSE, for Intrusion Detection and Prevention Systems Extraordinaire), but we didn't get the required amount of signatures on our petition. If you'd like to donate money toward the effort, operators are standing by.

Intrusion Detection/Prevention Systems

As with many products in the security industry, the most innovative products start life as pet projects from talented hackers. As part of the community of security professionals, these tools are almost always posted for the world to review and use in the form of open-source applications. These solutions result in a quality product and have an extensive community of end users who share configuration tips and usage notes. Most of the problems you'll encounter during installation or use have already been solved or discovered. However, in some corporate environments, the lack of a single entity to get on the phone in the middle of the night for emergency support might make a CISO nervous. Several commercial packages provide this accountability and add many enhancements not available in their open-source counterparts. In the following sections, we present the most influential open-source tools and their commercial contemporaries.

Snort

Snort (www.snort.org) is the most commonly used open-source network intrusion detection package available. Written by Marty Roesch, it is a signature-based solution that has a huge user base and is supported very well by the public community. Snort was originally intended as a packet sniffer. In November 1998, Marty Roesch wrote a Linux-only packet sniffer called APE. Despite the great features of APE, Marty wanted a sniffer that also does the following:

- Works on multiple OSs
- Uses a hexdump payload dump (TcpDump later had this functionality)
- Displays all the different network packets the same way (TcpDump did not have this)

Marty's goal was to write a better sniffer for his own use. He also wrote Snort as a libpcap application, which gives Snort portability from a network filtering and sniffing standpoint. At the time, only TcpDump was also compiled with libpcap, so this gave the system administrator another sniffer with which to work. Snort became available at Packet Storm (www.packetstormsecurity.com) on December 22, 1998. At that time, Snort was only about 1600 lines of code and had a total of two files. This was about a month after Snort's initial inception, and was only used for packet sniffing at this point. Marty's first uses of Snort included monitoring his cable modem connection and debugging network applications he coded.

Snort's first signature-based analysis (also known as rules-based within the Snort community) became a feature in late January 1999. This was Snort's initial foray down the path of intrusion detection, and Snort could be used as a lightweight IDS at the time. By the time Snort version 1.5 came out in December 1999, Martin had decided on the Snort architecture that is currently being used until version 2.0. After version 1.5 was released, Snort was able to use all the different plug-ins available today. The latest version of Snort is 2.1, which is a rework of the architecture and contains approximately 75,000 lines of code.

Signature updates are almost instantaneous thanks to a very active signature distribution list. Within hours of an issue being discovered (a new worm, virus, and so forth), Snort users post signatures designed to detect the malicious traffic. The availability of these particular signatures has been so universally accepted that many of the top commercial packages allow importing Snort signatures into their own signature database. Snort signatures are easy to write. The following is one of the default signatures for Code Red v2.

```
alert tcp $EXTERNAL_NET any -> $HTTP_SERVERS $HTTP_PORTS (msg:"WEB-IIS
CodeRed v2 root.exe access"; flow:to_server,established;
uricontent:"/root.exe"; nocase; classtype:web-application-attack;
reference:url,www.cert.org/advisories/CA-2001-19.html; sid:1256;  rev:7;)
```

All "$" values in the preceding code are defined in your snort.conf. This signature tells Snort to log an alert for any traffic from the external network on any port going to our defined HTTP servers on the defined HTTP ports with "/root.exe" in the URL string. Since Code Red v2 tries the following URL string while propagating:

```
GET /scripts/root.exe?/c+dir HTTP/1.0
```

the previous rule would put an entry in alert.ids in the log directory that would look like:

```
[**] [1:1256:2] WEB-IIS CodeRed v2 root.exe access [**][Classification: Web
Application Attack] [Priority: 1]04/04-23:43:00.538443 211.38.132.221:4493
-> 211.38.45.165:80 TCP TTL:123 TOS:0x0 ID:57686 IpLen:20 DgmLen:112 DF
***AP*** Seq: 0xEF40ABB9 Ack: 0xEF287695 Win: 0x4470 TcpLen: 20
```

In addition to the basic Snort features, Snort can be set up to provide real-time alerts. This provides you with the ability to receive alerts in real time, rather than having to continuously monitor your Snort system. Logging support is extensive as well. Snort can log alerts to databases such as MySQL and MSSQL, text files, and syslog servers. It can log with SNMP traps and e-mail alerts as well. Figure 9.2 shows Snort's basic architecture and alert logging capabilities. Snort has packet logging and packet sniffing capabilities as well (see reference to Snort in Chapter 2 under *Packet Sniffing*).

Figure 9.2 Snort Architecture and Alert Logging Capabilities

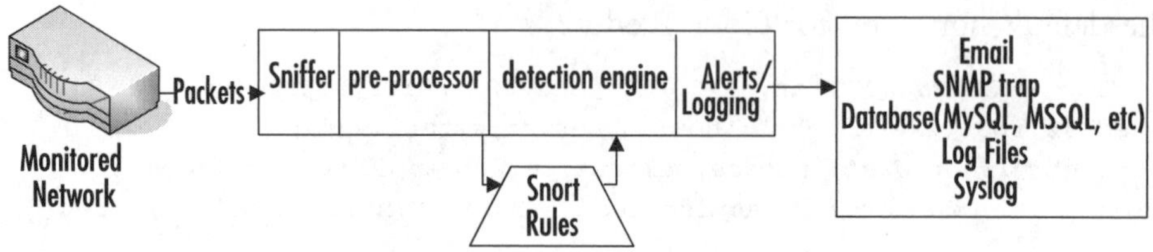

Tools of the Trade...

Can't Snort Enough?

Looking for more information about Snort? The tool is really very powerful and we could go on for pages and pages about it. In fact, you could probably write an entire book just about the Snort IDS. Luckily, you don't have to; it has already been written and released in August 2003 (*Snort 2.0 Intrusion Detection*, ISBN 1931836744), written by actual members of the Snort.org team. Within the (over 500!) pages, readers are given invaluable insight into the code base of Snort, and in-depth tutorials of complex installation, configuration, and troubleshooting scenarios. A CD containing the latest version of Snort as well as other open-source security utilities accompanies the book. One review from Richard Bejtlich (influential security expert and author of the TaoSecurity.org security journal) states, "I've read the best IDS books, and used IDS technology, since 1998, and *Snort 2.0* is the first to give real insight into an IDS' inner workings."

Sourcefire

Sourcefire (www.sourcefire.com) is the commercial version of the popular Snort IDS, covered previously. This solution starts with the Snort engine, adds an intuitive user interface (instead of the sometimes difficult-to-use command-line interface), some fascinating data analysis, and slams it all onto some hardware that was hand-picked to provide a high-performance IDS environment. A nice advancement in the Sourcefire product line is the availability of a Gigabit-Ethernet version of their Network Sensors (NS). This means that if you are a large organization that uses GigE within the core switching layer, you don't have to slow your network down just to have effective inspection performed. Add to this the fact that multiple sensors can be load balanced and have automatic device failover, and you can see that the Sourcefire solution definitely deserves attention from any serious buyers.

To reduce the effectiveness of common IDS evasion techniques (detailed later in this chapter), the Sourcefire NS provides packet reassembly and fragment reordering. The NS uses a dual-NIC architecture to allow it to listen (undetectable) on one interface, while reporting the information back to a management console (MC) on the other interface. Speaking of management, the MC allows your numerous/multiple Sourcefire NS devices across your network to report their findings in a central data window. This "contextual intelligence," in the words of the Sourcefire marketing department, "finally enables users to protect the real assets on their networks instead of merely attempting to assess the hostility of the packets traversing the network."

> **NOTE**
>
> The name Snort came from the fact that the application is a "sniffer and more." In addition, Martin said that he has too many programs called a.out, and all the popular names for sniffers called TCP-something were already taken.

Cisco

Cisco has a product for virtually every niche of an enterprise network, so it shouldn't surprise anyone that Cisco has products in the IDS space as well. The older IDS offering from Cisco was a well-intentioned-but-lacking product called NetRanger. After the January 2003 acquisition of Okena, Inc., Cisco dropped the NetRanger product and quickly renamed the (far superior) Okena offering.

Cisco's host-based IPS product was dubbed the Cisco Security Agent, formerly known as Okena StormWatch. It is flexible enough to protect Windows NT, 2000, XP, and even some flavors of UNIX. The configuration console, however, runs on Windows 2000 Server. Like many other HIDSs, the agent installs on the host systems and receives configuration parameters from the console. These components communicate with each other over SSL. Administrators access the console through an HTTPS Web site. The important differentiator between the Okena (now Cisco) product is that it feels equally at home protecting workstations and servers. You can find out more about the newly renamed Cisco Security Agent at (better go grab a pencil—Cisco isn't known for easy to remember URLs): www.cisco.com/en/US/products/sw/secursw/ps5057.

Moving beyond HIDS and onto NIDS, Cisco has a wide range of products, some developed in-house and others acquired by buying entire companies. Cisco makes IDS modules for most of its nearly ubiquitous routers and switches. Many times you can add IDS features into a router or switch that you might already own with very little effort. Cisco also has stand-alone appliances with the sole purpose of providing IDS / IPS.

Cisco's network-based product is called IDS Sensor. It is designed to accurately identify and classify known and unknown threats targeting your network, including worms, denial-of-service (DoS), and application attacks. Cisco IDS uses an array of detection methods to accurately detect nearly all potential threats. Building on seven years of IDS experience, Cisco delivers a hybrid system using detection methods most appropriate for the threat, including stateful pattern recognition, protocol analysis, traffic anomaly detection, and protocol anomaly detection. You can find out more about the Cisco IDS at www.cisco.com/en/US/products/sw/secursw/ps2113.

Pulling the individual products together, Cisco's Threat Response software provides an automated, just-in-time analysis of each targeted host to determine whether a compromise has occurred. Only by investigating the host under attack can you efficiently uncover the real intrusions and address them quickly. Cisco even goes as far as claiming that their product virtually eliminates false alarms, escalates real attacks, and aids in the remediation of costly intrusions. Find out more about the comprehensive Cisco Threat Response system at www.cisco.com/en/US/products/sw/secursw/ps5054.

eEye

The eEye Blink product is one of the newest offerings in this arena. As this book went to press, the software was in the last phases of beta testing and should be released sometime in early summer 2004. For completeness, we've included the product in this section even though we don't have experience with it (we're not one of the beta testers). Therefore, instead of reviewing this product, we will just present the feature list from the software publisher and hope that it is available for trial download by the time these pages hit your favorite bookstore.

Blink will provide threat mitigation through multiple layers of security technologies. Using smart protocol analysis and application monitoring engines, Blink claims to protect against even unknown vulnerabilities. Security policies will be fully customizable and allow security administrators to lock down and secure against intruders and owner misuse. The following is a quick overview of the proposed features of Blink.

- **Intrusion Prevention Engine (Protocol Analysis)** Blink will reconstruct network traffic to analyze the protocol data to discover an attack in progress, responding to attacks by logging the attack, dropping the packets, or resetting the TCP session.

- **Intrusion Prevention Engine (Signature Checking)** As a secondary layer of defense, Blink should be able to block well-known attacks using pattern matching against a database of signatures.

- **Firewall Engine (Network Layer Protection)** Blink intends to ship with a limited firewall capability that can analyze each packet of incoming and outgoing network traffic. By monitoring all outgoing network traffic in real time and verifying that the traffic is coming from an approved application, Blink will be able to protect against Trojan code execution as well.

Internet Security Systems

Internet Security Systems (ISS), founded in 1994, is one of the larger fish in the IDS ocean. With 1200 employees in 27 countries, this is a far cry from a startup or open-source software. The ISS RealSecure suite of programs is designed to watch every corner of an enterprise network. The real value that sets ISS apart is its talented staff who make up the "X-Force" team of vulnerability researchers. The products that make up the RealSecure system are as follows:

- **SiteProtector** Provides centralized management for all ISS products. Event prioritization and correlation within the console allow on-site administrators to view real-time attack information and, if necessary, use filters to screen for exceptions and false alarms. SiteProtector also greatly automates the deployment of other RealSecure modules.

- **Server Sensor** The HIDS portion of the RealSecure system provides real-time intrusion monitoring, detection, and protection by analyzing events logs and inbound and outbound network activity on critical enterprise assets such as your payroll or HR servers. The Server Sensor combines its database of built-in signatures with protocol analysis and behavioral pattern sets to prevent known attacks and (with any luck) thwart some unknown attacks, too.

- **Network Sensor** The NIDS component of RealSecure comes in both 10/100 Ethernet and Gigabit Ethernet varieties. These sensors are then centrally administered and maintained through SiteProtector. The researchers in the X-Force (funny name, yes) provide security intelligence to ISS customers and issue "X-Press Updates" (yes, they might have gotten a bit too cute with the naming) to add to customer attack signature databases. Side note: For those of you searching for a stocking-stuffer this Holiday season, there were some ISS X-Force action figures (yes, action figures) produced as employee gifts. Check eBay for your very own four-inch security researcher sitting right there on your desk.

- **Guard** An inline Network Intrusion Prevention System (NIPS), RealSecure Guard actively protects network segments by automatically blocking malicious attacks. Unlike most IDS components that silently monitor a network segment on one port and send alert information on another port, the inline nature of RealSecure Guard means that all data flowing in to or out of your network must pass through this machine.

On the one hand, this provides for a very high level of security; every packet is inspected and must conform to a security policy before being passed through the device. The trade-off (and you could have seen this coming) is, of course, performance. You must make sure that the addition of this data choke point in your network architecture won't bring your speedy Internet connection to its knees.

The RealSecure product line can also be purchased pre-installed on a new line of ISS Proventia G-Series appliances. For further product information, deployment guides, whitepapers, and evaluation copies of RealSecure, please consult www.iss.net/products_services.

NOTE

Although RealSecure does offer many features to help you assess your network's risk, it does have some challenges that you will want to understand. Perhaps most importantly, this product does not come at a small price, especially when considering a large deployment on your internal segments. Even though this is a commercially supported product, you will need to decide if this product can fit your budget. Secondly, this application is not the easiest to deploy or maintain in your environment. Companies have spent large sums of money on the deployment of these systems. Oftentimes, ISS or third-party VAR consultants are required to assist in the deployments. This will only add to the cost and complexity of the product.

Network Associates

In April 2003, Network Associates (NAI) bought two companies: Entercept Security Technologies and Intruvert Networks. Entercept brought its host-based IDS products with it, and Intruvert brought its network-based products. By June, NAI had released its first product line and was doing well. In a bold departure from the rest of the herd, NAI indeed markets their products specifically as Intrusion *Prevention* Systems, which will remove the guesswork as to their approach and capabilities. Most other vendors, hoping to catch the buzz surrounding both acronyms, use IDS and IPS interchangeably.

Host-Based Products

The host-based products are specialized for each type of application. Each has been designed to protect the most common type of hosts that are attacked.

- **McAfee Entercept Web Server Edition** Anyone who has used (or is still using) the Entercept IPS software (pre-acquisition) will recognize it under the new name: McAfee Entercept Web Server Edition (WSE). Without a doubt, we can definitely say this is powerful software. Having installed Entercept on a large Web farm (and only after spending many hours in configuration), we can report to you that we sleep better at night knowing it is protecting our network (not to mention our teeth are whiter and our dishes are sparkling, but we digress). Since Web servers are externally accessible (by definition), they are within easy reach of attackers. Protection provided by firewalls and perimeter security is no longer enough, since they will happily allow traffic destined for port 80 straight through the front door of the firewall and knocking on the door of the server. Increasingly knowledgeable hackers have discovered ways around firewalls and existing detection systems to launch attacks, such as buffer overflows and worms, directly against Web servers. Entercept WSE proactively defends Web servers against the myriad of buffer overflow and privilege escalation attacks by preventing any (and we do mean *any*) unauthorized server processes.

- **McAfee Entercept Standard Edition** The McAfee Entercept Standard Edition is much like the WSE, but is meant for your more general-purpose (but critical) enterprise servers. With agents available for Windows NT and Windows 2000, Solaris 2.6, 7, 8, and 9, and HP-UX 11, McAfee Entercept is a formidable product offering.

- **McAfee Entercept Database Edition** A third variation on the same theme is the McAfee Entercept Database Edition. Building upon the protection capabilities of the core Entercept product, the Database Edition offers a wide array of prevention mechanisms to thwart the popular SQL Injection attacks of today with the as-yet-unknown attacks of tomorrow. McAfee Entercept Database Edition locks down a Microsoft SQL 2000 database to both enforce correct behavior and block abnormal behavior, putting it almost in the Application-Specific IPS category to follow.

- **McAfee Entercept Management System** The McAfee Entercept Management System is the hub of all Entercept data collection activities. Up to 5000 Entercept Agents can be managed on a single management server, which is great news for IT departments that are quickly running out of rack space in their data centers. Entercept is able to adjust security policies to all of your management agents, across Windows NT, 2000, HP-UX, and Solaris platforms.

You can find more information about Entercept at www.nai.com/us/products/mcafee/host_ips/management_system.htm. In addition, make sure to read through the FAQ located at www.nai.com/us/_tier2/products/_media/mcafee/entercept_faqs.pdf to find some great information on the Entercept "adaptive auditing" functionality, which allows it to easily "learn" the applications that are on your Web server or network file server. This minimizes the time it takes an administrator to set up a set of rules and allows for a faster overall security deployment. After determining a baseline for your server, a protective envelope is wrapped around your most valuable processes (if it's a Microsoft IIS server, we'd make sure to protect inetinfo.exe). Any time an application wants to write to the executing file or otherwise disturb the envelope, the Entercept manager has to approve the action. In this fashion, it is very possible that no unknown threat or vulnerability will be able to bring your Entercept-protected Web server down. (See Figure 9.3.)

Figure 9.3 McAfee Entercept

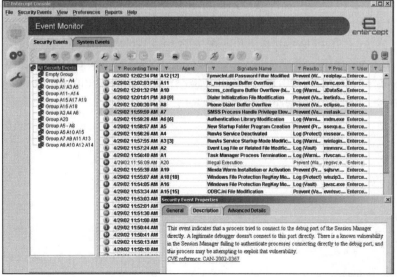

Network-Based Products

The network-based products are based on Intruvert's IntruShield product line before the acquisition. There are three products in the line-up. Each product has the same feature set but increases through the list in performance capabilities.

- **McAfee IntruShield** The McAfee IntruShield appliances vary in size and capacity to fit your different network needs. The IntruShield 1200 is designed for your branch offices, and includes two Fast Ethernet detection ports, a response port, a management port, and can still deliver 100 Mbps performance. The IntruShield 2600 is a slightly beefed-up box, intended for perimeter deployment. This appliance includes two Gigabit Ethernet and six Fast Ethernet detection ports, with three response ports, and a management port. With performance numbers near 600 Mbps, it has more than enough capacity to measure all but the largest Internet data pipes. The final and largest sensor offering is the IntruShield 4000, which is best suited for the core of your company's switching architecture where speed is in high demand. This device contains a whopping four Gigabit Ethernet detection ports, two Fast Ethernet response ports, one management port, and still manages to deliver up to 2 Gbps of performance. (See Figure 9.4.)

- **McAfee IntruShield Manager** Tying together all of your sensors into one management console, the IntruShield Manager runs on any Windows 2000 management station, supported by a MySQL back end database. You'll need additional IntruShield Manager installations for networks with more than six sensors. This software sets itself apart from many others by supporting an incredibly rich policy management framework, which allows for very granular access control. CISOs will be able to tailor security policies down to the individual business unit or geographical location sub-division.

Figure 9.4 McAfee IntruShield

Equally interesting to note is the ability for the IntruShield solution to be integrated into your existing (and perhaps much larger) network management system. IntruShield Manager supports the forwarding of alert messages via SNMP to applications such as HP OpenView, IBM Tivoli, or Computer Associates' Unicenter TNG (see Chapter 6 for more information). Find out more about the IntruShield line of products, acquired from IntruVert, at www.nai.com/us/products/sniffer/network_ips/category.htm.

Notes from the Underground…

Merger Mania

Confused about the many logos beneath the NAI umbrella? In April 2003, Network Associates acquired Entercept Security Technologies and the product was renamed McAfee Entercept. Why not call it NAI Entercept? Good question. The name Network Associates came about through the merger of McAfee Associates and Network General (known for their popular Sniffer tool) in December 1997. Since then, the company has been NAI and the products have generally carried the McAfee name. Ready for another one? McAfee IntruShield appeared on the NAI Web site after the

Continued

acquisition of Intruvert Networks, also in April 2003. If IDS really *is* dead (as some misguided analysts claim), why would NAI purchase two leading IDS technologies in the same month? IDS, whether morphed into IPS or an as-yet-unseen technology, will be around for the next few years—you can count on it.

Sana Security

The Primary Response intrusion prevention software from Sana Security is based on the work of Dr. Steven Hofmeyr, while at the University of New Mexico. There he studied ways to replicate the powerful adaptive and defensive qualities of the human immune system to digital networks. It is this research that is the basis for the Sana Profile (SP) technology that learns normal OS and application activities by observing low-level code paths in running programs. Much more than just examining the currently running process list in Task Manager, SP performs deep inspection on the interdependencies of system-level calls and studies the "normal" process spawning sequences. Once the learning mode has concluded, any anomalous activities can be detected and blocked at the kernel level. If the code path that a Web server takes is strangely altered suddenly, Primary Response will detect that as a possible remote code exploit. If a new process is spawned, or an authorized process is spawned in an unusual sequence, Primary Response will also flag that malicious activity. Service packs or patching of the OS will cause Primary Response to "re-learn" the code paths of authorized activities, and thus it is safe to install the software on production servers without fear of having incompatibilities between your IPS and your day-to-day systems management.

Because of the detailed system-level inspection the software performs, Sana Security is able to claim that they can stop zero-day attacks (so called because within the first day of a vulnerability being announced and before others can issue updates to their databases, a "zero day" exploit can attack your network). Primary Response works in a tiered architecture, with a centralized management console and agent software installed on your various servers. Up to 7000 agents can communicate with the management console using SSL encrypted channels and can alert different users or groups depending on the nature of the malicious activity detected. Agent software is available for Windows as well as Solaris platforms, and Primary Response is the first protection software specifically designed to work with IIS 6.0 (in native mode, not isolation mode), which comes with Windows Server 2003. (See Figure 9.5.)

Figure 9.5 Sana Security Primary Response

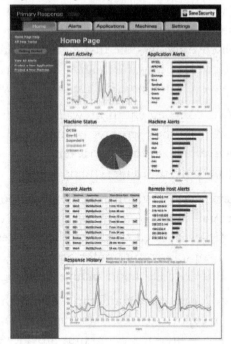

Symantec

In July 2002, Symantec bought Recourse Technologies and its ManHunt product. This acquisition pushed Symantec toward the top of the market with a product that could perform well, even at gigabit speeds. Symantec paired the network-based ManHunt with their existing host-based Host IDS. Adding ManTrap in September 2002, Symantec launched their Enterprise Security Suite. The suite of products allows you to watch the critical portions of your network infrastructure, as well as confuse and distract your attackers using one of the very few commercial honeypot implementations.

- **ManHunt (from Recourse)** Providing a high-speed NIDS that is able to perform real-time attack correlation and proactive prevention, ManHunt protects large networks from internal and external intrusions and DoS attacks. Using anomaly detection, ManHunt is able to look at network traffic and determine what seems outside of the "norm" of legitimate traffic. By doing this, an educated guess can be made that anything that is outside of an established range of network traffic is an anomaly, and all anomalies are (or might be) new, as-yet-unknown attacks. This helps to eliminate the inherent time-delay vulnerability in signature-based intrusion detection products. One unique feature that we enjoyed discovering was the traffic rate monitoring capability, which allows for detection of slow, methodical stealth scans and DoS attacks that can cripple even the most sophisticated networks. (See Figure 9.6.)

- **Host IDS** As a complement to firewalls and other access controls, the HIDS component of the Symantec solution enables administrators to develop proactive policies to stop hackers, or authorized users with malicious intent, from misusing systems.

- **Intruder Alert** The central management component from Symantec, Intruder Alert will sound an alarm or take other countermeasures according to pre-established security policies when an attack is detected. From a central console, administrators can create, update, and deploy policies, and securely collect and archive audit logs for incident analysis.

- **Decoy Server (formerly ManTrap)** Although more appropriately listed in the honeypot category, ManTrap is a great addition to the Symantec family of products. ManHunt provides early detection of internal, external, and unknown attacks by monitoring attempted connections to fictitious network resources. By creating a realistic "mock" network environment, the ManHunt solution serves as an enticing target for potential attackers.

Figure 9.6 Symantec ManHunt

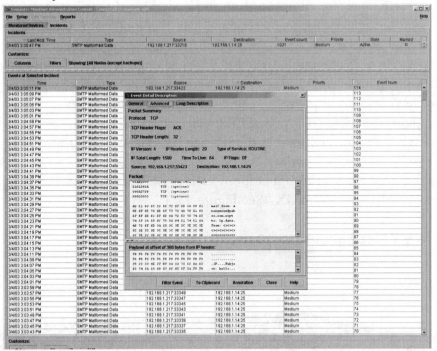

For more information on the complete Symantec solution to intrusion detection and prevention, visit http://enterprisesecurity.symantec.com/content.cfm?articleid=1608. Make sure not to miss the excellent article on "The Importance of Layered Security," featured at http://enterprisesecurity.symantec.com/article.cfm?articleid=769.

TippingPoint

The TippingPoint UnityOne offering comes in an impressive range of hardware performance, from the low-end UnityOne-200 meant for branch offices (up to 200 Mbit/sec), to the mind-boggling data center speeds of the UnityOne-2400 that just screams at 2.0 Gbit/sec. UnityOne uses a combination of software and high-performance ASIC design to offer a (in their words) "Threat Suppression Engine (TSE) that enables intrusion prevention at multi-gigabit speeds." Having the inspection software in ASIC form greatly improves speed over software-only solutions. As mentioned previously, knowing the composition of Windows and UNIX servers in your environment can greatly reduce false positives. To that end, TippingPoint includes a network discovery tool that allows UnityOne to automatically tune to the segment in which it is placed.

As an inline device, the stability and robustness of these appliances is definitely something to consider; you don't want anything that will quit on you and bring your entire network to a screeching halt. TippingPoint has you covered there as well, with an automatic failover of the appliance to a regular Layer 2 switch in case of malfunction. In addition, many appliances can be interlinked for redundancy. With over 850 attack signatures out-of-the-box, TippingPoint places a substantial amount of research behind their "security intelligence" by tapping into exploit researchers at SANS, CERT, and SecuriTeam. An innovative add-on module to UnityOne, released in the last half of 2003, is called the Peer-to-Peer (P2P) Piracy Prevention option. The device can be set to completely limit (or set quotas on) P2P file-sharing applications such as KaZaa, Gnutella, Limewire, Bearshare, iMesh, and WinMX. (See Figure 9.7.)

Figure 9.7 TippingPoint UnityOne-2400 Appliance

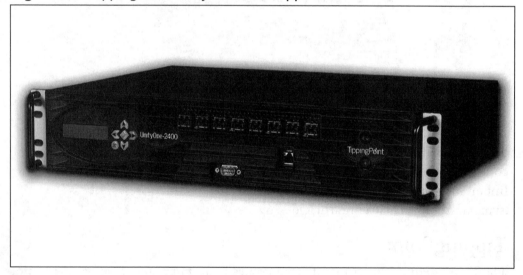

NOTE

Just as we were going to press, Elisa Lippincott, marketing manager for TippingPoint, wrote us and let us know that they have expanded both their low-end and high-end offerings. A small-office 50 Mbps UnityOne-50 appliance and the industry's first 5.0 Gbit/sec IPS, the UnityOne-5000, will be available in Q3 of 2004.

Application-Level Firewalls

The tools presented in this section are different because they are not IDS solutions that have evolved into IPS. Rather, they have always been a form of intrusion prevention and were all recently introduced to the market. They specialize in addressing the nature of "good traffic" that is allowed through the firewall, but might have "bad content." Some have called these "Application-Layer IPSs" but we believe they are really more of a firewall. The major features that these firewalls have in common are summarized in Table 9.2.

Table 9.2 Common Web Application Firewall Features

Vulnerability	Attack Method	Ease of Exploit
Buffer Overflow	A common type of input validation attack that overflows a buffer with excessive data. Successfully executed, the hacker can run a remote shell on the machine and gain the same system privileges granted to the application being attacked.	Difficult to write your own; Very easy to use a precompiled exploit found in chat rooms
Parameter Manipulation	An input validation attack that illegally modifies data that is passed to a server-side script. Without proper validation of query parameters passed to CGI scripts, a hacker can gain unauthorized system privileges.	Easy to manipulate parameters; difficult to get additional privileges because of it.
Hidden Form Field Manipulation	Modifying the contents of a hidden field in an attempt to trick the application into accepting invalid data.	Easy to manipulate hidden fields; difficult to force application to accept invalid data.
Cross-Site Scripting (XSS)	Tricking the user's browser into sending an attacker confidential information that can be used to steal that user's identity.	Very easy—can be accomplished as simply as posting malicious JavaScript code in a public chat room.

Continued

Table 9.2 Common Web Application Firewall Features

Vulnerability	Attack Method	Ease of Exploit
SQL Injection	An input validation attack that sends SQL commands to a Web application, which are then passed to a back-end database. Successfully executed, the hacker can gain access to a sensitive information store.	Easy to inject commands; sometimes difficult to know which commands to use for desired results.
Directory Traversal/ Forceful Browsing	Allows access to certain parts of the Web site that aren't meant for public consumption. This can sometimes happen by random guessing of unlinked directory names, or by causing the Web server to enumerate the directory names.	Easy to perform, if Web server is configured for directory browsing or has a vulnerability that allows browsing.
Authentication Hijacking	If the identity management of a Web application is handled by cookies or URL values with weak encryption, a logged-in user (with low privileges) might hijack the session of another currently logged-in user (with higher privileges) by changing parts of his session cookie to impersonate the other user.	Difficult to discover; once found, however, this is very easy to exploit and can have disastrous results (especially if an administrator is logged in at the time).
Error Triggering Information Leaks	Submitting malformed data to an application with the goal of generating errors and gaining sensitive information about the application environment.	Easy to perform, if application is poorly configured with detailed error reporting.
Server Misconfiguration	Exploiting misconfigurations, including the failure to fully lock down or harden the Web server, disable default accounts and services, or remove unnecessary functionality.	Easy to attempt (defaults are well known and documented) if allowed by server admin negligence.

Because of the examples of Web-delivered worms in 2003, more and more companies are beginning to feel the pressure to have an additional layer of security between the traditional (port/protocol-based) firewall and the Web server.

Richard Stiennon, an analyst at the Gartner Group (you remember—the folks who said IDS was dead?), advises: "You've got to have a Web application firewall. New e-commerce services will just be too vulnerable without something like that." He goes on to offer, "My advice is: Buy a Web application-specific firewall today and install it in front of all your Web servers as soon as you can." While we believe that a well-configured HIPS can greatly reduce this threat, a layered, defense-in-depth strategy of network-based firewall, then application firewall, then HIPS is a recipe for peace of mind.

This emerging market is definitely going to see some acquisitions very soon. As the importance of Web-delivered applications (and the security of those Web applications) increases, watch for the big players in the market to swoop in on the market leaders and affix their brand name to a winning technology. We present, for your consideration, a selection of Web firewalls and a brief note on their capabilities (although they can be largely summarized in Table 9.2). If you manage any size Web farm, you should definitely evaluate one of these technologies before the next worm tests your defenses for you!

eEye

Hardly anyone would argue if we said that the team over at eEye are experts at finding vulnerabilities in Microsoft's IIS Web server. Therefore, it makes sense that they would be experts at making software to prevent all these vulnerabilities. Rather than address the more generic problem of Web vulnerabilities, eEye has chosen to concentrate its efforts on just the IIS Web server, with much success.

The SecureIIS product integrates as an ISAPI—an Information Services Application Programming Interface—that plugs into IIS itself. Instead of sitting in front of your Web farm, SecureIIS is integrated much like modules integrate into Apache; every time a Web request is made, SecureIIS inspects the request for known vulnerabilities and malformed data, and then decides whether to allow the request to be serviced by IIS, or to block the request. Instead of relying on a database of known attack signatures (that usually require frequent updates), SecureIIS inspects Web traffic for common attack methods such as buffer overflows, parser evasions, high-bit shell code, and directory traversals.

Through the SecureIIS management console, shown in Figure 9.8, you can control all of your IIS Web servers. Once settings are made for one server, they can be exported and pushed out to the others. All blocked requests are logged so that you can troubleshoot legitimate requests and keep a vigilant eye out for malicious activity. Since SecureIIS runs in concert with IIS, it has access to

HTTPS Web requests *after* they have been decrypted, allowing these to be monitored as well. Other products that sit in front of the server (and do not terminate the SSL session themselves) will be blind to these attacks.

As an added feature, you can also have SecureIIS monitor arbitrary files on the Web server file system, looking for any additions, modifications, or deletions that are unauthorized (like someone attempting to delete your HTML, or attempting to add something to your knowledge base remotely). Commercial licenses of SecureIIS can be ordered online for $995 per server. Noncommercial use for one Web site is absolutely free with the SecureIIS Personal Edition.

Figure 9.8 eEye SecureIIS

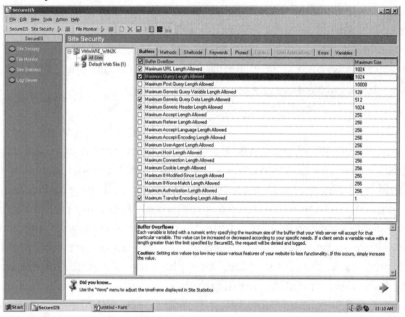

Hogwash

Back in 1996, Jed Haile and Jason Larsen had a problem. They were at Idaho State University and had a mission-critical Web application hosted on an ancient version of Microsoft IIS. Due to some tight integration, they were unable to patch the old NT machine and they couldn't migrate the application. Knowing they had vulnerabilities, they could not just leave the matter as-is (the box was being hacked daily). They needed a way to intercept packets on the way to the Web server, but without installing anything on the Web server itself. They needed to do it that night and without any budget money. Over one weekend, Jason created a basic packet inspection engine and married that to some filtering intelligence to come up with a method to clean up malicious packets; he called it Scrub.

Years later, Jason came across Snort and was impressed by its inspection engine (see Figure 9.2). He replaced his own "Cheap and Dirty detection engine" with Snort, and renamed his project SnortScrub. Fast forward to modern times and many different contributions later, and what you have is a way to "scrub" incoming Web packets of anything malicious that has an existing Snort signature. As a nod to the pink pig that is the Snort mascot, he renamed his creation Hogwash. If you'd like to try your hand at some open-source intrusion prevention, we'd recommend getting your feet wet with Hogwash.

KaVaDo

With both a scanning and a protection component, KaVaDo can protect your Web farm from both sides. Their ScanDo product will perform an assessment of your Web application security and then feed the results to the Web application firewall, InterDo, using what they call "AutoPolicy" technology. By setting up your policy in the InterDo Enterprise management console, you can manage many InterDo installations across your organization. To provide the most granular configuration, InterDo allows you to define "pipes" that identify the flow of information into your Web farm. Once traffic matches a particular pipe, it is inspected using the rules for that information path. The software will block a large amount of known attacks, and you can configure it to protect against a number of potential attacks by just using some common sense when creating your pipes. For those who want to do a little custom-integration programming work, you could even use the Pipes SDK to allow your program to dynamically create and modify the InterDo pipes. Unlike some of the other technologies listed here, InterDo works with not only Microsoft IIS, but also on Apache and Netscape Enterprise Servers, on both Linux and Windows, and is even Check Point OPSEC certified.

NetContinuum

Unlike previously mentioned software solutions, the NetContinuum NC-1000 is a hardware appliance that solves many of today's Web farm needs all in one box. The NetContinuum solution starts with a fully ICSA-certified firewall to protect against the usual network-borne attacks discussed in Chapter 3. To this, they add their Web Cloaking technology, which hides the details of the back-end application that is servicing the Web requests. This is an important step in preventing information disclosure. During the learning mode (called Dynamic Application Profiling), the NC-1000 inspects all traffic going to and from the Web server, attempting to determine the correct and legitimate dialogues allowed with each particular Web application. Explicit rules can be set using the management console, shown in Figure 9.9 (a command-line interface is also available for those who prefer it). Rather than tax the individual Web servers with the HTTPS encryption, you can use the NC-1000's Instant SSL features to quickly terminate SSL tunnels at the appliance, and then pass unencrypted Web requests back to the Web server. This allows for deep packet inspection even on HTTPS-protected requests, since the NC-1000 has access to the unencrypted request contents before they are passed along to the Web server.

The NC-1000 will allow you to extend the concept of NAT to Web sites, but using Web Address Translation. This allows you to expose internal company applications without disclosing internal resource names (Web server hostnames). To help with new compliance laws, the NC-1000 also provides centralized logging for your entire Web farm, and can even set up different log files for different Web applications—even those running on the same Web server. This can greatly help troubleshooting efforts, since you can weed out requests that weren't destined for a particular Web application and concentrate on the offending packets. However, by far the best feature of the NetContinuum Web Security Gateway is under the hood and (perhaps) little-appreciated. A custom, purpose-built ASIC chip performs all the TCP session setup and tear-down, attack prevention, and SSL encryption. This powerful piece of silicon has 48 hyperthreaded processors embedded, and a beefy 280 Gbit/sec nonblocking switching fabric to ensure fast throughput. Moreover, if high availability is your concern, the NC-1000 is able to perform Active/Active and Active/Passive failovers with another appliance.

Figure 9.9 NetContinuum Web Security Gateway Management Console

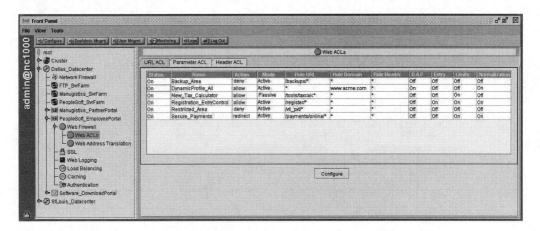

Sanctum

The AppShield software can either be purchased as a stand-alone, or pre-loaded on the AppShield appliance (a SunFire V100). During learning mode, which leverages their patented Policy Recognition Engine, you can set an internal IP address to be a "trusted source" for the basis of creating a policy. Any Web requests from this machine will be considered genuine, and thus a policy will be built around what this machine does and does not request from your Web servers. Sanctum AppShield comes with high praise, as being the first security product to achieve the Certification for Web Application Policy Enforcement from ICSA Labs. All of the Top 10 Web application vulnerabilities published by the Open Web Application Security Project (OWASP) are addressed by AppShield out of the box. AppShield is also OPSEC certified and can seamlessly integrate with your IBM Tivoli network management framework or other SNMP-based management software. It is no surprise that AppShield won the *Network World* Best of the Tests award for 2003 in the Security Infrastructure category (www.nwfusion.com/best/2004/0223securityinf.html). With no software updates or patches to download, ever, the AppShield solution is a comforting one. With a long track record for excellence, Sanctum truly shows that they were the innovators in this arena, with their first version of the product released back in 1999.

Notes from the Underground…

Sanctum Patents Web Application Scanning

In June 2003, the U.S. Patent and Trademark Office issued Patent No. 6,584,569 to Sanctum for "describing a process for automatically detecting potential application-level vulnerabilities or security flaws in a Web application." Unlike the product patents with which we are most familiar, this was a *method* patent, which means that the very process of probing a Web server for application vulnerabilities (something that all of the VA tools listed in Chapter 2 and most of the tools in this section do) is patented. This could cause quite an uproar in the industry if Sanctum finds a way to enforce their patent against all these other vendors. Could you imagine if every time you wanted to scan your own Web farm (using a tool other than AppShield of course), you would have to pay a royalty to Sanctum? Join in on the thought-provoking discussion located at www.securityfocus.com/archive/107/349930.

Teros

The Teros Secure Application Gateway is an all-in-one solution for networks that need protection from today's complex Web-based attacks. Teros CEO Bob Walters says, "With the advent of Web services, IT departments are now faced with the prospect of deploying yet another single function device to protect XML traffic. In response, a new class of security appliance, called an application security gateway, has emerged. These appliances provide unified protection for both HTML and XML applications, while performing additional security and networking functions currently handled by single-purpose products."

Teros' Secure Application Gateway solution is available on a family of appliance platforms to meet all performance and availability requirements. All Teros security appliances are purpose-built and integrate Teros' award-winning application protection to secure any Web infrastructure against known and unknown attacks. Both families of Secure Application Gateway appliances offer models integrating hardware-based SSL acceleration and FIPS 140-2 Level 3 Secure Key Management. One unique feature that the Teros offers is the ability to sift through the Web server responses on the way to the client, and filter out any information that has been predetermined to be of a sensitive nature. You can instruct Teros to look for credit card information or social security numbers (using pattern matching), and it will prevent any accidental information disclosure from getting to the outside world. The e-commerce functions are so well thought out, that the Teros gateway can recognize American Express, Diners Club, Discover, JCB, MasterCard, and VISA account numbers and prevent them from being viewed by the remote user. The software actually calculates a credit card checksum and uses this to recognize sensitive information. A random collection of 16 digits (with appropriate hyphens) will be passed by the Teros gateway, but a valid MasterCard account number will be stopped dead in its tracks. This means that even if someone were able to compromise your Web application's logic and convince your Web site to spit out a customer's credit card number, the Teros would prevent that from happening. You can also set the Teros to allow credit cards, but to only allow one per HTML page. This would allow normal order processing, but prevent an attacker who has managed to use SQL poisoning to get a list of thousands of credit card numbers from ever seeing that list. (See Figure 9.10.)

Figure 9.10 Teros Application Protection System

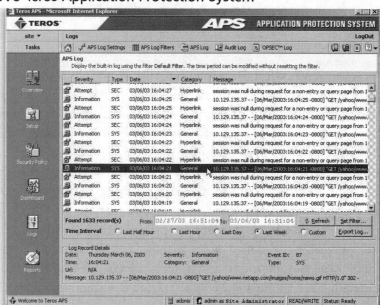

Whale Communications

There is little doubt that the application firewall has a place in today's networks. Elad Baron, CEO of Whale Communications, notes that "When network attacks became prevalent, companies installed TCP/IP firewalls and IDSs. But, today, devastating worms and viruses attack at the application level ... Against such problems, TCP/IP firewalls and IDS are powerless and do not offer protection; to regain security you need an application-level firewall." The e-Gap Application Firewall from Whale Communications is delivered as a robust hardware appliance and promises to deliver tight control over your Web applications by using "Air Gap technology." The device has an impressive list of features, including an automatic learning mode that can generate and enforce rule sets that are tailored to your Web application, encryption, PKI, and HTTP payload screening wrapped up in one integrated software/hardware platform.

The truly ingenious feature in this appliance is an honest-to-goodness physical "air gap" (most often found in military networks) between the two networks that the unit bridges. By using two internal single-board computers inside the appliance, the e-Gap Firewall can perform all of the security inspection on the internal (shielded) computer without fear of being attacked itself. A patent-pending analog switch connects a 512 KB memory bank to one and only one computer at a time using a SCSI interface. Only application layer data is transferred in real time through the analog switch, and the switch itself has no operating system, no TCP/IP address, and no programmable units.

With most other security software, the underlying operating system can still be undermined no matter how many safeguards are in the protection software itself. Because of this air gap, the appliance doesn't rely on the security of the underlying operating system of the external computer; it does all the sensitive operations and stores encryption keys on the internal, shielded computer, behind the physical gap. Find out more about the gap and how it can protect your network at www.whalecommunications.com/site/Whale/Corporate/Whale.asp?pi=35. (See Figure 9.11.)

Figure 9.11 Whale Communications' e-Gap Application Firewall

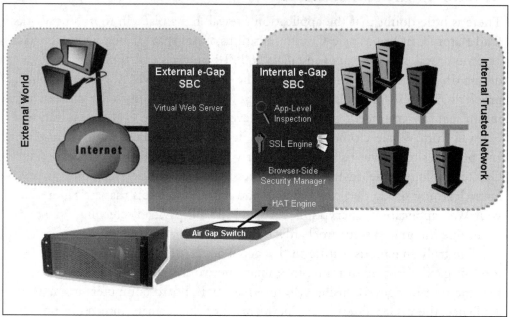

Honeypots/Honeynets

Honeypots are the youngest of the different intrusion prevention components described here; however, they are maturing very fast. As the fallout from the worms of 2003 is discussed and analyzed, many will begin to see the deceptive nature of honeypots to be useful in researching the next big "Slammer" type of worm. By monitoring which remote hosts "take the bait" and begin to attack fictitious systems, it becomes very easy to classify those hosts as 100-percent hostile (an honest user wouldn't be sending packets to a fictitious machine, now would he?) and take corrective defensive actions—or sometimes even offensive action if you want to be really nasty about it—in response to that information.

ForeScout

The ActiveScout solution, from ForeScout, is a very aggressive honeypot. While most honeypots will just lure an attacker in and distract and/or confuse the attacker, ActiveScout will "actively" solicit an attacker's probing and react to any exploit attempts. The logic behind this is blindingly simple. On unused, externally facing IP addresses, ActiveScout advertises the availability of services that are attractive to attackers. When a potential attacker performs a port scan as part of his reconnaissance effort, he will find a wealth of open services (but not all) on the ActiveScout-enabled ports. In response to his probing, ActiveScout will respond with a specially tainted packet. Should that tainted packet ever be used to establish another connection, the software can determine with 100-percent certainty that the user is malicious, since no genuine request would have been routed to the ActiveScout IP addresses in the first place. Once it has been determined that there is a malicious user knocking on the door, ActiveScout will block that IP address across all machines, to prevent further probing or attacks. Because of this methodology, ActiveScout is uniquely able to stop zero-day attacks, no matter what their payload happens to be. This is because the inspection software doesn't even check the packet's payload, but instead works off the behavior that the attacker has shown.

ForeScout CEO T. Kent Elliot states that "ForeScout's Anti-Hacker and Anti-Worm solutions are based on a patented technology called ActiveResponse. One of the key distinguishing features of the technology is the ability to BLOCK zero-day attacks." If there is a probe, ActiveScout responds with the "bait," which is a tainted packet. When the attacker takes the bait and responds using the tainted packet, he is blocked. "The key to the ActiveScout and WormScout solutions is accuracy. One-hundred percent of ForeScout's installed base has the automatic blocking capabilities turned on. This is a testament to the accuracy of the detection mechanism that makes the data actionable." With most other IPS technologies, customers are sometimes gun-shy to enable full blocking because they are worried about false positives (mistakenly blocking legitimate traffic). Because of the high confidence that the software has in identifying attackers, this is not an issue. In fact, 75% percent of their customers don't have an IDS at all; they just use ActiveScout.

Tools and Tips...

Stop Worms from Spreading

A spin-off product, WormScout, uses the same ActiveResponse technology that is so effective on the perimeter of the network and applies it to smaller segments without your internal infrastructure. If you have studied the recommendation in Chapter 11, you know the importance of segmenting your important internal networks. Let's say that you have a Sales VLAN, an Accounting VLAN, a Mobile User VLAN, and a general user VLAN. What happens if an infected mobile user, dialing in through the VPN and without the proper security patches that the in-house computers enjoy, connects to your network with a vulnerable service running or with a live worm? When the user connects, immediately the laptop starts to infect the other users in the Mobile VLAN. It is not long before the self-propagation routines in the worm start to attack the rest of your networks, from the inside! Even after you spent all that time and effort on blocking the vulnerable port at the firewall, the worm was still able to get inside your network.

With WormScout, you are able to quarantine the worm to just one small segment of your network. At each choke point (or segmentation point) in your network, you would install WormScout. There, it would advertise a large number of potentially vulnerable ports to that segment. If a worm infection does begin from within that segment, WormScout will receive a probe from the worm. Like before, the ActiveResponse technology will respond with a tainted packet. When the worm responds to this tainted packet, WormScout will know with certainty that this is malicious traffic, and will prevent all of this traffic from escaping this segment. The nice part is that, in contrast to ActiveScout where the entire machine is blocked, with the internally minded WormScout product, only the malicious port and traffic are blocked. This means that instead of having your entire network overcome with SQL Blaster, you just have the Mobile User VLAN under attack. In addition, instead of cutting off the entire VLAN, you just filter out any attempts to spread the virus to other parts of the network, while allowing these (infected) users to still access other network resources. (See Figure 9.12.)

Continued

Figure 9.12 ForeScout WormScout Enterprise Manager

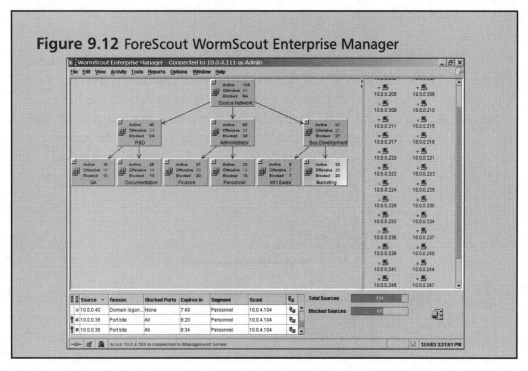

Honeyd

Honeyd (www.citi.umich.edu/u/provos/honeyd) is a small server process that creates virtual hosts on a network. The hosts can be configured to run arbitrary services, and their personality can be adapted so that they appear to be running certain operating systems. Honeyd enables a single host to claim multiple addresses. From a defense point of view, it deters adversaries by hiding real systems in the middle of virtual systems. A short list of features includes:

- Simulates thousands of "virtual hosts" at the same time.

- Configuration of arbitrary services via simple configuration file.

- Simulates multiple operating systems.

- Simulation of different routing topologies.

- Subsystem virtualization:

  - Run real UNIX applications under virtual Honeyd IP addresses: Web servers, FTP servers, and so forth.

  - Dynamic port binding in virtual address space, background initiation of network connections, and so forth.

Sebek

Sebek (http://honeynet.lss.hr/tools/sebek) is a tool designed for data capture; it captures all of the attacker's activity on the honeypot without the attacker knowing it. The Sebek client covertly sends the recovered data to the Sebek server, as seen in Figure 9.13. Typically, the Sebek client is not installed on the same machine as the Sebek server. The whole point is to not let the attacker know that he is being watched. If the Sebek Server is on the compromised machine, the attacker will find the data pretty quickly and make a quick exit. Now what fun is that?

Figure 9.13 Sebek Architecture

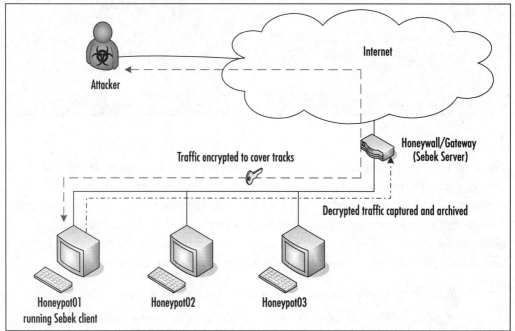

Tarpits

Tarpits reverse the normal assumption that connections should be optimized for maximum speed and maximum throughput. For unused IP addresses, you really shouldn't expect any connections. Tarpits are configured to listen on those unused IP addresses. A tarpit will listen on certain ports, or all ports for that matter, waiting for a connection. During the three-way TCP handshake, the tarpit negotiates low-bandwidth connection settings (such as tiny TCP transmission windows); this results in slowing the transmission rate of the attacking machine. Furthermore, a tarpit will never send back an ACK (acknowledgment) packet to the transmitting machine, and thus the built-in transport-layer retransmission features will retry every transmitted packet over and over. This also serves to tie up the attacker for up to several hours.

The spread of worms on the Internet continues to be a major issue, affecting hundreds of thousands or even millions of network hosts around the world. The outbreaks of MS Blaster and Nachi/Welchia should be proof enough of that. The concept behind a tarpit is fairly simple—connections come in, but they don't get back out. An August 2003 posting to SecurityFocus.com explains the process of slowing network-based worms in much greater detail (www.securityfocus.com/infocus/1723). Tarpits can be very valuable to a security administrator, especially if you route a large range of addresses through a concentration point. A tarpit placed at the concentration point can slow information scans and stop new attack vectors before they cause problems.

ipt_TARPIT, an IPTables Patch

IPTables is a very commonly used firewall on Linux. It is command-line driven, usually by a predefined script. Most scripts are written to allow specific traffic to pass and block everything else. IPTables uses the concept of "targets" for its rule actions. Examples of IPTables targets are accept, reject, and drop. ipt_TARPIT (www.netfilter.org/patch-o-matic/pom-extra.html#pom-extra-TARPIT) is a patch for IPTables. It adds a TARPIT target to IPTables. If an attack matches a certain pattern, the connection can be tarpitted.

For example, to significantly slow Code Red/Nimda/Blaster/Nachi-style scans, you can forward unused IP addresses to a Linux box not acting as a router. Enable IP forwarding on the Linux box, and add the following lines to your IPTables startup script:

```
iptables -A FORWARD -p tcp -j TARPIT
iptables -A FORWARD -j DROP
```

Figure 9.14 shows how this would work. This would cause any TCP connection coming into the Linux box—which would be bad traffic since we're routing all unused IP addresses to the tarpit—to be tarpitted. The scan performance on the attacker's side would become so slow that the scan would take days to complete even a small number of IPs, if not fail. The attacker would get bored or impatient before he discovered the Web server toward the end of the scan.

Figure 9.15 Example ipt_TARPIT Deployment

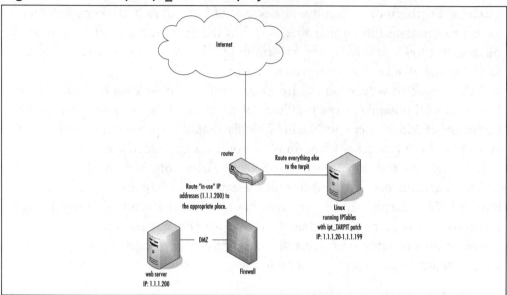

LaBrea

LaBrea (http://labrea.sourceforge.net) takes over unused IP addresses and creates virtual servers that are attractive to worms and hackers. The program answers connection attempts in such a way that the machine at the other end gets "stuck," sometimes for a very long time. LaBrea works by watching ARP requests and replies. When LaBrea sees consecutive ARP requests spaced several seconds apart without any intervening ARP reply, it assumes that the IP in question is unoccupied. It then creates an ARP reply with a bogus MAC address, and fires it back to the requester. The nearest router takes note of the reply and forwards all traffic destined for that IP to the bogus MAC address.

Subverting an IDS/IPS

IDSs only see what they are looking for. As long as traffic is massaged to stay out of the IDS's alert context, most attacks will go unnoticed. For example, a port scan of a single system timed over many days would not cause an alert. Viruses, worms, and script kiddies won't take the time to use the following techniques. Their method is to smash in, make the kill, and hope nobody is watching. *Finesse* is not a word in their dictionary.

Port Hopping

Some ways of avoiding detection are simple and easy to do. Some IDS signatures only look for activity on a certain port to identify the attack. For example, BackOrifice connections use port 31337 by default. Simply changing the port to another port would leave most IDSs clueless. You should review critical signatures for easy ways to get around them.

Fragmenting

Packet fragmenting is another method that is often used. Low Maximum Transmission Units (MTUs) allow a malicious payload to be spread over many tiny packets that have to be reassembled to read them. Some IDSs will reassemble packet streams, but if the attack is spread over a long enough time, the IDS gives up and stops reassembling that session. There are a couple techniques that use fragmentation in different ways to evade IDS, including:

- Fragmentation overlap
- Fragment overwrite

Fragmentation overlap involves sending packets so subsequent fragments overwrite data from previous fragments, changing the attack signature enough for the IDS to ignore it and the destination to receive the attack.

For example, PacketA could have the payload of "GET /scripts/root," PacketB could have a payload of "t.exe /cc," and PacketC could have a payload of "c+dir." The IDS would see the request as "GET /scripts/roott.exe /ccc+dir," but when reassembled on the destination the packets would be reassembled as "GET /scripts/root.exe /c+dir," a typical Code Red check for vulnerability.

```
PacketA:     GET /scripts/root
PacketB:     t.exe /cc
PacketC:     c+dir
```

Fragmentation overwrite involves subsequent fragments overwriting an entire previous fragment, instead of just a portion. To extend the previous example, the packets could have the following payloads:

```
PacketA:     GET /scripts/root
PacketB:     xyxyxyxyxyxyxyxy
PacketC:     .exe c+dir
```

PacketC would be set to overwrite PacketB. The destination would receive the URL correctly, but the IDS sees a long URL that doesn't match any of its signatures.

Doug Song's FragRoute (www.monkey.org/~dugsong/fragroute/) is a utility that will implement the fragmentation overlap and fragment overwrite attacks for you. FragRoute intercepts, modifies, and rewrites egress traffic destined for a specified host, implementing most of the attacks described in the Secure Networks "Insertion, Evasion, and Denial of Service: Eluding Network Intrusion Detection" paper of January 1998 (found at www.securityfocus.com/library/745). It features a simple rule set language to delay, duplicate, drop, fragment, overlap, print, reorder, segment, source-route, or otherwise monkey with all outbound packets destined for a target host, with minimal support for randomized or probabilistic behavior.

Flooding

When all else fails, attackers will overwhelm the IDS with a multitude of useless attacks and bury the real attack in the fray. Anyone who is responding to such an attack likely won't go through 1000 alert messages for well-known attack vectors—like Code Red. It's easy to assume that someone just brought up an infected machine and there is little cause for alarm. Surges of this type are common.

In March 2001, ISS X-Force reported a new attack tool that can be used to launch a stress test against many popular IDSs. Called Stick by its creators, the tool reduces performance, and/or denies service to many commercial IDS products. Stick directs thousands of overt attacks at IDSs. The additional processing required by IDSs to handle the new load causes a DoS to occur.

Stick does not employ any new methods, nor does it expose any new flaws in signature-based IDSs. Stick uses the straightforward technique of firing numerous attacks from random source IP addresses to purposely trigger IDS events. The IDS will attempt to keep up with the new flood of events, but if incoming events cross the IDS detection threshold, a DoS might result. The effectiveness of the Stick attack is a function of the attacker's available bandwidth. Stick is essentially a flooding tool. If a lot of bandwidth is available to the attacker, he or she might be more successful. Stick is available at www.euro-compton.net/stick/projects8.html.

Summary

This chapter took you through an understanding of Intrusion Detection System (IDS) basics and types of components within IDSs. It presented comparisons of some of the many IDS solutions available. You learned how attackers fool IDSs and navigate around them. You should now be able to decide what type of IDS will work well in your environment. Once the IDS is implemented, regular maintenance and attention will return many benefits that make IDSs a permanent part of "defense in depth."

Checklists

Deployment Checklist

Planning Many people try to skip this part and go straight to the installation. Many problems can be identified and resolved in the planning stage. If discovered later in the deployment, money and time could be wasted.

- Determine Scope of Policy
    - Identify what the sensor will be looking for.
    - Decide how the sensor will react to attacks. Alert? Log? Block Access?
- Set Response Procedure
    - Establish a primary response person.
- Research and Architect
    - Gather network topology information.
    - Identify type(s) of sensors to be deployed.
    - Determine whether the attack responses will be sent over the monitored segment or a different segment.
- Design Topology
    - Identify assets that need to be watched.
    - Determine where the sensor will be placed.

- Determine where the management station(s) will be placed.

Pre-Installation Once the design and research have been completed and the deployment locations are identified, put together a "shopping list" and get quotes from several vendors if possible.

- Purchase
    - Ensure timely ship date. Delayed ship dates lead to delayed deployments.

Installation Once the equipment has been delivered, installation can begin. Make sure you have reviewed the installation documents by now.

- Build
    - Remove any unnecessary services from each sensor. Do not connect any sensors to the network until the sensor can be hardened.
    - Make sure each sensor is running the same version of software and watch for the appropriate attacks.

- Test
    - Attach to a test segment and send a few attacks by the sensor. Adjust as needed.
    - Check for false positives and adjust as needed.

- Deploy
    - Once tuned to an acceptable level, move the monitored interface to the live network.

Post-Installation

- Review Design

Routine Maintenance

- Review IDS logs for irregular activity.
- Follow up on every alert. Real attacks can be buried in a surge of false attacks. If a signature is alerting too often, adjust the sensitivity to an acceptable level.

- Review for false positives. Adjust the signatures to reduce the number of false positives.
- Check sensors regularly. Run an attack by one and see if it alerts on it.

Solutions Fast Track

Understanding Intrusion Detection System Basics

☑ There are several different components available within IDS environments. Your environment will dictate which ones (network-based sensors, host-based sensors, hybrid sensors, honeypots, tarpits) will work for you and which ones will not.

Comparing IDS/IPS Products

☑ Many open-source products are very useful and can add tremendous value. They tend to be less "point-and-click" than commercial solutions.

☑ Choosing the right solution for your environment will provide you with a truly usable resource and will help justify expanding later, if warranted.

Subverting an IDS/IPS

☑ Attackers will use many different techniques to fool your IDS. Be prepared for the attacks and don't rely solely on the IDS to find the attacks.

☑ IDS evasion techniques will constantly be evolving. Follow them; learn them. They will be used against you.

Links to Sites

- **www.nai.com/us/products/mcafee/host_ips/category.htm**
  NAI's Host Intrusion Prevention Web site. This site features information on the McAfee Entercept agent and console.

- **www.nai.com/us/products/sniffer/network_ips/category.htm**
  NAI's Network Intrusion Prevention homepage. Old-time network
  engineers will notice that the Web address contains a reference to the
  former Network General's Sniffer; NAI has owned NG since the late
  1990s and has continued to develop the line.

- **www.cisco.com/en/US/products/sw/secursw/ps2113/
  products_data_sheets_list.html** Cisco's IDS information page. This
  page gives you a starting point for examining Cisco's IDS/IPS products.

- **www.netfilter.org/patch-o-matic/pom-extra.html#pom-extra-
  TARPIT** TARPIT patch page. You'll find information about this patch
  for the IPTables firewall on this page.

- **http://labrea.sourceforge.net** LaBrea homepage. This site has good
  information about how tarpits work.

- **http://honeynet.lss.hr/tools/sebek** Sebek homepage.

- **www.citi.umich.edu/u/provos/honeyd** Honeyd homepage.

- **http://enterprisesecurity.symantec.com/content.cfm?
  articleid=1608** Symantec's Enterprise Security page. You'll find information about all the products available from Symantec.

- **www.iss.net/products_services** ISS RealSecure Guard.

- **www.snort.org** Snort Web site. This site has many add-ons and
  enhancements to Snort. Good documentation is available as well.

- **www.sourcefire.com** Sourcefire, the commercial version of Snort.

- **www.syngress.com/catalog/sg_main.cfm?pid=2440** *Snort 2.0
  Intrusion Detection* book, over 500 pages of valuable information on the
  Snort IDS.

- **www.monkey.org/~dugsong/fragroute** Doug Song's FragRoute
  utility will allow you to try your hand at fragmentation overlap and
  overwrite attacks.

- **www.forescout.com/products.html** ForeScout ActiveScout and
  WormScout.

- **www.whalecommunications.com** Whale Communications' e-Gap
  Application Firewall.

- **www.teros.com/products/appliances/gateway/** Teros Secure Application Gateway.

- **www.sanctuminc.com/solutions/appshield/** Sanctum AppShield and AppScan.

- **www.sanasecurity.com/products/** Sana Security Primary Response host-based intrusion prevention.

- **www.netcontinuum.com** NetContinuum NC-1000 Web Security Gateway.

- **www.kavado.com/ProductsInterdo.htm** KaVaDo, InterDo, and ScanDo.

- **www.eeye.com/html/Products/SecureIIS** eEye SecureIIS.

- **http://hogwash.sourceforge.net/** Hogwash, a Snort derivative.

Mailing Lists

- **Focus-IDS@scurityfocus.com** This mailing list is vendor neutral. You'll find lots of discussions relating to IDS.

- **www.snort.org/lists.html** Several discussion lists that are actively used by other Snort users worldwide.

Frequently Asked Questions

The following Frequently Asked Questions, answered by the authors of this book, are designed to both measure your understanding of the concepts presented in this chapter and to assist you with real-life implementation of these concepts. To have your questions about this chapter answered by the author, browse to **www.syngress.com/solutions** and click on the **"Ask the Author"** form. You will also gain access to thousands of other FAQs at ITFAQnet.com.

Q: Where is the best place to watch for traffic?

A: That really depends on your network layout. Some networks are routed and have several "choke points" or aggregation segments through which all traffic passes. Common places for IDS components are behind and in front of Internet points of presence, inside a DMZ, behind a VPN switch that is used for remote access and VPN-based WAN links, and on uplinks for a data center.

Q: Since I watch my firewall logs, do I really need an IDS?

A: Yes! You might be able to identify some attacks from firewall logs, but many attacks are buried in legitimate connections. Most firewalls only log connections and not packet contents.

Q: My IDS has been running for a few weeks and I don't have the time to look through all 10,000 alert e-mails that it has sent to me. Which IDS package should I buy that has fewer alerts?

A: Tuning is so important to an IDS deployment yet it is often overlooked. Most administrators believe that they can just install the IDS and walk away from it. That is not true. In most sophisticated burglar alarms, you can't simply buy one off the shelf at the supermarket and plug it into the wall outlet. You need to plan where the equipment will be placed and tune the motion sensors so that it triggers on human intruders but allows your dog to walk around the house freely. The same is true for IDS. A properly tuned IDS should only be sending out alert e-mails for critical issues. If you are receiving a high number (it is not unheard of to receive 100 to 200 e-mails/day from some IDS) of messages, you haven't done your homework.

Q: What legitimate services should I be cognizant of when I "flip the switch" and engage my IPS' blocking mode?

A: Remember to consider automated update methods (such as Microsoft Windows Update, Symantec LiveUpdate, and so forth), your own scheduled tasks, and your nightly backup routine. If you do a different backup method only monthly (perhaps full backup monthly, differential backups every other day), make sure you consider whether the monthly backup needs more or less rights than the daily, quick backup.

Q: My router has some IDS features; why would I want to dedicate a whole machine to this?

A: The router has plenty to do with routing packets without trying to compare each one to a database of signatures. As far as databases go, the one provided with router-based IDS solutions is woefully inadequate. Only the very obvious attacks will be picked up, at the expense of slowing all packets.

Q: Which ports should I allow through the firewall and into my honeynet?

A: One of the most important concepts of a honeynet is that it is not to be trusted. It should be a completely separate entity from your production network. Ideally, you should have a dedicated T1 or DSL line for this network to keep it far away from your "good" servers. If possible, noncontiguous IP address space is desirable to keep attackers from associating your network with the honeynet. Since you know the honeynet might be compromised, you don't want to provide a jumping-off point for potential attackers to reach your internal network. If a completely new Internet connection is not feasible, a dedicated DMZ interface on your firewall (one that is *not* shared with other servers) can be substituted. Do not allow *any* packets to flow from this DMZ to your internal network.

Chapter 10

Perimeter Network Design

Solutions in this Chapter:

- Looking at Design Principles
- Designing an Internet Access Network
- Designing Internet Application Networks
- Designing VPN and Remote Access Termination Networks

Related Chapters:

- Chapter 1 Designing Perimeter and Internal Segments
- Chapter 3 Selecting the Correct Firewall
- Chapter 4 Firewall Manipulation: Attacks and Defenses
- Chapter 5 Routing Devices and Protocols

Introduction

Most computer networks can be categorized by the function they perform and the services they provide. Perimeter networks can be defined as any network that provides services to any other user or network of unknown security status. These provided services might include Internet access to corporate networks, public access to Internet applications, or possibly even remote access or VPN services. Networks of unknown security status to which those services are provided can be anything from the public Internet, the home networks of corporate users, or even the private networks of partner organizations. The category of perimeter network includes many different types of network functions; however, the one common function found in perimeter networks is a connection point to less trusted networks. Given this fundamental attribute, it is important to have security as one of the primary objectives when designing perimeter networks. Firewalls, Intrusion Detection Systems (IDSs) and Intrusion Prevention Systems (IPSs), filtering routers, and network segmentation are just some of the devices and techniques that are used in designing secure perimeter networks. And while a perimeter network is by no means the only location in your network architecture where security is paramount, perimeter networks are probably the most important place to implement security devices.

In this chapter, we focus on some of the main issues relating to designing perimeter networks. We discuss the general design principles commonly used when designing all network architectures and consider how those principles change when applied to designing perimeter networks. We also discuss the different types of security devices most commonly used to protect your perimeter network, including firewalls, IDS, and IPS, and some of the most common secure design techniques such as network segmentation and filtering. We discuss the techniques of choosing the best type of firewalls and IDSs for the job, and consider the optimal location for security devices within an overall perimeter network design. To end the chapter, we cover three examples of classic perimeter network design challenges, an Internet access network, an Internet application network, and a remote access service network, detailing the design characteristics of each and going over the basic considerations made in their designs.

Looking at Design Principles

As with any complex system, the design of computer networks begins with the careful consideration of many factors to ensure that the result performs optimally.

Even though computer networks are constantly evolving and changing with the advance of technology, good network design principles are just as relevant now as they were in the early days of computer networking. In this section, we look at some of the more accepted network design principles and see how they apply to secure perimeter network design. We discuss firewall placement and selection, IDS placement and selection, and proper network segmentation using DMZ networks, service networks, and filtering routers.

Most network design professionals will tell you that to design an optimally performing network you have to start at the top. For some, the top is the application using the network, and for others, the top extends past the application to the users of that application. What most will agree on is that competent network design principles start by considering the purpose of the network. Whether that network is a corporate network supporting file and print sharing along with Internet access, an Internet application network supporting a busy e-commerce application, or an ISP network supporting data transport around the globe, the important thing to consider is the applications and users themselves, including the technical goals and business objectives that the network will be used to accomplish. This network design technique is generally called the top-down network design philosophy. Practitioners of top-down network design first focus on collecting information that will allow them to determine the requirements for capacity, functionality, performance, availability, scalability, affordability, manageability, and security. With these requirements complete, top-down network designers proceed to create logical network designs that encompass the specific needs of the application or user base. Only after the logical design has proven to meet requirements, do they proceed to the physical design phase where real network devices are introduced.

In designing perimeter networks, a slightly modified top-down design philosophy is necessary. Because of the prevalence of interconnected networks and Internet applications in today's perimeter network architectures, most designers of perimeter networks put an equal amount of emphasis on designing for security as they do designing for application requirements. As always, a balance must be struck between what can sometimes be two opposing needs. Secure network designs generally are costlier, necessitate more equipment, and are often more difficult to manage and maintain than are designs built strictly for application performance. These additional costs must then be balanced against the possible consequences and costs of an insecure perimeter network that may allow unauthorized or malicious access to private networks and resources. It may be difficult to express the costs of a security breach in terms of dollars and cents because the effect of a security breach can range from data being lost or destroyed to the loss of reputation and media exposure if valuable information or applications are compromised. In most scenarios, a balance between security and application performance can be arrived at that both protects private networks with strong perimeter network security and maintains acceptable levels of application performance.

Selecting and Deploying Firewalls

Firewalls are probably the most common network security device, and these days one can be found on almost any network. There are many different types of firewall devices that are based on various platforms and architectures. The technology behind firewalls has progressed steadily through many evolutions of performance, functionality, and price. Firewalls today are faster, more capable, and cost less than the devices of only a couple of years ago. Firewalls have also progressed beyond the corporations, government entities, and ISPs who were among the first implementers of firewall technology. The explosion of broadband Internet connectivity has created a demand for basic firewall devices in small offices and homes that has been met by simple hardware firewalls that cost less than $100 and various software firewall applications. This explosion of firewall technology will only continue as networks become more interconnected and the devices themselves become faster, contain more features, and become more cost effective to deploy on a wider scale.

Firewalls in general are meant to be points of control between two network security zones through which all network traffic must pass. At this point of control, firewalls perform a variety of functions on passing traffic. The two main functions most conventional firewalls perform are enforcing security policies and logging. By enforcing security policies, firewalls decide whether to allow network connections. These decisions are based on rules that the administrator has configured into the firewall or rules that the firewall has configured based on past connections. For example, an administrator might configure a rule to allow HTTP traffic on TCP port 80 from hosts inside the firewall to hosts on the Internet, or a firewall might create a dynamic rule to allow traffic to an internal host from a host outside the firewall based on an established session. Firewalls also have the capability to log all aspects of traffic flow between the networks they join. Logging can be the key to determining traffic patterns and for forensic analysis. Firewalls are such a powerful tool in securing your network that they are often considered the most important security devices you can implement. And while this might be true, it's important to also remember that a firewall alone does not provide complete network protection.

In this section, we look at how you can use firewalls to protect your perimeter networks. We look at where in your overall perimeter network design a firewall is most effective, and how to determine which type of firewall is best for your network design.

Placing Firewalls for Maximum Effect

Because perimeter networks are fortified boundaries between networks of different security levels, firewalls are a key component in a good perimeter network design. A good firewall implementation is designed to keep out all network traffic that is not specifically allowed, and this key tenet should be the overall goal of your perimeter network design as well. A good perimeter network design should aim to control all points of access to the perimeter network, and firewalls are responsible for maintaining the security policies at those access points. Firewalls should be placed at any access point to your perimeter network as well as between any network segments within your perimeter network architecture. Multiple firewalls or firewalls with multiple interfaces can be used to create different security zones for different types of traffic that might require different security policies. For example, a public zone that contains Web servers should be segmented from any higher-level security zones like a management network, backup network, or data access network (see Figure 10.1).

Figure 10.1 Typical Internet Application Network Design

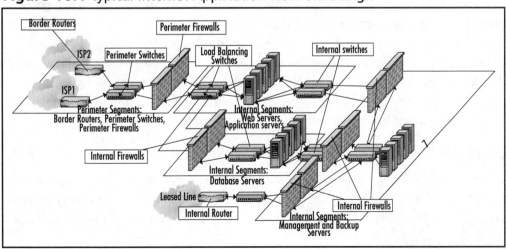

Eliminate Single Points of Failure

Because a firewall is a single point through which all network traffic must pass, it is also an easy place to have a single point of failure in your network architecture. To avoid this common failure point, most of the current enterprise class firewalls have the capability to be deployed in a redundant or high availability mode. This configuration usually allows the firewall pair to seamlessly transfer session information to one another so that traffic flow is not disrupted should one device fail. Implementing high availability firewalls increases network reliability and provides another level of defense against some types of network attacks. If one firewall is compromised and fails, the other will automatically resume protecting the network.

Determining the Right Type of Firewall for Your Perimeter Network Design

There are many different types of firewalls, and each has unique strengths and weaknesses. Deciding on the right type of firewall for the job depends on the details of the situation where it will be used. Requirements for low network latency, high network capacity, the network protocols in use, and the applications being placed behind the firewall all play a major role in deciding which type of firewall is best suited for a particular design.

Firewalls are generally classified by the methods they use to enforce security policies, by how they handle network traffic, and by the physical configuration of the device. In this section, we look at the various classifications of firewalls, examining the strengths and weaknesses of each, and give examples of where each type of firewall best fits into a perimeter network design.

Packet-Filtering and Proxy-Based Firewalls

When classified by the way in which they enforce security policies, most firewalls fall into at least one of three categories. The first category is packet-filtering firewalls. This type of firewall operates at the network or IP level of a network stack.

It examines a network packet's IP content and filters traffic based on addresses, ports, and packet options. This category includes stateful packet inspection firewalls, which maintain a state table of authorized connections and use this table to deny traffic that doesn't match with expected session states of existing connections. Stateful packet inspection firewalls are a very common type of firewall in use today. Because packet-filtering firewalls operate at the network level, they are usually very high-performance firewalls. So much so that some manufacturers of stateful packet inspection firewalls claim that their devices can perform at wire speed, meaning that traffic flows though the device with no noticeable delay. Packet-filtering firewalls are excellent solutions when application performance is an important requirement, such as when designing a network to host an Internet application such as an e-commerce site.

The second category of firewall is the application-proxy firewall. This type of firewall works at the application layers of a network, and actually terminates all incoming and outgoing connections at the firewall. If the connection is permitted, the application-proxy firewall then initiates a connection to the destination host on behalf of the source host. Application-proxy firewalls are able to make sure traffic flowing through them conforms to network security policies, and that functions within a protocol or application conform to specified security policies as well. For this reason, application-proxy firewalls are considered more secure than packet-filtering firewalls. Unfortunately, by the vary nature of application-based firewalls, they must be able to understand the application before they are able to proxy it. It is nearly impossible to create proxies for each individual application that exists, so most application-proxy firewall vendors provide proxies for the most common Internet applications.

The third category of firewalls is the circuit gateway firewall. This type of firewall works at the transport layer of a network and filters traffic based on addresses. A circuit gateway firewall is intended to create a virtual circuit between source and destination host allowing for a more seamless connection. Most circuit gateway firewalls are implemented using SOCKS, an IETF approved standard for application proxies. The SOCKS implementation uses sockets to keep track of separate connections and requires a SOCKS-compatible client on the source host system. Even though most common Web browsers include a SOCKS client, circuit gateway firewalls are more commonly used in corporate Internet access scenarios where the administrator has control over the client system.

Server-Based Firewalls and Firewall Appliances

When classified by the physical configuration of the firewall, there are two general types of dedicated firewall devices. The first is a server-based firewall. A server-based firewall runs on a secured or specially modified common operating system like UNIX, Linux, Solaris, or Windows NT/2000 running on commodity server hardware. The second type of firewall configuration is known as a firewall appliance. Firewall appliances are purpose-built hardware devices that run proprietary operating systems.

Each firewall configuration has strengths and weaknesses and it is important to consider these when choosing the type that is right for your perimeter network design. The strengths of server-based firewalls are that they are generally more customizable and have a higher degree of complexity owing to the fact that they run on commodity server hardware on top of a general operating system. Server-based firewalls also generally have more internal storage for logs and are easier to upgrade than firewall appliances are. Some of the weaknesses of server-based firewalls are cost (server-based firewalls generally are more expensive solutions), performance (server-based firewalls are usually slower than most firewall appliances), and manageability; because server-based firewalls run on common operating systems they become vulnerable to any weakness discovered in the operating system platform. To maintain a server-based firewall, patches and updates for both the firewall software and the underlying operating system must be tracked and applied religiously. Still, server-based firewalls are generally the only firewall configuration that supports application proxy and circuit-gateway firewall solutions, which is still the highest level of firewall security available.

The strengths and weaknesses of a firewall appliance are mainly based on the purpose-built hardware that runs the device. Firewall appliances derive their major strength from the fact that most of the network logic and firewall functions happen on purpose-built hardware and not up through the network stack of an operating system. This fact makes these devices capable of handling traffic at higher rates of speed and in higher quantities than server-based firewalls can. These devices have become extremely prevalent in high traffic applications such as Internet application and ISP networks because of their high-performance characteristics. Unfortunately, the purpose-built hardware platform is also a weakness for firewall appliances. Proprietary hardware generally makes these devices less upgradeable than server-based firewalls, and is less likely to have standard server features that can be convenient, such as a hard disk drive for log storage.

Examining Routing Firewalls and Transparent Bridging Mode Firewalls

When classified by the way in which a firewall deals with network traffic, two general types of firewall configurations have become prevalent in most firewall solutions. The more traditional configuration is the routing firewall. Because most firewalls manipulate packets at the network layer and higher, they generally are placed in a location between different networks and are responsible for routing packets between two or more interfaces and network numbers; hence the classification of routing firewall. More recently, firewalls have taken their game down a level to the data link layer. This type of firewall still inspects a packet's IP information and is a single point through which all traffic passes; however, this type of firewall bridges traffic at the data link layer and hence is known as a bridging firewall or transparent firewall.

A bridging firewall is a relatively new configuration that does offer a couple of advantages in some circumstances. Primarily, a bridging firewall can be inserted into any network environment without any serious reconfiguration of network numbers or default gateways. This makes a bridging firewall an excellent device to use for quiet monitoring of network traffic or to protect a device within a complex network environment where configuration changes aren't possible. Another benefit of bridging firewalls is that the firewall itself might not need to have an IP address at all, and in this configuration the device is totally transparent to the network and any potential attacks or threats. However, this configuration is slightly more difficult to manage, as any configuration would be done through a serial terminal CLI.

Routing firewalls are still the standard for most firewall configurations and probably will continue to be based on the fact that routing-based firewalls allow for features that are very important in many network designs. NAT, multiple interfaces and networks, and ease of management are all strong features not available in pure bridging firewalls.

Tools & Traps…

Bridging Firewalls Can Help Fix a Problem Quickly

Because bridging firewalls do not require any changes to existing network infrastructure, it is possible to deploy one in front of an entire network in minutes. It is a good thing to have handy when an emergency requires that strict policies be implemented immediately. Keep a bridging firewall configured and ready to deploy and you will be prepared for the next time the fire alarm goes off.

Including IDSs and IPSs in Your Design

While firewalls might be considered the foundation of your network security design for their capability to secure all access points to your perimeter network, IDSs and IPSs are fast becoming just as widely deployed for their capability to examine traffic as it flows through your network to detect possible attacks. Additionally, the increasing threat of DoS attacks, DDoS attacks, and self-replicating Internet worms and viruses has also lead to intrusion detection/prevention systems becoming more common in a complete perimeter network design. Where IDSs were once almost exclusively used to detect rogue traffic patterns that matched a preconfigured set and to send alerts, new generations of IDS/IPS are increasing in features, functions, and performance to the point where IDS/IPS are now actively denying traffic that matches patterns or is a statistical anomaly. Perimeter network designers are increasingly dovetailing IDS and IPS with existing firewall solutions to create layered security solutions that are more effective than firewalls alone.

There are two main techniques for IDSs and IPSs to detect intrusions. The first technique is a knowledge-based technique. IDSs based on a knowledge-based technique work by examining traffic at the network layer and above and comparing patterns within those network packets to known attack or intrusion signatures. This technique is the most commonly used technique in IDSs today because it is very accurate. Knowledge-based IDSs are very good at detecting traffic that matches signatures they know about. However, just because these systems are accurate doesn't mean they catch all intrusions and attacks. A knowledge-based system has to be updated continually with the latest signatures to keep up to date.

Another technique for IDS design is a behavior-based system. A behavior-based system works by examining traffic patterns and comparing them with historical trends. Alerts are generated on any traffic patterns that are out of the ordinary. Behavior-based IDSs can be very good at catching all attacks and intrusions; anything that looks out of the ordinary will generate an alarm. Unfortunately, behavior-based IDSs generally aren't as accurate as knowledge-based systems, and tend to generate many false alarms as well.

Where Is an IDS Most Effective?

Most IDSs have traditionally been deployed behind the firewall in a passive role, monitoring all traffic as it flows past the firewall into the network through mirrored ports on a switch or via a tap device inserted directly between the firewall and core switches. However, newer IDS and IPS devices are designed to connect directly between the perimeter firewall and network switches, intercepting all network traffic. This position puts these devices in a better location to prevent intrusion and attack traffic by dropping the offending packets. More and more devices are also being designed for deployment outside the perimeter firewall between the perimeter router and the perimeter firewall. These devices are designed to stop DoS and DDoS attacks before they reach your firewall device.

The optimal location for an IDS or IPS depends on its features and functions. An IDS with passive monitoring and alerting capabilities won't need to be in a position to deny traffic. Its optimal location is behind the perimeter firewall closest to the data that is protected. An IPS that is capable of stopping DoS and DDoS attacks should be deployed on the perimeter network between the perimeter router and perimeter firewall where it can do the most good. In addition, an IPS that can match traffic patterns quickly and accurately enough to deny intrusion attempts as they happen should be deployed inline to all network traffic right behind the perimeter firewalls in a redundant configuration to eliminate any single points of failure.

Creating Network Segments

One of the methods commonly used for alleviating network congestion and network segmentation can also be used to increase the security of perimeter networks. Network segmentation is the practice of dividing your network architecture into sections, and is usually implemented to reduce the size of broadcast domains and to increase network efficiency. In designing perimeter networks, network segmentation is implemented to separate networks based on content and use. This technique enables network security devices to be implemented at the boundaries between network segments, which allows for more control over network traffic that reaches critical information assets.

Network segmentation can be implemented in a variety of ways, and it is important to consider which method best meets your perimeter network design goals.   In this section, we discuss the various methods and tactics used to properly implement network segmentation, and a couple of different ways to consider network segmentation in your perimeter network architecture.

Securing Your Perimeter Network with VLANs and Routers with Access Control Lists

Implementing network segmentation means dividing your network into smaller pieces, which can be done by either physically separating your networks or using VLANs. Physically separating your networks is probably the most secure method of segmentation, but it is also the costliest in terms of additional NICs, switching infrastructure, and increased management. For this reason, most networks use VLANs. VLANs are a technology that is supported on most enterprise-class switches and allows different ports on the same switch to be assigned to different virtual networks. Traffic on one VLAN can't traverse onto other VLANs without being routed by a Layer 3 network device. This allows for network segmentation without implementing additional switches; however, it is important that some security considerations be taken before implementing VLANs.

Primarily, all switches should be properly secured at the switch OS level. Implementing VLANs on an improperly secured switch provides little security improvement, as the switch might be easily compromised and reconfigured. In addition, all VLANs should be created specifically for the networks to which they will belong, and the default VLAN should either be removed or configured with no member ports. Finally, all unused ports on your VLAN switch should be configured to belong to no VLANs at all. These techniques will help keep your VLAN configurations secure and your network properly segmented.

Because each network segment becomes its own network broadcast domain, traffic cannot freely travel between network segments. To get from one segment to another, all traffic must pass through a Layer 3 network device like a router, routing firewall, or a switch with Layer 3 capabilities. It is this fact that makes network segmentation such a useful technique for secure network design; it presents the perfect opportunity to control the flow of traffic. While we have already discussed the importance of implementing firewalls at every major network boundary, another method for controlling traffic between network segments is ACLs on the routers that direct traffic between them. ACLs are similar to packet-filtering firewalls in that they prevent or authorize traffic based on rule sets. These rule sets reference IP network and address information, and protocol details and control network traffic based on these parameters. ACLs and router security are covered in more depth in Chapter 5, "Routing Devices and Protocols."

Segmenting Using DMZ Networks and Service Networks

DMZ, as many people know, is actually a military term for *demilitarized zone*. The military definition of DMZ means a zone, or area, from which military installations, operations, and forces are prohibited. This area generally separates two opposing forces and is owned by neither. The term *DMZ* first became commonly used in describing a particular part of a network that was in many ways similar to a military DMZ. The network segment between a gateway router and a firewall was generally unprotected and separated "us" from "them." More recently, the term *DMZ* has evolved to describe a zone on the network that isn't necessarily unprotected, but still exists as a buffer between areas of dissimilar control.

When segmenting perimeter networks, there are various ways to separate the architecture. The first technique involves segmenting the network based on the function and location of the resources within each segment. Resources that need to be available to users and networks of unknown security status are regularly designed into a DMZ network, and that approach can also be used to segment a perimeter network internally. Servers and resources such as Web servers, e-mail gateways, and anonymous FTP servers that require constant access via public networks would be segmented from other areas of the perimeter network that might include database servers that contain Web server display data, or private FTP servers. This technique can aid in segmenting the network based on utilization because servers that are publicly available would be separated and protected from servers that still need to be accessed by known users from outside your security domain.

Another approach to segmenting a perimeter network is to consider the services provided by the various resources on each segment, and segment the network accordingly. Each network segment would be defined based on the services the resources within that network provide. This approach allows very tight control over the traffic flowing between each of the network segments because each segment only provides one type of service. However, this approach can also lead to a large number of network segments if too many services need to be provided, and a large number of network segments can mean additional network security devices and management overhead.

Designing an Internet Access Network

An Internet access network is one that connects a trusted network to the public Internet. This type of perimeter network is probably one of the most common types of perimeter networks deployed and is most often used to connect the trusted networks of businesses or public institutions to the Internet. The Internet has become so prevalent and necessary in daily business functions that most Internet access networks are also considered mission-critical resources, meaning that their design must be fault tolerant, highly available, and secure. The Internet access network is mainly designed for network hosts on the trusted network to make requests and access information on the public Internet. An Internet access network is not designed to allow any access from the public Internet to reach the trusted network. This type of perimeter network is called an *Internet application network*. We discuss design considerations for Internet application networks in the next design example.

In this section, we look at designing a typical Internet access network for a sample company of 250 people using a top-down network design approach while keeping security a top priority. We begin by looking at the typical types of information that we need to collect to design the appropriate solution, and from there we progress to a logical network design that can be easily translated into a physical network architecture design.

What to Consider when Designing Internet Access Networks

When designing an Internet access network, the first step is to collect requirements. These requirements can generally be broken down into two types: business requirements and technical requirements. Business requirements include things like project budget, project goals, project schedules, and the scope of the project. Technical details include requirements for network availability and performance, network manageability and usability, and most importantly of all in an Internet access network design, network security.

Collecting business and technical requirements requires diligence and patience. All requirements should be recorded and documented. Only after all of the business and technical requirements have been collected can we begin translating those requirements into technical details that we can then use to create our logical network design. A good place to begin collecting the requirements is in assessing the business requirements and scope. Are we designing an Internet connection network for the entire organization or for a small field office? Other important considerations are the budget and schedule of the project.

Business requirements play a big role in influencing the types of technologies used when translating the technical requirements into a logical and physical network design. With a good understanding of the business requirements, collecting the technical requirements allows us to delve one level deeper into the design process. The technical requirements will dictate the level of network availability and performance. These requirements will help us answer questions like "Does the level of availability require redundant Internet connections, and how much capacity will our Internet connections need to accommodate the application performance required?" Technical requirements will also allow us to decide important factors like usability and manageability. What protocols and application will be allowed? Will caching and/or proxying of the Internet connection be necessary? Finally, the technical requirements will also translate directly into considerations for network security. What types of firewalls will be necessary? Will they be redundantly deployed and configured? How will logging and auditing of Internet access be addressed? Will usage be authenticated, and if so, how? How will IDSs or intrusion prevention be integrated into the design? The answers to all of these questions should be contained in the technical requirements, and as the design progresses a matrix that maps the technical decisions to business and technical requirements should be created to make sure all requirements have been accommodated.

Once all of the business and technical requirements have been considered, the next step is designing the logical network and physical networks. For this example, we will assume that we have collected the small set of business and technical requirements listed in Table 10.1.

Table 10.1 Technical Decisions to Requirements Map

Business Requirements	Technical Requirements	Technical Decisions
Internet access is mission critical.	Bandwidth necessary is 5 Mbps.	Multiple Fractional T3 circuits.

Continued

Table 10.1 Technical Decisions to Requirements Map

Business Requirements	Technical Requirements	Technical Decisions
IMAP e-mail clients, Web browsing allowed. No IM or other network applications allowed.	IMAP and HTTP will be the only protocols allowed.	Redundant firewalls with appropriate rule configuration.
	Detect possible network intrusions.	Implement IDS.
	Allow Web browsing un-authenticated but log all browsing activity.	Implement Web proxy server.
	Log all firewall events and unauthorized activity.	Implement syslog server and configure firewalls.
	Secure perimeter network devices.	Routers and switches configured to guard against DoS attacks.
	Redundant and secure routing protocol needed.	BGPv4 implemented for redundant dynamic routing. BGPv4 also supports authentication.

Designing the Logical and Physical Networks

With the business and technical requirements captured and translated, the next step in designing an Internet access network is the logical network design. For this task, most network architects use a visual design application such as Microsoft Visio or SmartDraw. These tools allow you to visually lay out your network design and choose the optimal placement for your firewalls, network switches, proxy or caching servers, and IDSs. Once complete, a logical network design should show at a high level how the Internet access network works, and should demonstrate each of the technical and business requirements. Logical network diagrams do not detail the exact device models and port-level connections; these details are contained in the physical network design.

For this example, we have included redundant border routers connecting to different ISPs. If possible, we would also try to ensure that each ISP uses a dif-

ferent local service provider for connectivity to the location. We have specified
an IDS and installed it on the perimeter network, outside the firewalls, where it
can detect any intrusion attempts. We have also specified redundant firewalls to
provide extremely reliable access to the Internet (see Figure 10.2).

Figure 10.2 Basic Internet Access Logical Network

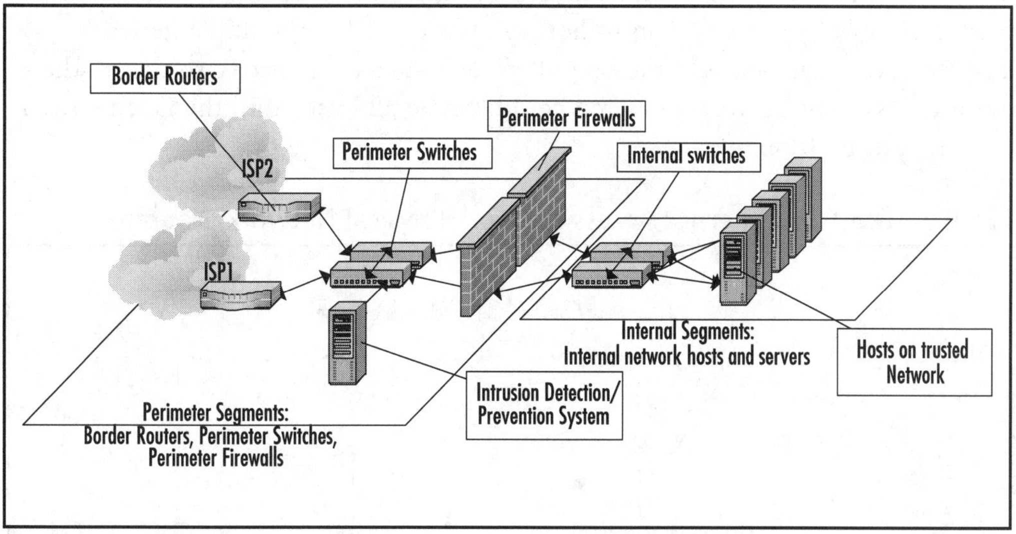

With a logical network design complete, the next phase of the network design
is the physical network design process. The physical network design process
includes choosing actual device models. This process can be time consuming, but
should be facilitated by the fact that your logical network design shows how the
devices need to function, and all of the requirements have been translated into all
of the performance, capacity, cost, and manageability details for the device. Most
network architects have a good understanding of the current network devices
being manufactured, including an understanding of features, functions, and limitations in the real world. However, if this is not the case, you will have to do extensive product evaluation to make sure that the devices you choose really can
perform up to the specifications detailed in the design process so far. How will the
firewall perform at your level of utilization? Will the logging and auditing tools
selected provide the information needed? Questions like these can be answered
during an evaluation process so that come implementation time, you can be assured
that your devices will function to your specifications. With the device selection
complete, a physical network diagram can be created with details about device
models and port-level connections and configurations of devices themselves.

The physical network diagram brings more detail to the design (see Figure 10.3). It specifies the actual devices being used and details where all the devices connect down to the port level. This diagram shows that the Web proxy and caching server is set up behind the redundant firewalls in addition to a syslog server. Each server is multihomed to separate switches to provide reliable service in the event of a device failure. Each host system would then be connected to one of the switches. Because most host systems don't have multiple network adapters, each switch would only be filled to 50-percent capacity, so that in the event of a switch failure, one switch could handle all hosts until the failed switch was brought back online.

Figure 10.3 Basic Internet Access Network Physical Network Diagram

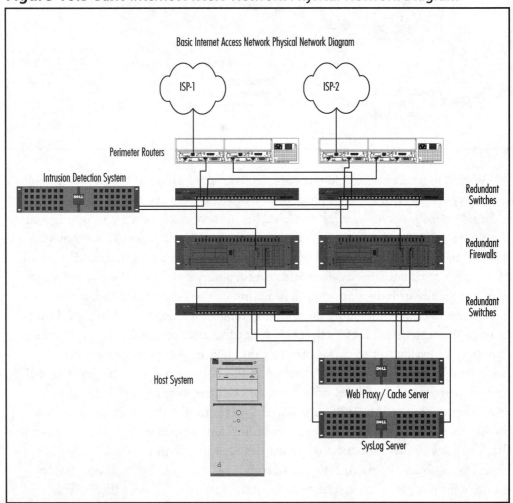

Designing Internet Application Networks

An Internet application network is a type of perimeter network that allows hosts on the Internet to access resources on your network. Typically, these resources are Web sites, e-mail servers, DNS servers, FTP servers, or a similar type of public Internet service. To provide these services securely, an Internet application perimeter network is used to support Web servers, e-mail servers, and FTP servers outside the protected internal network. Internet application networks generally have specific requirements depending on the application hosted; however, there are some common features to most Internet application networks, which we examine in this section. In most cases, Internet application networks are considered mission critical and must be designed with fault tolerance and application availability in mind. Internet application networks by definition are available to any Internet host, which means that network security is also a top design priority.

In this section, we examine the process of designing a typical Internet application perimeter network. Using a top-down design process, we consider the case of a sample e-commerce Internet application where downtime can mean lost revenue, and stored credit card payment information requires enhanced security. We start by collecting the typical types of information necessary to design our solution, and progress down to a logical network design and finally to a physical network design.

What to Consider when Designing Internet Application Networks

When designing an Internet application network using a top-down network design approach, the first step is to collect both business and technical requirements. In the case of an Internet application network, business requirements include things such as project scope, budget, and schedules. It is also important to understand the Internet application from the business perspective. What does the application do? How is it used by customers and end users? What are the ultimate goals that the application is trying to accomplish? What level of application availability must be maintained? What type of data will be stored and transmitted? Understanding these aspects of the Internet application will give you a framework upon which you will be able to begin to build your network design.

After collecting business requirements, the next step in the design process is to collect technical requirements. A good place to start gathering technical requirements is by examining the application from a technical perspective. Which protocols will the application use? How will those protocols flow between layers of the application? What is the expected utilization of the application and what resources are necessary to support that utilization level? All of these questions will lead to technical requirements that must be accommodated in your network design. For our example, we will use the small set of business and technical requirements listed in Table 10.2.

Table 10.2 Sample Technical Decisions to Requirements Map for Internet Application Network

Business Requirements	Technical Requirements	Technical Decisions
Mission-critical e-commerce application.	Bandwidth must be scalable and burst-able for dynamic growth.	Data center location with plenty of available band width.
Application will process credit card transaction.	HTTP and HTTPS are primary application protocols.	Multiple firewall layers with appropriate access controls.
Application will be database driven.	Detect possible network intrusions.	Implement IDS.
Application will store customer information.	Application will have three tiers: Web servers, application servers, and database servers.	Segment network based on services to provide superior application performance and security.
	Log all firewall events and unauthorized activity.	Implement syslog server and configure firewalls.
	Secure perimeter network devices.	Routers and switches configured to guard against DoS attacks.
	Redundant and secure routing protocol needed.	Obtain an Autonomous System number and implement BGPv4 for redundant dynamic routing. BGPv4 also supports authentication for added security.

Logical and Physical Network Design

Once the business and technical requirements have been mapped to technical decisions, we can proceed to create a logical network diagram (see Figure 10.4). For our example, we have segmented our network by services to increase performance and security of the network infrastructure. We have also secured each of the segments with a firewall between the network boundaries to ensure traffic passing between the segments meets our defined security policies. Redundant Internet access from multiple ISPs and BGPv4 provides reliable access to the Internet. Finally, a management network is created for backup, maintenance, and monitoring of the application. Access to the monitoring network is provided by a dedicated leased connection, which allows the tightest possible rule set at the Internet-facing firewalls.

Figure 10.4 Sample Internet Application Network—Logical Network Diagram

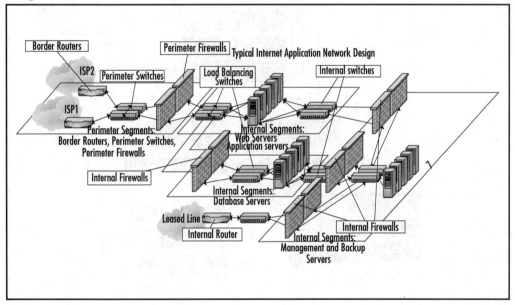

After completing the logical network design, a physical network design can be completed (see Figure 10.5). This level of details provides information on exactly how the networks defined in the logical diagram will be implemented. In our example, firewalls with multiple interfaces and load-balancing switches are used to segment the network according to service type using VLANs, and servers are multihomed to multiple networks to increase security and performance.

Figure 10.5 Sample Internet Application Network—Physical Network Diagram

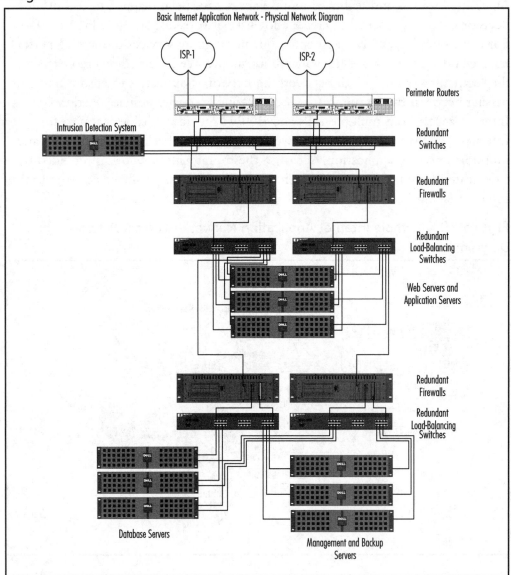

Basic Internet Application Network - Physical Network Diagram

Designing VPN and Remote Access Termination Networks

A VPN or remote access termination network is a perimeter network that connects remote users to your network via VPN or POTS (Plain Old Telephone Service) dial-in. This type of perimeter network has become very common as the need for access to information has grown. It is most commonly deployed by companies or organizations that want to increase employee productivity by providing them access from their home offices or that have many traveling employees such as sales resources who require remote access from locations outside the corporate network. VPN and remote access termination networks are also commonly deployed by organizations that have multiple trading partners with which they exchange information on a regular basis. This type of perimeter network allows a firewall to be placed between the endpoint of a VPN or RAS server to ensure that traffic passing to the internal network conforms to security policies.

In this section, we examine a VPN and remote access termination network for a sample company of 250 traveling employees and five remote manufacturing partners. We start by collecting all of the requirements, both business and technical, and translating those into technical decisions. We will create a technical decision matrix to make sure all requirements have been satisfied. We will then proceed to create logical network diagram and a physical network diagram of the final perimeter network design.

What to Consider when Designing Remote Access Termination Networks

One of the first things to consider when designing a VPN and remote access termination network are the business requirements driving the need for the network. Who are the end users of the VPN or dial-in connections? What is the security status of the network from which they will be connecting? How important are the VPN and remote access services to the organization? The answers to these questions will lead to your set of business requirements.

Once the business requirements are complete, gathering technical requirements begins. It will be important to establish various technical details that will stem from the business requirements already gathered. Which applications and protocols will the users need to use? How will these users or organizations authenticate to your network? How will usage be monitored and audited? If

VPNs are to be established, how will key negotiation and encryption policies be established? There will more than likely be multiple rounds of requirements gathering for any project, because inevitably the process of gathering technical requirements uncovers hidden business requirements that then must be considered. Although sometimes frustrating, this process is normal, and eventually all business and technical requirements will have been collected. When all requirements have been collected, we can move forward to make technical decisions based on the requirements. For our sample, the technical decision matrix shown in Table 10.3 will be used.

Table 10.3 Sample Technical Decisions to Requirements Map for VPN and Remote Access Termination Network

Business Requirements	Technical Requirements	Technical Decisions
VPN and remote access is mission critical.	Bandwidth necessary is 5 Mbps.	Multiple fractional T3 circuits.
250 RAS clients using dial-in and dynamic VPN clients.	48 POTS dial-in lines will be needed to handle ~20% of users dialed in.	2 x 24 line voice PRI terminating to dedicated RAS server.
Five partners with static VPN tunnels using Web services.	Clients will be authenticated.	Implement IPSec VPN tunnels with VPN concentrator.
RAS clients will be able to use IMAP e-mail clients and will be able to access Web-based document management system.	Allow Web browsing unauthenticated but log all browsing activity.	Redundant firewalls with appropriate rule configuration.
Log and audit all RAS activity.	Log all firewall events and unauthorized activity.	Implement syslog server and configure firewalls.
	Secure perimeter network devices.	Routers and switches configured to guard against DoS attacks.
	Redundant and secure routing protocol needed.	BGPv4 implemented for redundant dynamic routing. BGPv4 also supports authentication.

Logical and Physical Network Design

Once all of the requirements are collected and translated into technical decisions, we can begin to create a logical diagram of the network design (see Figure 10.6). In our example, a VPN concentrator and dedicated RAS server with 48 POTS lines will handle both dial-in users as dynamic VPN clients. The VPN concentrator will also be the endpoint for the five IPSec VPN tunnels to partner networks. All users will be authenticated via an LDAP server on the internal segment, and the firewalls are configured to restrict traffic that does not conform to the security policy.

Figure 10.6 Sample Remote Access Termination Network—Logical Network Diagram

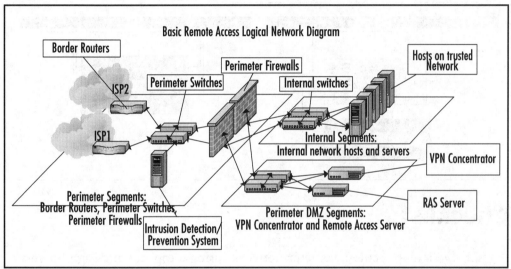

With the logical network diagram and design created, a physical network diagram is created to detail how all of the actual components will integrate together (see Figure 10.7). Multiple interfaces on redundant firewalls segment the network into security zones. The perimeter segment includes the border routers, perimeter switches, and IDS, while the perimeter DMZ segment contains the termination endpoints for all RAS connections and VPN tunnels. All devices are multihomed to independent switches for reliability and performance.

Figure 10.7 Remote Access Network—Physical Network Diagram

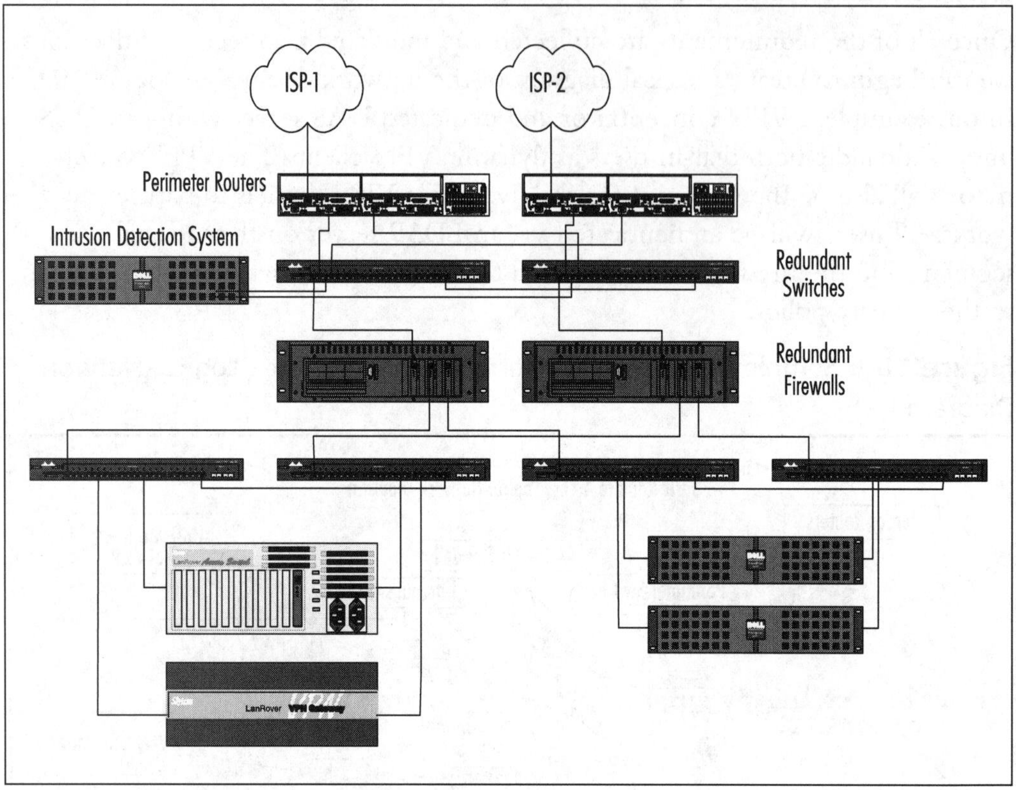

Checklist

☑ Designing secure perimeter networks using a top-down design process

- Examine and collect business requirements.

- Examine and collect technical requirements.

- Create a technical decision matrix to verify all requirements have been accommodated.

- Create a logical network diagram that encompasses

- Create a physical network diagram.

Summary

Perimeter networks can be defined as any network that provides services to any other user or network of unknown security status. Firewalls, Intrusion Detection Systems (IDSs) and Intrusion Prevention Systems (IPSs), filtering routers, and network segmentation are just some of the devices and techniques that are used in designing secure perimeter networks.

One of the best design principles to use when designing perimeter networks is the top-down design method. Practitioners of top-down network design first focus on collecting information that will allow them to determine the requirements for capacity, functionality, performance, availability, scalability, affordability, manageability, and security. With these requirements complete, top-down network designers proceed to creating logical network designs that encompass the specific needs of the application or user base. Only after the logical design has proven to meet requirements do they proceed to the physical design phase where real network devices are introduced. In designing perimeter networks, network security should be given an increased priority.

Firewalls are probably the most common network security device, and these days one can be found on almost any network. Firewalls in general are meant to be points of control between two network security zones through which all network traffic must pass. Firewalls also have the capability to log all aspects of traffic flow between the networks they join. There are many different types of firewalls, and each has unique strengths and weaknesses. Deciding on the right type of firewall for the job depends on the details of the situation where it will be used. The first category is packet-filtering firewalls. This type of firewall operates at the network or IP level of a network stack. It examines a network packet's IP content and filters traffic based on addresses, ports, and packet options. The second category of firewall is the application-proxy firewall. This type of firewall works at the application layer of a network, and actually terminates all incoming and outgoing connections at the firewall. If the connection is permitted, the application-proxy firewall then initiates a connection to the destination host on behalf of the source host. The third category of firewalls is the circuit gateway firewall. This type of firewall works at the transport layer of a network and filters traffic based on addresses. A circuit gateway firewall is intended to create a virtual circuit between source and destination host, allowing for a more seamless connection. Firewalls can be server based, running on top of a security hardened operating system, or a firewall appliance, a purpose-built hardware device that runs a custom operating system dedicated to firewalling. Firewall appliances derive their major strength from the fact that most of the network logic and firewall functions happen on purpose-built hardware and not up through the network stack of an operating system. This makes these devices capable of handling traffic at higher rates of speed and in higher quantities than server-based firewalls can. The strengths of server-based firewalls are that they are generally more customizable and have a higher degree of complexity, owing to the fact that they run on commodity server hardware on top of a general operating system. Server-based firewalls also generally have more internal storage for logs and are easier to upgrade than firewall appliances are.

While firewalls might be considered the foundation of your network security design for their capability to secure all access points to your perimeter network, IDSs and IPSs are fast becoming just as widely deployed for their capability to examine traffic as it flows through your network to detect possible attacks. There are two main techniques for IDSs and IPSs to detect intrusions. The first is a knowledge-based technique. IDSs based on a knowledge-based technique work by examining traffic at the network layer and above and comparing patterns within those network packets to known attack or intrusion signatures. Another technique for IDS design is a behavior-based system. A behavior-based system works by examining traffic patterns and comparing them with historical trends. Alerts are generated on any traffic patterns that are out of the ordinary. Behavior-based IDSs can be very good at catching all attacks and intrusions; anything that looks out of the ordinary will generate an alarm. Unfortunately, behavior-based IDSs generally aren't as accurate as knowledge-based systems, and tend to generate many false alarms as well.

One method commonly used for alleviating network congestion, network segmentation, can also be used to increase the security of perimeter networks. Network segmentation is the practice of dividing your network architecture into sections, and is usually implemented to reduce the size of broadcast domains and to increase network efficiency. In designing perimeter networks, network segmentation is implemented to separate networks based on content and use. Network segmentation can be done by either physically separating your networks or by using virtual local area networks (VLANs). Physically separating your networks is probably the most secure method of segmentation, but it is also the costliest in terms of additional network interface cards (NICs), switching infrastructure, and increased management. For this reason, most networks use virtual local area networks (VLANs). VLANs are a technology that is supported on most enterprise class switches and allows different ports on the same switch to be assigned to different virtual networks. Traffic on one VLAN can't traverse onto other VLANs without being routed by a Layer 3 network device.

Segmenting your network using demilitarized zone (DMZ) networks and service networks is also an effective method for segmenting perimeter networks. The term *DMZ* first became commonly used in describing a particular part of a network that was in many ways similar to a military DMZ. The network segment between a gateway router and a firewall was generally unprotected and separated "us" from "them." More recently, the term *DMZ* has evolved to describe a zone on the network that isn't necessarily unprotected, but still exists as a buffer between areas of dissimilar control. Another approach to segmenting a perimeter network is to consider the services provided by the various resources on each segment and segment the network accordingly. Each network segment would be defined based on the services the resources within that network provide.

The first of three design examples we tackle in this chapter is an Internet access network. An Internet access network is one that connects a trusted network to the public Internet. The Internet access network is mainly designed to allow network hosts on the trusted network to make requests and access information on the public Internet, and generally does not allow hosts on the public Internet to access hosts or applications on the trusted network. When designing an Internet access network using a top-down network design approach, the first step is to collect requirements. These requirements can generally be broken down into two types: business requirements and technical requirements. Business requirements include things like project budget, project goals, project schedules, and the scope of the project. Technical details include requirements for network availability and performance, network manageability and usability, and most importantly of all in an Internet access network design, network security.

The second design example is an Internet application network. An Internet application network is a type of perimeter network that allows hosts on the Internet to access resources on your network. In the case of an Internet application network, business requirements not only include things like project scope, budget, and schedules, it is also important to understand the Internet application from the business perspective. After collecting business requirements, a good place to start with gathering technical requirements is by examining the application from a technical perspective. Internet application networks by definition are available to any Internet host, which means that network security is also a top design priority.

The final design example is a VPN and remote access termination network. A VPN or remote access termination network is a perimeter network that connects remote users to your network via VPN or POTS (Plain Old Telephone Service) dial-in. This type of perimeter network has become very common as the need for access to information has grown. It is most commonly deployed by companies or organizations that want to increase employee productivity by providing them access from their home offices, or that have many traveling employees such as sales resources who require remote access from locations outside the corporate network. Even though most users of this network will be authenticated, it is still very important to secure this type of network because the networks you are connecting to are not under your control and therefore cannot be trusted.

Solutions Fast Track

Looking at Design Principles

- ☑ Firewall selection and placement is a critical piece of perimeter network design. The right type of firewall for your application depends on the details of the situation where it will be used.

- ☑ While firewalls might be considered the foundation of your network security design for their capability to secure all access points to your perimeter network, Intrusion Detection Systems (IDSs) and Intrusion Prevention Systems (IPSs) are fast becoming just as widely deployed for their capability to examine traffic as it flows through your network to detect possible attacks.

- ☑ In designing perimeter networks, network segmentation is implemented to separate networks based on content and utilization.

- ☑ The network segment between a gateway router and a firewall was generally unprotected and separated "us" from "them." More recently, the term *DMZ* has evolved to describe a zone on the network that isn't necessarily unprotected, but still exists as a buffer between areas of dissimilar control.

Designing an Internet Access Network

☑ When designing Internet access networks, it is important to consider the types of applications that will be used by the internal hosts and configure firewall rules appropriately.

☑ When all business and technical requirements have been collected, create a technical decision matrix to make sure all of the requirements have been accommodated.

☑ After all of the requirements have been met, start by creating a logical diagram to show the high-level network design. After completing the logical diagram, design a physical diagram to document the details of device models and connections.

Designing Internet Application Networks

☑ When designing an Internet application network, it is important to examine the application completely for business and technical requirements.

☑ After all requirements have been gathered, make sure you have accommodated them all by creating a technical decision matrix.

☑ Create logical and physical network diagrams to show the details of the network design.

Designing VPN and Remote Access Termination Networks

☑ When designing a VPN and remote access termination network it is important to consider the users of the service. Plan which application and protocols will be allowed to traverse network boundaries based on user needs.

☑ Make sure all requirements are met by creating a technical decision matrix.

☑ Create a logical and physical network diagram to finish you network design.

Links to Sites

- **http://www.ietf.org** Internet Engineering Task Force Web site provides texts for all network RFCs and Internet drafts.

- **http://www.sans.org/rr/** The Sans InfoSec reading room contains articles and papers that relate to many networking and security subjects.

- **http://www.checkpoint.com** Check Point Software Technologies is the market leader firewall maker.

- **http://www.netscreen.com** Netscreen Technology makes firewalls and VPN devices.

- **http://www.cisco.com/en/US/products/hw/vpndevc/index.html** Cisco Security and VPN devices homepage.

Mailing Lists

- **http://www.checkpoint.com/services/mailing.html** Mailing lists for Check Point firewalls.

- **http://honor.icsalabs.com/mailman/listinfo/firewall-wizards** Mailing list that discusses issues related to firewalls.

- **http://www.qorbit.net/mailman/listinfo/nn** List for Netscreen support and communication.

- **http://www.securityfocus.com/subscribe?listname=129** Security Focus list concentrated on firewalls. Security Focus also maintains various other lists, including BugTraq.

Frequently Asked Questions

The following Frequently Asked Questions, answered by the authors of this book, are designed to both measure your understanding of the concepts presented in this chapter and to assist you with real-life implementation of these concepts. To have your questions about this chapter answered by the author, browse to **www.syngress.com/solutions** and click on the **"Ask the Author"** form. You will also gain access to thousands of other FAQs at ITFAQnet.com.

Q: What is a perimeter network?

A: Perimeter networks can be defined as any network that provides services to any other user or network of unknown security status.

Q: What are the different types and classifications of firewalls?

A: There are three common types of firewalls. The first category is packet-filtering firewalls. The second category of firewall is the application-proxy firewall, and the third category of firewalls is the circuit gateway firewall. Firewalls can also be classified by the physical attributes. Host-based firewalls run on a security-hardened operating system, and firewall appliances run on purpose-built hardware.

Q: How is network segmentation used in secure perimeter network design?

A: Network segmentation is the practice of dividing your network architecture into sections, and is usually implemented to reduce the size of broadcast domains and to increase network efficiency. In designing perimeter networks, network segmentation is implemented to separate networks based on content and use. Network segmentation can be done by either physically separating your networks or by using virtual local area networks (VLANs).

Q: What are the different types of Intrusion Detection Systems (IDSs)?

A: There are two main techniques for IDSs to detect intrusions. The first is a knowledge-based technique. IDSs based on a knowledge-based technique work by examining traffic at the network layer and above and comparing patterns within those network packets to known attack or intrusion signatures. Another technique for IDS design is a behavior-based system. A behavior-based system works by examining traffic patterns and comparing them with historical trends.

Q: What is the top-down network design philosophy?

A: Practitioners of top-down network design first focus on collecting information that will allow them to determine the requirements for capacity, functionality, performance, availability, scalability, affordability, manageability, and security. With these requirements complete, top-down network designers proceed to creating logical network designs that encompass the specific needs of the application or user base. Only after the logical design has proven to meet requirements do they proceed to the physical design phase where real network devices are introduced.

Chapter 11

Internal Network Design

Solutions in this Chapter:

- Design Principles and Examples
- Proper Segmentation and Placement

Related Chapters:

- ☑ Summary
- ☑ Solutions Fast Track
- ☑ Frequently Asked Questions

Introduction

Many network administrators believe that once they've protected their network from the outside world, they've done their job. However, according to the 2001 National Retail Security Survey, employees' account for 47 percent (nearly half) of all retail loses. This could be translated to the statistic that a network protected only from the outside only provides 50-percent protection.

Before this statistic frightens you into locking up the candy jar on your desk, keep in mind the old German proverb, "Opportunity makes thieves." You can keep the honest people in your office honest by removing the obvious security holes from your network. Behold! Lead not your end users down the path to corporate espionage and identity theft. Keep them from the temptation that is the employee payroll file. And verily, protect them from reading the CEO memo to the Board. When the CFO complains about the cost, pick up your wooden staff and proclaim, "Sinner, how canst thou put a price on saving souls? I do the Lord's work." This routine might actually buy you enough time to construct a valid plan or it might get you sent to a windowless room with soft walls (in which case it will probably be your only chance to take a vacation without having to carry your pager). Good network security doesn't just happen. It takes careful planning, a solid knowledge of your current infrastructure, a thorough understanding of your company's business process, and the proper budget.

Most businesses do not produce Information Technology (IT) as their core deliverable. Consequently, IT expenditures fall into the "cost center" category. This already makes it hard to sell IT projects, but security is an intangible product, making it an even harder sell. The CFO can see the results from a faster server, but he cannot see, taste, feel, hear, or smell "safer." Successful completion of an expensive security project will usually only garner employee indifference at best. Does this mean that you should drop the project? Absolutely not! When someone steals intellectual property from the company, management will look squarely to IT for not protecting them. Network administrators need to attack this problem proactively and provide a solid solution for security holes with sufficient documentation. If the CFO doesn't want to pay for it, you at least have a shield for when the hammer falls.

Design Principles and Examples

Nothing good comes from a bad design, and the worst designs come from networks formed with no planning at all. If we may borrow a page from sports psychology, we need to visualize our goal before we start. Ask yourself, "What does this network need to do?" Often, end users conduct their business based on the capabilities of the network, but a well-designed network should work transparently. Marshall McLuhan noted with television, "The medium is the message." Unlike television networks, computer networks should *facilitate* the work and not *become* the work. Once you've answered what the network should do, now you can focus on the "how." Network engineers could debate this point, but the network design should start from the "inside out." Plan your internal networks and then work on connecting your LANs to each other and to external networks, such as the Internet.

The lessons from Chapter 7 should guide your initial designs. Your first design pass needs to connect each station to the network as cleanly as possible. Once you've accomplished this, now consider adding fault tolerance to the network. Examine the important links, such as backbone connections between floors and buildings in your campus model. What happens if one of these links malfunctions? How can you prevent a single failure from crashing your network? You need to answer these questions during this phase of your planning.

Notes from the Underground…

SPOF-Busters

Although it might not be the most popular Halloween costume, I like to regularly don my Ghostbusters-inspired SPOF-Buster costume and hunt through wiring closets for the evil critters. I'm talking, of course, about SPOFs—Single Points of Failure. You should, at any time, be able to bust down the doors of your wiring closets and Network Operation Centers (NOCs), and point out the nasty SPOFs. We actually make a sport of it. We trade networks for the day with a stack of bright orange sticky-notes. When we see a SPOF in the other's network, we slam a sticker on it and rack up the points. Costumes optional.

Firewall Placement and Selection

Firewall placement is probably the single most important task in infrastructure security. This section will give you a chance to apply what you learned from Chapter 3, in a design situation. Firewalls, even more so than routers, demark where the public network ends and your private network begins. What is a firewall? Briefly, a firewall is a device used to prevent unauthorized access into a protected network from some other network. Usually, this "other network" is the Internet. What isn't a firewall? A firewall is not a magic bullet that will solve all of your security issues.

Perimeter Placement

Given the simplified definition of a firewall, most of these devices will eventually find themselves at the network's edge. First, let's examine a simple network in Figure 11.1. This network shows a group of workstations on the third floor connected to the mail server on the first floor with a Gigabit Ethernet connection.

Figure 11.1 Sample Network

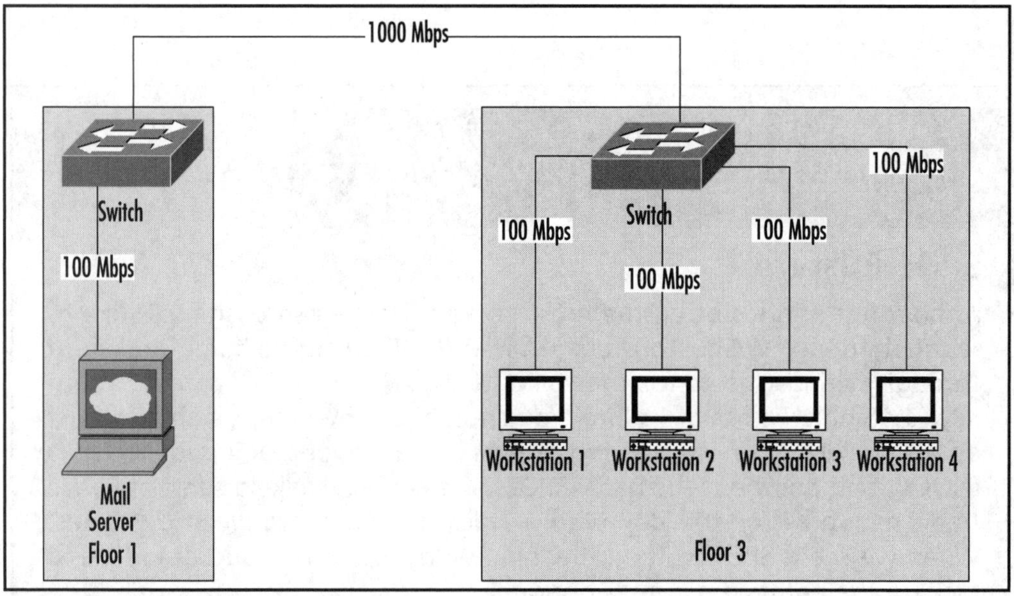

From an internal standpoint, this network looks fine. However, what about Internet mail and Web access? Most modern networks need access to external resources such as these. So far, our sample network has perfect security from the outside world by virtue of not having any connections to the outside world. We could connect our sample network to the Internet with merely a router and no firewall, but this would leave the network with very little protection. If we apply some of what we learned from Chapter 3, we know that we need a firewall with an ICSA rating of either Small/Medium Business (SMB) or Corporate, since the Residential certified firewalls do not need to support internal servers and we need support for the first floor mail server. We can choose from dozens of models to suit our modest needs in this example.

For this example, let's choose a very basic firewall with just an external and an internal interface. Since public addresses have a high recurring cost, we should make sure that our firewall also performs Network Address Translation (NAT), so that we can use one or two public addresses for Internet access instead of a unique public address for each device in the network.

Tools & Traps...

Private Addressing

NAT allows a device such as a router or firewall to proxy Internet connections for the network devices behind it. The NAT device keeps track of the Internet connections going through it, and directs the traffic to the proper recipients. The host machines on the Internet only see the IP address of the NAT device and not of the actual machine requesting the connections. For this to work properly, each machine behind the NAT device needs an IP address unique within the company network that isn't publicly routed. In 1996, The Internet Engineering Task Force (IETF) ratified Request for Comment (RFC) 1918 (www.ietf.org/rfc/rfc1918.txt?number=1918), "Address Allocation for Private Internets," to give network engineers a list of IP addresses from which to choose when creating NATed networks. The IETF felt the need to make this document nine pages long, but the relevant section takes all of three lines on page three:

```
10.0.0.0      -    10.255.255.255      (10/8 prefix)

172.16.0.0    -    172.31.255.255      (172.16/12 prefix)

192.168.0.0   -    192.168.255.255     (192.168/16 prefix)
```

Continued

www.syngress.com

> These three lines list the permissible private networks when using NAT to connect to the Internet. Please note, however, that you can subnet these networks to fit your own needs. For example, even though the "10" network uses an 8-bit subnet mask by default, you can divide this range into 65,536 networks, each with 254 hosts, by using a 24-bit subnet mask.

Once we connect our network to the Internet, we should get a configuration that looks similar to Figure 11.2. This figure depicts a network with a DS-1 (1.54 Mbps, also referred to as T-1) connection to the Internet through a router. The router then connects to the external interface of the firewall, while the firewall's internal interface links to the sample network. For minimum security, the firewall should only allow Simple Mail Transfer Protocol (SMTP) traffic into the mail server, but deny all other inbound traffic. The mail server will also need to send mail, so the firewall should also allow SMTP traffic out from the mail server. If the network users require Web access to the Internet, the firewall should at least allow HyperText Transfer Protocol (HTTP) out to the Internet.

Figure 11.2 Sample Network with Firewall

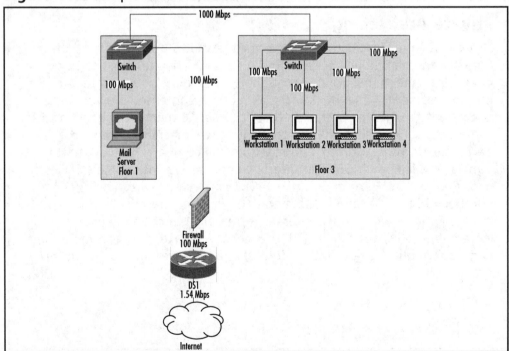

This looks pretty good, but can we do better? Our firewall rules allow traffic into the mail server on port TCP 25, the standard SMTP port. This seems harmless enough; however, this rule assumes that the mail server can safely handle SMTP traffic. As we know, Microsoft issues patches on almost a weekly basis to correct security problems, but other vendors also have problems. For example, in September 2003, CERT released an advisory that all versions of Sendmail earlier than 8.12.10 have a serious flaw that needs patching (www.kb.cert.org/vuls/id/AAMN-5RGP4Q). A hacker could potential exploit this flaw merely by sending an e-mail message to an e-mail server. Since the mail server sits directly on the trusted network, a hacker could use the compromised mail server as a launching point for attacking the rest of the network.

Let's upsize our firewall to include an additional interface. Previously, the firewall in Figure 11.2 of our sample network had only two interfaces:

- Inside
- Outside

More sophisticated firewalls add a third choice called a *demilitarized zone*, or DMZ. Some advanced firewalls can have multiple DMZ interfaces instead of merely a single DMZ interface. Figure 11.3 shows our new network, now with a DMZ and an SMTP proxy. In this design, the firewall sends all inbound e-mail to the SMTP proxy server. The SMTP proxy server masquerades as the real mail server for the purposes of virus and content filtering and many other functions. Once the SMTP proxy server has confirmed that the mail has passed its inspection, it sends it back through the firewall, which passes the data to the real mail server. This prevents Internet traffic from entering the protected network directly. If the SMTP proxy is compromised, it has limited access to launch an attack against the protected network since all of its traffic is processed by the firewall before gaining access to the protected network. Internet access for the workstations continues to pass through the firewall as in the previous example of Figure 11.2, although this network configuration no longer requires a connection between the second and third floor switches, as the firewall now provides this connection.

Figure 11.3 Sample Network with DMZ

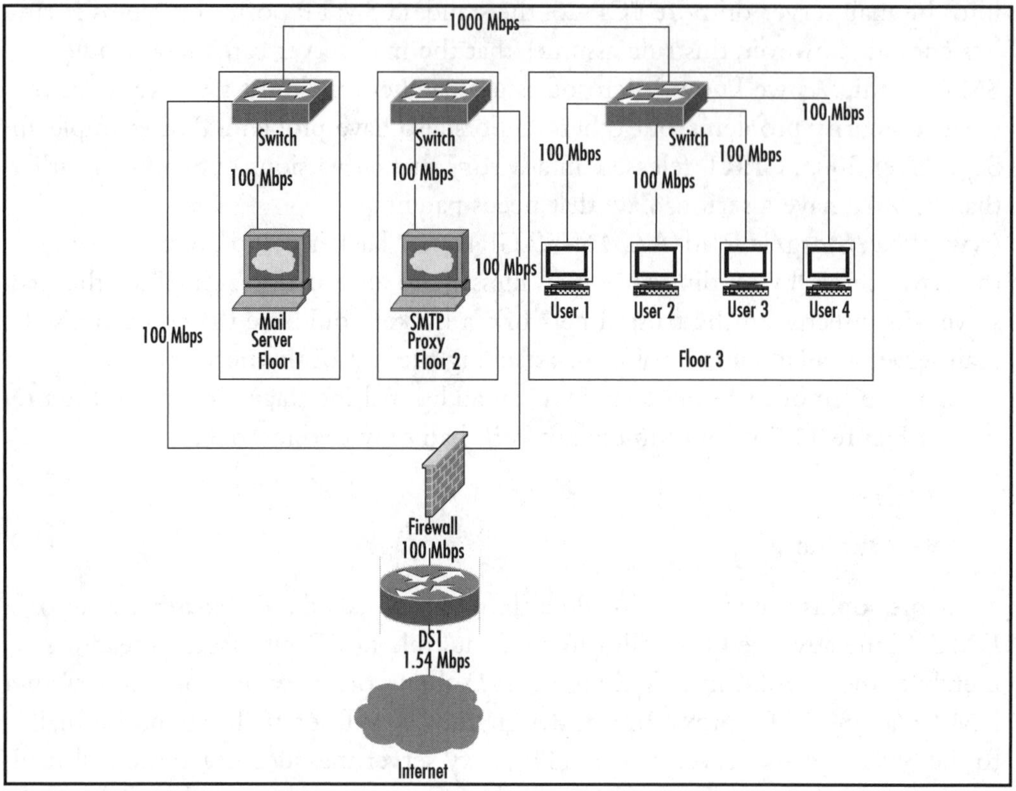

Internal Placement

Most firewalls exist on the edge of the campus network, but sometimes a company needs protection from itself. Let's rip this next example from the headlines. Ten Wall Street banking firms have recently settled a case for $1.4 billion brought against them by the New York State Attorney General (www.forbes.com/markets/newswire/2003/05/01/rtr959208.html). Attorney General Eliot Spitzer contended that the firms mislead investors into buying stocks in which the firms had a significant interest. To avoid future lawsuits, these firms now need to keep their banking operations separate from their analysis operations. The new, segmented design is illustrated in Figure 11.4. This network example separates these two entities, but still gives the Legal department access to both.

Figure 11.4 Internal Firewall Placement

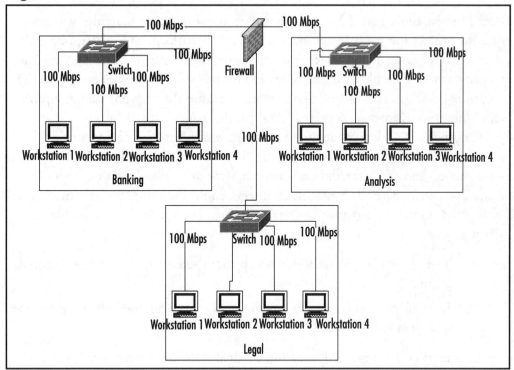

Figure 11.4 has a firewall clearly at the core of the network. All communication between the three departments, Analysis, Banking, and Legal, must cross the firewall. For this example, the firewall rules would:

- Disallow any traffic from Banking to Analysis and from Analysis to Banking.

- Allow two-way conversations between Banking and Legal and Analysis and Legal.

This firewall has three interfaces, but we wouldn't consider any interface necessarily as internal, external, or DMZ.

Network engineers have other choices beyond firewalls to separate departments. Engineers have optimized firewalls to allow the flow of certain traffic under stringent controls. This level of security usual comes at a high cost, and since it requires more processing power than normal switching or routing, it also has lower performance than most routers or switches.

IDS Placement

Being the paranoid sort, I have a Martian protection charm hanging over my door to protect me from (drum roll) Martians. It works great—so far, I haven't seen a single Martian anywhere near my house, so it must be working. Network security works a lot like my anti-Martian charm. Network engineers set up the security and then they assume that it works because they haven't had any problems. Intrusion Detection Systems (IDS) fill this gap.

Originally, IDS devices analyzed network traffic patterns against known attacks. If the current network traffic matched any of the patterns, the IDS would send an alert through a predefined channel, such as a console, syslog, pager, e-mail, or other method. Network engineers could then use this information to craft a plan to defend against the attack. Unfortunately, the alerts resembled car alarms:

- They happened so often for no apparent reason that everyone ignored them.

- Even if the event were legitimate, by the time anyone got there, the car was already vandalized.

Engineering has improved since the original IDSs were introduced, and the new devices give far fewer false positives and in some cases can actually stop intrusions themselves. Many people in the industry now call these devices Intrusion *Prevention* Systems (IPS) since they not only detect the threats, but also stop them in their tracks. Some IDSs can additionally prevent attacks by reconfiguring access control lists (ACLs) on switches and routers, dynamically rewrite firewall policies to exclude the suspect traffic, and even drop the offending packets. Of course, multiple manufacturers offer IDS/IPS products, and each product has its own strengths and weaknesses. Some vendors even have multiple IDS and IPS products, each occupying a separate niche. For example, Cisco classifies IDS products as either a Network Intrusion Detection System (NIDS) or a Host Intrusion Detection System (HIDS). A NIDS is usually a network appliance that plugs into the network and monitors traffic. A HIDS is usually a software agent that runs on a server and alerts the network administrator to attacks, prevents these attacks from succeeding, or does both. Chapter 9 covers these two types of systems in depth.

Host Intrusion Detection System Placement

Network admins install HIDSs on servers and workstations that need extra protection above what the OS and AV software can provide. Examples of this include McAfee Entercept from Network Associates, and the Cisco Security Agent, formerly Okena StormWatch. This type of software examines all of the activity on the host, disallows anything that it feels compromises the security of the host, and sends an alert to inform the administrator about the attempted breach. Often, normal operations cause *false positives*, events that the agent thinks are security intrusions, but are really normal operations. Network administrators must tune the agents for their own environment to reduce the number of false positives.

Figure 11.5 HIDS Placement

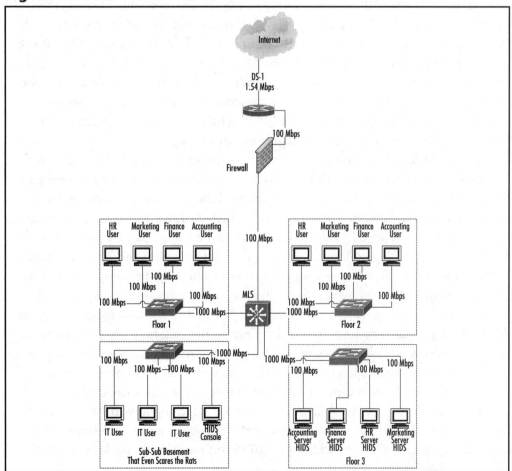

Figure 11.5 shows suggested HIDS placement: you'll notice that all of the servers have an agent on them. Chapter 2 discusses asset inventory, which you can use to determine exactly which servers need agents. Even though we quickly discovered the agent placement, the placement of the HIDS console, however, might not jump out at you in Figure 11.5. In this instance, we've placed the HIDS console with the IT department. In this example, the console could have stayed with the servers, but since you probably wouldn't keep your keys with the lock that they open, you might want to consider moving the console away from the machines that it protects. In our configuration, we have a Gigabit Ethernet connection to the highly desirable IT subbasement where we've located the console. This gives us a reliable connection that the communication between the HIDS and the console will not saturate. Since, in this example, the connection goes through a multilayer switch, we can add filtering rules that only allow HIDS traffic between the HIDS agents and the console. For example, Entercept's HIDS agents use either TCP port 5000 or 5005 (version dependent) to communicate with the console, so the network administrator could easily set up a filter on the MLS only to allow those ports from the agents to the console. This will add an additional layer of protection against tampering. The HIDS console should also have an agent installed on it to harden the console itself. The Cisco Security Agent uses standard SSL traffic (TCP 443), which can make it harder to filter since many Web sites use SSL for legitimate business.

Figure 11.5 only installs HIDS agents on the servers. What about the workstations? HIDS generally work by preventing unauthorized activity. Server data changes constantly, but the configuration and functions remain static. A workstation, however, can change with the wind, which makes a HIDS on a workstation much more of a challenge, but perhaps even more important. Do you think that one of your travelling colleague's notebook computer with the built-in wireless card has less of a chance of getting hacked than one of your company's servers that never ventures beyond the firewall? Infected notebooks can bypass containment faster than a cold through a Kindergarten and it can take longer to fix the damage than it takes to lose the sniffles. Due to the difficulty (or perhaps to a lack of a perceived market), some companies only make HIDS agents for servers and not workstations. Therefore, if you feel that you need the protection of a workstation HIDS, shop around carefully before you make a decision.

In addition to affecting your choice of product, using a workstation HIDS will probably also affect where you place the console. Figure 11.6 shows that with the addition of the workstation HIDS on a notebook, we have created a

DMZ for our console. We could have left the console in its former location and put in a firewall rule to allow traffic from the notebook to reach the console. However, this creates an opening from the outside world directly into a high-security machine nestled snugly in the center of the protected network. Granted, the console should have an agent on it, making it one of the most secure hosts in the company, but that should not stop us from taking the extra step if possible. In this configuration, we lose the Gigabit Ethernet link to the console, but properly tuned HIDS agents should never saturate a 100 Mbps link. With this new configuration, if anything happens to compromise the HIDS console, the firewall can still protect the inside network. We will discuss this in more depth in Chapter 6, "Secure Network Management."

Figure 11.6 HIDS Placement with Notebook

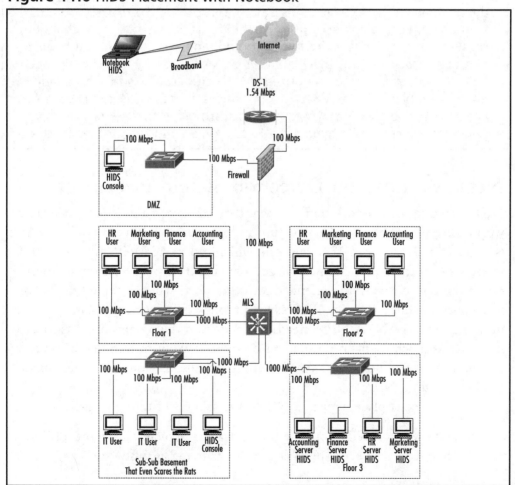

Test, Test, and Retest

Security is a double-edged sword. A workstation HIDS is a powerful weapon against hackers and even your own users. A workstation HIDS can stop your users from getting into the holiday spirit by preventing them from installing kitten screensavers, the latest version of *DOOM*, and a million other pieces of unauthorized software. Used properly, it can lock down the configuration better than a Group Policy object (GPO), which can save the IT department from having to constantly re-image wandering machines. However, this same control could prevent your road warrior from using PowerPoint for that big sales presentation or changing his IP address to access the hotel's broadband connection. You need to test *everything* on the machine that an end user could possibly need before sending the machine out into the cold, cruel world. This includes all of the applications and network interfaces. In many cases, a HIDS is not like antivirus software that you can just turn off with a password. If you find that you can easily bypass the HIDS, you should try another product.

Network Intrusion Detection System Placement

NIDSs need to see network traffic so that they can analyze it. Most modern networks use a fully switched infrastructure and virtual local area networks (VLANs) (see Chapter 7 for a detailed discussion), which can make it difficult for a NIDS to see most of the traffic. Many managed switches have port mirroring/monitoring options so that traffic intended for other ports will get copied to the mirrored port. In addition, many VLANs have promiscuous ports that can see traffic from multiple VLANs. A NIDS needs to connect to these types of ports so that it can see as much traffic as possible. In Chapter 2, we went into depth about setting up this type of port for network sniffing operations—the same information can be used for a NIDS.

As to the exact placement of a NIDS, two schools of thoughts exist:

- One wants a NIDS outside the firewall, as depicted in Figure 11.7, so that it can see every possible attack occurring against a site.

- Then there is the school of thought that says that a NIDS should connect inside the firewall, as depicted in Figure 11.8, so that it only reports the attacks that have entered the protected network.

Figure 11.7 NIDS Outside Firewall

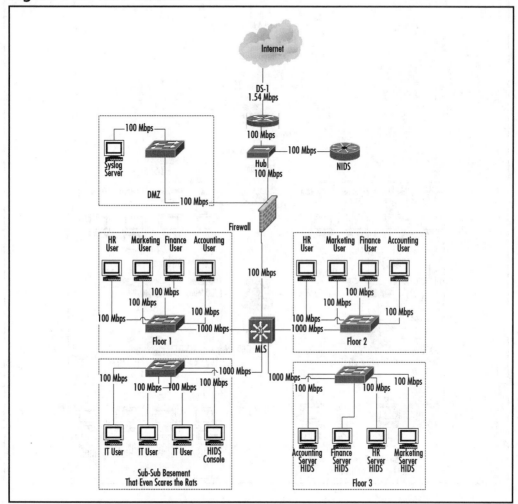

Figure 11.8 NIDS Inside Firewall

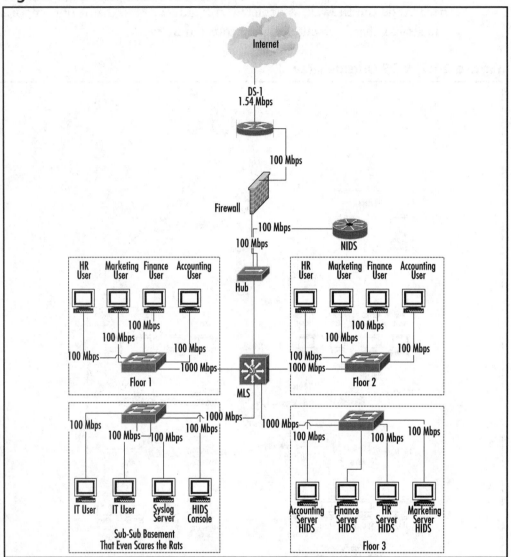

Both methods have pros and cons. Outside the firewall, a NIDS can see attacks from the moment they start, giving a network administrator the maximum amount of time to react to the situation and prevent any damage. However, a NIDS outside the firewall will report minor attacks that the firewall would have stopped easily. For example, a properly configured firewall should stop the SQL Slammer worm (www.microsoft.com/technet/security/

bulletin/ms02-061.asp) dead in its tracks, but a NIDS outside the firewall will see and report this problem. Just as with the "Boy who cried wolf," a network administrator could eventually start ignoring all problems that this NIDS reports just because of the sheer volume of trivial events.

Depending on your network configuration, a NIDS inside the firewall, such as in Figure 11.8, might see an attack from one source that a NIDS outside the firewall would miss. Many network administrators terminate their virtual private network (VPN) connections *behind* the firewall. Any attacks routed through a compromised VPN client will bypass all firewall protection entirely, which will also bypass a NIDS in front of the firewall. A NIDS on the same network segment as the company servers would have a perfect vantage point to see attacks coming from this source, since the hacker would probably try to crack the servers as part of the incursion. Terminating the VPN connection in front of the firewall can mitigate some of these problems, but often this requires opening so many holes in the firewall for the VPN connection that the firewall has trouble stopping the attacks. Most VPNs have split tunneling deactivated by default, which prevents the VPN client from accessing any other Internet traffic outside of the secure tunnel. In most cases, this prevents someone from actively controlling the compromised VPN client while it's attached to the VPN tunnel. This, however, does not stop a machine infected with a worm, such as MS Blaster, from infecting unprotected machines on the inside network.

Notes from the Underground...

What's "a Lot?"

We talk about a large volume of alerts, but what does that really mean? A NIDS on an active network could easily accumulate five events a second. Most of these would—or should—fall into the trivial category, but an improperly configured policy could easily start dumping all of these to your e-mail or pager. Many policies have time components so that one event could have a different significance at 10:00 A.M. than at 2:00 A.M..

Fine-tuning the reporting mechanism on a NIDS can greatly reduce the number of "false positives" and trivial events that get reported, but that also minimizes the benefits of having the NIDS outside the firewall. Minor event-gathering events often precede a full-scale attack, so a network administrator must carefully tune the reporting engine or he will miss the early part of the attack and miss the opportunity to defend against the attack before it escalates.

Given the many opportunities for bypassing a corporate firewall, a network administrator needs a tool harder to bypass. Since a HIDS sits directly on a protected box, this makes it extremely difficult to successfully attack a HIDS-protected machine. Any important server or workstation should have a HIDS on it, especially if it sits in a DMZ or service network. Most HIDSs use a console to configure them, so if a hacker compromises the console, he can easily compromise all the protected machines. Therefore, the console should also have a HIDS on it. The HIDSs from both Cisco and Network Associates, for example, use this as the default configuration. In addition, you should take great care in placing the console on a secure segment, perhaps using VLANs or a multilayer switch to prevent as much traffic as possible from reaching the console. For example, the console could sit on an administrative VLAN with no Internet access and that can only see protected servers internally. This makes it difficult for anyone to tamper with the console.

A NIDS inside the firewall, such as was shown previously in Figure 11.8, will see a significantly reduced number of attacks, which means that it will also require less tuning, thereby speeding the installation. Since this device sits behind the firewall, any attacks that this device reports have already made it through the firewall and need immediate attention. False positives here can mean the difference between a full night's sleep and an unproductive trip to the office at 2:00 A.M. For these reasons, you must filter carefully here.

Please note that Figures 11.7 and 11.8 still make reference to HIDSs. A secure network does not need to make a choice between a HIDS and a NIDS—it should have both. Moreover, the NIDS diagrams do not reference a console. Network administrators configure most NIDSs directly, either through a command-line interface (CLI) or through a Web browser. The NIDS will need to send alerts, though, which means that it could need access to a mail server, pager gateway, or syslog server depending on the alert mechanism used. These two figures show suggested placements of the syslog server for collecting alerts. With the NIDS inside the firewall in Figure 11.8, the NIDS can stay in the protected network since the NIDS does not need to cross the firewall. In Figure 11.7, with the NIDS outside the firewall, setting up the syslog server in a DMZ or service network makes more sense so that we minimize the amount of "dirty" traffic coming into the protected network.

Proper Segmentation

A great network doesn't just happen—but a bad one does. Some of the worst network designs have reared their ugly heads because of a lack of forethought as to how the network should ultimately look. Instead, someone said, "Get these machines on the network as cheaply and quickly as possible."

Segmenting a network involves balancing the following items:

- Security
- Speed
- Cost
- Convenience

The highest security network would have a firewall between every server and workstation on the network, but that would slow the network to a crawl, be extremely expensive, and require an inordinate amount of time to configure. The best network design will balance all four criteria. Any network that emphasizes one aspect too heavily will most likely contain serious design flaws.

Tools & Traps…

Hardware Firewalls for Every PC

3Com makes a family of network interface cards (NICs) that have firewall functionality embedded in the hardware (www.3com.com/products/en_US/prodlist.jsp?tab=cat&pathtype=purchase&cat=134482&selcat=Firewalls+%26+Filters&family=134494). A network administrator would use 3Com's Embedded Firewall Policy Server to configure and control up to 1000 of these devices from a central location. This family of product makes it affordable to add hardware firewall protection to almost any PC in the enterprise. 3Com does not offer a Gigabit version of this card, which might make it impractical for extremely busy servers at the core of

Continued

a network. However, this shouldn't limit its use of servers that primarily handle Internet traffic, since the Internet connection at most companies carries less than 100 Mbps of traffic.

Let's ease into segmenting the network with an easy requirement first: Layer 2 segmentation. Assuming that you're building your network around Ethernet, you will want to use switches exclusively instead of hubs. This immediately puts each host into its own collision domain as discussed in Chapter 7. This is something that you'll want to do regardless of any other requirements for the network. Moving up the difficulty ladder, consider the physical topology of your campus. Use a diagramming program such as Visio and other tools, as discussed in Chapter 2, to map out the locations of all of your network devices. Now, start placing switches in logical locations, keeping in mind the availability of resources where you want to place the switches. For example, Figure 11.9 shows a typical main server room, or "Main Distribution Frame" (MDF). This diagram tracks everything of significance in the room. This includes racks, outlet size and location, uninterruptible power supply (UPS), server, and phone switch (PBX). Figure 11.9 shows specific dimensions so that there are no surprises when it comes time to place equipment and run cabling. Figure 11.9 also includes a text key with instructions for items that the diagram cannot make clear visually. The important detail that this diagram does not show is the distance to any hosts that connect to the switches in the racks. Distance can vary by the equipment used, but you can usually assume that you can get 100 meters using copper and at least 500 meters with fiber when planning the network.

NOTE

Remember, before you buy any equipment, you should confirm that your environment will accommodate the equipment that you've selected.

Figure 11.9 Sample MDF

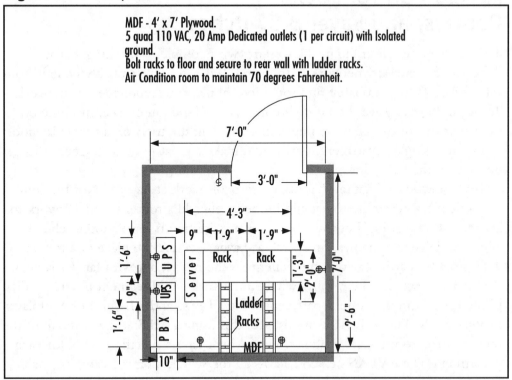

The complete physical campus diagram will require a similar sketch of every closet and then an overview drawing to show how each closet attaches to the other closets. This final drawing will need to account for the distances between the closets so that you can make sure that you have not exceeded any distance limitations. This diagram works very well for populating your wiring closets and server rooms, but it doesn't replace diagrams that represent the topology of your network. For example, as much detail as this diagram has, it does not show the IP addresses or operating systems of any servers or the type of switches in the racks. This information will prove vital when it comes time to connect all the different devices into a cohesive network.

This next step requires a little more thought than the previous steps did. We now have to consider traffic patterns. We just designed a completely switched network, which greatly reduces our collisions, but we haven't addressed any other issues such as broadcast storms. Layer 2 segmentation does nothing to control this, so to solve this problem, we need to move to Layer 3 and perform subnetting.

Access Control Lists, Routers, and Layer 3 Switches

The network design in Figure 11.10 starts with complete switching, but it doesn't end there. Any network with over 100 devices will probably benefit from subnetting. We can probably find some logical places to subdivide our network. To do this properly, we should now consider the function of each machine on the network. For example, we might find that half the users on a particular floor belong to a single department. This would make a great place to segment the network at the Layer 3 level.

As discussed in Chapter 7, routing protocols work at Layer 3. Not too long ago, a network administrator would immediately add a router to the network to accomplish subnetting, but today, network administrators have another choice. Mid- to high-end switches can switch at Layer 3, taking the place of a router. This provides a switch with same benefits as the router, but with far less latency than a router would add. A fully switched network could segment physically disparate users from the same department using VLANs and a Layer 3 or Multilayer Switch (MLS). Figure 11.10 demonstrates this using a MLS at the core. All of the users connect to the same switches, all of which have a specific VLAN for each department. These VLANs extend across all the switches on the campus. Each VLAN gets its own subnet, which the MLS routes. For added security, the MLS can even prevent traffic from crossing subnets so that each user group can only see its own traffic.

Pay close attention to the phrase "for added security." Some network administrators assume that because each group has its own subnet that these groups automatically cannot see each other. VLANs need routing information to see other VLANs, so initially, they don't see each other. However, they also probably don't see the Internet traffic, necessitating the administrator to add routing information to the VLAN. Assuming that the network administrator routed everything properly, all the VLANs now accidentally see each other. At this point, the network administrator can either:

- Remove the unwanted routing information
- Configure the filtering on the MLS if it supports it

Most administrators should opt for the latter, since it will provide higher security and will look like a purposeful separation of the networks. Using a deficient routing table can often look like a mistake to new administrator that might get "fixed" accidentally.

Figure 11.10 Network Segmentation Using VLANs

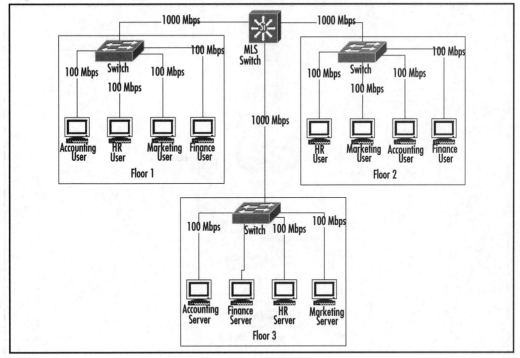

Different manufacturers have different mechanisms for filtering traffic, but most companies use some form of access control lists (ACLs). ACLs allow network administrators to use rules similar to those on firewalls on routers and some high-end switches. An ACL can take the form of a simple filter that prevents traffic from one subnet from reaching another, or it can get as granular as specifying which protocols can interoperate between specific hosts. For example, RFC 2827, "Network Ingress Filtering: Defeating Denial of Service Attacks which employ IP Source Address Spoofing," offers simple advice for filtering traffic at routers. This works especially well on exterior routers attached to the Internet when combined with the advice from RFC 1918, "Address Allocation for Private Internets." We can see a simplified version if we look at Figure 11.11.

Figure 11.11 Simple Network with ACL

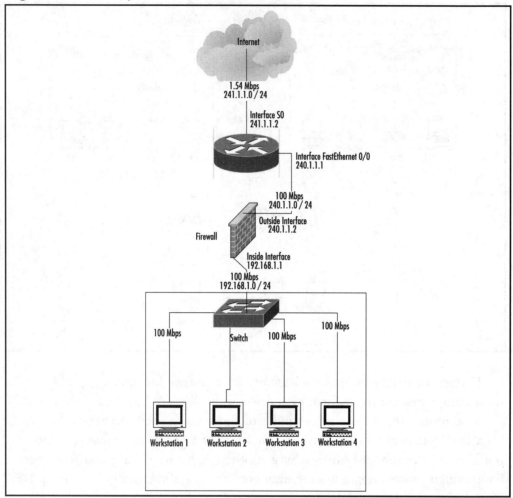

The sample network in Figure 11.11 has a router connecting to the Internet through a serial interface (S0). The serial interface has an address on the 240.1.1.0 network with a 24-bit subnet mask. The ISP in this example has given the network administrator the 241.1.1.0 network with a 24-bit subnet mask to use as the company's public addresses. The company attached a firewall to the Fast Ethernet interface of this router and then used NAT to give the internal 192.168.1.0 network Internet access. Based on this scenario, the network should never see traffic from the 241.1.1.0 / 24 range enter the network from the S0 interface of the router. In addition, the network should allow not traffic from any private network (RFC

1918) entering from the interface. Using RFC 2827 as our guide and Cisco's IOS syntax, we could construct an ACL that looked like this:

```
access-list 1 deny  10.0.0.0 0.255.255.255
access-list 1 deny 127.0.0.0 0.255.255.255
access-list 1 deny 172.16.0.0 0.15.255.255
access-list 1 deny 192.168.0.0 0.0.255.255
access-list 1 deny 240.1.1.0 0.0.0.255 any
```

This ACL also includes the reflexive addresses, 127.0.0.0 / 8, which, like the RFC 1918 addresses, should never arrive from the outside interface. Finally, we must apply this to the serial interface by entering the following commands at the router:

```
interface Serial0
ip access-group 1 in
```

ACLs can also restrict traffic based on protocols, ports, and specific hosts. In addition to stopping traffic from entering a network, they can also stop traffic from leaving a network. For example, we could have applied the previous ACL to the interior port of the router using the commands:

```
interface FastEthernet 0
ip access-group 1 out
```

Notice that since we've applied this to the inside interface, we had to swap the word *in* for *out*. Now, the router allows the restricted traffic to enter through the interface attached to the Internet, but then the router stops this traffic from exiting. These two examples achieve the same basic result—blocking spoofed traffic—but the second example consumes additional router resources since two interfaces have to deal with the traffic before dropping it.

The previous examples use ACLs at the network edge, but ACLs can work at almost any Layer 3 boundary. For example, an ACL crafted from RFC 2827 can prevent spoofing on an internal router connecting departments just as easily as on an external router. ACLs can also restrict access on a more granular level. ACLs from many vendors can filter on protocols, ports, and specific hosts. This allows for a granular approach to security similar to what we would see from a firewall.

Tools & Traps...

Dropping Traffic

When constructing an ACL, try to eliminate unwanted traffic as soon as possible. This means revising campuswide ACLs so that restricted traffic never makes it past the first hop of your network. Every additional hop that the traffic takes wastes bandwidth and processor cycles. Whenever you create an ACL, examine your campus diagram and ask yourself, "Can I block this traffic upstream instead?" If you can, move the ACL. If not, you have a keeper—probably. Don't forget that most ACLs include an "invisible" *deny all* statement, so you might have to add a generic *permit* statement at the end to handle normal traffic. Just don't be too generous with your permits: a *permit ip any any* statement set in the wrong place can make the rest of your ACL worthless.

Use of DMZs and Service Networks

Network administrators consider themselves at war with users, hackers, their bosses, vending machines, and most everything else they encounter, so it shouldn't surprise anyone that they borrow military terms. Politicians use the term *demilitarized zone*, or DMZ, to refer to a region devoid of weapons with heavy barriers on the outside separating warring factions. In computerese, a DMZ refers to a network protected from the outside network, but also protected against from the inside.

Previously, Figure 11.3 showed a sample network with a DMZ. The SMTP proxy server sits behind the protection of the firewall, but this server must also cross this same firewall to send information to the mail server on the inside network. The SMTP Proxy server finds itself "surrounded" by the firewall. The firewall protects the SMTP relay server, but if the machine falls to the hacking hoards, the firewall will now protect the inside of the network from the compromised proxy server.

What happens to a DMZ that actually gets settlers? In the computer world, we call this a *service network*. Service networks often resemble DMZs because they are surrounded by a firewall, but just as a continent differs from an island by virtue of size, a service network differs from a DMZ by the number of machines protected. Usually, these machines serve a common purpose, such as a Web server farm or a bank of mail servers. Many administrators don't consider themselves up to the challenge that service networks and DMZs represent, but they are not that much different from regular networks.

Configuring the Hosts

Even though these have special names, DMZs and service networks are really just networks. Configure the machines just as you would on the inside of your network. These machines will have their own subnet distinct from the rest of your network, and any communication between this network and any other network will require routing or Layer 3 switching. Since these machines will contact users from a public network, you should harden these machines as much as possible. This includes performing the following actions:

- Applying all the latest patches
- Disabling any unnecessary services
- Fully configuring all applications
- Tightening all the rights

Each operating system and application will have a set of steps unique to it regarding hardening. Finally, you should install a HIDS on these machines whenever possible for the highest possible level of protection.

Tools & Traps…

Information for Hardening Microsoft Products

Microsoft's TechNet (www.microsoft.com/technet) contains a wealth of information for securing Microsoft's products. Given Microsoft's current reputation for security, going to this site might seem like taking an oath of loyalty from Benedict Arnold, but you can hardly beat the developers for information about their own products. The page www.microsoft.com/ technet/security contains links to security checklists for most of Microsoft's products that really require it.

Administrators refer to a severely hardened server as a *bastion host*. These machines usually run a single application, such as a Web server, and have all other functionality disabled. Since the administrator has disabled so much of the operating capabilities, troubleshooting these machines takes much longer than their unhardened brethren do. During the hardening process, take careful notes as to what you've done to the machine because you might have to back out some of your work to get your application to function if you go too far.

Damage & Defense...

Install First, Harden Second

Some hardening procedures make it very difficult or even impossible to install new software. If you plan to create a bastion host, install all of your applications before you begin hardening it. Better yet, consider using a HIDS instead of creating a bastion host. A HIDS on a properly configured box can provide as much protection as a bastion host, and give you reporting functionality. A HIDS also has the ability to quickly deactivate in case you need to make changes to the host. Try making changes quickly to a bastion host. If you do need to deactivate a HIDS, isolate the machine from the rest of the network, if possible, so that it does not become compromised during this period.

Configuring the DMZ and Service Network

Once you have your hosts configured, you now have to tie them together into a cohesive unit. Figure 11.12 shows a simple service network and its relation to the inside network and the Internet. This diagram closely resembles Figure 11.3, except that the DMZ in Figure 11.12 contains more machines.

Figure 11.12 Sample Service Network

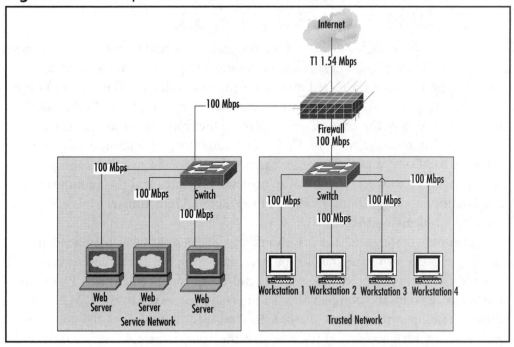

The service network uses a simple Layer 2 switch to connect all the machines and then connects to the other networks using the firewall as both a filter and a router. If the service network contained enough machines, you could subnet them, VLAN them, or both. In Figure 11.12, the firewall uses 100 Mbps links to connect to the inside network and the service network, but only high-end firewalls can actually process traffic fast enough to take advantage of links this fast. Keep this in mind when planning the service network. In most cases, traffic to the Internet will never approach 100 Mbps, but traffic from the inside could easily move that quickly. If you need extremely fast access to the service network from the inside of your campus, you might have to use a high-end firewall or even split the service network into several smaller networks and use multiple firewalls to create your DMZ. An NIDS on this network can help identify a situation before it becomes a problem.

Configuring the Firewall for the DMZ and Service Network

Anyone can go to the local computer store and buy a $30.00 piece of equipment that calls itself a firewall. These boxes come preconfigured to allow all traffic out and nothing in to the protected network. This works fine for the average home user, but many network administrators give their corporate firewalls the same treatment. Typically, the firewall will let any traffic from the protected network out to the Internet and into the DMZ. The administrator will limit inbound traffic to the DMZ and the protected network to specific machines and protocols. This seems to work well because no one complains and the administrator can continue to play CounterStrike uninterrupted. Unfortunately, this can create security problems later.

A properly configured firewall should give users only what they need and nothing more. This usually takes some trial and error, but the added security will pay for itself. For example, why does an end user need an open SMTP port to the Internet when the company has an internal mail server in the DMZ? He doesn't. The open port allows the user to send mail that bypasses the company's mail server, which avoids any filtering that the company might have configured. Since most new viruses have their own SMTP engines, this open port also allows an infected machine to further spread across the Internet.

A similar situation exists for the DMZ and service network. A mail relay machine needs very few ports to fulfill its function. For example, it might need to get DNS information and SMTP from the outside and transfer SMTP with the inside. As an administrator, you might take the attitude, "Why should I protect the Internet from my own machines?" The extraneous port or protocol that you don't block could be the one that your hacked mail server uses to communicate back to the hacker. This can open a reflexive hole in the firewall that the hacker can then use to start attacking your inside network directly from the DMZ. Once the hacker has compromised your DMZ, he has a pretty good start on cracking the rest of the network.

Checklist

☑ Keep all systems patched and up to date.

☑ Review security logs daily.

☑ Review maintenance logs daily.

☑ Review firewall policies and ACLs regularly to check for tampering and configuration errors.

☑ Avoid single points of failure (SPOF) wherever and whenever possible.

☑ Use only RFC 1918 addresses for private networks.

☑ Consider using firewalls internally for high-security departments or segments.

☑ Use Host Intrusion Detection System (HIDS) agents on critical servers and workstations.

☑ Heavily test any HIDS installation thoroughly before deploying the system into the field.

☑ Placing a Network Intrusion Detection System (NIDS) in front of a firewall will produce different results than placing one behind a firewall, so study the differences carefully before placing the unit.

☑ A properly segmented network balances speed, security, cost, and convenience.

☑ Before you buy anything, make sure that the physical space where you to plan to install any piece of equipment will accommodate the equipment.

☑ Use virtual local area networks (VLANs) to increase security and to reduce broadcast traffic.

☑ Don't be afraid to use access control lists (ACLs) on the inside of the network to increase security.

☑ Any resources accessible from the Internet should reside on a demilitarized zone (DMZ) or service network.

☑ Before hardening any system, try to install all applications. This will get much harder after hardening the system.

Summary

A network designer must plan every aspect of the network to maintain proper security. The network design needs to account for how the users will use the resources and the placement of assets. The network administrator will use this information to create a functional network that meets the basic connectivity needs of the organization.

Once the network engineer has a basic network, he can then start adding security components to the diagram. Most engineers start with adding firewalls to the perimeter of the network, although some highly secure networks could require internal firewalls as well. Networks that require a separation between entities, but also require high-performance connections, could opt for routers, multilayer switches, VLANs, or both instead of an internal firewall. This configuration sacrifices some security, however, as these higher performance options usually do not have the same tolerances as high-end firewalls. ACLs on routers and multilayer switches can help to make these devices almost as secure as firewalls.

Network engineers should consider using a DMZ or service network for servers that need to accept traffic from an unprotected network, such as the Internet. DMZs and service networks are usually local area network (LAN) segments that connect to both the inside (protected) network and the outside (unprotected) network through a firewall. This limits the exposure of the machines on these segments from most unwanted traffic from the outside, while also protecting the inside network from these machines should they fall to a hacker.

After the network engineer has hardened the network, he now needs a mechanism for ensuring that his protective measures work. Classic Intrusion Detection Systems (IDSs) provide this function. The newer systems even prevent the security breaches from happening in the first place. IDSs fall into two basic categories: Host and Network. Host Intrusion Detection Systems (HIDSs) are usually software agents installed on key hosts, configured by an external console, that prevent unauthorized access to these hosts and report the intrusion. A thorough network evaluation, as discussed in Chapter 2, will help determine what hosts need protecting. Once the engineer makes this determination, he can install the agents on the hosts.

NIDSs are either appliances or hosts with special software installed that examines network traffic for possible attacks. Some NIDSs can report about attacks in progress, and can also prevent these attacks from succeeding by taking reactive measures, such as reconfiguring a router or firewall. A network engineer can install a NIDS either in front of or behind a firewall. A NIDS in front of a firewall will see many more trivial events than a NIDS behind the firewall will, but a NIDS behind a firewall might not see an attack in progress because the firewall might block the offending traffic. The location of the NIDS, therefore, will vary with the needs of the particular network.

Solutions Fast Track

Design Principles and Examples

- ☑ Firewalls at the perimeter.

- ☑ Firewalls can divide interior networks that need high security.

- ☑ When using NAT internally to conserve public addresses, choose networks listed in RFC 1918.

- ☑ Intrusion Detection Systems (IDSs) fall into two categories: Host Intrusion Detection Systems (HIDSs) and Network Intrusion Detection Systems (NIDSs).

- ☑ IDSs need careful installation and "tuning" to avoid false positives.

- ☑ HIDSs are software agents that protect important hosts.

- ☑ HIDSs need a secure console for configuration.

- ☑ NIDSs are network appliances that analyze traffic to look for and prevent breaches.

- ☑ NIDSs can work in front of or behind a firewall depending on the traffic that you need to examine.

- ☑ If connected to a switch, a NIDS needs a promiscuous port to see as much traffic as possible. This port should span all VLANs if possible.

Proper Segmentation

- ☑ Networks need careful planning.

- ☑ Segmentation must balance security, speed, cost, and convenience.

- ☑ Network interface cards (NICs) with embedded firewalls can give every host a hardware-based firewall for high-security environments.

- ☑ Consider your physical environment first and map everything.

- ☑ Consider the "political" environment next.

- ☑ Use routers, Layer 3 switches, or multilayer switches to subdivide large networks.

- ☑ No subnet should have more than 100 devices in most cases.

- ☑ ACLs can provide firewall-like features at the core of your network without having to actually use a firewall.

- ☑ RFC 1918 and RFC 2827 make basic ACL suggestions.

- ☑ Hosts in a DMZ or service network should be hardened through advanced configuration techniques or with a HIDS.

Links to Sites

- **www.ietf.org** The Internet Engineering Task Force (IETF) homepage. The IETF maintains the authoritative list of RFCs, the documents that set the standards for the Internet.

- **www.ietf.org/rfc/rfc1918.txt?number=1918** RFC 1918, "Address Allocation for Private Internets." This document lists the network addresses that network engineers can use when creating private networks that use NAT to connect to the Internet.

- **www.forbes.com/markets/newswire/2003/05/01/rtr959208.html** Reuters article detailing network changes due to a $1.4 billion lawsuit. This article has very little technical information, but it does show how the business needs to drive network designs.

- **www.microsoft.com/technet/** Microsoft Security Bulletin MS02-061. This page links to a patch to fix the SQL Slammer worm vulnerability in Microsoft SQL 2000 and MSDE, and the site describes the nature of the vulnerability.

- **www.3com.com/products/en_US/prodlist.jsp?tab= cat&pathtype=purchase&cat=134482&selcat=Firewalls+%26+Filt ers&family=134494** Embedded Firewall Products. This page links to

3Com's embedded firewall product line. Basically, these products are NICs with built-in firewalls.

- **www.microsoft.com/technet** Microsoft TechNet. Technical information and "Best Practices" for Microsoft products.

- **www.microsoft.com/technet/security** Microsoft Security Checklists. Security checklists for Microsoft's server products, including Windows servers and Internet Information Server (IIS).

Mailing Lists

- **www.securitypipeline.com/newsletter.jhtml** *Security Pipeline Newsletter.* Newsletter designed to summarize the latest security threats to the computer industry.

- **www.cisco.com/tac/newsletter/signup** *Cisco Technical Assistance Center (TAC) Newsletter.* The official newsletter from Cisco's Online Technical Support Department.

- **www.securityfocus.com/archive** SecurityFocus Mailing List Directory. This page lists all the available mailing lists from SecurityFocus, a clearinghouse of security-related information owned by Symantec.

- **http://networkperspectives.rsc01.net/servlet/website/ ResponseForm?gHpEu7-zNIlJkpIL-.26** Subscription for the monthly e-publication from Network Associates, *Network Perspectives.* NAI makes Entercept, a popular HIDS.

- **www.bluecoat.com/news/index.html** Homepage for Blue Coat Systems, a manufacturer of security proxy devices. You can sign up for Blue Coat's "Security News and Updates" from this page. Note: some of you might know Blue Coat by its former name, CacheFlow.

Frequently Asked Questions

The following Frequently Asked Questions, answered by the authors of this book, are designed to both measure your understanding of the concepts presented in this chapter and to assist you with real-life implementation of these concepts. To have your questions about this chapter answered by the author, browse to **www.syngress.com/solutions** and click on the **"Ask the Author"** form. You will also gain access to thousands of other FAQs at ITFAQnet.com.

Q: My network is completely flat, all on one hub, and has no segmentation. Where should I place my NIDS?

A: You have a very easy network to monitor, but a very inefficient topology. After reading Chapter 7 (you did read it, right?), if you are still unable to convince the money folks to let you purchase a mid-range network switch, you can still use NIDS on any port of your hub. One has to wonder, however, if they will let you purchase any NIDS equipment if they won't let you purchase a switch!

Q: If I already have NIDS in my network, do I also need HIDS? What about the reverse—I have HIDS on a couple of servers; do I still need NIDS?

A: In our opinion, both are necessary and very informative. If we had to pick one, however, we would put a couple of HIDS agents on our most important servers and make sure they were protected first. Then, we would worry about the rest of the network. If you have the resources, you should have both. Use the attack signatures from your NIDS to guide your rule creation on the HIDS. You can use the HIDS rule exceptions (for normal activity) to dictate the exceptions on your NIDS as well.

Q: I love network design and this is by far my favorite chapter in this book. Where can I go to share my love of design with others?

A: Lucky for you, there is a certification that (albeit vendor-based) has a strict design emphasis. The Cisco Certified Design Associate (and Design Professional) are certification programs that discuss the concepts in this chapter at great lengths. You can find other Syngress titles on CCDA and CCDP at www.syngress.com.

Q: My company is a financial institution similar to the ones discussed in the Merrill Lynch article in *Forbes* magazine. Are there any current federal mandates or SEC regulations on internal networking?

A: Not yet, but you can believe with the events of 2003 that this is on the regulatory agency's radar and will soon find its way into the laws. Spend the time to properly deploy internal firewalls today and you'll be a shining star when the regulations go into place next year or the year after. Who knows—you might even be rewarded for your proactive design by a (gasp!) raise.

Q: My campus network has multiple buildings with people from each department scattered throughout each building. Can I segment my network by department?

A: Yes, you can. The simple way to do this would be to use a separate switch for each department and then trunk each individual departmental switch back to larger departmental switches at the core of the network. You could then use routers, firewalls, or multilayer switches to connect these core switches to each other. If your network design can tolerate a lower level of security, VLANs are a better way to handle this situation.

Q: I have a firewall on the outside of my network, so I was wondering how any dangerous traffic could get into my network?

A: As-of-yet unknown operating system or protocol vulnerabilities can make even "safe" traffic dangerous once someone learns how to exploit these vulnerabilities. Beyond this, many networks terminate virtual private network (VPN) connections inside the firewall, so any compromised remote machine can now wreak havoc inside the network. Notebook computers that get infected at a user's home can also quickly infect an unprotected network once the user reconnects the notebook to the corporate network.

Index

~~Acknowledgements~~ *Liner Notes*

Brian Kenyon (lead guitar) — Mom & Dad for providing me the best base on which to build my life; Lauren for making my life better each day and being the best thing that has ever happened to me; Bartlett for always being happy to see me (thump, thump); Dave and Heather for patience and understanding during my lack of contact; Charly and Joe for constant support, love and inspiration; Troy & Tommy – my (much) older, extended brothers – to another year at angel's stadium ,very large bar tabs, king & do, and our circle bar; Erik for always being a great friend and having an answer when needed; Dave/Pete/Ryan/Donny(cakes) – "while you are at the bookstore buying this you should pick up a..." for a lifetime of friendship i dedicate chapter 12 to all of you (my best to Pete and Shauna); Larry M. – my chief counsel and mentor, better times and years to come; Nate for getting me started in tech (damn you!) and years of support, Jody for being a much better writer, justin – thanks for cleaning up my work and making this book look good; Andrew & Something Corporate for writing remarkable, inspiring music that makes me rethink my career choice everyday (Like i needed that while i was writing); CBK, Jan, Stevens (Rub), Barnes, Boston, Adam, Uy, Will, O'Dea and GK for making work fun (well, sometimes); Tesar for your patience and understanding; Andrew, Catherine, Amy and the rest of the Syngress team –thanks for your guidance, support and for giving our thoughts a voice; Birkholz – all my love, even though you con'ed me into writing this, my best to you and shelly; to all of my family, near and far, thanks for your love and support; to all of my friends – without you, life would be an empty room without windows; to my Friend and Co-Author Steve – it wasn't always pretty but we got there, and had some fun arguments along the way (anti-spoof), i wouldn't have it any other way

Steven Andrés (keyboards) — To Nona Livia, this book is for you—Li manco più ogni giorno. To my Mom, thanks for being my rock of support all my life, for teaching me good from bad, and that angels really do live among us. To Dad watching down from Sailor's Heaven, thanks for buying me my first Texas Instruments computer, and your enduring love. To tia Petty, tio Juanca, Kimberly, Michelle, Fede, and my new nephew due in a few months—we are so lucky to be so close. To Adri, Paola, Alba, Joe, Tania, and the rest of the clan in Buenos Aires—I hope to see you all soon, and NO I cannot help you with your anti-virus software (ha ha). To my friends who have been there for me, I thank you for putting up with me (and for all the road trips, apologies for the snoring): Chris "mister sandro", Pete "bella daddy", Dave "walrus", Jay & Backer, Steck & Tasha, John "leftnut", Duane & Laura, Daryl, Justin, the other Justin, Bill, the other Bill, Caso & Chipol, Lauren (my reality tv addiction therapist), G-Mo (remember virutalwestwood?), Hertz (and Zeus), Payrovi (remember rosarito?), Castro (remember Drake stadium?), Sanchez (remember Cabo? both times?), Lesa & Renee and the Delta Terrace ladies, Lt. Neal, Steve Peterson (damn Republican), Mark Green (and baby), Telly McGill (army), Jeff Fralich (zoolander), Brandon Ray (flash mastah), the MSN security team (you call that a data center?), Justin Dolly (out of the dog house yet?), the Niuhi nerds, the Scooby gang, the Call One veterans, the Mesa crowd, the Phi Psi crew, the La Salle alums, Linkin Park, bailey, ben, blanca, bartlett, kona, and gwen. To Andrew, thanks for teaching me that you can actually write a book while it is being stocked on the shelves. To birkholz, for giving me a chance. To Larry, where would I be without your guidance and support (and blue shirts)? To the 'stoners Jan, CBK, CK, GK, JMR, Uy, Modea, Kolesar, Simmons, Rub, Barnes, Beets, Barry, Jefe, Tom— thanks for making me smile when i wanted to scream. To those i've mistakenly omitted, my apologies. To those i've intentionally omitted, stop calling me. To my fellow authors, thanks for making my writing seem childlike in comparison. To my friend and graduate of the "Steve's Former Boss" support group, thanks for being there, making me laugh, giving me guidance, and being wrong about so many things (anti-spoof is dumb) and predictably forgetting the rest (the rails were funny, you have to admit).

Jody Marc Cohn (drums) — I'd like to thank my family who continues to tolerate me even though I daily redefine the term "bastard." To my parents, Ken & Ava, for working hard to raise the clan; To my wife, Michele, who loves me even though I haven't done any work around the house since – ever; To my children, Ryan & Bryn, whom I hope remember how much I love them the next time that they watch the menendez brothers biography; To Seth & Heather, sorry for . . . everything; To Stacy, Carlee, and Joe, welcome to the family – yes, insanity is contagious, but it works slowly so make the best of the time that you have left; To Phyllis and Bob, Thanks for always being there; To Stephanie, who still makes me laugh after all of these years; To Heide, Joan, Artie, Sydney, and Ilene, who have given me hope that intelligence runs in the family, so my kids have a chance even though it may have skipped me; To David, for getting me started in IT – I'll never forgive you! To Shawn, who proves that you don't have to work hard to be successful; To Dan, who inspired me to write despite my lack of talent; To Hewab, for making my views look moderate. To my partners, Girdner & Mike, thanks for carrying me. To my co-authors, I am not worthy. Thank you so much for your help.

Nate Johnson (cowbell, "We need more Cowbell!!") — I'd like to offer my deepest gratitude to my beautiful wife Nicole for her love and understanding and to the apple of my eye- Riley for being so damn cute, making me laugh, and making everyday amazing; to Mom and Dad for everything you have done- you are our heroes; AJ, Julie, Matt, Mike, Ama, Amy, Anthony, Alexis, Makenna, Kyle, Benjamin, Trevor, and Noah for reminding me to focus on the big picture; Ray, Joan, and Grammy for all of their help and loving support. When it comes to this book, Praise be to Kenyon for bringing me into this "cosa nostra". I've really enjoyed the experience. Personally, I'd like to send to thank (from the beginning): Brasil for moving me; Susie B for aiding me – without you I'd still be there; CS and KAUCR for the memories; Everyone on the bench at T.Tech Svc; Hossein, Renee, and Karim; Allen F for opening my mind to the possibilities; Alfred and Kenyon for bringing their A game and for being the type of guys you are friends with your whole life; Grig "The Cobra", Dave "The Tiger", John "The Walrus", Bradley "the Prariedog", Todd "The Weasel", Jim "the Rat Dog"; James "The Rooster", George "The SeaUrchin", and Wayne "The Shark" – I've never had more fun working so hard; Megan for giving me the opportunity, Derek for making it possible and Adi, Jeff, Cheryl, Kevin, and John for making it happen; Last but not least - huge props to Greco for starting it up and being a stellar business partner. To everyone else I've worked with, played with, and learned from - Thank you!

Justin Dolly (Uileann Pipes) — To Mum & Dad for being the best there is; Annette & Jarlath for being my chief counsels and ever-present sounding-boards; Michaela for making me laugh; Ro, Gordo and Ferg for unwavering friendship; Moira (Sr. Sebastian) - this is all because you encouraged me (it's all your fault!), To Betty, Cliff and Dee for letting Cartman sing in Spain...and most of all, to Orlaith for love and support I can't do without. Steve, BK, Erik, David L., Stu, Partick H. for being great guys, not just great geeks. Letty, you got me into this... Dan, you were the catalyst. TC for friendship and technical knowledge in the early days. Debbie, Terri, Sara, JohnBoy, DaveO and Eden. To those that inspire me, Beckett, Joyce, Van the man, Lyle, Miles, Christy, Colum McCann and Paul Weller - please keep it comin' (except for those of you who are no longer with us, you're off the hook!). Robert U, Robin, Jesus, Belinda, Kim, Herman, Anjoo, Andrea - thanks - sorry to make your lives more complicated every day! To the following - thanks for being who you are...KD, Nader, Ed, Sammy, Adrian, ctuft, Maley, AJ, Ivan, Alicia (hope the leg gets better soon), Anne & Tom (all the best), Dr. Sherwood for putting my hand back together and to Wanda who helped me learn to use it again; and finally to Bill Clinton, who gave me my Green Card!

Syngress: *The Definition of a Serious Security Library*

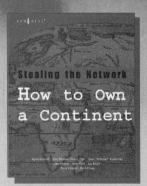